MW01006241

FLAMES BEYOND GETTISBURG

The Confederate Expedition
to the Susquehanna River, June 1863

Scott L. Mingus Sr.

SB

Savas Beatie

New York and California

Originally published as *Flames Beyond Gettysburg: The Gordon Expedition, June 1863* (Ironclad Publishing, 2009, Vol. 5, Discovering Civil War America series)

Cataloging-in-Publication Data is available from the Library of Congress.

ISBN 978-1-611210-72-9

05 04 03 02 01   5 4 3 2 1
First Savas Beatie edition, first printing

SB

Published by
Savas Beatie LLC
521 Fifth Avenue, Suite 1700
New York, NY 10175

Editorial Offices:

Savas Beatie LLC
P.O. Box 4527
El Dorado Hills, CA 95762
Phone: 916-941-6896
(E-mail) editorial@savasbeatie.com

Savas Beatie titles are available at special discounts for bulk purchases in the United States by corporations, institutions, and other organizations. For more details, please contact Special Sales, P.O. Box 4527, El Dorado Hills, CA 95762, or you may e-mail us at sales@savasbeatie.com, or visit our website at www.savasbeatie.com for additional information.

Dedicated to my late parents, Staff. Sgt. Robert Earl Mingus and Mary M. (Williams) Mingus, who provided the inspiration for me to begin a life-long love for history and our American heritage.

Thanks Mom and Dad!

"Pennsylvanians. . . . Show yourselves what you are—a free, loyal, spirited, brave, vigorous race. . . . The time has now come when we must all stand or fall together in defense of our duty that posterity shall not blush for us."

— Gov. Andrew G. Curtin, Pennsylvania, USA

"These Pennsylvanians were not in sympathy with my expedition."

— Brig. Gen. John B. Gordon, Georgia, CSA

"When the history of our great victory at Gettysburg comes to be written, this little skirmish will be found to have sustained an important relation, and with no small degree of complacency will those men who so faithfully watched the rebel approach, reflect on the part they played in the drama."

— *Columbia* (Pa.) *Spy*, July 11, 1863

Contents

Contents (continued)

MAPS

MAPS (continued)

Photos and illustrations appear throughout
the book for the convenience of the reader

Acknowledgments

I am grateful to so many people for their assistance and support. First, and foremost, is my wife Debi, who has patiently put up with my endless babbling about the Civil War, endured several car rides to check out obscure locations associated with troop movements, and cheerfully endorsed the time I spent researching and writing this book. I also thank God for my children. Scott Jr. donated his graduate research paper from Millersville University, which was the genesis for this book. My son Tom frequently accompanied me touring sites associated with this story. I also thank my daughter Melissa, whose sweet disposition always kept me smiling throughout the months of research and writing.

I appreciate all those who contributed material for this project. Researcher and author David Ward shared his vast knowledge of Pennsylvania-related Civil War manuscripts and letters. Al Gambone freely shared his perspectives on Maj. Gen. Darius N. Couch, personalizing a copy of his excellent biography of the enigmatic general. James McClure, editor of the York Daily Record, graciously shared sources he used for his excellent series of York County histories. Tom Ryan of Delaware, author of an article on the bridge burning for the Washington Press, freely shared his notes that I later incorporated into the driving tours. Brian Kesterson provided input on the 17th Virginia Cavalry, including the James Hodam manuscript in his possession. Rob Wynstra directed me to the William D. Lyon papers at Navarro College and provided an Alabama newspaper article that held additional information. Gregory C. White shared his research on Georgians at Gettysburg and sent materials from the

University of Georgia's Hargrett Library. Chris Brantley, compiler of source material for Gordon's Brigade, gave me valuable leads.

Guy Breshears exchanged information with me regarding Maj. Granville Haller. Several descendants of leading characters offered information and encouragement, including Haller's great-grandson Martin N. Chamberlain, the Emmick brothers, and the Rev. Elijah White IV of Virginia. Richard C. Wiggin graciously gave me permission to quote the informative July 1, 1863, letter Annie Welsh sent to her husband, Brig. Gen. Thomas Welsh at Vicksburg.

June Lloyd, Lila Fouhrman-Shaull, and the volunteers at the York County Heritage Trust were quite helpful, as was John Heiser, librarian of the Gettysburg National Military Park and York County historian Thomas L. Scheafer. Tom Buffenbarger at the U.S. Military History Institute in Carlisle guided me to several resources in their collection, as did Timothy Smith at the Adams County Historical Society. Kevin Shue of the Lancaster County Historical Society assisted in researching local accounts and gave me permission to quote from Sidney Myer's diary and J. Houston Mifflin's letters. Bob Schmidt of Historic Wrightsville provided encouragement, as did members of Rivertownes and the Columbia Historic Preservation Society. Jim Brown allowed me to quote the Phebe Angeline Smith letter from his collection. Chris Vera provided access to letters and documents at the Columbia Historic Preservation Society.

Several people critiqued parts of the manuscript, including primary proofreader David Wieck. Additional input and suggestions came from Licensed Battlefield Guide Phil Cole (publisher of three of my books on human interest stories from Gettysburg and Antietam), Lancaster County historian Ronald Young, wargamer Doug Rogers, and living historians Ken Miller and J. David Petruzzi. Ivor Janci published my four books on miniature wargaming and has been a constant source of encouragement. Eric J. Wittenberg, noted author and cavalry expert, proofed the text and provided several good sources for cavalry-related material.

Finally, I would like to thank the good folks at Savas Beatie for their encouragement and support of this second edition. It's not often that an author gets to rewrite a previously published book and make it even better, and I thank Theodore P. Savas, managing director for Savas Beatie LLC, for believing in this project and for making so many useful suggestions. His marketing director, Sarah Keeney, is a whiz at promotion and her efforts on behalf of this book are commendable and very much appreciated. I would also like to thank graphic designer Ian Hughes of London, England, for designing the cover using

Bradley M. Schmehl's impressive painting *Columbia Bridge Burning*, and talented cartographer Steven Stanley for his wonderful maps for this edition (with the exception of the Skirmish of Wrightsville map, which is from the studio of Tom Poston). Modern photography was supplied by Dr. Thomas M. Mingus, and Chapter 11 was co-written with Professor Scott L. Mingus, Jr.

My father, Staff Sgt. Robert E. Mingus, a decorated veteran of World War II's European Theater, offered tremendous love, support, and enthusiasm for the project. He and my Mom gave me the early training and inspiration for a life of research and study, both personally and professionally.

Finally, thank you, dear readers, for your interest in these long-ago events, when the path of the Gordon Expedition was marked by flames beyond Gettysburg.

Scott L. Mingus, Sr.
York, Pennsylvania

Abbreviations found in the footnotes

ACHS: Adams County Historical Society
CVHS: Codorus Valley Historical Society
CWTI: *Civil War Times Illustrated*
FCHS: Franklin County Historical Society
GDAH: Georgia Department of Archives and History
GHS: Georgia Historical Society
GNMP: Gettysburg National Military Park
JMSIUS: Journal of the Military Service Institution of the United States
LCHS: Lancaster County Historical Society
LOC: Library of Congress
NARA: National Archives and Records Administration
SHSP: *Southern Historical Society Papers*
OR: *Official Records of the War of the Rebellion*
USMHI: United States Military History Institute
YCHT: York County Heritage Trust

Foreword

There have tens of hundreds of books written about the Battle of Gettysburg since it was fought in early July 1863. Many of them deal with obscure aspects of that pivotal Civil War campaign, and it has seemed for a long while as if nearly every possible nook and cranny of the campaign has been filled. Given that fact, one might wonder what ground remains unturned, what aspect of this campaign remains ripe for a book-length study? On the large-scale front, nearly everything worthy of coverage has been the subject of at least one book-length study. The truth is that, save for micro-tactical histories of disparate elements of the battle, there are precious few subjects remaining worthy of in-depth exploration. Given the avalanche of Gettysburg titles, it is somewhat surprising that one major portion of the Gettysburg operation failed to receive the attention it deserved.

In the days leading up to the battle itself (July 1-3, 1863), an expedition unfolded that nearly changed the entire course of the campaign. One brigade of Georgians under Brig. Gen. John B. Gordon, part of Maj. Gen. Jubal A. Early's Division, Lt. Gen. Richard Ewell's Corps, supported by Virginia artillery and cavalry, passed through the south-central Pennsylvania countryside. Intent on mischief, the Georgians seized the town of Gettysburg, engaged Pennsylvania emergency militia forces, and set about wreaking havoc all the way to the bank of the mile-wide Susquehanna River. Beyond beckoned the state capital at Harrisburg. At that point, General Gordon . . . well, to tell more would be tantamount to inserting a spoiler and ruining one of the better told stories of the always-fascinating Gettysburg saga.

Scott L. Mingus Sr. has penned a first-rate study of Gordon's Pennsylvania operation. His compelling book *Flames Beyond Gettysburg: The Confederate Expedition to the Susquehanna River, June 1863* represents the culmination of years of digging through obscure files in order to cobble together this previously untold story. Scott's fascinating narrative fills a large but rarely obvious gap in Gettysburg historiography by giving this episode the attention it has so long deserved. In addition to all the remarkable characters and personalities you will meet along the way, *Flames Beyond Gettysburg* provides detailed tactical discussions of the fighting, places the expedition in its proper historical and social context, and demonstrates how Gordon's Georgians impacted the outcome of the campaign.

In addition, Scott provides us with detailed driving tours so that you may visit the sites so vividly described in his narrative. It is as if he is saying, "Follow in the footsteps of Gordon and his Georgians and track them all the way to the banks of the Susquehanna River, where you can see the true highwater mark of the second Confederate invasion of the North."

Flames Beyond Gettysburg is a worthy addition to the body of Gettysburg knowledge and should be necessary reading for any serious student of this pivotal campaign of the American Civil War.

Eric J. Wittenberg
Columbus, Ohio

Chapter 1
Lee Looks North

Invasion Plans

It was the humid, rainy late spring of 1863, the third year of the increasingly brutal American Civil War. The military outlook for the Union Army of the Potomac had grown more uncertain as the war dragged on. Following yet another devastating defeat by Confederate General Robert E. Lee and his Army of Northern Virginia in May at Chancellorsville, this Federal army was in disarray. Leading generals openly sniped at each other in the press and often in front of subordinates. Senior officials in Washington, including President Abraham Lincoln, feuded with the army's commanding general, "Fighting Joe" Hooker, who seemingly refused to fight or make any aggressive moves to keep Lee off-balance. The War Department's policy decisions were being challenged by military officers and disputed by the Northern press.[1]

Disillusioned Federal soldiers questioned the competence and courage of their generals. Morale sank because of Hooker's perceived bungling of repeated chances for victory at Chancellorsville. Discipline began to slip, desertion rates increased, and recruitment declined in many states. As veteran regiments and artillery batteries mustered out when their terms of enlistment expired in the

---

1 Lincoln outlined his expectations for Hooker in a remarkable letter in January 1863 in *The War of the Rebellion: A Compilation of the Official Records of the Union and Confederate Armies*, 128 volumes (Washington, D.C.: Government Printing Office, 1889), volume 25, part 2, p. 4, (hereafter cited as *OR*) including a command to "beware of rashness, but with energy and sleepless vigilance go forward and give us victories." After Hooker's devastating defeat at Chancellorsville, several senior officers (in particular Henry Slocum and Darius Couch) wanted George G. Meade to assume command of the army.

weeks following Chancellorsville, considerably fewer soldiers than expected re-enlisted. In March, the Federal government had approved the Enrollment Act, opening the way for a conscription draft to fulfill the need for additional manpower. As a result, the peace movement gained momentum across a broad spectrum of society, giving anti-war "Copperheads" a wider audience for their rhetoric. The previous September at Antietam, the Army of the Potomac thwarted Lee's invasion of Maryland, but failed to take advantage of its first good opportunity to destroy his army. Two-and-one-half years of killing, suffering, and hardship spawned discouragement and frustration toward the war for many Northerners. Early thoughts of a quick victory had long since vanished. The casualty lists grew numbingly longer, and now, there was no end in sight.[2]

To many Southerners, this was an opportune time for another invasion of the North. It was not a fresh idea. During his Valley Campaign in May 1862, Thomas J. "Stonewall" Jackson informed a Confederate congressman that if he had forty thousand men, he would "raise the siege of Richmond and transfer this campaign to the banks of the Susquehanna," a broad river flowing southeasterly through central Pennsylvania. Reinforcements were not forthcoming, and Jackson moved his command to the Richmond area to assist Lee during the Peninsula Campaign.[3]

After a series of Confederate victories forced Maj. Gen. George B. McClellan's Army of the Potomac to withdraw, Lee adopted Jackson's general idea and studied an invasion. After bullying John Pope's army at Second Manassas, Lee suddenly turned northward, apparently heading for Pennsylvania. His men had developed a marked attitude of invincibility and were in high spirits as they entered Maryland. Even the ghastly losses at Sharpsburg on September 17 did not dim their confidence. There, they

2 National Archives and Records Administration (NARA), Provost Marshal General's Bureau, 1863-1865, Record Group 110. On March 3, 1863, the Thirty-seventh Congress passed the Enrollment Act, which imposed military service on males aged 20-45 for three years or until the end of the war. Men could avoid the draft by paying $300 to hire a substitute soldier. To some, this gave the impression that this was a rich man's war and a poor man's fight.

3 *Southern Historical Society Papers*, 52 volumes (Richmond, Va.: Southern Historical Society, 1876-1943), 40: 164-65. Alexander R. Boteler was a Confederate congressman from Jefferson County, Virginia. On May 30, Jackson appointed his close friend as a volunteer aide-de-camp, giving him the rank of colonel. Jackson for some time lobbied Boteler to convince President Jefferson Davis to support an invasion plan. With Lee's endorsement and leadership, this culminated with the Maryland Campaign in September.

withstood repeated attacks by McClellan's much larger Federal army, retiring from the blood-drenched fields on their own initiative. Just days before that great battle, Lt. Gen. James Longstreet's soldiers marched within ten miles of Pennsylvania before withdrawing toward Sharpsburg.[4]

After their decisive victory at Fredericksburg in December, Lee and Jackson again contemplated an invasion. They would push well beyond Maryland into the lush Pennsylvania farmlands, forcing the Army of the Potomac to come to them. Their eyes were on targets of political and strategic importance, among them Harrisburg. The seizure of the capital of the North's second most populous state could stimulate cries for a negotiated peace and increase European pressure on Washington. Jackson advocated breaking up Pennsylvania's coal mining operations and cutting off fuel supplies vital to Northern war efforts. In late February, he directed topographical engineer Jedediah Hotchkiss to draw a detailed map of the Valley of Virginia up to Harrisburg and beyond to Philadelphia. He warned Hotchkiss to keep the preparations "a profound secret."[5]

The Keystone State was a logical objective. Confederate strategists believed the southern tier of Franklin, Adams, and York counties to be ambivalent to the Union cause. Much of its population was of German or Scotch-Irish ancestry, typically hard-working people with thriving farms and well-stocked larders. Southern sympathizers in the region had openly supported the controversial Fugitive Slave Law. Bounty hunters and slave traders from below the Mason-Dixon Line freely roamed the area before the war. Maps were plentiful and detailed, and the vast road network was conducive to the movements of thousands of soldiers.[6]

---

4   OR 19, pt. 1, 839. On Sept. 12, 1862, Longstreet and the divisions of Brig. Gen. John Bell Hood and Maj. Gen. David R. Jones marched to Hagerstown, Maryland, roughly six miles south of the Mason-Dixon Line and eleven miles from Greencastle, Pennsylvania.

5   Clement A. Evans, *Confederate Military History* (Atlanta: Confederate Publishing Co., 1899; reprinted in 1975 in Dayton, Ohio, by Morningside Bookshop), 3: 375-76. Hotchkiss attended college in New York near the Pennsylvania coalfields. After graduating in 1846, he spent a year as a schoolteacher in the Lykens Valley in Pennsylvania, an anthracite region. He studied the mining industry and geology of the coal deposits. After completing the term, he and a fellow teacher walked the Cumberland Valley and explored the area well into Maryland and Virginia. His firsthand knowledge of the region helped him draft his detailed maps. Pennsylvania boasted 2.9 million residents in 1860, second only to New York in population.

6   Generals Gordon and Early consulted an 1860 map of York County by Shearer & Lake. General Isaac Trimble worked for the railroad in south-central Pennsylvania prior to the war.

This agricultural breadbasket of the North was rich with bountiful orchards and well-cultivated farms brimming with food and much-needed horses and mules. Several prosperous towns invited tributes that could be levied to raise cash, supplies, and other useful goods. Escaped slaves might be recaptured and returned to the South, a political concern not lost on wealthy plantation owners who wielded considerable clout in Richmond. Perhaps the coal industry, so critical to the North's industry and war machine, could be damaged; three-quarters of the country's production came from Pennsylvania mines.[7]

Despite the abortive Maryland Campaign, by the spring of 1863 strong public sentiment in the upper South pressed Lee to move his army into the Northern heartland. That would provide devastated Virginia farmers much needed relief from the rigors of feeding and supporting the soldiers for another summer campaign. Two years of fighting and supply raiding depleted previous harvests, because both Union and Confederate forces repeatedly crisscrossed the upper counties. Fields and orchards had been replanted, and civic officials were eager to allow the farmers a season of uninterrupted agriculture. If Lee remained in the North for an extended period, the Federals would be compelled to follow him, removing their resource-draining presence from the Old Dominion. Let the Yankee farmers feed both armies for a summer, thought many in Richmond. In some circles, there was a growing belief that just one more victory in the East might even end the bitter war. Virginia newspapers were vehement in sounding the trumpet for another invasion to relieve pressure on Richmond, as Jackson had suggested during the Peninsula Campaign. Jackson was mortally wounded at the battle of Chancellorsville and died shortly thereafter, but his invasion idea lived on.[8]

Southern military advisers believed that the summer would bring another major Federal push to take Richmond. If Lee instead moved north, surely the Yankees would strip troops from Washington's defenses to try to corner Lee.

7 James A. Kegel, *North With Lee and Jackson* (Mechanicsburg, Pa.: Stackpole Books, 1996), 47-48. Pennsylvania mined sixteen million tons of coal in 1860, or 78.3% of the country's production. More than half of the coal in the U.S. was anthracite (hard coal) from ten northeastern Pennsylvania counties, directly in line with the Cumberland Valley. Anthracite burned hotter and produced less smoke and flame than bituminous (soft coal), making it a logical choice for industry, trains, and ships, including the Union Navy blockaders.

8 "Pennsylvania Reaction to the Confederate Invasion," Vertical files of the Library of the Gettysburg National Military Park (GNMP). *Richmond Whig; Richmond Daily Dispatch; Staunton Observer*, various issues, Feb.-June 1863.

Isolating the Federal capital might spark loud cries throughout the North to shift troops from the West to aid Hooker. If this happened, the Southerners could perhaps break Union Maj. Gen. Ulysses S. Grant's tightening grip on Vicksburg, Mississippi. Its loss would split the Confederacy in two as the Yankees gained full control of the Mississippi River.

For some time, Lee conversed with his staff regarding a growing concern. While the Army of Northern Virginia was consistently winning battles, the South did not have the sustainable strength in manpower, logistics, or resources to prevail in a prolonged war. Time was of the essence. Lee expressed to Jefferson Davis that it was wise to "carefully measure and husband our strength." The falling aggregate of available combat soldiers indicated to Lee that his army was growing weaker, and fresh recruits were not adequately resupplying its ranks. A protracted battle of attrition would only bring ruin and, in the end, the Confederacy would lose.[9]

To many in its military, the only real opportunity for victory was in seizing the initiative. Brigadier General John B. Gordon of Georgia related the prevailing philosophy for another invasion. "In the logistics of defensive war, offensive movements are often the wisest strategy. Voltaire has somewhere remarked that 'to subsist one's army at the expense of the enemy, to advance on their own ground and force them to retrace their steps—thus rendering strength useless by skill—is regarded as one of the masterpieces of military art.'" Adding one more significant win to the string of previous tactical successes might finally lead to the desired strategic triumph. Peace Democrats, other war-weary groups, certain religious organizations, and influential newspapers might form a powerful lobby and force Lincoln to negotiate a peace settlement. The Confederacy might attain status as an independent legal nation in the eyes of the world.[10]

Pressure mounted on the Confederate government to do something to relieve the threat on Vicksburg. In mid-May, Lee took a train to Richmond to meet with President Jefferson Davis and Secretary of War James Seddon to discuss an invasion. He soon returned to Fredericksburg to start planning tactical details with his staff. On May 27, Union intelligence officers informed Washington that plans were afoot in Richmond for Lee to go on the offensive.

9 *OR* 27, pt. 3, 880-82.

10 John B. Gordon, *Reminiscences of the Civil War* (New York/Atlanta: Charles Scribner's Sons, 1903), 137.

Three days later, Lee reorganized the Army of Northern Virginia. He appointed one-legged Lt. Gen. Richard S. Ewell to lead the Second Corps and high-strung Lt. Gen. A. P. Hill to head the new Third Corps, in effect splitting the late Jackson's old command. Longstreet retained his First Corps.[11]

Lee's army could easily reach Pennsylvania from deep within Virginia by following the Shenandoah Valley, which runs northeasterly to the Potomac River. In Maryland, it becomes the Cumberland Valley, situated between Blue (North) Mountain and South Mountain. In turn, the valley leads to Harrisburg in central Pennsylvania. This lush and fertile region reminded an observer of a dagger pointed straight at the Yankees' heart. Steep mountains to Lee's right flank would screen his forces from pursuit. Cavalry and mounted infantry would safeguard mountain passes that the enemy might use to attack Lee's army, which would be vulnerable when strung out in long columns. The politicians and the War Department approved the plan, but insisted that Lee leave several brigades to guard Richmond. Confident that the Federals would make no aggressive moves to attack the capital, Lee wrestled with Davis and his war managers over which specific commands would stay behind.[12]

Once his army's final composition was set, Lee estimated it would take roughly two weeks to march into Pennsylvania and threaten Harrisburg. He expected minimal resistance from badly outnumbered Federal troops stationed in the Shenandoah Valley. Lee's religious faith bolstered his confidence that a second incursion into the North would be successful. The disjointed and confused Army of the Potomac could not stop his victorious army, as an unseen God was guiding its fortunes. Nor could any militia or amateur home guard thwart Lee's ultimate goal, no matter their strength. He stated, "There never were such men in an army before. They will go anywhere and do anything if properly led." On May 31, he wrote his wife Mary, "I pray that our merciful Father in Heaven may protect and direct us! In that case, I fear no odds and no numbers."[13]

After entering Pennsylvania, his advance elements would focus on collecting supplies and disrupting supply routes, telegraphs, and railroads.

11 OR 25, pt. 2, 810.

12 John W. Urban, *Battle Field and Prison Pen* (Philadelphia: Hubbard Bros., 1882), 186; OR 27, pt. 3, 927; 25, Pt. 2, 810-16.

13 Robert E. Lee, Jr., *Recollections and Letters of General Robert E. Lee* (Indianapolis: IndyPublishing.Com, 2002), 79.

These linked the West with New York, Philadelphia, and other wealthy eastern cities. Surely Hooker's army would follow Lee, especially when Northern newspapers began clamoring for action. If Lee was correct, he could, at the time and place of his choosing, determine the circumstances for a pitched battle. His opponent, Joseph Hooker, enjoyed a reputation as an aggressive fighter at the division level, with some skills when leading a corps. His perceived success led to his installation as commander of the Army of the Potomac, replacing Maj. Gen. Ambrose Burnside after the ill-fated Rappahannock Campaign. Hooker was a gifted administrator whose reforms initially worked wonders for the badly demoralized soldiers. However, when commanding an entire army in combat at Chancellorsville, he exhibited uncertainty. Lee suspected that Hooker's indecision regarding Confederate intentions would aid his army in reaching Pennsylvania unmolested. He was correct. Unknown to Lee, on September 12, 1862, just before Antietam, Hooker wrote, "To my mind the rebels have no more intention of going to Harrisburg than they have of going to Heaven." His opinion had not changed, nor had Lee's objective.[14]

North to the Mason-Dixon Line

While Lee and Confederate authorities contemplated an invasion of Pennsylvania, most of the Army of Northern Virginia remained stationary near Fredericksburg. Major General Jubal A. Early's 7,200-man division, including John Gordon's brigade of six crack Georgia regiments, camped on a low ridge near Hamilton's Crossing. Organized by Brig. Gen. Alexander Lawton in early 1862, the battle-tested brigade fought in the Seven Days' Battles against George McClellan and at Second Manassas against John Pope, where Lawton assumed divisional command after Ewell was wounded at Groveton. At Sharpsburg, the Georgians formed the apex of Jackson's line. Attacked near farmer David Miller's cornfield, they suffered massive casualties, including acting brigade commander Col. Marcellus Douglass and five of six regimental leaders. Farther south, near the Piper farm, Colonel Gordon and his 6th Alabama lined the infamous "Sunken Road." He received five painful wounds, but greatly impressed his superiors and peers with his courage and charisma. While Gordon recovered, Lee promoted him to brigadier general on November 1,

---

14 *Ibid.* Robert E. Lee to Mary Lee, May 31, 1863; Jacob H. Stoner, *History of Franklin County and the Cumberland Valley, Pennsylvania* (Chambersburg, Pa.: The Craft Press, 1947), 368.

1862. The next spring, a healthy Gordon assumed command of Lawton's Brigade shortly before the Chancellorsville Campaign.[15]

John Brown Gordon was born February 6, 1832, in Upson County in rural Middle Georgia. The fourth of twelve children of a minister, he was an outstanding student at the University of Georgia, but withdrew during his senior year. Instead, he studied law and passed the bar exam before briefly becoming a journalist covering politics in the state capital, Milledgeville. Gordon and his father developed several profitable coal mines in Georgia, Alabama, and Tennessee. Elected as captain of a group of mountain men known as the "Raccoon Roughs," Gordon offered his services to Georgia upon secession. However, all volunteer quotas were full so his coonskin-capped volunteers were not accepted for duty. He then telegraphed several Southern governors, being rewarded when Andrew B. Moore commissioned him as major of the 6th Alabama Infantry.

When Gordon finally went off to war, he received an emotional farewell from his mother, a parting that "nothing short of death's hand can ever obliterate from my heart." Holding John in her arms, "her heart almost bursting with anguish, and the tears running down her cheeks," she asked God to take care of him. She added, "Go, my son; I shall perhaps never see you again, but I commit you freely to the service of your country."

The six-foot tall, ramrod straight Gordon proved to be one of the best citizen-soldiers in the army. His tactical judgments often exceeded those of professionally trained officers. He rose from captain to corps commander by the end of the war, a rare feat in the Confederacy. Gordon was a captivating orator and brilliant negotiator, skills that contributed to his successful military career. He devoted much time and attention to his adoring wife Fanny. Much to Jubal Early's consternation, she often accompanied her husband on campaigns, leaving their two boys under the care of his mother and "Mammy Mary," a slave. However, Fanny stayed put that summer.[16]

---

15 OR 25, pt. 2, 810. Ewell was wounded at Brawner's Farm on Aug. 28, 1862. Lawton temporarily replaced him in divisional command and Col. Marcellus Douglass became acting commander of Lawton's Brigade. On May 20, 1863, Lee notified President Davis that he wanted to place Gordon in charge of Rodes' Brigade, leaving Lawton's position vacant. However, he finally named Gordon to the Georgians. The War Department confirmed Gordon's appointment on June 6, 1863. OR 27, pt. 3, 865.

16 Gordon, *Reminiscences*, 1-10. Cavalry leader Nathan Bedford Forrest also rose through the ranks from private to corps commander.

Brig. Gen. John B. Gordon led a mixed force of infantry, artillery, and cavalry for much of the Gettysburg Campaign. Troops under his command were the first to occupy Gettysburg, York, and Wrightsville, Pennsylvania. *Library of Congress*

Now her beloved husband prepared for yet another campaign. Private G. W. Nichols of the 61st Georgia wrote:

> Here in this camp our regimental chaplains held divine services day and night. Our beloved General Gordon was often among the worshippers. He had become almost an idol in the brigade with officers and men, often leading in the prayer and exhortation service. A great many professed religion, joined the church and were baptized. The last of May we drew plenty of clothing and shoes. Every gun was examined and if they were not all right we had to get one that was. Our cartridges boxes were filled, and we knew something was up… On the first day of June we were ordered to cook two days rations, which we did.[17]

Well after dark on June 3, elements of the Army of Northern Virginia broke camp near Fredericksburg and headed northwest toward Culpeper. The next night, Maj. Gen. Robert Rodes' division of Ewell's Corps left after dark to avoid the watchful eye of Union observation balloonists. John Gordon's 2,500 veterans also prepared to depart Hamilton's Crossing. The 13th Georgia was his most seasoned regiment, having mustered into service in July 1861 at Griffin. Reduced by attrition to a little more than three hundred men, the diverse command contained companies from ten counties in Middle Georgia. A 39-year-old lawyer and blacksmith's son, Col. James M. Smith, Jr., rode at their head. The Democrat had unsuccessfully run for Congress in 1855, and he still harbored political ambitions.[18]

The 26th Georgia was another veteran regiment. It was organized in Brunswick in October 1861 with men from southeastern Georgia, a thinly settled area with few schools. Early in life, most of the backwoodsmen had learned how to handle guns. As a result, they could "kill the fleet-footed deer, panther, wolf, bear, wild-cat, and fox running at break-neck speed or could take off a squirrel's head with the old plantation rifle. . . . When the Twenty-sixth had to fight the enemy, it always punished them severely. It always had the ground well strewn with dead and wounded." More than three hundred and twenty

---

17 Alton J. Murray, *South Georgia Rebels: The True Wartime Experiences of the 26th Regiment Georgia Volunteer Infantry* (St. Mary's, Ga.: s. n., 1976), 127.

18 OR 27, pt. 3, 5-7, 70; Strength estimates are from John W. Busey and David G. Martin, *Regimental Strengths and Losses at Gettysburg* (Hightstown, N.J.: Longstreet House, 1982), 286.

marksmen marched under the proven leadership of 28-year-old Col. Edmund Nathan Atkinson, a grandson of a former president of the University of Georgia, Moses Waddel. The wealthy son of a Camden County plantation owner, Atkinson was an 1856 graduate of the Georgia Military Institute in Marietta. At the start of the war, he was one of the few people in southeastern Georgia proficient in drilling troops and moving a military command from one point to another. He was wounded at Sharpsburg and again at Fredericksburg, where he was captured while commanding the brigade. After being paroled and exchanged, he returned to active duty.[19]

The remaining four regiments in Gordon's Brigade had been reorganized from previous commands. Within Col. Clement Anselm Evans' 31st Georgia, Company C was a group of Alabamians from five counties who called themselves the Mitchell Guards. The regiment organized in October 1861 as the 27th Georgia, but was redesignated the 31st Georgia the following May. The smallest in the brigade with fewer than 300 men, it served as the brigade's provost.[20]

The rest of Gordon's regiments each counted between 300 and 400 fighting men plus scores of cooks, hospital stewards, surgeons, teamsters, artificers, and other noncombatants. The 38th Georgia was originally part of Wright's Legion, a command comprised of infantry, cavalry, and artillery battalions. The legion was dissolved in the spring of 1862 and its foot soldiers redesignated as the 38th Georgia, with new recruits swelling its ranks. Because of injuries, death, and incompetence, the senior officers were no longer with the regiment. Accordingly, 21-year-old Capt. William L. McLeod had commanded the regiment since October. He had been recommended in January 1863 for promotion to lieutenant colonel. However, some of his men protested and signed a petition, citing "his extreme youth… want of judgment & stability…injustice to men & officers being subject to extreme prejudices which in our opinion unfits him to command brave & true men… gambling with his men and officers." Despite his shortcomings, many of his three hundred and fifty hard-edged soldiers regarded him as a solid fighter. One peer called

19 G. W. Nichols, *A Soldier's Story of His Regiment, 61st Georgia* (Kennesaw, Ga.: Continental Book, 1961), 115.

20 The 31st Georgia was organized in November 1861 to defend Georgia's gulf coast with men from five counties in Alabama and eight in Georgia—Muscogee, Monroe, Stewart, Pulaski, Chattahoochee, Harris, Decatur, and Terrell.

McLeod "a gentleman of the highest tone." A slave named Moses accompanied him to cook and maintain his equipment.[21]

Rounding out the brigade were two regiments also reorganized in the spring of 1862 and redesignated as the 60th and 61st Georgia. In the summer of 1861, William H. Stiles organized the six-company 4th Georgia Battalion at Dalton with recruits from several northwestern counties. They initially served on the Atlantic Coast at Hilton Head, South Carolina, where they came under fire from the Federal fleet during the loss of Fort Walker. Four new companies, including the "Irwin Invincibles" of Henry County, Alabama, were added to the undersized battalion to form the 60th Georgia. W. B. Jones now commanded the regiment. The 7th Georgia Battalion formed at Eden on September 10, 1861, and mustered into service in October. It was reorganized in May 1862 as the 61st Georgia with additional volunteers from south-central Georgia. General Gordon called its commander, Col. John H. Lamar, "a most promising young officer" who had gained a reputation as being cool-headed under fire. Lamar lost part of a finger at Fredericksburg.[22]

Thirty-year-old Col. Clement Evans of the 31st Georgia recorded in his diary on June 4: "6 o'clock p.m. Tents are all down & packed. Baggage in the wagons, arms stacked & all ready to move." During the evening, the men piled logs in heaps near their hillside camps and set the wood on fire, using the towering pillars of flames to mask their departure. Starting at 1:00 a.m. to avoid detection by Union balloonists, the brigade marched sixteen miles past Spotsylvania Court House over "very rugged country" to Gordonsville. According to Evans, the hike was "most disagreeably dusty and fatiguing… poor fellows, we have done very little marching in six months and their feet were badly blistered."[23]

21 Michael W. Hofe, *That There Be No Stain Upon My Stones: Lieutenant Colonel William L. McLeod, 38th Georgia Regiment, 1842-1863* (Gettysburg, Pa.: Thomas Publications, 1995).

22 OR 37, pt. 1, 352. The companies of the 60th were from Bartow, Dooly, Fannin, Gilmer, Meriwether, Paulding, Troup, Walker, and Whitfield counties. Lamar's 61st regiment was from Tattnall, Bulloch, Brooks, Montgomery, Quitman, Bibb, and Wilkes counties.

23 Robert Grier Stephens, Jr., ed., *Intrepid Warrior: Clement Anselm Evans* (Dayton, Ohio: Morningside Press, 1992), 183. This book, written by his grandson, contains Evans' wartime diary. Evans was born Feb. 25, 1833, in Stewart County, Georgia. He studied at the Augusta Law School and was admitted to the bar at the age of 18. By 21 he was a county judge, and by 25 a state senator. Evans was commissioned as major of the 31st Georgia on Nov. 19, 1861, and advanced to colonel on May 13, 1862. He temporarily commanded the Georgia Brigade from September through November 1862.

Private Nichols of the 61st recorded, "We left our camp about dark. . . . The first little branch that we came to every man was trying to walk the foot-logs, when General Gordon jumped off his horse and waded the branch back and forth, to show the boys how to wade." During daylight, the brigade camped in dense woods. Ewell banned campfires to avoid alerting the enemy.[24]

Once safely away from the Federals, Ewell ordered daytime marches. To keep his men relatively fresh, he did as Stonewall Jackson had done and issued orders to halt every two miles for a ten-minute rest break. Twenty-year-old Pvt. Isaac Gordon Bradwell of the 31st Georgia liked the routine and noted, "By doing this, we could march all day, and the boys who were well could keep up. We had but few stragglers. The wagon trains kept up and we drew rations regularly. We made excellent time." General Gordon wrote his wife after three days on the road, "Our march since the first day has been much more agreeable & less fatiguing. Rain has fallen & dust settled. Short marches too now . . . only 8 to 10 miles per day." The brigade marched north through Sperryville, where ladies lining the street served cold water to the appreciative men. Gordon camped three miles beyond Little Washington.[25]

More Rebels soon left Fredericksburg, and Washington buzzed with rumors as to Lee's intentions. Few soldiers or officers knew their mission or destination. Early's Division reached Culpeper on June 7 and camped for two days. "How far we will go, no one seems to know—I doubt if Genl. Lee himself knows," John Gordon informed Fanny. "I have no doubt however that we shall succeed in making Hooker fall back to Manassas or beyond there." A captain in the 26th Georgia penned an optimistic letter that later appeared in a Georgia newspaper:

> I cannot tell you where we are going, but you will no doubt hear of us before long. We are on the road to the Potomac, and if "Fighting Joe" don't mind, we will run into him. We have a large army, and it is in the finest condition I have ever seen it. We march from 20-25 miles each day, so that it will not take us long to get to Baltimore or Washington, or somewhere up there. There is a

---

24 Murray, *South Georgia Rebels*, 128.

25 John Gordon to Fanny Gordon, June 7, 1863. Courtesy of Hargrett Rare Book & Manuscript Library / University of Georgia Libraries; Isaac G. Bradwell, "Capture of Winchester, Virginia and Milroy's Army in June, 1863," *Confederate Veteran*, Vol. 30, No. 9 (Sept. 1922), 330.

really big fight or long march on hand, without doubt, for we drew three days' rations today—one of flour and two of hard bread. I expect to march 30 miles tomorrow. I will drop a line every opportunity, but don't think I will have a chance to do so until after the fight. Do not be uneasy or pay any attention until you know what you hear is true.[26]

When Federal intelligence officers realized that large numbers of Confederates had left their camps, including Ewell's entire corps, the War Department ordered General Hooker to find the missing Rebels and determine their course. Union scouts detected a major concentration of enemy cavalry near Culpeper, and Hooker sent much of his cavalry there with orders to destroy or disperse them. The summer campaign opened with a long bloody tactical draw on June 9 at Brandy Station, where Union cavalry under Brig. Gen. Alfred Pleasonton surprised Rebels under Maj. Gen. James E. B. Stuart. Ewell's Second Corps left Culpeper the next day heading for the Shenandoah Valley. Lt. Col. Elijah V. White's 35th Battalion, Virginia Cavalry, a command General Ewell personally requested to escort his forces, screened the corps' movement.[27]

Intelligence gathered in Richmond and from Southern deserters indicated to Union officers that Pennsylvania appeared to be the primary target. Secretary of War Edwin M. Stanton warned Harrisburg to prepare for a possible invasion. On June 10, he assigned a capable and experienced officer to organize the defenses along the Susquehanna River. Major General Darius Nash Couch, although he was the senior corps commander in the Army of the Potomac, resigned command of the Second Corps on May 22 in protest of Hooker's bungling of the Chancellorsville Campaign. He despised Hooker and was unwilling to continue serving under him. A 40-year-old New York native, Couch possessed considerable combat experience and strong organizational skills. He and his West Point roommate, Thomas J. Jackson, graduated in the talented Class of 1846 that included twenty-two future Civil War generals including George McClellan, George Pickett, A. P. Hill, Cadmus Wilcox, and

26 *Columbus* (Ga.) *Daily Sun*, June 28, 1863. Letter by an unknown captain in the 26th Georgia, June 8, 1863.

27 OR 27, pt. 1, 29-33; Pt. 2, 752; Frank M. Myers, *The Comanches: A History of White's Battalion, Virginia Cavalry* (Baltimore: Kelly, Piet & Co., 1871), 103-104, 188. White's battalion was detached from William E. "Grumble" Jones' brigade.

Maj. Gen. Darius N. Couch commanded the Department of the Susquehanna during the Gettysburg Campaign. The former leader of the Army of the Potomac's Second Corps, he had resigned in protest of Hooker's generalship. *Library of Congress*

John Gibbon. Couch had fought Mexicans, Seminoles, and Rebels. Few questioned his competence, dedication, or zeal.[28]

Couch's command assignment was the huge newly formed Department of the Susquehanna, nearly 34,000 square miles stretching from Johnstown and the Laurel Highlands east to the state line. Arriving in Harrisburg in the early afternoon of June 11, he established headquarters in the Old State Capitol Building. After conferring with Republican Governor Andrew G. Curtin and his advisers, Couch started planning how best to protect his sector. The veteran general pitched into his new role with vigor and efficiency. He assigned several former or current army officers to his staff.[29]

Meanwhile, Ewell's Confederates streamed toward the Shenandoah Valley. The only significant Union opposition was a relatively untested 7,500-man force under Maj. Gen. Robert H. Milroy near Winchester, an important logistical center in the Shenendoah's northern reaches. Ewell led more than twice that number, the majority being veterans of multiple campaigns. John Gordon counted 188 officers and 2,194 men in his brigade, down somewhat from May 31 levels because of exhaustion, foot-soreness, and straggling.[30]

On June 12, Gordon's Brigade entered the Valley at Chester Gap in the Blue Ridge Mountains. The lead elements reached Front Royal about 5:00 p.m. "after a most exhausting march of 17 miles in about six hours." According to Private Gordon Bradwell, "The weather was hot and the roads dry and dusty. This dust, worked up by the wagon trains and artillery, settled on us until we were as brown as the dust itself. General Gordon," added the private, "riding along by us, said in a loud voice: 'Boys, if your mothers could see you now, they wouldn't know you.' Some of us were limping along on blistered feet, and the General greatly endeared himself to us by his conduct on this occasion. Getting down from his horse, he mounted a private soldier in the saddle, while he fell into ranks with a gun on his shoulder and trudged along with us."[31]

28 OR 27, pt. 3, 54-55; A. M. Gambone, *Major General Darius Nash Couch: Enigmatic Valor* (Baltimore: Butternut and Blue, 2000), 137-38. Descendants claim the general pronounced his name Duh-RYE-us Couch (rhymes with ouch). Couch supported Democrats but maintained a cordial and effective working relationship with Republican Governor Andrew Curtin.

29 OR 27, pt. 3, 55.

30 *SHSP*, 4: 241-281. Gordon's Brigade was the largest command in Early's Division.

31 John Gordon to Fanny Gordon, June 13, 1863. Courtesy of Hargrett Rare Book & Manuscript Library, University of Georgia Libraries; Bradwell, "Capture of Winchester," 330.

Gordon and his dust-caked legions camped just east of the South Branch of the Shenandoah River. At 3:00 a.m. on June 13 they forded both branches and marched on the Valley Pike toward Milroy's outer defenses, three miles southwest of Winchester. The Rebels had no love for the Federal commander and looked forward to whipping him. One Confederate described Milroy as nothing more than a "bombastic coward and cow-stealer." Gordon attacked about 4:00 p.m., deploying a line of skirmishers and holding two regiments (the 13th and 31st Georgia) in reserve. After his men advanced several hundred yards he ordered the remaining regiments into battle line. Milroy's skirmishers retired behind a stone wall but were driven off quickly, as was a nearby battery Gordon hoped to capture. "For a short time the fighting was fast and furious," recalled Private Bradwell, "but the enemy could not stand against charge and yelling, and they broke immediately for the cover of their fortifications." Howling Confederates advanced almost a mile before Union counterattacks, the normal course of confusion and chaos, and the gathering darkness halted their progress. Gordon suffered seventy-five casualties, including several "efficient officers" whose loss would affect the upcoming campaign.[32]

On June 14 Abraham Lincoln asked department commander Maj. Gen. Robert Schenck to extricate Milroy from Winchester to safety at Harpers Ferry. "He will be gobbled up if he remains," observed the president, "if he is not already past salvation." Lincoln's plea was too late. That same day, the divisions under Early and Johnson, both of Richard Ewell's Second Corps, shattered the Winchester defenses, sending Milroy "skedaddling" to the north during the night. Gordon advanced on Fort Milroy at daylight battling premonitions of death, only to discover the fort was empty. He sent a detachment to occupy it and take down its garrison flag. Milroy retreated toward Harpers Ferry but was cut off and soundly defeated near Stephenson's Depot. Union losses were heavy, and included more than 3,000 men killed, wounded, and captured, twenty-three pieces of artillery, 300 loaded supply wagons, and 200,000 rounds of small arms ammunition. Gordon's Brigade moved rapidly in the direction of firing and helped collect prisoners and horses.[33]

Flushed with a successful debut at the head of a corps, Ewell asked his men to join him in thanking their Heavenly Father. In acknowledgment of Divine

---

32 Myers, *The Comanches*, 188; OR 27, pt. 2, 491; Bradwell, "Capture of Winchester," 331.

33 Benjamin F. Keller, Jr. papers, Civil War files, Bullard County (Ga.) Historical Society.

favor, regimental chaplains were instructed to hold religious services as time permitted. Perhaps even more than victory Ewell's soldiers thanked God for the captured food and supplies. Lieutenant Benjamin F. Keller Jr. of the 60th Georgia reported that Gordon's Brigade dined well on "very fine beef."[34]

Soundly defeated, what was left of Milroy's command scattered in the mountains and several soldiers from his 87th Pennsylvania fled to their hometowns of Gettysburg and York. The general and his remaining 2,500 demoralized men eventually regrouped, some in Maryland and others at Bloody Run, Pennsylvania. They posed no further hindrance to Lee. Ewell assured his corps that its decisive victories should "strengthen the reliance in the righteousness of our cause, which has inspired every effort of our troops." Confederate confidence continued to rise.

The Shenandoah Valley now was essentially clear of Federals and the road to Pennsylvania was wide open. John Gordon, who was anxious to take the offensive, would later write that "The hungry hosts of Israel did not look across Jordan to the vine-clad hills of Canaan with more longing eyes than did Lee's braves contemplate the yellow grain-fields of Pennsylvania beyond the Potomac." After a two-day respite, his brigade headed north to Shepherdstown, West Virginia, and its important ford into Maryland.[35]

Meanwhile, more than 1,200 Confederate mounted infantry under Brig. Gen. Albert G. Jenkins, a former U.S. congressman from northwestern Virginia, entered Pennsylvania on June 15 and rode sixteen miles north of the Mason-Dixon Line into Franklin County. For the next week Lee's army would march unmolested toward the North's heartland. Many believed he was heading straight for Harrisburg. Much of the populace was aghast that the Southern army was now so close at hand. The hard face of war was about to become much more personal for Pennsylvanians.[36]

34 OR 51, 1,055; 27, pt. 2, 53, 464; 491; 27, pt. 3, 5-7, 70, 894-95. Schenck is pronounced "scank."

35 George R. Prowell, *History of the Eighty-seventh Regiment, Pennsylvania Volunteers* (York, Pa.: York Daily Record, 1901); Gordon, *Reminiscences*, 139; OR 27, pt. 2, 53; 27, pt. 3, 895. Bloody Run is now called Everett.

36 OR 27, pt. 3, 186. Jenkins also served in the Confederate Congress.

Chapter 2

Pennsylvania's Response

Preparing for the Rebels

While Confederates marched freely through the Shenandoah Valley, Pennsylvania Governor Andrew Curtin warned his citizens that Harrisburg could be targeted, or perhaps Pittsburgh or even Philadelphia. He ordered increased security measures in those cities. In Washington, Henry W. Halleck, the general-in-chief of the U.S. Army, grew concerned that the Rebels might turn westward and cross the Ohio River. From there, they could return to the South through West Virginia. He dispatched Maj. Gen. William T. H. Brooks, a veteran of the Army of the Potomac, to organize Pittsburgh's defense. Brooks assigned engineers to locate and plan forts around the city. Soon thousands of civilians began constructing these works. Commerce halted as Pittsburgh's merchants and mechanics organized into defense companies. Officials ordered all bars, restaurants, and saloons to close, stopping the sale and distribution of liquor and spirits.[1]

In towns across the threatened section of Pennsylvania, newspapers and local officials urged constituents to enroll in home guard companies. Because these did not require long-term military commitment, the response was significant. A Johnstown politician proudly declared that he could personally muster between five hundred and a thousand men to defend his borough. Altoona and other nearby towns responded with thousands of volunteers for

---

1   OR 27, pt. 3, 54-55, 169; Samuel P. Bates, *Martial Deeds of Pennsylvania* (Philadelphia: T. H. Davis, 1876), 171.

regional duty. On June 14, Blair County leaders organized home guards under the command of Col. Jacob Higgins, late of the 125th Pennsylvania. The roster included a few men, recently discharged from the Army of the Potomac, who served under Higgins at Chancellorsville. However, most of the others were either too young or too old for military service, or had been turned down for health reasons. They fortified several mountain passes in the region while stealing poultry and hams from local farmers. Near McKee Gap, campfires built by hungry recruits triggered a small forest fire. Area farmers sarcastically dubbed Higgins' soldiers "The Chicken Raiders."[2]

Residents in Franklin County did not wait for the government to react. On the morning of June 15, refugees from Virginia and Maryland crowded the streets of Chambersburg, the county seat and one of the largest towns in the fertile Cumberland Valley. They brought unwelcome news that the Rebels were not far off. A newspaperman described the ensuing exodus: "Nearly every horse, good, bad, and indifferent, was started for the mountains as early on Monday as possible, and the negroes darkened the different roads northward for hours, loaded with household effects, sable babies, etc., and horses, wagons, and cattle crowded every avenue to places of safety."[3]

Fear increased when more than forty Federal supply wagons galloped through Chambersburg at 10:00 a.m., confirming civilian reports that Confederates were approaching Pennsylvania. The townspeople had never before witnessed "such wild excitement and consternation." A few careening wagons lost their wheels and crashed. Exhausted horses fell dead in the streets. Angry teamsters swore at the top of their lungs at balky animals while whipping them with the lash. As the grand stampede continued, eyewitnesses reported that every man and horse was "animated with the singular desire of salvation from Rebel clutches." Order was restored only when a provost lieutenant brandished a cocked revolver and ordered the teamsters to halt. The extraordinary spectacle alarmed Chambersburg's residents. When more than one hundred fleeing New York cavalrymen later dashed through town, "The skedaddle commenced in magnificent earnestness and exquisite confusion."[4]

---

2   Vertical files, GNMP; Sylva Emerson website, *A Brief History of Blair County, Pennsylvania*.

3   *Chambersburg Repository*, June 16, 1863; Bates, *Martial Deeds*, 169-70.

4   *Chambersburg Valley Spirit*, July 8, 1863; *Chambersburg Repository*, June 16, 1863; Rachel Cormany diary, Franklin County (Pa.) Historical Society.

Confederate cavalry under Brig. Gen. Albert G. Jenkins raided Franklin County, Pennsylvania twice in mid-June 1863, taking horses, supplies, and livestock from the region.

By mid-afternoon the army wagons and a long stream of refugees "of every age and size, and beasts and four-footed things innumerable" approached Harrisburg. The Camelback toll bridge across the Susquehanna presented "a scene of ceaseless activity" and a financial windfall for its owners. Throughout the sultry day a cloud of dust "rose constantly far down the valley, reaching forward and across the stream, as far in the opposite direction as the eye could penetrate." Fine dust enveloped the people, vehicles, and livestock until "thick folds wrapped them like a garment." By nightfall the long trek amid rumbling wagons had dulled the senses of the weary travelers. Many collapsed from exhaustion after entering the city. Eventually, 1,800 black refugees crowded into the capital, where they joined thousands of whites who had fled their homes. Businesses closed as Harrisburg prepared for the approaching enemy.[5]

In Gettysburg that same day, Alice Powers recorded her thoughts about the frightened populace:

> Our streets were thronged with the frightened colored citizens, starting with terror-stricken women and children toward the Susquehanna, with the hope of reaching its opposite bank if possible. They were burdened with all sorts of household goods. The children clung to the skirts of their mothers weeping, and the aged tottered on frantic with fear. Some in their poverty were obliged to walk, others drove 'sorry nags' in all sorts of vehicles and yet others dragged their belongings to the railroad to ship them, so that they might go by train in the morning. A more sad and pitiful scene than that Monday night witnessed cannot be conceived.[6]

A Philadelphia newsman commented on another aspect brought about by the flood of civilians: the lack of services. "There is scarcely a negro left in any of the border counties of Pennsylvania," wrote the reporter. He continued:

> In traveling from town to town, your reporters go unshaved and hungry, and do penance for their sins. The cooks in the kitchen and the knights of the razor have fled. At Mechanicsburg yesterday we made a dinner of peanuts, the hotel proprietor declaring that his assistants had vanished. At York the same story was told, and at Carlisle there was no variation. It is very sad to witness the troubles of these people. Not infrequently the refugees move in families, and while the father carries a child, the mother is burdened with a few cooking utensils and some necessary articles of clothing. Thus we have met them, trudging through dark woods on deserted railroads, or hiding temporarily behind bushes until they ascertained that we were not Rebels. Along the turnpike they go in gangs, seldom asking favors, and nearly always having sufficient money to pay for their meals. They find no shelter from white citizens."[7]

---

5   Robert G. Crist, "Highwater 1863: The Confederate Approach to Harrisburg," *Pennsylvania History*, Vol. 30, No. 2 (April 1963), 167-68; Bates, *Martial Deeds*, 170; *Philadelphia Inquirer*, June 30, 1863. The wagons were from Col. Andrew T. McReynolds' brigade, Milroy's division. The bridge was privately owned by the local McCormick family, which published the *Patriot and Union* newspaper. Tolls for the week ending June 12 were $271.05 (a typical week's gross). The next week, as refugees flooded into Harrisburg, receipts totaled $1,180.40. Gambone, *Major General Darius Nash Couch*, 153-54.

6   *Gettysburg Compiler*, June 24, 1903.

7   *Philadelphia Inquirer*, June 30, 1863.

Concerned about the Rebels' northward thrust, President Lincoln issued a proclamation requesting 100,000 volunteers spread across four states to serve for six months "to repel the threatened and imminent invasion of Pennsylvania." Governor Curtin called for 50,000 men as his state's quota. He admonished his constituents, "Pennsylvanians. . . . Show yourselves what you are—a free, loyal, spirited, brave, vigorous race. . . . The time has now come when we must all stand or fall together in defense of our duty that posterity shall not blush for us." Curtin sought help from Governor Horatio Seymour of New York. Although an outspoken critic of Lincoln's war policies, the Democrat dispatched 6,000 well-equipped militiamen to Harrisburg. Residents admired the New Yorkers' fancy uniforms and outward military appearance, but soon discovered they were better foragers than soldiers. Couch dispatched some of the militia toward Chambersburg to counter the Rebel threat.[8]

New Jersey's governor, Joel Parker, offered up the 27th New Jersey Infantry, a veteran but untested regiment of nearly 800 soldiers. The unit was stationed in Cincinnati while completing its nine-month enlistment term and would not arrive in Harrisburg until June 26. Several other governors scrambled to raise additional troops for Pennsylvania's defense, but none could be ready in time. "There is danger that we may be disposed to rely too much on General Hooker's army, and not sufficiently upon our own strength and resources, which alone should be equal to the task if stout hearts direct them," warned the editor of the *Philadelphia Press*. "There is a danger that, having been so frequently alarmed by reports of previous raids which have proved unfounded, our people may allow themselves to rest in a false sense of security. There is danger that, from these causes, the response to the Governor's proclamation may not be so prompt and unanimous as the emergency demands."[9]

---

8   H. M. M. Richards, *Pennsylvania's Emergency Men at Gettysburg* (Reading, Pa.: s. n., 1895), 6. Seymour strongly opposed the Emancipation Proclamation as unenforceable and politically motivated. He actively supported the Union and helped New York raise troops. He ran for the Democratic presidential nomination in 1868, but lost to Ulysses S. Grant. Richards claimed that the New York militia's "whole time seemed to be taken up in foraging; in many cases brow-beating helpless persons, and in wondering how soon they would get home."

9   OR 27, pt. 3, 142-43, 164-67, 184-85, 190-91, 201, 222-23, 1080; *Philadelphia Press*, June 16, 1863. The 27th New Jersey served only three days in Harrisburg before returning home to be mustered out on July 2, 1863.

Fear Turns to Reality

Advanced Confederate scouting parties entered Pennsylvania on June 15, following the refugees by mere hours. Behind them rode Brig. Gen. Albert Jenkins' veteran brigade of mounted infantry. His poorly disciplined horsemen included several companies that had served as independent partisans in the mountainous terrain of northwestern Virginia. They seized Greencastle after routing New York cavalry and capturing a lieutenant. After destroying the railroad depot and cutting telegraph wires, they rode northward. Shortly before midnight, two companies of the 14th Virginia Cavalry entered Chambersburg's nearly empty square. Many inhabitants already had fled, leaving clothes and household utensils scattered in the streets.

"As matters look now, all south of the Susquehanna will be swept," General Darius Couch warned Secretary of War Edwin Stanton. Couch decided to use the river as his main defensive line, holding all bridges and fords, and requested permission to draw from Federal supplies in Philadelphia, including 10,000 rifles and full equipment and 2,000,000 rounds of small arms ammunition. Couch initiated efforts to construct breastworks and rifle-pits along Harrisburg's riverfront and on the opposite bank. That night the general wired Stanton, "The enemy are following my pickets 9 miles south of Chambersburg, and apparently moving north in three columns; one to Chambersburg, one to Gettysburg, and the other in the direction of the coal mines. Infantry reported with them. I shall have but little to resist them, I fear."[10]

On Tuesday, June 16, General Jenkins dispersed his Rebel regiments throughout the area to procure supplies and damage the infrastructure of military value. A detachment ripped down telegraph wires and burned the Cumberland Valley Railroad bridge near Scotland, five miles northeast of Chambersburg. Squads tore up track, bent rails, and destroyed rolling stock and equipment. Virginia horsemen plundered abandoned houses throughout the countryside.[11] Jenkins dispatched several patrols that collected local blacks

---

10 *OR* 27, pt. 3, 79, 129, 131, 162, 914.

11 *Richmond Daily Dispatch*, April 5, 1896. The newspaper translated extracts from the diary of German-speaking Lt. Hermann Schuricht of the 14th Virginia Cavalry. See Schuricht's article, "Jenkins's Brigade in the Gettysburg Campaign," *SHSP*, 24 (1896) and the *Chambersburg Repository*, June 16, 1863. The paper reported that a few empty houses were robbed of clothing,

suspected of being escaped slaves, or "contraband." The wagons of captives being sent south into slavery included Pennsylvania-born freemen. Worried that they too would be captured, a few white government employees headed for safety.[12]

Early on Wednesday morning, Jenkins moved his headquarters to a downtown hotel. He ordered the townspeople to turn in their weapons, and eventually his men collected five hundred assorted firearms, as well as swords and pistols. Lieutenant Hermann Schuricht and Company D loaded the usable weapons into wagons and destroyed the rest. Jenkins ordered Chambersburg's shopkeepers to open their establishments from 8 until 10 a.m. to sell goods to his soldiers in exchange for Confederate money. Business was "brisk." He instructed the townspeople to provide rations for his hungry troopers, who "fared very well" according to Schuricht, despite the residents' adverse feelings. "However," he added, "a number of them, belonging to the peace-party, treated us kindly; especially were the Germans in favor of peace."[13]

While Rebels raided Chambersburg, efforts to raise troops continued in Harrisburg. An unusual group of volunteers responded to Governor Curtin's plea. Captain Charles C. Carson and a company of seventeen men, the youngest of whom as 68 years old, presented themselves for military service. Each senior citizen was a veteran of the War of 1812, and each wanted to serve his state and country again in another time of need. A color bearer carried a tattered flag once borne at the battle of Trenton by Pennsylvanians serving under George Washington. The old patriots asked for flintlock muskets. Then, using colonial commands and formations and with a drum and fife playing, marched to the rifle pits. Their bodies may have aged, but their spirits had not.[14]

Alarmed at the enemy incursion, officials boxed government archives for removal to safety. Overnight, workers loaded the 28,000 books of the state library and the oil portraits of past governors into railroad cars for transport to

kettles, and goods, and bureaus and cupboards ransacked and their contents strewn about. Provost guards protected the borough's empty houses, but country folk were not as fortunate.

12 Ted Alexander, "A Regular Slave Hunt," *North & South*, Issue 4, No. 7, 82-88. See also Franklin Repository, July 8, 1863; *Chambersburg Valley Spirit*, July 8, 1863, Rachel Cormany diary entry for June 16, 1863; and the Reverend Thomas Creigh diary, entries for June 26 and 27.

13 *Richmond Daily Dispatch*, April 5, 1896; Stoner, *History of Franklin County*, 369.

14 *Philadelphia Press*, June 24, 1863; Samuel P. Bates, *History of Pennsylvania Volunteers*, 1861-5 (Harrisburg: B. Singerly, 1868-71), 5: 1224-25; *Albany Evening Journal*, June 25, 1863.

Philadelphia. State cash and gold reserves were hustled off for safekeeping, as were the assets of several banks along the Rebels' possible invasion routes. Harrisburg's post office closed, and several merchants packed up their inventory and sent it to safety. Ironically, while many in Harrisburg prepared to leave, delegates arrived for the state Democratic Party's convention, where they would select Governor Curtin's opponent for the fall election. Some in the press accused the attendees of harboring "Copperhead" or pro-Southern views.[15]

Meanwhile, after hearing rumors in the forenoon on June 17 that a strong Yankee force was approaching Chambersburg, Jenkins withdrew his mounted command into Maryland. However, he did send foragers back into Pennsylvania. On Thursday, Col. Milton J. Ferguson and 250 men crossed the Cove and Tuscarora Mountains into Fulton County to raid for horses and supplies in McConnellsburg. They returned with $12,000 worth of cattle, 120 horses, and several young blacks seized from area farms and residences. Many Unionists perceived Jenkins' foraging activities to be a mere feint, because infantry had not crossed the border into the state. To Darius Couch, however, the presence of Southern horsemen in the Cumberland Valley was an ominous sign that General Lee indeed intended to launch a full-scale invasion of Pennsylvania. At that time Couch could count on fewer than 250 men in officially mustered Federal commands throughout the threatened area.[16]

Jenkins' raids generated headlines throughout the Keystone State, but the response to Governor Curtin's call to arms to combat the Rebels fell far short of expectations. Many residents were unsure whether they would be enrolled in the Federal army or as short-term state emergency militia, as had been the case in September 1862. Those who traveled to Harrisburg to enlist discovered they had to secure their own shelter and food until the question was settled. Fifty-seven Pennsylvania College students departed Gettysburg via train on June 17, along with more than two dozen other townsmen, including four students from the Lutheran Theological Seminary. They sang "The Battle Cry of Freedom" while embarking for the capital, where they joined thousands of other eager volunteers. However, confusion reigned as to both their expected term of service and status as Federal troops or state militia. According to young

---

15 *Philadelphia Press*, June 17, 1863. The convention nominated Judge George W. Woodward for governor.

16 *The Mercersburg Journal*, July 17, 1863.

drummer Henry M. M. Richards, "The streets of Harrisburg were filled with unorganized crowds, roaming about aimlessly. Utterly discouraged, many returned home. Finally order began to appear from well nigh chaos."[17]

Couch organized the remaining recruits into seven volunteer militia regiments of roughly 1,000 men apiece. They mustered into state service "for the duration of the emergency." In reality, Pennsylvania needed dozens more regiments to protect its cities, railroads, and military targets. Couch had experience commanding a division of infantry and later a corps against Lee's Army of Northern Virginia. He knew all too well that the handful of emergency soldiers being raised could not stop Lee's army. Additional enemy forces could appear almost anywhere along the Department of the Susquehanna's 180-mile border between slave state Maryland and free state Pennsylvania.[18]

In addition to sending New York militia to Franklin County, Couch assigned veteran officers to spearhead the defense of ninety miles of the Susquehanna River from its confluence with the Juniata River downstream to the Conowingo Bridge in Maryland. What Couch needed now was a strong leader with considerable military experience to defend York and Adams counties, which were likely Confederate paths to the Susquehanna. He selected Maj. Granville Owen Haller for this arduous task. Couch charged Haller with determining the best places to defend important towns, railroads, and other possible targets.

Granville Haller was born in York on January 31, 1819. His attorney father George died when he was just two years old, leaving behind a widow and four small children. His mother raised her family using rental income from several houses she inherited from her late husband. She sent the oldest Haller son to medical college and wanted Granville to attend the Lutheran Theological Seminary in Gettysburg. The younger son, however, preferred a military career to that of a minister and after he graduated in 1838 from York County Academy, the board of trustees recommended Granville for West Point. In a resolution passed October 23, 1838, trustee Charles Weiser praised Haller, calling him a young man of "excellent moral character" who possessed strong "habits of study and perseverance." However, U.S. Senator James Buchanan

17 *OR* 27, pt. 3, 857; *Gettysburg Compiler*, June 24, 1903; H. M. M. Richards, *Pennsylvania's Emergency Men at Gettysburg*, 5. Richards was a 14-year-old drummer in the 26th Pennsylvania Volunteer Militia. His older brother, Corp. Matthias H. Richards, served in the same company.

18 *OR* 27, pt. 3, 76-77.

Maj. Granville O. Haller commanded the headquarters guard of the Army of the Potomac at Antietam and Fredericksburg. During the Gettysburg Campaign he led the defense of Adams and York counties. *USAMHI*

appointed William B. Franklin, son of his recently deceased close friend, Clerk of the House of Representatives Walter Franklin.[19]

After Haller traveled to Washington and met with the secretary of war, he received an invitation to appear before a board of military officers. The result was a commission in November 1839 as a second lieutenant in the 4th U.S. Infantry. Haller fought Seminoles in Florida in 1840-41 and served with distinction at Monterrey, Veracruz, and other battles in the Mexican War in the same regiment as Ulysses S. Grant. Haller was brevetted captain "for gallant and meritorious conduct in the battle of Chapultepec," and promoted to captaincy in January 1848. Four years later, the Army brevetted Haller as major of the 7th U.S. Infantry and transferred him to Washington Territory, where he hunted down Indians who were part of localized insurrections. Haller routinely hanged their leaders as an example to others who did not obey the white man's law. In 1860 he served in California and Arizona Territory. One early historian described Granville Haller as a man whose "broad brow indicated a strong intellect, his eye shone clear and bright, and he was never afraid to look any man in the face."[20]

An avid chess player, Haller was keenly interested in strategy. After the Civil War erupted, army authorities ordered him to the East and promoted him to major of the 7th Infantry on September 25, 1861. He subsequently accepted an assignment to Maj. Gen. George B. McClellan's staff in the Army of the Potomac. Haller commanded McClellan's headquarters guard on the Peninsula and during the Maryland Campaign. He stayed in that role under subsequent commanders Ambrose Burnside and Joseph Hooker. In early May 1863, the outspoken Democrat returned to York to recover from disease contracted in the field.[21]

Haller did not have a formal command when the Rebels threatened Pennsylvania. As with dozens of other unassigned officers, he traveled to

19 Charles Weiser, Resolution of the York County Academy, Oct. 23, 1838, Granville Haller file, York County Historical Trust, York, Pa. The academy was a precursor to York College.

20 Clarence Bagley, *History of Seattle from the Earliest Settlement to the Present Time* (Chicago: S. J. Clarke, 1916), 2: 747. In October 1855 more than 300 Yakima Indians besieged Haller's two outnumbered companies at a ford on the Toppenish River. He lost five men killed and 17 wounded, plus his pack train, supplies and a mountain howitzer which he buried. Engineers surveying the right of way for a highway discovered the old relic in 1913.

21 John Gibson, *History of York County, Pennsylvania* (Chicago: F. A. Battey, 1886), 327. The headquarters guard was companies A, F, H, and K of the 93rd New York Infantry.

Harrisburg and offered his services to General Couch. Haller stood out in the crowd of ambitious men eager to resume their service. He was Regular Army, a career soldier with impressive credentials including years of combat experience against diverse enemies and organizational skills enhanced under McClellan. Couch designated him as an aide-de-camp. His selection to head the defense of Adams and York counties was widely applauded, except for an old associate, naval officer Clark H. Wells. He accused Haller of uttering disloyal remarks about the Union cause at Fredericksburg during the winter. The pair subsequently engaged in a series of unpleasant written exchanges concerning the veracity of the serious allegation. Wells elevated the issue to Secretary of War Edwin Stanton, eventually calling Haller a "traitor and unmitigated liar." In turn, Haller accused the Philadelphia Navy Yard executive officer of hallucinations and darkly noted his past mental instability.[22]

Haller met with Col. Levi Maish of the 130th Pennsylvania Infantry. Maish, who had been in Virginia visiting his brother after he fell wounded at Second Winchester, was on his way home to York when he "received a telegram from a prominent citizen of York, at Baltimore . . . informing me that Governor Curtin requested my presence at Harrisburg to assist in defending the State against invasion." Maish and Haller called upon Curtin, who directed them to "raise some emergency men." They took the earliest train back to York and on June 15—the same day that Jenkins' Rebel horsemen entered Pennsylvania—met with civic leaders to develop contingency plans should enemy raiders approach their bustling town of 8,600 people. A major regional commercial and railroad center, York boasted a large U.S. Army Hospital with hundreds of convalescing patients. As Couch later explained it, "York was a strategic point. It covered the approaches to [the] Columbia Bridge, one of the important crossings of the Susquehanna and it gave me more anxiety than any other point in Pennsylvania excepting Chambersburg."[23]

Major General William B. Franklin, the former commander of the Army of the Potomac's Sixth Corps and another York native, also counseled the leaders. Ironically, it was Franklin who years before had received the West Point appointment coveted by Haller. The two officers urged civil authorities to

---

22 Clark H. Wells, *The Reply to a Pamphlet Recently Published by G. O. Haller, Late a U.S. Major* (York, Pa.: H. Young, 1865), 13-16.

23 Guy Breshears, *Major Granville Haller: Dismissed with Malice* (Westminster, Md.: Heritage Books, 2006), 88-90.

recruit soldiers for state service and home guard companies. Haller emphasized the need to send out scouting parties toward Carlisle and fell trees to block key roads in the low mountains of northwestern York County. However, the latter request was never followed. The civic leaders did order all businesses, including taverns, to close by six o'clock each evening. Armed civilians soon patrolled York's streets.[24]

Haller toured the army hospital on Penn Common and met with chief surgeon Henry Palmer, formerly the chief surgeon of the famed "Iron Brigade of the West." Their primary conversation centered around the fighting ability of the convalescing soldiers who served as orderlies and stewards. Most had faced Lee's vaunted army before, and several had suffered serious wounds at Antietam. Major Palmer informed Haller that the invalids still had some fight left in them. After assembling them on the parade ground, the 35-year-old Wisconsin doctor read a telegram from Governor Curtin requesting volunteers. Palmer, who served as a volunteer surgeon during the Crimean War, challenged all who desired to serve to step forward one pace. To his delight, 187 men responded. This "Invalid Battalion" as they were soon called voted for their officers, selecting a sergeant of the 2nd Wisconsin as captain and a one-armed boy from Philadelphia as first lieutenant.[25]

24 Granville O. Haller, *The Dismissal of Major Granville O. Haller of the Regular Army of the United States by Order of the Secretary of War in Special Orders, 331, of July 25, 1863* (Paterson, N.J.: Daily Guardian, 1863), 61. That evening, Chief Burgess David Small convened a town meeting in the courthouse. Fifteen leading citizens (three from each ward) formed a "Committee of Safety" to coordinate the defense of York should the enemy approach. The committee met at 9 a.m. on Tuesday, June 16, and issued a proclamation urging citizens to obey Curtin's call. A company of six-month volunteers was formed under Capt. David Z. Seipe and sent to Harrisburg to enlist in the army. The committee authorized a $25 bounty for each volunteer. They also formed a company of mounted scouts to patrol the county. The committee met twice a day during the emergency (YCHT).

25 Haller, *Dismissal of Major Granville O. Haller*, 61; William J. Wray, *History of the Twenty-third Pennsylvania Volunteer Infantry, Birney's Zouaves* (Philadelphia: s. n., 1904), 151-52. A New York private was voted as second lieutenant of the invalid battalion. Many of the patients looked upon the entire affair as "a huge joke" or "scare of the Governor's." For several days, they lounged around the hospital during the daytime and then picketed at night. A sergeant of the 1st Maine Cavalry and a Philadelphia cavalryman served as scouts, patrolling the region west of York.

The Columbia Bridge

Among the military targets that Couch ordered Haller to protect was a massive bridge across the Susquehanna River connecting Wrightsville, thirteen miles east of York's Centre Square, with Columbia in Lancaster County. The only remaining span between Harrisburg and Maryland, it was sure to attract Confederate interest. A marvel of structural engineering designed by noted bridge builder James Moore, Jr., it was the longest covered bridge in the world at 5,629 feet long and forty feet wide. It rose fourteen feet above flood level and served as a vital route for commercial and military traffic.[26]

Until the early 19th century, the Wrightsville-Columbia crossing utilized a series of progressively larger ferries. However they had limits in speed and the amount and type of cargo they could carry. Winter storms, so frequent in the Susquehanna Valley, hindered ferry service. At times ice completely blocked the river. To minimize seasonal weather effects on commerce, local investors planned a covered bridge just north of Wright's Ferry. They hired the firm of Walcott & Slaymaker to build it. Workers constructed the impressive bridge from oak and pine harvested nearby. It opened to the public in 1814, providing a passageway for wagons, carriages, horses and riders, pedestrians, and related traffic. "When the project was started, it appeared so stupendous and so far above the reach of human exertion, that it was generally ridiculed for its extravagance," marveled one reporter. "The idea of building a permanent bridge over a bold, rapid, and turbulent stream of more than a mile in extent was too vast for minds only accustomed to contemplate ordinary difficulties. . . . The great enterprise, however, has been accomplished by a private company in about two years."[27]

The new bridge quickly turned a profit for its owners, who recouped their investment by charging a toll. However, the cold winter of 1831-32 saw heavy icing of the Susquehanna, and on February 18 ice floes crushed five spans and

26 Gibson, *History of York County*, 327; Robert H. Goodall, "The Second Columbia Bridge," *Journal of the Lancaster County Historical Society*, Vol. 57, No. 1 (1953). A second bridge connecting York and Lancaster counties was constructed in 1814 at McCall's Ferry. Shortly thereafter, ice destroyed it. The architect, Theodore Burr, also designed and constructed the Camelback Bridge at Harrisburg. A bridge at York Furnace, constructed in 1855, was carried away by a flood a year later. The April 16, 1856, *Baltimore Sun* reported "considerable damage was done to the Columbia bridge." However, workers quickly repaired it.

27 *Daily National Intelligencer*, March 13, 1815. The bridge was 30 ft. wide and 5,696 ft. long. It stood on 53 piers.

The Columbia Bridge was the longest covered bridge in the world. Shown in this 1850 engraving, the bridge had been rebuilt in 1834 after an earlier one was destroyed by ice floes. *Author's Collection*

carried them downstream. Over the next few days, other spans also failed, ultimately destroying the entire bridge. Confederate General John Brown Gordon was less than two weeks old when the first Columbia Bridge collapsed.[28]

Local businessmen decided to erect a new, wider structure about 1,500 feet downstream from the old bridge, closer to the ferry crossing. They planned to build it well above flood level, hoping to avoid future ice floes. Early investors in the Columbia Bridge Company and the bank that financed the project included Stephen Smith, one of the wealthiest black men in the country. By the mid-1830s, Smith held a $9,000 stake in the bridge company and an additional $18,000 investment in Columbia Bank stock. Engineering drawings were generated and construction began in mid-1832. The new bridge required twenty-seven stone piers to support the 200-foot long wooden spans. The builders, James Moore and John Evans, incorporated useful wood salvaged from the wreck of its predecessor. This second bridge opened for traffic on July 8, 1834. Two years later, famed generals William Henry Harrison and Andrew Jackson traveled in October from Philadelphia to York. The bridge's owners waived the toll for the dignitaries and their escorts, reaping a publicity bonanza from their passage.[29]

In 1835, while under state charter, crews dug a set of canals paralleling the Susquehanna River to permit the consistent transport of goods up and downstream. The goal was to reduce insurance companies' worries about summer low water levels exposing rocks that might sink boats. The North Branch Canal followed the eastern riverbank, extending the Pennsylvania Canal system's Main Line, Eastern Division. It ran from west of Harrisburg south to Columbia, where it terminated. Horses and mules towed the canal boats across the river on a bi-level towpath added to the south side of the bridge in 1840 at a

---

28 *Rhode Island American*, March 1, 1832, quoting the *York Republican*. "The destruction of the Columbia bridge, by the choking of the ice in the river, was a scene of terrific grandeur. The river, far and wide, presented a polar view; a sea of ice, crushing, crackling together in the excitement of its own rage. . . . We have never witnessed any scene, the sea excepted, which gave such an impressive view of human littleness or the fury of elemental war. About 2,500 feet or nearly one half of the bridge is gone, and the remaining portion is in all probability much injured."

29 *Baltimore Patriot*, July 16, 1834; *Philadelphia Inquirer*, Oct. 12, 1836. The long-time president of the Columbia Bridge Company, attorney Christian Brenneman, died suddenly on March 3 prior to the reopening of the bridge. Newspapers reported he expired from "agitation produced by an alarm of fire, occasioned by the burning of a chimney in the vicinity of his dwelling."

cost of $90,000. This arrangement permitted teams to pull boats in different directions simultaneously; the lower path going west to east and the upper, east to west.[30]

Once on the Wrightsville side, workers transferred the boats to a second canal, the Susquehanna and Tide Water. Commissioned by Baltimore businessmen and completed in May 1840, it ran forty-five miles south to the Chesapeake Bay at Havre de Grace, Maryland. Both canals were constructed of log cribbing filled with rocks, and, while they were roughly fifty feet wide, they were only five to six feet deep. The Columbia Bridge Company recouped its investment in the towpath addition by collecting fees from the canal boat operators.[31]

As the relatively new railroad industry emerged as competition for the canals, executives petitioned to use the existing bridge to cross the river, rather than construct another one solely for their purposes. The Columbia Bank and its insurers fretted that embers from the smokestacks of passing locomotives might ignite the wooden superstructure. A compromise was reached: The bank would allow the railroads to use their bridge for a fee, but engines would not be permitted to cross it. In 1850, the Baltimore & Susquehanna Railroad laid parallel sets of tracks on the oak deck and built a high partition to separate the new railway from the road. The bridge connected the B&SRR to the Philadelphia & Columbia Railroad on the eastern side. A turntable constructed in Wrightsville reversed the locomotives, and mules and horses towed the railcars across the bridge. Once in Columbia, a different engine picked up the cars, which then resumed their journey under steam power. Later that year, the Pennsylvania Railroad laid tracks parallel to the Susquehanna River that connected with the bridge's rails. The PRR erected a large depot, the Washington House, which featured a commanding view of the viaduct and river from its imposing front balcony.[32]

30 *Philadelphia Public Ledger*, May 10, 1837; *Philadelphia North American*, June 20, 1839.

31 More than 8,000 boats used the canal in 1855, but traffic declined sharply as railroads emerged as competition.

32 Undated transcript by P. H. Small of a newspaper article in a 1905 issue of the *York Dispatch* announcing the retirement of engineer George Small upon his 70th birthday. Hereafter referenced as "George Small, 1905 *York Dispatch*"; Gibson, *History of York County*, 327. A man named Sutton furnished the motive power for transporting the cars across to Columbia—ten mules.

In the middle of June 1850, a large fire of unknown origin broke out and destroyed several lumberyards lining the riverfront in Columbia. "The Columbia bridge over the Susquehanna was on fire several times," explained a Baltimore newspaper, "but was in each case fortunately extinguished before much damage was done."[33]

For three decades before the Civil War broke out the Columbia Bridge provided a major route to freedom for escaped slaves. The Underground Railroad thrived in this heavily Quaker, Lutheran, and Anabaptist region, where a deep and secretive network of "conductors" and "stations" offered security for those hoping to avoid roving bounty hunters. Lancaster County's black population included several descendants of early escapees. When the second bridge was constructed, Columbia's free black merchants regularly welcomed the runaways and helped them on a journey that often ended in Canada. Men such as lumberman and real estate entrepreneur Stephen Smith and businessman William Whipper provided the financial means to help the fugitives.

Particularly on the Wrightsville side of the river, the covered bridge was under constant scrutiny by spies working for slave traders, bounty hunters, informers, and others who stood to profit handsomely from any rewards paid for the capture and return of escaped slaves. In late April 1852, a Baltimore police officer murdered a fugitive during an attempt to arrest him at a lumberyard in Columbia. The shocking and scandalous incident drew national attention. Several Wrightsville residents were accused of being Southern sympathizers who willingly betrayed hidden blacks. At times, freight cars crossing the bridge carried living cargo hidden among more mundane lading. The most dangerous time for these former slaves was when railroaders unhooked the cars from the locomotives and then hitched up mules and horses. Occasionally, authorities searched the railcars before the workers towed them across the bridge. The fugitives had to be especially quiet while crossing the long tunnel-like viaduct, where any sound would echo and thus be amplified during the mile-and-a-quarter journey.[34]

---

33 *Baltimore Sun*, June 17, 1850. The fire destroyed the office of the *Columbia Spy*, as well Howard's Hotel, four houses, and the car sheds of the Baltimore & Susquehanna Railroad. The exertions of railroad employees, however, saved the railcars. Later that year the funeral train of President Zachary Taylor crossed the bridge en route to a brief stopover in York.

34 *Ohio Statesman*, May 18, 1852.

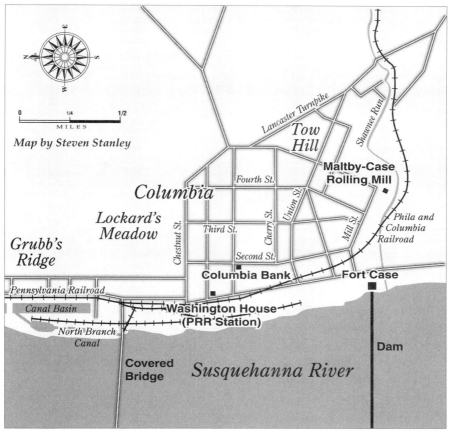

Columbia, Pennsylvania, on the eastern bank of the Susquehanna River, had once been considered as the site for the capital of the United States.

In addition to periodic inspection of railcars, authorities occasionally stopped eastbound wagons and carts in Wrightsville so that bounty hunters could perform their odious job and search for "contraband." Well coordinated Underground Railroad partisans in Columbia anxiously watched as traffic emerged from the bridge. Consignments for "respectable" businesses in Columbia and Marietta sometimes contained families or individuals illegally smuggled into Lancaster County. Several blacks and their descendants remained in the prosperous region as war approached. The 1860 census listed 169 blacks out of a population of 1,294 in Wrightsville. In Columbia, the figure was 437 of roughly 5,500 people. Many found employment in the industries flourishing along the riverbanks, spurred by the canals, railways, and road system.[35]

Columbia had grown into a bustling commercial and railroad center, second in the county to Lancaster in size and prosperity. Leading industries included iron furnaces, sawmills, flour mills, and a thriving railroad machine shop. The Maltby & Case Rolling Mill provided significant quantities of sheet iron for the railroads and the booming construction business. Many blacks toiled in this large facility, as well as nearby anthracite-fired furnaces. A newspaper editor was pleased to see black men laboring side by side with whites at all the furnaces in the region—digging ore, boating coal, standing at the helm of burden boats, piling blooms, pigs, and the like. He beamed, "This is just what I desire to see, and is what will make them respected as men."[36]

On Wrightsville's riverbank, Front Street bustled with activity. Several massive sawmills dotted the riverbank on both sides of the bridge entrance, providing a significant source of construction-grade lumber during the housing booms of the 1840s and 50s. Henry Kauffelt grew wealthy from his large mill along the Susquehanna and Tide Water Canal. His family members established partnerships in other business ventures, including another huge lumberyard co-owned with the Lanius family. By 1860, the 54-year-old Kauffelt was a leading citizen of Wrightsville. He was a director of the First National Bank. Millions of board feet of lumber came from Kauffelt's sawmills. The canals traditionally carried much of this wood, but the railroads were supplanting them. Kauffelt soon established a freight company, supplied with his own private boxcars.

Along with lumbering, other industries provided stable employment for Wrightsville's citizens, including two flourishing boat construction factories north of the bridge's tollhouse. A series of blast furnaces provided raw materials for Wolf's Iron Works. Laborers mined limestone from quarries along Kreutz Creek, just south of the lumberyards. In 1848, five brick limekilns were erected along Front Street to burn ground limestone to form processed lime for whitewash, plaster, and fertilizer. Canal boats carried the lime, among the finest

35 U.S. Census of 1860. Columbia's black population dropped from 943 in 1850 to 437 in 1860 when several black families migrated to Canada because of the Fugitive Slave Law.

36 *North Star*, Dec. 15, 1848. Blessed with considerable industry, Lancaster County was one of Pennsylvania's most populous districts with 116,000 residents according to the 1860 census. By contrast, neighboring York County counted 68,000 citizens and Adams County 28,000. Lancaster (17,603 residents) was larger than the state capital, Harrisburg (13,405).

in the world, south to Havre de Grace. There, work crews unloaded the lime and stored it for transoceanic shipment from Baltimore. Several small shops housed cigar makers and retailers, a business that boomed in the decade before the Civil War. Area farmers substantially increased their production of tobacco, a cash crop first introduced in the region in 1837. By the summer of 1863, ninety-five tobacco merchants operated in Lancaster County and more than 100 in York County.[37]

Many of Wrightsville's riverfront businessmen rebuilt their establishments following a significant fire on the night of August 28, 1862. The conflagration, fanned by strong winds, quickly spread among the lumberyards and warehouses. A lodge hall and a store were also consumed. In what would prove to be a twist of irony, Henry Kauffelt's sprawling warehouse on Locust Street was "saved by great exertion," as were some private residences.[38]

Defending the Bridge

The imposing bridge over the broad Susquehanna was vital to the region's economic health. It provided transportation between the neighboring counties and served as a connection point for the busy canals and railroads linking the East Coast with the riches of western Pennsylvania. During the Civil War, Federal troops regularly used the bridge to reach new posts. The government paid the Columbia Bank a small fee for every troop train that crossed the span, and business was usually brisk.

When Confederates invaded Maryland in September 1862, Pennsylvania's Governor Curtin feared that his state was Robert E. Lee's ultimate objective. He called for volunteers to form emergency militia regiments to repel the Rebels. Politicians and military strategists brooded over possible scenarios for such an incursion, fearing that Lee might try to cross the Columbia Bridge or Conowingo Bridge to threaten Lancaster and Philadelphia. Lancaster's Committee of Safety wrote letters to the chief burgess of Columbia, Peter Frailey, and to civil authorities in Conowingo, Maryland, expressing its desire

---

37 Gibson, *History of York County*, 355-56. In 1853, P. A. & S. Small distributed Connecticut leaf tobacco seeds to farmers in York and Lancaster counties. Small would purchase the tobacco harvests and resell the processed leaves to cigar makers, similar to his program of buying grain to resell to the flour mills. In 1860, York County growers produced 695,000 out of 3 million pounds of tobacco in Pennsylvania.

38 *Philadelphia Public Ledger*, Sept. 2, 1862.

that everything be done to defend the two bridges or render them impassable if necessary. The next day, Frailey responded that Curtin had assured him that the bridge would be protected until the enemy threatened to seize it. Then, it "shall be destroyed." Military authorities were to judge the necessity of such a drastic act, and the state would be held responsible for any resultant losses.[39]

After the horrendous day-long fight along the Antietam, the immediate threat to Pennsylvania abated when Lee withdrew into Virginia. Major General J.E.B. Stuart's cavalry raided Franklin and Adams counties that October, destroying railroad shops and depots in Chambersburg. Foraging patrols rode within four miles of Gettysburg, but Stuart did not come close enough to Columbia to threaten the bridge. However, over the winter, borough leaders remembered Frailey's plans to render the bridge impassable if another military emergency materialized. Concerned that future hostile action might target their bridge, on May 5, 1863, the bank depreciated its original cost of $157,000 to an asset value of $100,000. Insurance covered this sum, and even if the bridge were "destroyed tomorrow," the bank's credit would not be impaired.[40]

After the Rebels entered Pennsylvania in mid-June, bridge traffic increased substantially. Refugees crowded the roads, streaming toward Lancaster or Philadelphia and supposed safety. Columbia resident J. Houston Mifflin noted a dichotomy. Whites who could get a horse to haul their beds and children rode in relative comfort, while droves of poor blacks had to walk, often while carrying enormous loads, occasionally including parts of beds. Other blacks carried their children and household items as they trudged along the dusty turnpike.[41]

Carts, wagons, carriages, horses, trains—the tired and frightened throng used all available forms of transportation to cross the bridge. Tolls were a dollar for a freight wagon and six-horse team; thirty cents for a carriage or small wagon and two-horse team; sixteen-and-a-half cents for each horse and rider; and six cents for a pedestrian. The sudden windfall pleased Dr. Barton Evans and other Columbia Bank executives. Samuel Schoch, the cashier, kept a running tally of the receipts, and toll collector William McConkey worked overtime to keep traffic moving. However, Chief Burgess Frailey knew all too

---

39 Columbia Bridge correspondence, Sept. 1862, LCHS.

40 *Lancaster Daily Express*, May 9, 1863.

41 J. Houston Mifflin to Lloyd Mifflin, July 8, 1863, LCHS. Mifflin's usage of an archaic racial euphemism has been replaced with the more commonly accepted term "blacks."

well that the bridge might need to be rendered impassable if the Confederates continued their push into the heart of Pennsylvania. Borough officials discussed that possibility during their June meeting. An important question highlighted the agenda: Defend the bridge or destroy it? They soon reached a consensus to defend it.[42]

General Couch asked Columbia's leaders to send a delegation to Harrisburg to discuss the defense of the riverfront. Committee member George W. Haldeman recalled that Couch "impressed us with the necessity of keeping a sharp lookout for any advance of the Confederates," with particular emphasis on the route from York. On June 16 Couch appointed Col. Emlen Franklin to command the defenses of Lancaster County. He warned him it was of "vital importance" that the fords and passenger bridge be "effectively guarded." Franklin, formerly colonel of the 122nd Pennsylvania, had commanded a brigade at Chancellorsville before mustering out on May 16. Determined to fulfill his new orders, he recruited railroad work gangs, including several blacks, to build cursory defenses just west of Wrightsville.[43]

Couch authorized Maj. Charles C. Haldeman of Marietta, late of the 23rd Pennsylvania or "Birney's Zouaves," to raise troops to defend Columbia and the bridge, nearby dam, and fords along the Susquehanna up to Marietta. Lancaster County's quota was 2,154 men. However, in the city of Lancaster, a newspaper reported, "There is an apathy, especially among property owners, that is difficult to explain." At a public rally Chief Burgess George Sanderson urged every citizen to take up arms "in defense of our soil." Columbia and other nearby towns organized home guard companies. Columbia telegraph operator F. X. Ziegler recorded in his diary, "Big scare. Folks run hither and thither with long faces and terrible forebodings of evil."[44]

Doubtful he could defend the river crossings with untrained volunteers, Couch wired Secretary of War Edwin M. Stanton, "The country is so wild with rumors that I was compelled to use great caution in communicating with you. I

---

42 Vertical files, LCHS. Shoch was a 66-year-old former Columbia attorney who served forty years as the bank's cashier and/or president. He was a delegate to the 1860 Republican National Convention and an officer of the Wrightsville, York & Gettysburg Railroad (operated by the Northern Central).

43 *Columbia Spy*, June 20, 1863; George W. Haldeman deposition, Aug. 19, 1904, Columbia Historic Preservation Society; OR 27, pt. 3, 210.

44 OR 27, pt. 3, 132; *Lancaster Daily Express*, June 16, 1862; F. X. Ziegler Diary, 1854-67, entry for June 16, 1863, LCHS.

have made every exertion to protect the bridges across the Susquehanna, but they are to be fired, if it becomes necessary." He added that some citizens urged the government to raise "colored troops" for state defense. However, believing that this would be controversial, he stated that he had no authority to accept them. In reply, Stanton authorized Couch to receive any volunteers, "without regard to color."[45]

On Wednesday, June 17, Major Haller ordered Charles Haldeman to plan earthworks to protect the approaches to Wrightsville. He appointed chief engineer of the Reading & Columbia Railroad John Sheaff, civil engineer Edward K. Smith, and military officer James Barber to stake out fortifications that featured an inner line of earthworks behind rifle-pits. Scores of workers began taking shifts day and night to construct the works. According to the *Columbia Spy*, "The working party consisted of over one hundred negroes from Tow Hill, divided into reliefs. They have done excellent service, and the cheerfulness with which they shouldered the pick and shovel is in contrast with the reluctance displayed by many of our white citizens to shoulder the musket."[46]

Most of the blacks worked at the Maltby & Case Rolling Mill. In 1863, it was uncommon to see armed blacks serving as soldiers, but the sight was becoming familiar in Columbia. Eighteen men had left in early March to enlist in the 54th Massachusetts, comprised of black soldiers under white officers. This regiment would gain fame at Fort Wagner in South Carolina, where one Columbian would be killed. In June, twenty-three more blacks entrained for Boston to sign up for the 55th Massachusetts. Several of their neighbors also wanted to serve, but the three-year commitment was a hindrance. Emergency home guard duty provided a short-term option for many men.[47]

Their efforts did not go unnoticed. York lawyer James W. Latimer and a colleague, James Kell, took a train to Harrisburg to see Governor Curtin "to ascertain the facts regarding the rebel invasion." Peering out the window, Latimer watched the construction efforts in the fields around the turnpike. "They are digging rifle-pits and throwing up entrenchments at Wrightsville to protect the Columbia bridge and say they are acting under orders from Gen.

45 OR 27, pt. 3, 163, 203.

46 *Columbia Spy*, June 20, 1863.

47 *Columbia Spy*, March 21 and June 13, 1863.

Couch." He added ominously, "They have a force of men on the bridge night and day to destroy it if necessary."[48]

That same day Federal telegraph wires hummed with reports that two powerful Confederate infantry divisions were operating in western Maryland and several more were marching northward through the Shenandoah Valley. Clearly General Lee was on the offensive and the Army of the Potomac had been caught napping. Confusion about his intentions reigned in the field and in Washington. Hooker's chief of staff, Maj. Gen. Daniel Butterfield, pleaded with a colleague in the capital, "Try and hunt up somebody from Pennsylvania who knows something, and has a cool enough head to judge what is the actual state of affairs there with regard to the enemy. . . . We cannot go boggling round until we know what we are going after."[49]

York authorities authorized a $5,000 bounty to entice recruits to join the state militia. Similar bounties were passed in other towns. Among the early responders in Lancaster County to Curtin's call were two groups of collegians. Captain William A. Atlee raised a company entirely of students and professors from Franklin & Marshall College. Professor James Pyle Wickersham raised another small command at Millersville Normal School. On Wednesday morning the two companies received rifled muskets in Lancaster and marched to Columbia. They camped northeast of the town in "a beautiful ravine" known locally as Lockard's Meadow. Thankful townspeople catered lavishly to the collegians and turned out in droves to watch them train for war. The students proved more adept at drilling than did their teachers. The two groups soon engaged in a friendly rivalry as to their respective military prowess. Each volunteer was issued twenty musket rounds. A few veterans gave them cursory instructions on how to load the cartridges and ram them down the barrel of their rifles.[50]

The next day, Thursday, June 18, as three more companies of volunteers arrived in Columbia with a battery of field artillery, the students and professors marched across the bridge to Wrightsville. From a rise just west of town, Major

---

48 Ibid.; James W. Latimer to Bartow Latimer, June 24, 1863, YCHT.

49 OR 27, pt. 3, 174.

50 *Baltimore Sun*, June 19, 1863; Vertical files, LCHS. The 31-year-old Atlee was a captain in the 12th PVM during the Emergency of 1862. Lt. William A. Wilson was a professor of ancient languages and 2nd Lt. Peter Stocksleger was a student from Cashtown and a veteran of the Union army. He lost an arm fighting in the Carolinas and returned to school to complete his studies. Sgt. John G. Weinberger was assistant professor of mathematics.

Haldeman pointed out the main approaches an attacker might utilize, among them the turnpike leading to York thirteen miles to the west. Before long the collegians were hard at work digging rifle-pits along a ridge that curved in toward the Susquehanna River. Wrightsville's borough council appropriated $50.00 to purchase bread and meat for these young volunteers and their teachers. "Several hundred contrabands are now industriously employed in constructing rifle-pits and other fortifications on the York county side," observed a reporter, "and some hundred men are employed on the Columbia side in similar work." Unlike the students, they all needed to provide their own meals.[51]

While the collegians and blacks dug, reaction to the potential invasion was decidedly less vigorous in York. Navy officer and former resident Clark H. Wells wrote in January, "I believe there is nothing new in York: I have no affection for that place, as it contains a strong disloyal element, chiefly confined to those who have not shouldered the musket." Back from the state capital, attorney James Latimer wrote his younger brother that there was "not the least excitement" in York. Few were alarmed and nearly everyone appeared indifferent, as if there were no Rebels within 1,000 miles. "Either the people of Harrisburg are scared very badly about nothing and are making fools of themselves," continued Latimer, "or there is some considerable danger to be apprehended. Still many people here say it is nothing but a causeless fright among railroad men."[52]

Leading York businessmen discussed with the Committee of Safety how best to protect their factories and stores. Guards patrolled warehouses containing military supplies. The Northern Central Railway transported much of its excess rolling stock to Harrisburg and Columbia for safekeeping. Volunteers toting wooden guns drilled in Centre Square, including the Rev. William M. Baum of the Lutheran Church. Although newspaper advertisements asked for volunteers for military service, only a handful signed up—just enough for a single company to begin scouting the roads west and south of town. A staunch Republican, Latimer wrote with open disgust that

51 *Columbia Spy*, Jan. 9, 1886. Two members of Wrightsville's council finally were designated to procure food for the men working on the rifle-pits. The final bill came to $23.15 at a local merchant. They added a $6 surcharge for "services rendered." YCHT.

52 James Latimer to Bartow Latimer, June 18, 1863, YCHT; Haller, *Dismissal of Major Granville O. Haller*, 16.

Yorkers exhibited "the most extraordinary apathy" regarding the invasion. Nothing was being done despite widespread rumors the the Rebels might attack Harrisburg in a day or two. "If men won't go to the defense of their own State," Latimer complained, "they don't deserve to be called patriots. I am ashamed of myself and my town."[53]

The first enemy soldiers appeared in York County on June 18. A patrol of York home guards detained four Confederate riders just out of town. They proved to be from the 16th Virginia Cavalry of Jenkins' Brigade. Each man possessed a signed oath of allegiance, but local authorities believed the documents were a ruse to help the men in case they were captured. When the volunteer company headed to Harrisburg to be mustered into service, they took the Rebel scouts with them to Camp Curtin, where the Southerners were incarcerated.[54]

That same day, Maj. Granville Haller traveled by train from York to Wrightsville, where he and General Franklin viewed the massive bridge. They inspected the defenses three-quarters of a mile west of it, a good position against small raiding parties. Franklin pronounced this site, although unexceptional, as "unquestionably the best that could be secured" and its "defensive character well planned" and "properly constructed." He complimented the volunteers and their officers. That evening, Major Haldeman organized a home guard company in Columbia. A committee of local leaders provided the volunteers with two hundred Harpers Ferry rifles and ammunition.[55]

The defense of Wrightsville and Columbia remained a significant concern to Major General Couch. He ordered Col. Emlen Franklin to send all canal boats to the eastern riverbank to prevent their usage by Southern intruders. Couch also authorized him to organize additional defenders, stating, "Citizens should be turned out en masse to go right across the river to throw up rifle pits or breastworks—not interfering with travel until the last moment, as large quantities of stock will be crossing. Select reliable and energetic officers, or

---

53 James Latimer to Bartow Latimer, June 24, 1863, YCHT. Maj. Gen. William B. Franklin, in his hometown of York while awaiting a new assignment, authored an anonymous appeal to the citizens of York County on June 23 in the *York Gazette*.

54 *Harrisburg Evening Telegraph*, June 18, 1863. The prisoners were George Canard, Robert Robinson, and John Bowell of Company D; and Green Adkins of Company E.

55 *Columbia Spy*, June 20, 1863, and Jan. 9, 1886; Patrick McSherry, "The Defense of Columbia: June 1863," *Journal of the Lancaster County Historical Society*, Vol. 84, No. 3 (1980), 139.

citizens, to carry out the Governor's wishes and my own. In no event must the enemy cross these bridges. You should then make preparations accordingly." He added a caveat, "Get calm and determined men for your work." Haldeman and Franklin raised three more companies of home guards, which included several combat veterans from Franklin's defunct 122nd Pennsylvania, as well as the 135th.[56]

This was the first opportunity for many of these volunteers to serve as citizen-soldiers, although their ranks were peppered with former nine-month soldiers with some who had experienced combat. The companies occasionally drilled under the watchful eye of Charles Haldeman, which provided a welcome respite from the backbreaking construction work at the entrenchments. According to Samuel Wright, the editor of the *Columbia Spy*, "The officers have persevered in their efforts to obtain efficient organization in spite of every discouragement. Captain Haldeman occupies a very responsible position, and there is but one voice as to the manner of his government. He has done admirable service under very trying circumstances, and deserves the thanks of his fellow citizens." After chastising his fellow citizens for their "disjointed efforts" and lack of organization, he concluded, "We have made a fair beginning, and if the Rebels do not come in overwhelming numbers, are even now ready to give them a wrestle for the bridge. We will fight for it before we burn it."[57]

Just south of Columbia, a dam spanned the Susquehanna River and thus provided water for the canal basins. The structure also created a slackwater pool for the horses and mules on the bridge's towpath to pull canal boats across the broad waterway without having to fight a current. At normal or low water levels, the dam's six-foot high breast offered a way for Rebels to wade across the river. To prevent this, some of Franklin's volunteers began digging rifle-pits along the Columbia riverfront. Others erected a timber, masonry, and dirt fortification, which the citizens named "Fort Case" in honor of William G. Case, co-owner of the rolling mill. The 42-year-old industrialist was a captain in the 2nd Pennsylvania Volunteer Militia during the Emergency of 1862 when Stuart's cavalry raided southern Pennsylvania. Case recruited his workers to assist in the war effort, and formed segregated home guard companies. He

---

56 *OR* 27, pt. 3, 160; *Columbia Spy*, June 20, 1863.

57 *Columbia Spy*, June 20, 1863.

donated raw materials for the riverfront bastion and managed the construction project.[58]

A Lancaster reporter observed that these crescent-shaped works along Shawnee Run comprised a fort "of great strength." A solid masonry parapet (actually the masonry of the dam's abutment) facing the river contained two heavy guns, mounted in embrasures to enfilade the entire breast of the dam. The southern section was not complete, and no guns yet filled its several embrasures. A long section of freshly dug rifle-pits flanked the fort to the north, and additional fortifications were in its rear. Nearly six hundred sweating volunteers, black and white, labored to complete the eighty-foot wide Fort Case and its accompanying earthworks and rifle-pits. Editor Samuel Wright opined, "The work on the entrenchments was steadily continued, and the preparations for a determined resistance should the rebels make a dash in this direction are still being pushed with vigor." He added, "We have made a fair beginning and, if the Rebels do not come in overwhelming numbers, are even now ready to give them a wrestle for the bridge. We will fight for it before we burn it." A Marietta newsman believed, "Properly armed and manned, these would prove truly dangerous strongholds."[59]

Colonel Franklin ordered additional artillery pieces from the Frankford Arsenal in Philadelphia for the remaining gun embrasures. Work crews completed Fort Case on June 20. The next day officials affixed a U.S. flag atop a nearby large walnut tree at 6:00 p.m. to the cheers of the volunteers and nearly a thousand visitors. After several lengthy orations from civic leaders, guardsmen fired off a nine-gun salute in honor of the new flag. Captain Case and businessman H. R. Knotwell of the Shawnee Ironworks organized and paid for a festive ox roast for the laborers. The celebration included an "inspiring and spirited" invocation by a local Methodist minister, the Reverend H. R. Callway, asking for God's blessing. Choirs led the assemblage in patriotic songs. A reporter later observed, "Besides roasted ox, there were crackers by the barrel, cheese by the hundred weight, pickles by the keg, and other substantials in proportion."[60]

58 Case was the captain of Company A, 2nd Militia, during the Emergency of 1862. The regiment was mustered in for only two weeks before being disbanded after Antietam.

59 *Lancaster Daily Express*, June 29, 1863; *Columbia Spy*, June 20, 1863; *Marietta* (Pa.) *Mariettian*, July 4, 1863.

60 *Columbia Spy*, June 27, 1863, and Jan. 9, 1886; *Marietta* (Pa.) *Mariettian*, July 4, 1863.

The Rebels developed negative opinions about the Federal practice of using blacks as construction gangs. Near Harpers Ferry, an officer in John Gordon's 26th Georgia wrote that his regiment captured several hundred Union prisoners and "crowds of negroes, who were decoyed under promise of forty acres and a mule if they would take arms against the South. These poor deluded field hands the cowardly Blue Coats used for beast works, the same as Burnside used his field hands at Malvern Hill."[61]

The "beast works" in Columbia were now complete. An atmosphere of gaiety continued at Fort Case for several days. Pastimes in between military drills included fishing, card playing, and foraging in town for pies, cream, and delicacies. Companies formed glee clubs and music abounded, including "some good drummers and several very poor ones." Relatives, neighbors, and friends frequently paid their respects to the defenders. Someone asked a 12-year-old boy, visiting his older brother in the fort, if he realized that the Rebels might kill his brother if they attacked Columbia. The proud lad offered, "Yes, but we know he will die gloriously!" The horrors of war were far away, lurking in Virginia and places south, not in rural Pennsylvania on the peaceful banks of the broad Susquehanna. The reality of their plight had not yet sunk in and the partying continued.[62]

Across the river, work continued to strengthen Wrightsville's defenses. Colonel Franklin called for more volunteers to construct and man these expanded works. He ordered, "Each citizen shall provide his own arms and ammunition until a sufficient supply reaches this department, also his own rations for three days, to be carried with him; also entrenching tools, either an axe, shovel, or pick."[63]

In response to General Franklin's latest appeal, about 600 additional volunteers from nine Lancaster County home guard companies arrived. Franklin placed most of these fresh laborers in Wrightsville under the command of Capt. William Atlee of Franklin & Marshall College, while

---

61 Charles Thompson Stuart, *Autobiographical Sketch of The War Service of Charles Thompson Stuart*, Lieutenant, Company H, 26th Regiment, Georgia Volunteers (typescript in the Robert L. Brake Collection, USMHI, Carlisle, Pa.).

62 *Lancaster Daily Express*, June 23, 1863; Wilbur S. Nye, *Here Come the Rebels!* (Baton Rouge: Louisiana State University Press, 1965), 10.

63 Wilbur S. Nye and John G. Redman, *Farthest East* (Wrightsville, Pa.: Wrightsville Centennial Committee, 1963), 9. E. K. Smith, a wealthy lumberman, was a director of the Columbia Bank which owned the covered bridge.

scattering the others along the eastern riverbank from Bainbridge to Peach Bottom. Most of these new recruits had no uniforms and only carried shotguns or old smoothbore muskets used for hunting. A battery of three locally produced cannons had been obtained to augment the defenses of Columbia. Franklin initially placed two of these guns in newly completed Fort Case. On Sunday, June 21, Capt. E. K. Smith moved all three pieces to Wrightsville. He positioned them in the outer works facing west along turnpike in case of a Confederate advance from York. However, these field pieces were of little immediate use because they lacked sufficient ammunition and trained crews. Before long, horses dragged them back across the long bridge to Columbia for safekeeping.[64]

Curious residents watched the proceedings. Occasionally, the onlookers were strangers, clearly not inhabitants of the river towns. Authorities questioned many of them to learn why they were so interested in the new earthworks and the artillery. Most were immediately released and ordered to leave town. The Reverend A. P. Case, a traveling bookkeeping instructor, was among the first to be detained for suspicious activity. Authorities soon released him. On June 21, Corp. Peter Saylor of the provost guard arrested three men near Columbia. He hauled them off to a Lancaster jail when they could not provide a consistent story explaining their vagrancy. On Monday morning, Capt. Adolphus W. Bolenius, the Provost Marshal of the Ninth District of Pennsylvania, released the trio because there was no evidence of ill intent.[65]

Authorities detained a few others for suspicious actions. One drunken man in a York County bar bragged that he was really a member of the 9th Alabama Infantry, sent on a secret scouting mission by Robert E. Lee himself. He spent time behind bars until he sobered up, but his boasting fueled speculation about strangers and their intentions. Residents remained on full alert, especially with the increase in traffic of refugees streaming eastward from Adams and Franklin counties.

---

64 *Columbia Spy*, June 20, 1863. Eventually twelve volunteer companies worked on the earthworks—two from Columbia, five from Lancaster, and one each from Lititz, Bird-in-Hand, Churchtown, Millersville, and New Holland. Two of the cannon were cast in Lancaster and one in Columbia (the latter by Supplee & Brother). They initially only had enough ammunition to fire a ceremonial salute.

65 *Lancaster Daily Express*, June 22, 1863. The trio of loiterers was Joseph Lobbida, William Snyder, and John Donnelly. According to the *Columbia Spy*, June 28, 1863, they were deserters from the Union army. Guards escorted them to Harrisburg.

In Harrisburg that Sunday, Darius Couch wired Washington that he expected the Northern Central Railway to be cut, but "I will try and protect five of the important bridges north of the Maryland line." During the following week, officials initiated additional preparations to secure these bridges against malicious intruders. On Tuesday, the board of Columbia Bank unanimously passed a resolution calling for bank president Barton Evans and cashier Samuel Schoch to provide lunch at the bank's expense for the armed guards at the Columbia end of their bridge. Still more home defense companies arrived. Colonel Franklin detailed them to dig an 80-foot-long crescent of earthworks along Grubb's Ridge. These new dirt-and-lumber fortifications, just north of the bridge, were intended to protect additional artillery pieces once they arrived via railcar.[66]

While some citizens applauded Couch's actions, others doubted the necessity. According to historian Benson J. Lossing, "Stockades and block-houses were constructed along the line of the Northern Central Railway, between Baltimore and Hanover Junction; and at Philadelphia some pretty little redoubts were erected, at which the citizens laughed when the danger was over."[67]

Within a week, few Pennsylvanians would be laughing.

---

66 *OR* 27, pt. 3, 251. These were at Harrisburg or northward, plus the one at Columbia.

67 Benson J. Lossing, *Pictorial Field Book of the Civil War* (New York: T. Belknap, 1868), 3: 55. Blockhouses "built of stout hewn logs and pierced for musketry" guarded bridges near Gunpowder Falls and other places.

Chapter 3

The Rebels are Coming!

The Defense of Gettysburg

On the late afternoon of Thursday, June 18, Maj. Granville Haller climbed aboard a train at Wrightsville bound for Hanover Junction in southern York County. The major needed to post troops at the important railroad intersection and communications hub, which was just ten miles north of Maryland. After examining the surrounding terrain, Haller transferred to a westbound train for Gettysburg, an Adams County town of 2,400 people and the nexus for many important roads. Arriving early in the evening, he established headquarters in the Eagle Hotel, touted as being newly renovated with the installation of oil lamps in every room. It featured a new tavern and restaurant that now served meals in a first floor lounge. A newspaper advertisement boasted, "Every attempt has been made to satisfy the needs of the traveler and businessman."[1]

In his comfortable room, Haller lacked nothing for his personal comfort. What the hotel could not satisfy was his need for soldiers. However, a veteran officer approached Haller and offered his services. Gettysburg-born Charles McLean Knox, Jr., the youthful major of the 9th New York Cavalry and a brigade commander earlier in the year, was at his parents' home recuperating

---

1   *Adams County Sentinel*, June 27, 1863. *The Sentinel* was Gettysburg's Republican newspaper, owned and published by Robert G. Harper. The Eagle Hotel stood at the northeast corner of Chambersburg and Washington streets. Gettysburg had boasted a thriving carriage-making business for Southern customers. That market had since dried up. Another key industry, granite quarrying, had slowed because of a lack of construction during the war.

from dysentery. Now in much better health, the 1860 graduate of Columbia Law School and New York City resident became Haller's adjutant. His men referred to him as a "good and popular officer." Haller also gladly accepted the services of Capt. Samuel L. Young, another cavalryman convalescing from illness. A pre-war attorney from Reading and former aide to Maj. Gen. William H. Keim, Young became Haller's aide-de-camp. Haller took command of a small group of invalided soldiers, home recuperating from wounds or illness. He petitioned Couch for more troops.[2]

Meanwhile, Couch dispatched New York militia to the threatened Cumberland Valley, where Albert Jenkins' raiders suddenly returned after their two-day withdrawal into Maryland. A large force of Rebels crossed the state line to search for horses and livestock. Briefly occupying Waynesboro, they jumbled the type of the *Village Record* and overturned the cases. One side of the newspaper was printed on June 19; the reverse would not be completed until July 31 after weeks of effort to restore order. Lieutenant Hermann Schuricht's company of the 14th Virginia Cavalry rode into the countryside to seize horses and cattle. When a powerful nighttime thunderstorm surprised them, they took refuge on a large farm. They forced the proprietor to furnish rations for them and their horses. On Saturday, June 20, Schuricht's foragers captured several horses and some cattle. At noon they rode into the farmyard of an old Pennsylvania German, who shouted, "O mein Gott, die rebels!" Schuricht reassured the terrified farmer that he would not be harmed if he gave them dinner and furnished rations for their horses. The soldiers were subsequently "well cared for."[3]

Private James H. Hodam of the 17th Virginia Cavalry left a lengthy and fascinating account of one of his adventures in Pennsylvania:

---

2 *New York Herald*, Nov. 27, 1861; *History of the First Troop, Philadelphia City Cavalry, From its Organization, November 17th, 1774 to its Centennial Anniversary, November 17th, 1874* (Philadelphia: Hallowell, 1875), 71; Anonymous (A Private Recruit), "Philadelphia City Cavalry, Service of the First Troop, Philadelphia City Cavalry During June and July, 1863," *Journal of the Military Service Institution of the United States* (1908), Vol. 43, 283. The authorship is attributed to Persifor Frazer, Jr. The 40-year-old Young, formerly an associate judge, organized an independent company of cavalry during the Emergency of 1862. He had been an artillery officer in the Mexican War.

3 *Chambersburg Valley Spirit*, July 8, 1863; *History of Franklin County, Pennsylvania* (Chicago: Warner, Beers & Co., 1887); *Richmond Daily Dispatch*, April 5, 1896. On June 21, the 8th New York Militia ("Washington Greys") marched into Chambersburg to a rousing welcome. Brig. Gen. Joseph F. Knipe took command of the troops and armed civilians. The 71st New York Militia and a battery of two bronze howitzers arrived on Monday.

While on picket near Waynesboro early one morning, four or five people were seen running to a farm-house nearby. It was too dark to fully distinguish them, but from their actions we supposed it was a party of Federals interested in our movements. Five of us were sent to the house to look after them. We dismounted in the yard of a substantial farm building, and found no one about but three or four women, who seemed perplexed and frightened at our early visit. We were informed that the men had fled east with their most valuable property, and at first they denied that anyone was concealed on the premises; but learning that we intended no personal harm, and that our purpose was to search the house, they reluctantly told how, a few minutes previously, five persons, worn out with fatigue and hunger, had sought refuge with them and were now concealed in the upper part of the house.

With revolvers in hand, we cautiously ascended two flights of stairs to the dark garret, expecting every moment to encounter an armed foe. As we reached the floor, an Irish comrade put his foot into a crock of apple-butter sitting near the stairway; the noise and vigorous oath occasioned thereby were echoed by a wail of fear and distress from the darkest corner of the room, where, in a kneeling posture, instead of armed Yankees, we beheld four men and a woman, who proved [to be blacks]. On informing them that we were looking for armed men instead of such defenceless creatures, their fear was turned to joy and thanks. They were free negroes from Maryland, and had been told that if caught by the 'rebels,' they would be killed or taken South as slaves. They had been fleeing from the supposed wrath to come for three days without food or rest. Assuring them of safety from molestation by our people, we left them devouring with ravenous haste the food we divided with them. The women were much surprised when we returned downstairs without killing or making prisoners of the miserable fugitives. They gave us an excellent breakfast, and we departed, leaving the impression with them that the Southern soldiers were not all barbarians."[4]

Residents who fled the Waynesboro region, taking horses northeast through Gettysburg, relayed news that Rebels were approaching but exaggerated their strength and movements. A skeptical Haller rode out to the

4   George M. Vickers, ed., *Under Both Flags: A Panorama of the Great Civil War* (New York: Charles R. Graham, 1896), 78-79.

Monterey House, a tavern atop Monterey Pass, to obtain firsthand information spotted about 100 enemy troopers at the western foot of South Mountain, searching farms for horses. Haller rode back to Gettysburg and addressed a public gathering at the courthouse, "advising all able-bodied male citizens to arm themselves and to be ready, at a moment's warning, for the defense of their homes and of the State." According to teenager Tillie Pierce, most of the men "could not understand Major Haller when he wanted them to enroll themselves and go to Harrisburg. They well knew that here was the first exposed point, and their families and property peremptorily demanded their personal attention." A group of older citizens formed a home guard company, "armed to the teeth with old, rusty guns and swords, pitchforks, shovels, and pick-axes."[5]

To Haller's relief, there was a more useful military force in Gettysburg. Thirty-three-year-old farmer Robert Bell traveled to Harrisburg on June 15 in response to the governor's proclamation. He had been a lieutenant in an independent cavalry company during the Emergency of 1862 when J.E.B. Stuart's Confederate cavalry raided Franklin and Adams counties. Pleased with Bell's leadership experience and willingness to serve, Pennsylvania's adjutant general instructed him on June 16 to return home. He was to gather as many men and horses as possible to scout the roads westward to Chambersburg and as far south as Hagerstown, Maryland. Within a few days, Bell recruited 45 volunteers. The state provided uniforms, breech-loading Sharps and Burnside carbines, and Colt .44 revolvers, but the cavalrymen needed to secure their own horses. Thirty-three men provided their own mounts, and the Deputy Provost Marshal added seven more horses confiscated in Gettysburg from deserters and stragglers from the Union Army. A few men were veterans of an infantry regiment with local ties, but most possessed no previous military experience. However, nearly all were seasoned riders. While Virginia cavalrymen terrorized Waynesboro on June 20, Major Haller formally commissioned Bell as a captain and mustered his Adams County Scouts into state service as an independent company for a term of six months. He assigned them to Major Knox.[6]

---

5   Haller, *Dismissal of Major Granville O. Haller*, 66; Michael Jacobs, *Notes on the Rebel Invasion of Maryland and Pennsylvania and the Battle of Gettysburg* (Philadelphia: J. B. Lippincott, 1863), 9; *History of Cumberland and Adams Counties*, 153-160; Tillie Pierce Alleman, *At Gettysburg, or What a Girl Saw and Heard of the Battle* (Baltimore: Butternut & Blue, 1994), 18.

6   Haller, *Dismissal of Major Granville O. Haller*, 64-65; Robert Bell, "Co. B, 21st Pennsylvania Cavalry, Remembrances of 1863," *Gettysburg Star & Sentinel*, Jan. 17, 1883. In August, most of

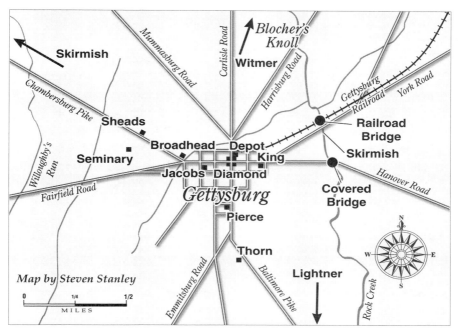

Ten roads radiating from Gettysburg made the town an important center of regional commerce. Some 2,800 people lived there according to the 1860 U.S. Census.

Haller relied on another group of Gettysburg volunteers as an important source of information. Earlier in the war, Capt. David McConaughy, a 40-year-old Republican attorney, enrolled some clients and other citizens into a rifle company. Now, with a new threat looming, McConaughy organized 30 to 40 civilian as scouts with each providing his own weapons, rations, and horses. Gettysburg, boasting a network of ten roads radiating from the town like spokes from a wagon wheel, previously attracted Confederate interest and was sure to do so again. Captain McConaughy, whom Darius Couch described as "quite reliable," sent scouts to tail Jenkins from Hagerstown into Pennsylvania. While Ewell's Corps marched through Maryland, Jenkins' horsemen probed eastward from Chambersburg. McConaughy's scouts patrolled the roads and hills, hoping to verify the size, strength, and destination of the Southerners.

the Adams County Scouts mustered into the newly organized 21st Pennsylvania Cavalry as Company B. Bell remained as captain and was eventually promoted to major.

They focused on the South Mountain gaps on the eastern side of the Cumberland Valley.[7]

General Couch soon sent more cavalry to Gettysburg. The previous week Governor Curtin appealed directly to the citizens of Philadelphia and exhorted them to close their businesses and come to Harrisburg to enlist. On June 16, after a wealthy member guaranteed funds to procure suitable horses, the famed First Troop, Philadelphia City Cavalry resolved to volunteer. This company was a civic institution, and its handsome show horses graced many parades and exhibitions. It had been organized in 1774 and financed by wealthy colonial patriot Robert Morris to serve as George Washington's personal bodyguard. It fought at Trenton and Princeton. Current members were scions of Philadelphia's high society, and some were descendants of the original troopers. The First City Troop saw action in the summer of 1861 in the Shenandoah Valley. Many members had since enlisted in the Federal army, several in the 6th Pennsylvania Cavalry. In the absence of the commissioned officers, Orderly Sergeant M. Edward Rogers now temporarily commanded the much depleted company.[8]

Volunteers, eager to prove their mettle, soon swelled Rogers' ranks. At 9 a.m. on June 17, 31 members and recruits proceeded to the street in front of their armory to select new mounts. There, about twenty dealers were hawking horses, many "utterly unfit for service, which they hoped to sell in the hurry of the emergency." Kicking chargers endangered the bystanders, while balky nags obstructed the street, preventing troopers from examining and exercising other potential mounts. However, by noon, the required number had been purchased

---

7 Peter C. Vermilyea, "To Prepare for the Emergency: Military Operations in the Gettysburg Area through June 24, 1863," *The Gettysburg Magazine*, Issue 32, 39 (2005); OR 27, pt. 3, 162. General Couch appointed McConaughy as a captain and aide-de-camp. One of the 63 men in McConaughy's early war Adams Rifles was John Burns, a veteran of the War of 1812. During the first day of fighting at the battle of Gettysburg, Burns picked up a musket and fought with the First Corps on McPherson's Ridge.

8 *History of the First Troop*, 71. Government officials wired Capt. Samuel Randall, "State unable at present to furnish horses—Troop should hold itself in readiness for service." W. O. Davis rose from his seat and offered to advance the funds to purchase the horses. In May 1861, the troop was attached to the command of Col. George H. Thomas, later famed as the "Rock of Chickamauga." It served in Carlisle, Shippensburg, Chambersburg, and Greencastle before being ordered on June 17 to cross the Potomac into western Virginia. After skirmishing near Falling Waters and Martinsburg, the troop rode to Charles Town. After heading to Harpers Ferry in late July, it guarded fords until its three-month term expired. The Troop was not needed during the Emergency of 1862.

and delivered to the Troop's stables. Each recruit also procured his own crisp new field uniform and arms, at a cost of 300 dollars apiece.[9]

The volunteers and their new horses entrained for Harrisburg at 1 p.m. on June 18. They arrived less than six hours later and roomed at the Buehler House, a leading hotel. The next day, their acting commander, Democratic U.S. Congressman Samuel J. Randall, and five additional men joined them. Thirty-four-year-old Captain Randall, a sergeant during the Philadelphians' 1861 sojourn in the Shenandoah Valley, met with Governor Curtin. He accepted the Troop into state service without formally mustering it. Couch averred, "I know we can trust to the honor of this corps without any oath." The troopers accepted no pay for their services and provided their own uniforms, arms and mounts.[10]

After receiving tents and ammunition from Couch on Saturday morning, the gentry and their horses, equipment, and supply wagons embarked on a train through York and Hanover Junction to Gettysburg. They arrived at 4:00 a.m. on Sunday, June 21, in a driving rainstorm. Because the station did not have facilities for handling carloads of horses, it took considerable time to unload them. The officers took up rooms in the McClellan House. The horses were quartered in the hotel's stable, while the troopers found what comfort they could in its hayloft. Later that morning, their bugler sounded "Boots and Saddles." The troopers assembled in the town square ("the Diamond") where residents warmly greeted them. One newspaperman deemed the Troop "an exceedingly fine body of mounted men" that "receive, as they deserve, expressions of admiration on all sides." However, innkeeper Charles Wills, noting that the well-groomed riders were expensively outfitted in white shirts and cuffs, likened them to mere "dandies."[11]

---

9 *History of the First Troop*, 71; *Philadelphia Inquirer*, June 19, 1863. This armory was on Twelfth Street below Chestnut. The men received a two-week supply of rations and their military accouterments.

10 *JMSIUS* (1908), Vol. 43, 282. One trooper was left behind because of illness, so only 35 men embarked for Gettysburg. Because the Troop had not been formally mustered into service, its men were denied Federal pension status as Civil War veterans.

11 Jones Wister, *Jones Wister's Reminiscences* (Philadelphia: J. B. Lippincott, 1920), 158; *History of the First Troop*, 71; *Gettysburg Compiler*, June 29, 1863; Charles Wills account, GNMP. The army arrested the Democratic paper's owner, Henry J. Stahle, after the battle of Gettysburg (possibly at the instigation of Radical Republican David McConaughy) for allegedly revealing the location of 95 wounded soldiers to the Rebels.

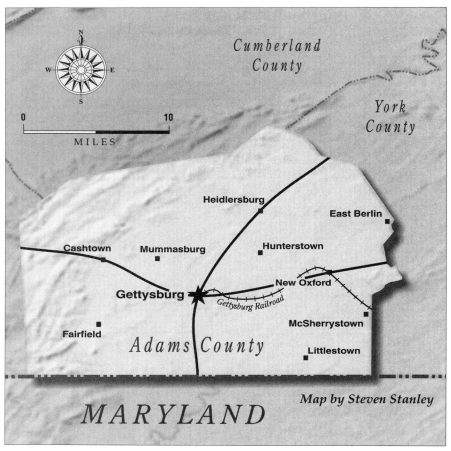

On Friday, June 26, 1863, Maj. Gen. Jubal A. Early's division entered the county from the west and marched toward Gettysburg using parallel roads.

Among those who welcomed the Troopers was "the gentleman in a silk hat with the umbrella, whom they soon came to cherish as Major Haller."[12]

Contact

While scouting toward Fairfield on their first day out in the field, Captain Randall and ten First City Troopers captured a pair of Rebels. One of the

12 *Philadelphia Press*, July 20, 1863.

Philadelphia cavalrymen suffered a freakish injury as he escorted the prisoners back to Gettysburg. About four miles from town near Wenny's Mill, Pvt. Edward W. White's horse became unmanageable. It ran against a tree, breaking the cavalryman's thighbone. An ambulance was dispatched to carry him to Gettysburg, where doctors set the limb that evening. Randall sent the troop's supply and baggage wagons and spare horses east to New Oxford to prevent their capture in case of a sudden attack.[13]

Fourteen members of Capt. John Scott's company of the Gettysburg Zouaves moved out the Chambersburg Pike fourteen miles into the mountains to bushwhack the Rebels. However, Bell's scouts turned them back. Later that same afternoon, mounted Rebels armed with rifles drove another home guard company armed only with pistols from the Monterey Pass. Responding to rumors of enemy troops approaching Fairfield, Major Haller led fifteen of Bell's cavalrymen and the remaining twenty-five First City Troopers out to investigate.[14]

About 6:00 p.m., they encountered 120 Confederate horsemen just east of Fairfield (also known as Millerstown), scouting the countryside for forage and remounts. The main body was stationed near a barn on the outskirts near Muddy Run, while detachments roamed the region. Haller now had firsthand knowledge that Rebels were east of the mountains. He hastened back to Gettysburg to wire the news to Couch. Haller's sudden departure sparked controversy among the First City Troopers. A Philadelphian sneered a month later, "Major Haller steadily looked towards South Mountain (the nest of the enemy) for some time; he acquired information so important as to call for his immediate presence at Gettysburg, and so the command devolved upon Captain Bell."[15]

Bell cautiously led the cavalrymen within a half-mile of Fairfield. The Philadelphian recalled, "Having less experience than his predecessor, and being naturally of a curious disposition, he pushed forward the men a section at a

13 *Gettysburg Compiler*, June 29, 1863; *JMSIUS* (1908), Vol. 43, 283. On Monday morning, Randall ordered two cavalrymen to escort White back to his house in Philadelphia. Randall accompanied them as far as Harrisburg to conduct "business of the troop." White arrived home late that evening.

14 Bates, *Martial Deeds*, 990; Haller, *Dismissal*, 62. Former constable John Burns was in this party.

15 *Philadelphia Press*, July 20, 1863.

time, joining the first section himself, and thus he entered Millerstown. He then ordered a mounted charge that swept through the village, driving the enemy back and capturing five prisoners. After a brief pursuit halted by twilight, the Federals returned to Fairfield, where they received food and praise from the citizens. Unlike Granville Haller, Bell made a strong initial impression on the Philadelphians, whose historian labeled him as "a brave, intelligent, and conscientious soldier."[16]

The Rebels withdrew along the Furnace Road to Monterey Pass, taking with them all the good horses they could find. Returning to General Jenkins, they reported the strong presence of Union cavalry patrols southwest of Gettysburg. Some officers surmised these Yankees were from the Army of the Potomac, while others remained convinced they were merely militia. Regardless, Jenkins' subsequent patrols proceeded cautiously as they scouted the mountain gaps.[17]

In Gettysburg that evening, Haller received more home guard volunteers when Captain Harvey Collins arrived with a company from Mountjoy Township and offered his services to the major. Editor Henry J. Stahle of *The Compiler* was impressed with what he saw and concluded, "The made a very soldierly appearance, and will do good service."[18]

One Monday, June 22, the First City Troop's supply wagons returned to Gettysburg from New Oxford. When Congressman Randall departed for Harrisburg on business, Haller dispatched the wagons to Hanover in southwestern York County and then turned his attention to slowing the Confederate thrust. Haller met with no success in York when he asked its Committee of Safety to assign men to fell trees along mountain approaches. However, Adams County residents enthusiastically fulfilled a similar request. Farmers living along the Monterey Pass quickly set about chopping down trees and blocking the gap as best they could. Gettysburg Zouave officer Joseph Broadhead was among a company of fifty men who volunteered to try to

16 Ibid.; *JMSIUS* (1908), Vol. 43, 283; *History of the First Troop*, 71; *Philadelphia Inquirer*, June 23, 1863. Some accounts place the Rebel raiding party at 160 men. Fairfield was also known as Millerstown.

17 Jacobs, *Notes on the Rebel Invasion*, 11. Jacobs wrote that the Rebels spent two hours in Fairfield from the time that Bell advanced until they withdrew. Haller refutes this in his *Dismissal* pamphlet. Orderly Sergeant M. E. Rogers commanded the First City Troopers in the engagement at Fairfield.

18 *Gettysburg Compiler*, June 29, 1863.

barricade the Chambersburg Pike. Some accounts suggest 70-year-old former constable John Burns accompanied the party.[19]

Shouldering axes and picks, the men walked westward until they reached the base of Rock Top, a high wooded peak on South Mountain.[20] They assumed the Secessionists were still on the reverse side of the gap, and so were startled to see a small group of Rebels riding down the road straight at them. The Southerners fired a few long-range warning shots which scattered the tree-cutters. About seventy cavalrymen leisurely followed the civilians eastward to Cashtown, a rural hamlet eight miles west of Gettysburg. They paused frequently to steal more horses and cattle before returning over the mountain pass to the Cumberland Valley after dark. Somehow, they missed encountering a patrol of First City Troopers that Haller dispatched to Cashtown. The Philadelphians returned to Gettysburg at midnight without spotting any Rebels.[21]

That same day, the New York militia stationed at Chambersburg retreated to Shippensburg when they learned of a powerful Confederate advance. Consequently, hundreds of residents abandoned their homes and businesses. They loaded wagons with necessities and family heirlooms and fled to Harrisburg or York. Chambersburg postmaster J. W. Deal was among those who departed, and he took the mailbags with him. Just north of Greencastle, Company I of the 14th Virginia skirmished with the 1st New York Cavalry, wounding one Yankee and killing Corp. William H. Rihl. Jenkins reentered Chambersburg about 10:45 a.m. with his band playing "Bonnie Blue Flag." Confederates broke into warehouses and began distributing large quantities of

---

19 Timothy H. Smith, *John Burns, The Hero of Gettysburg* (Gettysburg, Pa.: Thomas Publications, 2000).

20 Rock Top rises 410 feet above Cashtown, or 1,210 feet above sea level, according to *The History of Cumberland and Adams Counties*. At the time of the Civil War, Cashtown boasted "a fine church building, a well conducted hotel, a few good business houses and a number of comfortable private homes."

21 Sarah M. Broadhead, *Diary of a Lady of Gettysburg*, 1863, June 22 entry, typed manuscript of notes from the *Gettysburg Compiler*, ACHS; *History of the First Troop*, 72. As a child, Joseph Broadhead immigrated with his parents to America from England. The 32-year-old engineer on the Gettysburg Railroad returned home on June 15 with news that the Confederates were moving north across the Potomac River. Despite being blind in one eye, he was a lieutenant in the Gettysburg Zouaves during the 1862 Maryland Campaign. His 30-year-old wife "Sallie" had been a schoolteacher, but now stayed home to care for their 4-year-old daughter, Mary. They lived in a two-story brick home at 217 Chambersburg Street, west of the Diamond. A shell struck the house on July 2 and embedded in the wall.

flour and molasses. Squads cut down telegraph poles and destroyed wires. Southerners torched David Oaks' large warehouse, but citizens quickly extinguished the flames. Rebels burned buildings and property of the Cumberland Valley Railroad. However, the wood used to rebuild the bridge at Scotland was too green to ignite. Rebels sawed support timbers in a futile effort to drop the span into Conocheague Creek.[22]

Other Virginians terrorized the populace, demanding fresh bread and food and searching for hidden valuables. Occasionally, they ignited matches and threatened to burn residences or buildings. Some destroyed property deeds and other important papers. Many soldiers deliberately pastured their horses in wheatfields in preference to less valuable crops of timothy or clover. Others pilfered threshed wheat from barns to feed their mounts.[23]

At least one Southern newspaper had no qualms about what was transpiring in Pennsylvania, as evidenced in the *Richmond Daily Dispatch*:

> While we are manifesting a tender regard for the subsistence of the burly Dutch farmers that inhabit the Valley of Pennsylvania, the brutes who are on their side are endeavoring to starve all the women and children in the Southern Confederacy. This should not be our policy, had we the control of affairs, and it is very well for the broad-bottomed denizens of the Susquehanna that we have not. We should proclaim at once 'an eye for an eye, and a tooth for a tooth,' or rather, we should have half a dozen eyes for every eye, and half a dozen teeth for every tooth. This is the only way to bring the Yankees to their senses. Let them take their own physic, and they will soon find how bitter it is. Let them see and feel what war is, and they will discover that it is not such an agreeable pastime as they are wont to consider it when contemplating it from a distance.[24]

Excitement spread in the Old Dominion as rumors spread about Jenkins' foray. Judith White McGuire penned in her diary:

22 Amos Stouffer account, FCHS; *Chambersburg Valley Spirit*, July 8, 1863; Rachel Cormany diary. During a brief firefight, Rihl, a member of Capt. William Boyd's Company C of the 1st NY Cavalry, was shot in the face, and a nearby soldier was wounded. A monument along U.S. Route 11 commemorates Rihl as the first Union casualty of the Gettysburg Campaign.

23 *Lancaster Daily Express*, July 8, 1863.

24 *Richmond Daily Dispatch*, June 22, 1863.

There are also rumours that our army is in Pennsylvania. So may it be! We are harassed to death with their ruinous raids, and why should not the North feel it in its homes? Nothing but their personal suffering. I don't want their women and children to suffer; nor that our men should follow their example, and break through and steal. I want our warfare carried on in a more honourable way; but I do want our men and horses to be fed on the good things of Pennsylvania; I want the fine dairies, pantries, granaries, meadows, and orchards belonging to the rich farmers of Pennsylvania, to be laid open to our army; and I want it all paid for with our Confederate money, which will be good at some future day. I want their horses taken for our cavalry and wagons, in return for the hundreds of thousands that they have taken from us; and I want their fat cattle driven into Virginia to feed our army. It amuses me to think how the Dutch farmers' wives will be concealing the golden products of their dairies, to say nothing of their apple-butter, peach-butter, and their wealth of apple-pies.[25]

As a result of Jenkins' second foraging raid, officials across southern Pennsylvania stepped up precautions. Quartermasters at the Carlisle Barracks sent away their vast military stores. Patrols of armed guards secured arsenals. Trains removed most of the sick and seriously wounded soldiers from York's army hospital to safer locations. Dr. Alexander G. Blair took 64 soldiers, many still recovering from serious wounds suffered at Antietam and Fredericksburg the previous year, across the Susquehanna River to the Odd Fellows Hall in Columbia. They arrived at midnight and local ladies provided food and temporary bedding. Soon, the patients moved into a new school building. A bright red flag identified it as a temporary hospital in case Confederate artillerymen decided to shell the town.[26]

About 200 less seriously injured soldiers stayed behind in York. They resumed martial drills alongside Capt. Thomas S. McGowan's Patapsco

---

25 Judith White McGuire, *Diary of a Southern Refugee during the War, by a lady of Virginia* (Richmond: J.W. Randolph & English, 1889), 225.

26 *Columbia Spy*, June 20, 1863; J. Houston Mifflin to Lloyd Mifflin, June 8, 1863, LCHS. The original letter is at Franklin & Marshall College. Mifflin was a 56-year-old Columbian whose son Lloyd was a well-known poet and artist. Some accounts say the hospital flag was yellow. Another 14 patients from York arrived the next day. Dr. Samuel B. McCleery from Lancaster assisted Blair.

Guards, which protected the military hospital. The independent company organized at Ellicott's Mills, Maryland, on September 25, 1861, to serve three years. Early duties included patrolling the covered bridge over the Patapsco River. Later, the company guarded fords and railroad bridges at Harpers Ferry before arriving in York. When Jenkins invaded Chambersburg, McGowan's 60 soldiers and most of the healthier patients traveled by rail to Harrisburg, where they changed trains to Shippensburg. Marching to nearby Scotland, they guarded the railroad crew that rebuilt the bridge burned by Jenkins. When construction was completed, they returned to York.[27]

The railroads, so critical to Pennsylvania's infrastructure and to national transportation, were sure to be a primary target. Work gangs constructed defenses at vital bridges, railroad yards, tunnels, and other places of potential interest to raiders. Already, a Confederate cavalry brigade under Brig. Gen. John D. Imboden threatened the Bedford Valley and the critical Baltimore & Ohio Railroad, which linked the Midwest with the East Coast. Secretary of War Stanton ordered that all Federal property in Pennsylvania be made available to Couch. Supplies of guns, uniforms, ammunition, and shoes were brought out of storage for the new emergency regiments. War was coming to the heartland, and Couch was determined to have some semblance of an organized defensive force. However, Brig. Gen. J. W. Ripley, the army's Chief of Ordnance, wired the commander of the U.S. Arsenal at Bridesburg, Pennsylvania, "Issue no first-class arms on General Couch's requisitions until the second and third class arms are exhausted."[28]

In addition to his military preparations, Couch ordered farmers in the threatened areas to move their livestock to safety. If this was not feasible, they were to hide them and afford as little aid to the enemy as possible. Private weapons and ammunition were also to be secreted so that the Rebels could not use them against state or Federal troops. In some cases, shotgun and pistol-wielding civilians openly defied this order, patrolling their towns and guarding roads, public buildings, railroad depots, and bridges. Five thousand armed men from the central Pennsylvania counties bordering the Juniata River filled the local mountain passes and hastily erected military works to defend

27 Daniel Carroll Toomey, *The Patapsco Guards Independent Company of Maryland Volunteers* (Baltimore: s. n., 1993), 1-15.

28 *OR* 27, pt. 3, 250.

their towns. Couch derisively called them "an army of bushwhackers, commanded by ex-officers."[29]

Many of the regional "troops" were useless even as bushwhackers. In several cases, within days of answering the call to duty, these companies packed up and went home, dissatisfied with the terms of their service. At Cold Mountain Gap near McConnellsburg, Lt. Col. Jacob Szink telegraphed Governor Curtin's adviser, Col. Thomas A. Scott, "I want you to never send me any more militia. I have done my best to keep them but to no purpose…"[30]

Many Cumberland Valley inhabitants felt abandoned by the military. Chambersburg storeowner William Heyser complained in his diary: "We don't understand their plans. Neither do we understand why the State hoards all those soldiers about Harrisburg, leaving the Southern portion to the invaders." The questioning intensified when Rebel raiders confiscated more than $100,000 worth of merchandise and private property from the residents of Welsh Run in southwestern Franklin County.[31]

Couch indeed was willing to abandon much of south-central Pennsylvania in order to buy time, but he was determined that the Confederates would never cross the Susquehanna at any point along its course. In the forenoon on the 22nd wired this strategy to Secretary of War Stanton, noting that the "veterans" within his force were a few militia regiments, sprinkled with nine-month men. The New York troops presented a good appearance, but lacked confidence. Couch concluded, "My artillery is all raw; my cavalry the same… I speak of the quality and condition of my troops in order that you may not wonder why I do not boldly face them against the rebels in the Cumberland Valley."[32]

On Tuesday, June 23, Granville Haller telegraphed York's Committee of Safety, authorizing the remnants of the 87th Pennsylvania to obstruct the roads in northwestern York County leading to Carlisle. However, this plan was denied because Maj. Gen. Robert Schenk previously ordered Milroy's scattered men to regroup in Baltimore. Handbills distributed throughout the county proclaimed

29 OR 27, pt. 2, 213.

30 Vertical files, GNMP. Szink had served under Col. Jacob Higgins as lieutenant colonel of the 125th Pennsylvania in the Twelfth Corps. At Antietam, a shell fragment disabled him.

31 Diary of William Heyser, June 23, 1863, *Valley of the Shadow: Two Communities in the American Civil War*, Virginia Center for Digital History, University of Virginia.

32 OR 27, pt. 3, 264; Jack Brubaker, "Defending the Susquehanna," *Civil War Times Illustrated*, Vol. 47, Issue 3 (2003), 77.

an order from General Couch "directing that all horses, except those for cavalry or scouting purposes, and all cattle, be sent north or east of Harrisburg." However, many citizens ignored the directive, supposing that the Rebels were still far off.[33]

However, that same day a clash between Haller's inexperienced horsemen and Jenkins' veteran 14th Virginia Cavalry resulted in a fatality. At dawn of a clear and pleasant day, Company D left the Cumberland Valley for the Caledonia Furnace & Iron Works, a sprawling facility located on the western base of South Mountain near Black Gap. Along the way, they confiscated only 26 horses and 22 mules, because most locals had moved their animals to safety. Arriving at the foundry about lunchtime, the Southerners easily scattered its guard detail and narrowly missed capturing the owner, abolitionist Congressman Thaddeus Stevens, who escaped to Shippensburg. Rebels seized two of his riding horses and forty mules and horses belonging to his teamsters. Maj. James C. Bryan forced the frightened overseer, John Sweeney, to provide rations for his men.[34]

About 2:00 p.m., Bryan and 40 troopers headed toward Gettysburg, pursuing the guards and their horses. Two miles beyond the ironworks, they encountered a blockade where the turnpike entered dense woods. Bryan, an infantry officer detached from Rodes' Division, feared a trap, so he consulted with his subordinates before deciding to attack. He ordered Lt. Hermann Schuricht to take nine dismounted men to clear the blockade. Schuricht directed four cavalrymen to approach the barricade from the right of the road, where thick bushes provided cover. He and the other five carefully advanced through an open field to the left. He spied about twenty-five Yankees lying in ambush, but they hurriedly disappeared when his soldiers drew near.[35]

Schuricht's detail quickly removed the obstructions and, as soon as the road was clear, Capt. Robert Moorman and twenty-five troopers charged in pursuit of the Yankees. Schuricht followed with his squad as soon as their

---

33 Haller, *Dismissal of Major Granville O. Haller*, 61; Gibson, *History of York County*, 175.

34 The Caledonia Furnace & Iron Works, on Constitution Hill ten miles east of Chambersburg, was constructed in 1837. Solely owned by Stevens after buying out his partner James Paxton in 1848, the company drew iron ore and timber from a 20,000-acre plot in Green Township. Stevens invested $65,000 in the company, which had only recently begun generating annual profits. Sweeney (spelled Swaney and Sweney in some accounts) became superintendent in 1858.

35 James C. Bryan was the quartermaster of Edward O'Neal's Brigade.

horses were brought up. The fleeing foundry guards took refuge behind a small company of Union horsemen hidden deeper in the woods. The Federals withdrew after mortally wounding Pvt. Eli Amick. Major Bryan, recognizing the dangers of advancing any farther without support, halted the pursuit. The Virginians rode back along the turnpike and reunited with the detachment guarding the purloined horses. Shortly after passing Caledonia Furnace, they came under fire from hidden bushwhackers.[36]

The Union defenders likely included Daniel D. Gitt and 24 other men from Arendtsville, a village in northern Adams County. They formed a militia company under the command of Capt. Elias Spangler and Lt. Hiram Lady. Composed of old men, men not healthy enough for regular military duty, and those with physical limitations, the company did not wear uniforms but they did carry state-issued rifles. However, they had no ammunition, so Gitt bought powder and lead, and the women of the town made improvised cartridges, enough for three rounds per man.

Major Haller ordered Spangler's company to blockade the pass on South Mountain along the Gettysburg and Chambersburg turnpike. Spangler and Lady marched their men to the designated place and sent forward pickets to watch for the Rebels. Soon, a patrol of Bell's Adams County Cavalry passed by and headed farther west to watch for the enemy. Spotting the Rebel column approaching, the cavalrymen retired to Gettysburg to inform Haller. They notified Captain Spangler as they rode past his civilian company. Spangler ordered his volunteers to hide in the dense thickets on the slopes beside the road. Some of the men who were constructing the barricades had left their guns lying in the road. Just as the Rebels came into range, a few men raced out into the pike to retrieve the weapons. Seeing the commotion and the barriers, the Confederate cavalry vanguard halted. Some troopers cautiously rode forward, dismounted, and deployed on either side of the densely packed gravel roadway.

---

36 *Richmond Daily Dispatch*, April 5, 1896. Eli Amick, from Nicholas County, WV, had long been regarded as a bushwhacker. He appears in a March 15, 1862, list of "suspected and disloyal persons." *OR* 2, pt. 2, 26. The *Gettysburg Compiler*, March 17, 1900, describes a similar event. Robert Bell dispatched orderly Sgt. Hugh Bigham and four men 15 miles west of Gettysburg to observe the Rebels. They turned around when 50 Rebels approached. A detachment of 18 enemy cavalrymen pursued them. Bigham and his comrades, lacking weapons, raced away. The pursuit continued for miles, with the Rebels only a few hundred yards behind. Finally a well-placed shot by a bushwhacker brought down one of the pursuers and disorganized the rest.

They captured many of the Arendtsville pickets, who hid their guns and denied being connected to a military force.[37]

An hour after the brief encounter, Granville Haller learned that Confederate cavalry was moving eastward on the turnpike near Cashtown. He dispatched Major Knox and the First City Troop at a "sharp gallop" eight miles to the village, where they heard that Rebels now were near Henry Munshower's old stone tavern on the turnpike about a mile-and-a-half west of Cashtown. Darkness was fast approaching, so Knox could not investigate. He left ten men at the Jacob Mickley Hotel in Cashtown as videttes. The remaining troopers returned to Gettysburg at 9 p.m. They remained in the saddle all night, expecting to see the pickets driven in by the Rebels. Because their supply wagons were in New Oxford, the Philadelphians relied upon the generosity of the residents for their meals.[38]

Haller experienced another scare that evening. Gettysburg resident Jennie McCreary noted, "A report came that the rebels were at New Salem, five or six miles from here. Then all was excitement for nearly everyone thought that now they were coming here." Captain Bell arrayed the Adams County Cavalry in "line of battle (I suppose you would call it) ready to meet them when they came." When no Confederates appeared in Gettysburg after a considerable wait, Bell's men galloped out to New Salem, but soon found that they were again chasing rumors. McCreary didn't "believe there has been a true one for the last week, someone raises them to create excitement. However I am perfectly well satisfied, I like excitement as long as there is no danger."[39]

For generations south-central Pennsylvania consisted of a peaceful close-knit farming community dominated by descendants of German, Scots-Irish, and English immigrants. Agriculture formed the backbone of the local economy, and the many small villages served as gathering places for friends, families, and acquaintances. Strangers and outsiders were traditionally looked upon with suspicion. As news of the approaching Confederates spread far and wide, frightened residents exchanged tales around their village squares,

37 *Gettysburg Star & Sentinel*, July 29, 1883.

38 *History of the First Troop*, 72-73. Munshower's (spelled Moonshour in some accounts) old stone building is at the intersection of Bingaman Road and old Route 30. It was also known as Willow Springs Tavern.

39 Jennie McCreary letter to Julia Earnest, June 24, 1863, GNMP. New Salem is now McKnightstown.

churches, and market places. Gettysburg schoolteacher Sallie Myers reported, "Day after day the people did little but stand along the streets in groups and talk. Whenever someone heard a new report, all flocked to him. The suspense was dreadful."[40]

According to 37-year-old Fannie J. Buehler, wife of Gettysburg's postmaster, "There were daily, almost hourly, reports of raids into Penn'a, and once or twice some Cavalry came as far as Cashtown and retreated. At first we were very much frightened by the thought of Rebel soldiers invading our town, taking possession of our new court house and other buildings, and doing all kinds of bad things, such as we read of in the papers." Buehler's concerns lessened when, "As day by day passed, and they did not come, we lost faith in their coming, and it grew to be an old story."[41]

Many other Pennsylvanians also left vivid accounts of these trying times. Tillie Pierce remembered it this way:

We had often heard that the rebels were about to make a raid. . . . On these occasions is was also amusing to behold the conduct of the colored people of the town. Gettysburg had a goodly number of them. The regarded the rebels as having an especial hatred toward them, and they believed that if they fell into their hands, annihilation was sure. These folks mostly lived in the southwestern part of town, and their flight was invariably down Breckinridge Street and Baltimore Street, and toward the woods on and around Culp's Hill. I can see them yet; men and women with bundles as large as old-fashioned feather ticks slung across their backs, almost bearing them to the ground. Children also, carrying their bundles, and striving in vain to keep up with their seniors. The greatest consternation was depicted on all their countenances as they hurried along; crowding and running against each other in their confusion; children stumbling, falling and crying. Mothers, anxious for their offspring, would stop for a moment to hurry them up, saying: 'For de lod's

40 Salome Myers account, ACHS. The 21-year-old Myers, assistant to the principal of Gettysburg's public school, wrote, "We had a vague idea that the Rebels were a dreadful set of men, and we didn't know what horrid things they might do. So we kept in our houses out of their way."

41 Fannie J. Buehler, *Recollections of the Rebel Raid and One Woman's Experience During the Battle* (Gettysburg, Pa.: Star and Sentinel, 1900), 6.

sake, you chillen, cum right long quick! If dem rebs dun katch you dey tear you all up.'[42]

Alice Powers also left an account of the angst she and others felt about the approaching enemy and its impact on them:

Who that endured it can ever forget the depression of the last half of June, sixty-three? How our hearts quaked at the reports and counter-reports. It was certainly a time of 'wars and rumors of wars.' Everything but the bare necessities of living had been sent away for fear of the raiders, which were a constant menace. Merchants, dealers and tradesmen were idle. Women picked lint and prepared articles for the comfort of the brave boys of others in hospitals, and wept for their own." However, "there was a short lull in the excitement and time worn on slowly . . . there was not much business done about this time [except] to hear and tell something new.[43]

After his first week in Gettysburg, the press lauded Granville Haller, who "possesses high qualities for the post. His pleasant and gentlemanly manners have won for him many friends, and the desire is general that he be allowed to continue to direct operations here as long as the emergency may continue. All his dispositions are made with promptness and energy." His soldiers, however, did not inspire much confidence. The First City Troop had not seen active duty since the summer of 1861, and new recruits comprised nearly half of its current roster. For the most part, Bell's local cavalrymen were even less experienced. Sallie Broadhead confided in her diary, "Two cavalry companies are here on scouting duty, but they can be of little use, as they have never seen service. Deserters come in every little while, who report the enemy near in large force." Residents questioned why Hooker's Army of the Potomac had not yet responded.[44]

First City Trooper Jones Wister was a 24-year-old iron foundry owner from one of Philadelphia's leading families. The world-class cricket player noted that "during a week of skirmishing, the vigilance of our small command impressed

42 Alleman, *At Gettysburg*, 19.

43 *Gettysburg Compiler*, June 24, 1903.

44 *Gettysburg Compiler*, June 29, 1863; Broadhead diary entry for June 25, 1863, ACHS.

the Confederates with the belief that we were the outposts of General Meade's army, which was what we had been working for." A reporter described Bell's Cavalry as doing "very efficient service as scouts," performing "the hardest kind of service, coming frequently in contact with the rebels, making narrow escapes and bringing in valuable information."[45]

The intelligence garnered by these reconnaissance patrols indicated that, thus at least, they had only encountered enemy horsemen. Granville Haller knew enough to realize that Lee's Southern infantry would not be far behind the cavalry screen. The skirmishing convinced Haller of two things: more serious fighting was imminent, and his untrained cavalry was all that stood between Gettysburg and the advance elements of the vaunted Army of Northern Virginia.

---

45 Wister, *Reminiscences*, 159; *Gettysburg Compiler*, June 29, 1863. Wister operated the Duncannon Iron Works in Perry County along the Susquehanna River north of Harrisburg. Jones was the fourth son of William Wister, a prominent businessman, and was born in the old family mansion, "Belfield," in Germantown. George Gordon Meade would replace Joe Hooker on June 28, 1863, as commander of the Army of the Potomac.

Chapter 4

Invasion!

A Gray Tide Rises

Robert E. Lee expected that his cavalry commander, Maj. Gen. J.E.B. Stuart, would notify him as soon as Joe Hooker's Army of the Potomac crossed the Potomac River. Since he had heard nothing from Stuart since his own army entered Maryland, Lee inferred the enemy was still in Virginia. On Sunday, June 21, he issued General Orders Number 72 instructing his men to respect private property while they appropriated supplies deep in enemy country. Lt. Gen. Richard S. Ewell reiterated these instructions the next day and gave additional orders aimed at Pennsylvania's residents. "Citizens of the country, through which the army may pass, who are not in the military service," he explained, "are admonished to abstain from all acts of hostility, upon the penalty of being dealt with in a summary manner. A ready acquiescence in the demands of the military authorities will serve greatly to lessen the rigors of war."[1]

Early on June 22 Lee informed Ewell, whose corps was in northern Maryland, that "if you are ready to move, you may do so. . . . I think your best course will be toward the Susquehanna." Lee stipulated that "if Harrisburg comes within your means, capture it," and the "progress and direction will of course depend upon the development of circumstances." He closed with a benediction, telling his corps commander that he was "trusting in the guidance of a merciful God, and invoking His protection for your corps." Lee set in motion his plan to invade Pennsylvania. Ewell would split his force, advancing

---

1 *Staunton Vindicator*, July 3, 1863. General Orders #49.

through Chambersburg to Harrisburg with the divisions of major generals Robert Rodes and Edward Johnson. Major General Jubal Early's Division, its four brigades reduced to about 5,600 men, would form a separate expeditionary force operating on Ewell's right flank. Early was ordered to march to York to "support the attack on Harrisburg by breaking the railroad between Baltimore and Harrisburg, and seizing the bridge over the Susquehanna at Wrightsville."[2]

Rodes' Division entered Pennsylvania on the morning of the 22nd, the first Confederate infantry to cross the Mason-Dixon Line. David McConaughy's civilian scouts from Gettysburg soon spotted them and reported to Darius Couch in Harrisburg that 7,000 Rebels were now in Greencastle. That same Monday, Early's Division, delayed by days of rain and high water, finally entered Maryland. "We crossed the Potomac at Shepherd's town, Va., on the 22nd of June with flags fluttering and bands playing 'Maryland, My Maryland,'" recalled Sgt. Francis L. Hudgins of the 38th Georgia.[3]

According to Georgian Cpl. Joseph H. Truett, he and his comrades:

crost the Potomac River this morning and have marched all day and we will march tomorrow. I reckon I dont know where we are a going to nor how long we will stay in these diggins. I think that we will go to Pensilvaney before [we] stop if the yankees dont stop us and I dont think they is many of them clost to us at this time. Genral Lee has got old Hookers army engaged so he cant get to us and we just whipt out old Milroy and I dont think that he will attack us any more without he gets a heap the advantage and I dont think that Genral Ewell will let him get that. Ewell Corps is all that is along with us in Mariland. This is Jacksons old army and it is hard to whip. Lawtons old brigade is all [in] yet it is holding out finely. We have got a good account of herself.[4]

According to Federal scouts, "The rebel forces in and around Sharpsburg are exclusively employed collecting plunder in Pennsylvania and Maryland. A

---

2 *OR* 27, pt. 2, 316; pt. 3, 914; *SHSP*, Vol. 4, 241-281. Early's field return on June 20 at Shepherdstown listed 487 officers and 5,124 men. He had detached the 54th North Carolina from Col. Isaac E. Avery's brigade and the 58th Virginia from Brig. Gen. William "Extra Billy" Smith's brigade to Staunton, Va., to escort prisoners from Milroy's force. He left Smith's 13th Virginia Regiment in Winchester.

3 F. L. Hudgins, "With the 38th Georgia," *Confederate Veteran*, Vol. 26 (1918).

4 Gregory C. White, *A History of the 31st Georgia Volunteer Infantry* (Baltimore: Butternut & Blue, 1997), 83, citing Joseph H. Truett letter, June 22, 1863, Georgia Department of Archives and History.

large train just passed the Shepherdstown Ford into Virginia, and also a large drove of beeves. This plunder is guarded from Shepherdstown by infantry, which, after a short absence, returns." Telegraph wires hummed with news that Early was once again advancing northward.[5]

Brigadier General John Gordon's six infantry regiments tramped through the southern Cumberland Valley on the afternoon of June 22. Following the losses at Second Winchester and sick men left behind there, his force now numbered 175 officers and 1,860 men. Hundreds were veterans of Lee's first invasion, and most carried reliable English-made Enfield rifles. Many of the Georgians wept openly as they passed the Sharpsburg battlefield, where so many comrades had perished. The somber soldiers marched three miles past Boonsboro and camped along the Hagerstown Road. Shortly afterward, Ewell detached Col. William Henderson French's 17th Virginia Cavalry from Jenkins' Brigade and assigned them to Early to screen his advance.

Many of these troopers were rebellious and free-willed and displayed but little discipline. Colonel French's command of about 240 men demanded Early's personal attention as it "was in such a state of inefficiency," a characteristic he associated with irregular "wildcat" troops. When Early encountered the 51-year-old French heading to the rear, the colonel claimed he was "very much fatigued" and needed to rest. After shaming his old acquaintance into going forward with his regiment, Early decided to accompany it for several days hoping to instill "some ideas of soldiering into the officers' heads."[6]

The following morning, June 23, the bulk of Early's Division marched northward through Cavetown, Smithsburg, and Ringgold en route to Waynesboro, Pennsylvania. Gordon's Brigade took a parallel route through Leitersburg toward the same destination. Private George F. Agee of the 26th Georgia noted that residents in the region "had put up long poles, upon the top of which was mounted an old cow's head with horns. This was for scare-crows, as they called them, to keep the hawks from the chickens. We boys would halloo and ask what had become of old Joe Hooker, and then answer their own

5 OR 27, pt. 3, 162; pt. 2, 25-27. "Beeves" was a colloquial term for cattle. Scouts erroneously reported to Brig. Gen. Daniel Tyler, commanding the Eighth Corps cavalry, that Early had 34 guns and 15,000 infantrymen.

6 Jubal A. Early to Henry B. McClellan, Feb. 2, 1878, Manuscript M1324a6, Library of Congress. Before the war French represented Mercer County in the Virginia legislature.

question by saying he is on top of the pole." The Confederates elicited anger and hatred from most residents. Agee added, "The women would get so red hot you could see their eyes sparkle."[7]

A reporter in Frederick noted, "Refugees, who arrived here this evening from near the Pennsylvania line, state that this morning at nine o'clock Early's Division of Ewell's Corps passed through Smithsburg on their way to Chambersburg. They had with them 16 pieces of artillery, two regiments of cavalry, and 11 regiments of infantry, in all about 8,000 men."[8]

Hundreds of refugees crowded the roads ahead of Gordon and Early, including scattered groups of Milroy's defeated Union soldiers. Desperate to return home after the Winchester debacle, they pushed their way through throngs of frightened citizens without pausing to assist them. Shortly before noon, civilian scouts raced into Waynesboro with the alarming news that Rebel infantry was approaching. John Philips, cashier of the First National Bank, hastily gathered up money and valuable documents. He headed east with his wife and son across Monterey Pass to Fairfield in neighboring Adams County. Philips encountered Maj. Granville Haller and informed him that 3,000 Rebels occupied Waynesboro.[9]

After establishing headquarters in the town hall in the early afternoon, the 46-year-old Jubal Early, an antebellum attorney, placed Waynesboro under martial law. A Confederate flag soon fluttered atop the building while military bands played in the square. Early stripped Chief Burgess Jacob R. Welsh and the town council of civil authority and transferred it to his provost marshal. He instructed former Union soldiers and local "stay-at-homes" to canvass the town for bread and meat for his men. Women baked bread while guards enforced his demands. Some officers accosted Josiah F. Kurtz on the steps of the National Hotel. They demanded he furnish the names and addresses of Waynesboro's

---

7   *The Sunny South*, July 20, 1901.

8   *Cleveland Plain Dealer*, June 25, 1863. Union spies confirmed Early's passage and the troop count. According to Bartlett Malone of the 6th NC (Avery's Brigade), the division found a "good meney [sic] Secesh" in Smithsburg. *The Diary of Bartlett Y. Malone* (Chapel Hill: The University of North Carolina, James Sprunt Historical Publications), Vol. 16, No. 2, 1919, 36. In Smithsburg, only four miles from decidedly Yankee-leaning Waynesboro, few espoused the Union cause. Residents of the two villages often quarreled over secession. Stoner, *History of Franklin County*, 368.

9   Stoner, *History of Franklin County*, 381-82; 369-70; Haller, *Dismissal of Major Granville O. Haller*, 68.

Maj. Gen. Jubal A. Early commanded a 6,000-man expedition to the Susquehanna River during the Gettysburg Campaign. *Library of Congress*

wealthiest citizens. When he refused, one Rebel drew a sword and attacked Kurtz, leaving a severe gash in his hand. Kurtz hastily left town for Somerset, 100 miles distant, where he remained until the invasion was over.

Early ordered the bars closed and all whiskey supplies destroyed. Several distillers in Washington and Quincy townships hid barrels of whiskey in out-of-the-way places. In some cases they dug pits and buried them. Confederate officers soon discovered most of the stashes and smashed in the barrelheads. However, a few "Louisiana Tigers" from Brig. Gen. Harry Hays' brigade found liquor and started robbing citizens of clothing, money, watches, and possessions. A particularly favorite sport was to relieve the Pennsylvanians of their high top hats and other headgear, and then mock them.[10]

Meanwhile, Gordon's Brigade was still on the road from Leitersburg. The Georgians approached the state line late that afternoon. Long after the war Gordon Bradwell left an account of what some of his comrades were up to as Pennsylvania drew near:

> In every regiment, I suppose there were some who were unworthy and even a disgrace to the service. In my company was a short, stocky fellow of German descent, who was always among the stragglers in the rear when there was any fighting to do and ahead us of when we were on the retreat. This knock-kneed, slew-footed fellow was a natural thief, always drunk when he could get liquor to drink, a consummate coward and dodger; but when under the influence of spirits a very dangerous man. Some wag dubbed him 'Old Webfoot,' and the name was so appropriate as to stick.
>
> Near the public road and just a few feet from the State line stood a very substantial residence, evidently the home of well-to-do people. 'Webfoot' fell out of the ranks of the stragglers when he saw the house and entered it, demanding in his abrupt manner something to eat. The folks treated his request with contempt, refusing to give him anything; whereupon he went through the dining room and pantry, taking the best of what he found. Not satisfied with this, he examined the premises and found concealed in the basement, under a quantity of hay, a span of splendid dappled iron-gray horses, very suitable for artillery service. This he reported to our quartermaster, whose duty it was to impress horses for the army, and in a short while the horses were led out and inducted into the Confederate service."[11]

Gordon's Georgians arrived in Waynesboro before nightfall and joined in the fun. One of his officers admitted his part in relieving some "dreadfully frightened" locals of their footwear. "They expected they were to be the victims

---

10 Stoner, *History of Franklin County*, 369-78. This account draws upon the reminiscences of Lida Welsh Bender, which appeared in the June 24, 1925, issue of *The Outlook*.

11 *Confederate Veteran*, Vol. 30, No. 10, Oct. 1922, 370.

of the most atrocious barbarity. In Waynesboro," he continued, "we made the people hand over what boots and shoes they had, also other articles that were needed for the comfort of the soldiers." Private George F. Agee noted, "The first night we spent in Pennsylvania was between Ringgold and Waynesboro. Here we drew two days of confederate grub, which was beef and bread." Some soldiers were billeted in area homes, but many slept in open fields and yards. Sixteen-year-old Lida Welsh, daughter of the deposed chief burgess, heard hundreds of men "singing familiar old hymns" after chaplains led them in prayer.[12]

That evening Gordon wrote his wife that the residents were "indifferent as to the result of the war" and would be delighted to see it end. He also mailed Fanny a pair of size four shoes, a gift from his ordnance officer Lt. William D. Lyon. They were too large, explained the general to his wife, but she could exchange them as needed. He had been unable to find the right size pair of gloves and also failed in his quest to secure a piece of nice black silk in Maryland, he continued, because Rodes' Division had already swept the area. Gordon and his jubilant but foot-weary men settled down for their first night on Pennsylvania soil.[13]

"The next morning," according to Agee, "There was a general order read that we must not forage or plunder or even leave the line of march." Early and Gordon departed after leaving a guard detachment at the town hall, still under the Confederate flag. Agee added, "We marched through the town of Waynesboro, which seemed to be a very pretty little town. . . . Curiosity to see the rebels they had heard so much about brought, I suppose, every old man, woman and child in the place. The doors, piazzas, and windows were crowded plumb full." Agee and his comrades had nicknamed Pvt. James Ervin Spivey "The 26th Georgia's Bull" for his peculiarly strong voice. G. W. Nichols recalled, "Erv could 'halloo' the queerest that I ever heard any one. It was kind of a scream or low, like a terrible bull, with a kind of a neigh mixed along with it, and it was nearly as loud as a steam whistle." His friends called for him to give the residents an example, so Spivey "brought forth that unearthly yell and in less time than it takes to tell the story there was not a living soul to be seen—the

---

12 *Mobile Advertiser & Register*, Aug. 9, 1863 (written by "an Alabamian in Lee's army," ascribed to Lt. William D. Lyon); *The Sunny South*, July 20, 1901; Bender, June 24, 1925, *The Outlook*.

13 John Gordon to Fanny Gordon, June 23, 1863. Courtesy of Hargrett Rare Book & Manuscript Library and University of Georgia libraries.

doors and windows slamming and a general scuffle as if a cyclone had come in their midst."[14]

Agee got a chuckle when he and his comrades drew "near the outskirts of town," where Agee "stepped onto the piazza and asked the lady of the house, who was peeping through a small crack she had left ajar, to please give me some of the latest newspapers. She left and in about a minute returned with several and handed them to me. They bore the date of 1842, the year I was born." Young Lida Welsh, who lived close by, complained, "The steady tramp of the men and continuous rumble of artillery and heavily loaded wagons over our narrow stony street became almost intolerable, and we were relieved when the last straggling soldier and the last rumbling wagon had vanished over the hill north of town."[15]

West of Early, Richard Ewell's lengthy column snaked its way through Chambersburg. "There was but little confusion or noise, nothing but the tramp, tramp of thousands of feet, and the continual monotonous rattle of canteens and equipment," reported a local newsman in the *Valley Spirit*. Ewell ransomed the prosperous town for supplies, money, and food. "One of the most amusing features of his [Ewell's] several requisitions was a demand for the immediate delivery of nine barrels of sauerkraut," wrote Alexander K. McClure, who continued:

He knew that sauerkraut was regarded as a very valuable antiscorbutic, and as some of his troop suffered from scurvy because of their unwholesome rations, he assumed that sauerkraut would be an invaluable remedy for those who were threatened with that malady. He was quite incredulous at first, when informed that sauerkraut was a commodity that could not be kept in midsummer, and that such a thing was unknown even in the German communities where sauerkraut was one of the great staples of the table. If there had been a barrel of sauerkraut in Chambersburg in midsummer he could have scented it any place within a square, and he finally abandoned that

---

14 Stoner, *History of Franklin County*, 386; *The Sunny South*, July 20, 1901; Nichols, *A Soldier's Story*, 142. According to *The History of Zephyr Hills*, 1821-1921, for his assistance in one of the battles in the Early's Valley Campaign, "'The Bull' was given a citation and presented with a gold fountain pen engraved with his name and the date of that battle, September 4, 1864." After the war Spivey and his brother John became Baptist preachers in Oakdale, Ga.

15 Bender, June 24, 1925, *The Outlook*. According to an 1868 atlas, the Welsh family lived on Mechanic Street (Quincy Road).

feature of the requisition when told that it was not an article that could be concealed in hot weather."[16]

One reporter observed that the Rebels were in good spirits. Many loudly boasted about what they intended to do while in Pennsylvania, and invariably denounced the Yankees as cowards. Some asked frightened residents how far it was to Harrisburg and how many defenders were stationed there. Others bragged, "Here's your ragged rebels; we are going to Harrisburg to capture your Dutch militia, and the boys that carry the big Knapsacks." Several laughed about the futile attempts to reunite the country, "Now that we are in the Union, guess you are satisfied." Jubilant soldiers teasingly pushed the men in front and shouted, "On to Richmond!" Two parallel columns of Confederates filled the lower Cumberland Valley. While Ewell occupied Chambersburg as a base to threaten Harrisburg, Early's Division marched northward toward Quincy. He sent some of the 17th Virginia Cavalry eastward to secure the South Mountain passes toward Fairfield.[17]

Terrified country folk exaggerated that a 30,000-man force under Ewell was now between Chambersburg and Carlisle, heading straight for Harrisburg. A deserter from the 44th Georgia of Law's Brigade arrived in Gettysburg later that day. He brought news that Ewell in reality had six brigades with 12,000 men at Hagerstown back on Sunday when he and 50 companions deserted.[18]

David McConaughy's scouts, meanwhile, busily monitored Ewell's and Early's commands. Messengers dashed across the mountains from Chambersburg northward to telegraph stations along the Pennsylvania Railroad, where they confirmed to General Couch the enemy movement through the Cumberland Valley. It now appeared that the Rebels were not turning toward Pittsburgh as some had believed, although John Imboden's Confederate cavalrymen sent a scare in that direction when they raided the Baltimore & Ohio Railroad in Bedford County. While the Army of the Potomac dawdled with indecision, Ewell's Confederates moved steadily toward the

---

16 *Valley Spirit*, June 5, 1863; A. K. McClure, "Maneuvering for Battle," in *Old Time Notes of Pennsylvania* (Philadelphia: John Winston, 1905), Vol. 2, 93-94.

17 *Lancaster Daily Express*, July 11, 1863.

18 *Albany Evening Journal*, June 25, 1863. The party of deserters hid for a night in the mountains before heading for Frederick; their goal was to go to Baltimore. The writer instead chose to go north to Gettysburg. Scouts captured him there and escorted him to Harrisburg.

Susquehanna bridges. They clearly intended to force the surrender of one of the North's most important state capitals and railway centers.

More refugees poured into Harrisburg, especially frightened blacks. The *Telegraph* reported, "Contrabands are arriving here constantly, and it really is a distressing sight to see women and children huddled in wagons, bringing all their worldly possessions with them." Newspaper advertisements called for workers to erect further defenses at $1.25 per day. Working feverishly, refugees and residents strained to strengthen the fortifications that protected the city from an attack from the south. In an effort to defend the Camelback toll bridge and the nearby Cumberland Valley Railroad Bridge, engineers supervised the construction of Forts Washington and Couch on heights overlooking the Susquehanna River near White Hill.[19]

A Dutchman's Pride

The vast majority of those serving in the ranks of Lee's army had never crossed the Mason-Dixon Line, and so were now getting their first look at storied Pennsylvania, a cradle of the American Revolution. They gawked at the verdant farmlands and well-maintained orchards of the Cumberland Valley. A culture of prosperity and abundance was evident. Pennsylvania truly appeared to be a land liberally flowing with milk and honey. Men who had barely scratched out a living farming the red clay of rural Georgia marveled at the rich black topsoil that promised an abundant harvest. Many homes were solidly constructed from fieldstone or brick; some dated from the colonial era. The wooden houses were nearly all well-kept and nicely whitewashed, glimmering in the sunshine. The massive bank barns were substantially more imposing than Southern counterparts. Modern farming implements and machinery often filled the barns and farmyards. Reapers and other new equipment were a novelty to be inspected as time (and the officers) allowed. One Georgian commented, "A Dutchman's pride is in his large well-filled barns." However, some passing Rebels kept a nervous eye on them, fearing they might be convenient hiding places for bushwhackers.[20]

19 *Harrisburg Telegraph*, June 24, 1863. White Hill now is Camp Hill.

20 *Savannah Daily Republican*, July 20, 1863. The author, Capt. Virgil A. S. Parks of the 17th Georgia, was in Benning's Brigade, but his comments are illustrative of the Rebels' general

John Gordon viewed "a panorama both interesting and enchanting" for several miles. Scores of prosperous farms, irrigated by clear streams and crystal springs, lay in the valley amid broad green meadows with luxuriant grasses. Huge barns prominently dominated the landscape in all directions. Harvested shocks already dotted some broad grain fields, while others were "clad in golden garb," waving their welcome to the reapers and binders. To Gordon, this valley of "universal thrift and plenty" awakened conflicting emotions. The scenery evoked images of the Shenandoah Valley before the ravages of war and the constant tramping of armies left that region wasted and bare. He noted, with a touch of sadness, that both valleys were "filled with big red barns, representing in their silent dignity the independence of their owners." They each contained old-fashioned brick or stone mansions, although they were as dissimilar in architectural style "as Teutonic manners and tastes differ from those of the Cavalier."[21]

One Alabama bachelor marching with Gordon kept his eyes on the girls, many of whom he found to be vulgar and not as pretty as the ladies of Savannah. However, he thought he had made quite an impression on one young lady, who was "exceedingly obliging" in the way of bread, butter, milk, and complimentary remarks. The soldier had no doubt that he could have "made a rebel of her" had he tried. While she was the most attractive girl in the region, he would not consider her good-looking outside of Pennsylvania. However, as with all Yankee girls, she had a degree of sharpness and wit, as well as great confidence that the Union army would soon drive the Rebels out of her state. As he said goodbye, she naively told him "to be sure and call and see her on my return if I was not in too big a hurry." He added, "I did not happen to come back by that road or I certainly should have accepted her invitation." The farmers and townsmen evoked an entirely different reaction from the young officer, who called the men he encountered "the most cowardly wretches I ever saw." The Dutchmen desired to save their property from impressment "on any terms," and they "would tell any tale and act any part to affect that result."[22]

Now well within enemy territory, Jubal Early authorized his soldiers to seize supplies from Pennsylvania farms, mills, and storehouses. Dozens of

---

impression as they tramped through Pennsylvania. Parks, a native of Texas who grew up in middle Georgia, died at Gettysburg.

21 Gordon, *Reminiscences*, 140-41.

22 *Mobile Advertiser & Register*, Aug. 9, 1863.

foraging patrols roamed the scenic landscape and visited many of the unsuspecting owners. They offered certificates drawn on the Confederacy in exchange for provisions, which Early's quartermaster, Maj. C. E. Snodgrass, sent southward in a steady procession of heavily laden wagons.[23]

In most instances where residents had abandoned their homes, the Confederates obeyed Lee's orders to respect private property. The 31st Georgia halted and rested near one such vacated farm. Some soldiers entered the yard to pick ripe cherries. Fearing they might be tempted to create additional mischief, Col. Clement Evans went to investigate. He found his men in the rear of the farmhouse near an underground milk and butter-house. Evans was relieved that, although the door was unlocked and the soldiers knew the cellar was well stocked, they had not touched anything. However, he believed "the citizens supply our troops too liberally with whiskey—surely they can ruin our army by a liberality of that sort unless the orders are enforced."[24]

Gordon's ordnance officer, Lt. William Lyon, "never enjoyed myself more than I did on that march." He passed through "the most beautiful and highly cultivated country that I ever saw. It was literally a land of plenty." Gordon's Confederates, many of English or Scotch-Irish descent, marveled at the quaint Germanic people they encountered. To Lyon, the residents were "very much frightened of our appearance" and "fully expected to be the victims of the most horrible atrocities. They brought out in the greatest abundance everything that they had to eat or drink and would not be prevailed upon to pay for it."[25]

Corporal Joseph H. Truett of the 31st Georgia wrote, "The Pennsylvania women would give us anything to eat that they had and we made milk and butter and chickens and eggs. We lived on the best that there was in the state and when we would get to a town we would press all of the sugar, coffee, and whiskey and shoes that was in the towns. We took wagons, horses, beef cattle, and everything that we wanted to supply the army."[26]

---

23 Jubal A. Early, *War Memoirs: Autobiographical Sketch and Narrative of the War Between the States* (Philadelphia: J. B. Lippincott, 1912), 254-55.

24 Stephens, *Intrepid Warrior*, 213.

25 William Dunn Lyon to George Lyon, July 18, 1863, William D. Lyon Papers, Pearce Civil War Collection, Navarro College, Corsicana, Texas. Clement Evans colorfully described Lyon in his diary (Stephens, *Intrepid Warrior*, 340-41). Lyon was killed in "a drunken spree" (possibly by a sharpshooter) at Third Winchester on Sept. 19, 1864.

26 White, *A History of the 31st Georgia*, 84, citing Joseph H. Truett letter, June 22, 1863, GDAH.

Many citizens tried to appease the advancing columns of Confederates in the hope that their buildings and families might be spared. One of Colonel French's wildcat Virginia cavalrymen, Pvt. James H. Hodam, wrote that the countryside abounded "chiefly in Dutch women who could not speak English, sweet cherries, and apple-butter." In that part of Pennsylvania, the cherry crop was immense and ancient trees laden with ripened fruit often overhung the highway. Early's infantrymen frequently broke off great branches and devoured the cherries as they marched along. Women and children stood at their front gates holding large loaves of bread and crocks of apple butter in an attempt to dissuade the grimy invaders from entering their premises.[27]

Jenkins' cavalry, part of which screened Jubal Early's advance, often accentuated fearful residents' perception that they might turn on their hosts at any time if more and more luxuries were not produced. A Pennsylvania newsman claimed that many cavalrymen behaved like common thieves. It was "not unusual" for them to accost residents who were walking in the road or sitting inside their houses. A squad would ride up, present a pistol to the terrified civilian's head, and demand his money, hat, coat, boots, and even his pantaloons. They forced some men to walk home in a state of nudity. If the victim refused to cooperate, he "would get a taste of real lead." The stereotype of the Southern "criminal" was perpetuated in streetside conversations and even in church sermons.[28]

Private G. W. Nichols of the 61st Georgia claimed that as Gordon's Brigade tramped through one town, a little girl exclaimed, "Why mamma, they haven't got horns! They are just like our people." Early's division quietly passed through Quincy and Altodale, where curious crowds peered at miles-long column of soldiers. Farmers along the route soon learned to hide their livestock. Nichols added, "Our quartermaster and commissary departments took every cow, sheep, horse, mule and wagon that they could lay their hands on, besides bacon and flour. Foraging was strictly prohibited among the men in line. The cavalry and commissary department did the work. We boys, with guns,

---

27 James Harrison Hodam manuscript, excerpted from Kesterson, *Campaigning with the 17th Virginia Cavalry: Night Hawks at Monocacy* (Washington, W.V.: Night Hawk Press, 2005) and Richard Wheeler, *Eyewitness to Gettysburg* (Edison, N.J.: Blue & Grey, 1994), 82.

28 *Lancaster Daily Express*, July 8, 1863. Certain irregular "cavalry" preceded Lee's army, including Mosby's Rangers and John H. McNeill's partisans. These independent commands also terrorized the populace.

had more strict orders here than we ever had in our own country; we just had to stay in line, and sometimes we almost suffered for water."[29]

Jubal Early finally halted his forces at Greenwood, a rustic village eight miles east of Chambersburg on the western approach to South Mountain. They camped in the shadow of Chestnut Ridge along the turnpike that ran eastward to Gettysburg. The easternmost regiment reached John Dillon's farm near Newman's Gap, establishing vidette posts on top of the mountain.[30]

Some of Gordon's Georgians found a "legal" way to get around Lee's orders to respect private property. Camping in open pastoral country, they ascertained that there was no wood nearby for campfires. Several soldiers asked General Gordon for permission to burn a few rails from an old-fashioned fence near the camp. He agreed, but stipulated they could only take the top layer of rails. The remaining barrier would still be high enough to answer the farmer's purpose. When morning came, the fencing had nearly all disappeared, but each man declared that he had taken only the top rail. To Gordon, it was "a case of adherence to the letter and neglect of the spirit; but there was no alternative except good-naturedly to admit that my men had gotten the better of me that time."[31]

That evening, Col. Clement Evans wrote his wife Allie about the "poor class of people" who had visited the 31st Georgia's camp to hear the regimental band. He described the mountain women as "pretty coarse," and "their hands are large & rough, fingers blunt at the ends. They have evidently been accustomed to labor."[32]

The Comanches

Driving refugees before them, the lead elements of the Army of Northern Virginia steadily advanced deeper into Pennsylvania. However, three brigades of J.E.B. Stuart's cavalry did not accompany Ewell. Stuart commenced a series

29 Nichols, *A Soldier's Story of his Regiment*, 115. Altodale is now known as Mount Alto. During the Civil War era it was also known as Funkstown, after its founder, John Funk.

30 *Gettysburg Compiler*, June 29, 1863. These videttes were likely atop Green Ridge.

31 Gordon, *Reminiscences*, 144-45. The location of this incident is unclear. Many of Gordon's campsites were in open pastoral country. His June 26 camp at Gettysburg on the G. Wolf farm is another strong possibility.

32 Stephens, *Intrepid Warrior*, 218.

Lt. Col. Elijah V. White was in command of the 35th Battalion, Virginia Cavalry, a unit later called as "White's Comanches" because of its penchant for lightning-quick raids and ear-piercing war cries.

Loudoun County Historical Society, Leesburg, Virginia

of moves that placed his force well behind Union lines. However, Robert E. Lee retained other horsemen to screen his army and disrupt Federal communications. Among these was the 35th Battalion, Virginia Cavalry, which had been detached from William "Grumble" Jones' brigade after Brandy Station and assigned to the Second Corps. Colorful 31-year-old Lt. Col. Elijah Veirs White commanded this battalion of five companies from Virginia and one from Maryland.[33]

Born August 29, 1832, at his parents' 700-acre "Stoney Castle" plantation near Poolesville, Maryland, "Lige" White was educated in the north, attending Lima Seminary in New York and Granville College in Ohio. After fighting abolitionists in Kansas in 1855-56, he returned to the East. He subsequently married a Maryland girl and purchased a 355-acre farm near Leesburg in Loudon County, Virginia. A large, blue-eyed man with a ruddy complexion, White's charismatic personality and booming voice commanded respect. A. P. Hill considered him to be "a trump and one of the best cavalry officers we have." White's appearance, with his gold-braided uniform and plumed hat, fit the popular image of a Southern cavalier. Because his home was often behind Federal lines, he moved his wife Sarah Elizabeth and their child to "Fruitland,"

---

33 Jones' and Jenkins' brigades screened Lee's army. To the west, John Imboden's brigade threatened the Baltimore & Ohio RR. Stuart took with him the brigades of Fitzhugh Lee, John Chambliss, and Wade Hampton, leaving Beverly Robertson's brigade with Lee.

the commodious home of a friend, David Coffman, near Ida in rural Page County. It was deep in the Shenandoah Valley and presumably beyond the reach of White's vindictive pro-Union Loudon neighbors.[34]

White's hard-hitting, hard-drinking men possessed more combat ability than military precision or discipline. They later earned the nickname "White's Comanches" for their wild war cries and lightning-quick raids on Federal communication lines. Many had seen action across northern Virginia, where they gained a reputation for efficiency and daring. They often struck without warning and then faded into the shadows. Union cavalry patrolled wide sectors searching for these partisans, but found only rumors and inconsistent speculation as to their whereabouts.[35]

In the spring of 1863, the 35th Battalion joined the Army of Northern Virginia. They fought at Beverly Ford and Brandy Station in early June and lost two company commanders and 88 men out of 267 engaged. Following his decisive victory over Milroy at Second Winchester, General Ewell granted White's request to take his remaining cavalrymen on a raid to wreck railroad and telegraph lines near Harpers Ferry to sever Federal communications. The objective was the Baltimore & Ohio Railroad depot at Point of Rocks, Maryland, about twelve miles east of Harpers Ferry.[36]

After leaving enough soldiers to guard the Blue Ridge passes, White and about 150 horsemen departed camp at Snickersville, Virginia, at 8 a.m. on June 17. They crossed the Potomac at Grubb's Ford, three miles west of Point of Rocks, and destroyed rails and ripped down telegraph wires. About 5:30 p.m., Lt. Joshua R. Crown and 62 men of Company B galloped toward the Frederick Road. Despite being outnumbered two-to-one, they easily drove off Maj. Henry Cole's Union cavalry near the mouth of Catoctin Creek. Crown's detachment chased the Yankees four miles toward Frederick, capturing 37 of them in a running fight that continued into the night. They returned in the darkness to Catoctin Station and attacked a Federal supply train loaded with provisions for

---

34 Files of the Loudoun County Historical Society, Thomas Balch Library, Leesburg, Virginia.

35 Confederate Brig. Gen. Thomas Rosser termed White's battalion the "Comanches" later in 1863 during the Mine Run Campaign. At Brandy Station, Capt. George Chiswell of Company B received a severe wound that put him out of the war and Lt. Joshua Crown assumed command. Lt. Harrison M. Strickler replaced Capt. John H. Grabill of Company E, captured that day at Beverly Ford.

36 *Richmond Times-Dispatch*, July 19, 1910.

the garrison at Harpers Ferry. Three other supply trains had passed through the station before Crown arrived.

Meanwhile, Elijah White led his command on a wild twilight dash down the Chesapeake & Ohio Canal towpath into Point of Rocks. They routed Union Capt. Samuel Means' Loudon Rangers, which hailed from the same county as many of White's men. Riding to the B&O depot, the Confederates found the final train in the supply convoy still there. After capturing the engineer, conductor, and 15 terrified passengers, cavalrymen removed burning coals from a furnace in one of the passenger cars. They scattered them on the floors of all 18 cars, including several filled with barrels of flour destined for Harpers Ferry. Fanning the flames, soon they had fires roaring in each car.[37]

The soldiers stuck the locomotive's throttle wide open and sent the blazing train careening down the tracks. They captured and burned three army wagons, along with considerable baggage and camp equipage. The panic-stricken depot telegrapher erroneously notified John W. Garrett, the president of the B&O Railroad, the Rebels had carried off Means' entire company. In reality, they killed four, wounded 27, and captured roughly a hundred soldiers from the three companies of Federal cavalry dispatched from Harpers Ferry. White had not lost a single man or horse. After destroying more rails and telegraph wires, the raiders disappeared about 10 p.m., dashing away in the darkness to safety across the Potomac. They were back in camp by nine the next morning, even as additional Yankee patrols futilely sought them. White's battalion made the 57-mile round trip in only 25 hours.[38]

After resting and recruiting for a few days, White led some 280 free spirits into Chambersburg on June 24, where Ewell ordered them eastward to meet Jubal Early in Greenwood. After setting up camp, White periodically sent scouting patrols across South Mountain to feel the strength of the Yankee outposts. His men joined Jenkins' 17th Virginia Cavalry in cautiously pushing

37 At the outbreak of the Civil War, the B&O RR stationmaster at Point of Rocks was Noble Means, Capt. Samuel Means' brother. The Loudon Rangers were for the most part from the western part of Loudon County, separated by a low mountain range from the Southern sympathizing eastern townships.

38 *New York Herald*, June 20, 1863, OR 27, pt. 2, 770-77; Myers, *The Comanches*, 188-91; John E. Devine, *35th Battalion, Virginia Cavalry* (Lynchburg, Va.: H. E. Howard, 1985); Edward G. Longacre, *The Cavalry at Gettysburg* (Lincoln: University of Nebraska Press, 1986), 138-39. Some accounts list White's strength at 262 men, although Busey and Martin, *Regimental Strengths and Losses at Gettysburg*, suggest 276. On June 23, privates John Breathard and James Hoskins of Lt. Joshua Crown's Company B were captured near Chambersburg.

ever eastward along the turnpike. A detachment surprised one of Captain Bell's Adam's County scouts, Harvey Cobean, who was unaware Rebels were coming up behind him. He turned his horse's blind eye toward the enemy, "slipped his horse pistols and saber through a nearby fence, and coolly collided the enemy." He managed to escape and ride back to report the incident to Bell.[39]

Later that day, Maj. Granville Haller dispatched his aide, Capt. Samuel Young, with a squad of First City Troopers to relieve Bell's pickets at Cashtown. Several times Rebel patrols probed the vidette post. Alarms sounded in Gettysburg throughout the day as scouts reported that a large body of Rebel infantry and artillery was approaching. Several skeptical residents downplayed these warnings because of past exaggerated threats. Consequently, they went about their daily business. However, many of the remaining blacks bundled up their possessions and hurriedly left town to avoid captivity.[40]

The Emergency Men

Union commanders prepared for the inevitable. Maj. Gen. Darius Couch, commanding the Department of the Susquehanna, knew that the Army of the Potomac could not reach Pennsylvania fast enough to repel the invasion. He responded by shifting emergency militia to key locations to slow down the Rebels and buy time for Hooker's arrival. These temporary militia regiments often consisted of young boys, old men, shopkeepers, and farmers, sprinkled with army veterans. Officers were often chosen because of political ties, friendships, social standing, or, in some cases, past military achievements.

One such hastily raised regiment was the 26th Pennsylvania Volunteer Militia. Its commander was Col. William Wesley Jennings, the 24-year-old son of a wealthy Harrisburg factory owner. In May 1861, Jennings used his family's longstanding relationship with Gov. Andrew Curtin to secure a commission as

---

39 William Alonzo Scott, *The Battle of Gettysburg* (Gettysburg, Pa.: s. n., 1905).

40 History of the First Troop, 71; Haller, *Dismissal of Major Granville O. Haller*, 66. Peter C. Vermilyea, in his essay "The Effect of the Confederate Invasion of Pennsylvania on Gettysburg's African American Community," (*Gettysburg Magazine*, No. 24) states that the 1860 Census enumerated 186 blacks in the borough, 8% of the population. According to Tillie Pierce, many blacks were certain that the Rebels had "an especial hatred toward them, and believed that if they fell into their hands, annihilation was sure." Some of the refugees came back after Lee retreated to Virginia. However, many never returned. Tax rolls for autumn 1863 list only 22 families (64 people) still in Gettysburg. Ten years later, only 74 pre-war blacks appear in the 1870 census.

Col. William Wesley Jennings commanded the 26th Pennsylvania Volunteer Militia during the Gettysburg Campaign. A veteran of the Army of the Potomac, he did not have sufficient time to properly train his untested militia before they were rushed to defend Gettysburg.

Sketch by Zac Bretz, based upon a wartime photograph

a first lieutenant in the "Locheil Grays," Company F of the 25th Pennsylvania. In July 1862, Curtin commissioned him as a colonel and ordered him to raise a nine-month regiment, the 127th Pennsylvania. Jennings was slightly wounded in the thigh at Fredericksburg and emerged unscathed from Chancellorsville. After mustering out in May, he returned to the service when Curtin asked him on June 22 to command one of the new emergency regiments.[41]

Jennings' previous combat experience and gift for rhetoric inspired his 743 men. One of his drummers remarked, "Thoroughly capable, and brave, he was held in highest esteem by all." Jennings had an accurate view of the combat proficiency of his recruits, calling them 700 civilians in soldier suits. Company officers ranged from 41-year-old Harrisburg engineer James L. Pell to a 21-year-old dentist from Catawissa, Elias C. Rishel, who was wounded at Chancellorsville. Several others had also served under Jennings in the 127th Pennsylvania.[42]

---

41 William S. Nye, "The First Battle of Gettysburg," *CWTI*, Vol. 4, No. 5 (Aug. 1965), 13. Jennings was born July 22, 1838, in Harrisburg. His father William owned a large iron foundry near Harrisburg. At twenty-two, the younger Jennings established his own successful business. His grandfather, yet another William Jennings, raised a militia company in the War of 1812 from the Juniata Valley.

42 Richards, *Pennsylvania's Emergency Men at Gettysburg*, 7; Regimental muster rolls and card file, Pennsylvania State Archives, Harrisburg.

After organizational meetings and muster ceremonies on June 22, the militiamen received new uniforms, rifled muskets from a nearby armory, and shiny new black leather knapsacks. They began two days of cursory drilling at Camp Curtin north of Harrisburg. One of the starry-eyed recruits in Company F was 20-year-old Samuel W. Pennypacker, who enrolled in Phoenixville. While volunteers such as the future governor of Pennsylvania conversed eagerly of expected military success, the few combat veterans were grim. They knew it was unrealistic to expect these boys to stop the cream of Lee's army when the Army of the Potomac had failed to do so. Pennypacker later admitted that he was so inexperienced that he was clueless as to how to affix his bayonet; let alone load, aim, and shoot his musket at a target.[43]

Very early in the morning of Wednesday, June 24, while Jubal Early's division prepared to depart Waynesboro, officers roused Jennings' militiamen out of bed. They ordered them to "cook two days rations, and to be ready to march by six." Couch wired Maj. Granville Haller, "Would it do to send a Regiment of Infantry to Gettysburg?" Haller responded, "Please send a Regiment, it will restore confidence and rally the people to take arms." Couch replied, "Colonel Jennings will use his best efforts to hold the country, harass the enemy—attacking him at exposed points or falling back in order—and advancing his force or part of it, making flank attacks etc., doing everything in his power to weaken, mislead the enemy and protect the country." When news of the untrained regiment's impending arrival reached Gettysburg, a skeptical Sallie Broadhead remarked, "We do not feel much safer."[44]

Colonel Jennings and his green recruits boarded Pennsylvania Railroad cars and headed toward Gettysburg. Company A was raised there by Capt. Frederick Klinefelter. The steam train crossed the Susquehanna and, according to Pennypacker, "finally started off on the road to York, amid the cheering of all on board. We travelled along very slowly, sometimes stopping for a half an hour or more, and then creeping on at such a snail's pace that it was very tiresome. I

43 Samuel W. Pennypacker, "Six Weeks in Uniform . . . Gettysburg Campaign, 1863," *Historical and Biographical Sketches* (Philadelphia: Robert A. Tripple, 1910), 340-43. Pennypacker wrote his lengthy narrative on Nov. 22, 1863, while the events were fresh in his mind. It is the best surviving account of the 26th PVM.

44 William Henry Rupp diary, Special Collections, Musselman Library, Gettysburg College; Haller, Dismissal, 65; Broadhead diary entry for June 24, 1863, ACHS. She noted, "We were getting used to the excitement, and many think the enemy, having been so long in the vicinity—without visiting us, will not favor us with their presence."

remember very distinctly in what a glorious humor we all were, without any anxiety except to reach the end of our journey. At nearly every house which we passed the women came to the windows and waved their handkerchiefs, and then all set up such a cheering, hurrahing, and tigering that it was enough to deafen one."

At several places in northeastern York County the train passed squads and companies of Col. William B. Thomas's 20th Volunteer Militia regiment. To Pennypacker, "their camps looked so pleasant upon the green, that the idea passed through my mind of how nice it would be to be stationed in some copse or grove for a few weeks and guard a bridge or something of the kind, then return home" to brag to those friends who had not enlisted. In downtown York, they saw a large contingent of paroled Union soldiers going into camp while awaiting transportation back to their various states.[45]

After leaving York, Pennypacker observed that the countryside south of town "seemed to be exceedingly dry, and the crops, which were then nearly ready to harvest, were generally very poor." The train passed scores of large bank barns, mostly painted red in the Pennsylvania German style. Soon, it arrived at Hanover Junction, where the locomotives were changed. The regiment headed west on the Hanover Branch Railroad, with many soldiers riding in open coal cars for the next leg of the trip. Twelve-and-a-half-miles later, they arrived in Hanover. Company I had been raised there by Lt. Col. Joseph S. Jenkins, who "had the faculty of making himself disagreeable to everyone." The train stopped at the depot for half an hour, "a time of great excitement" according to Pennypacker. A crowd gathered to welcome the soldiers, who asked, "Are there any Confederates in the neighborhood?" No enemy was reported nearby. Crews divided the train into two sections, and Jennings sent a portion of the regiment on ahead toward Gettysburg while he awaited a second locomotive for the remaining cars.[46]

A railroad mishap in Adams County delayed the regiment's arrival. Shortly after passing through New Oxford, the lead section struck "a poor woman's cow" on the tracks near Swift Run, six miles east of Gettysburg. The

45 Robert L. Bloom, "We Never Expected a Battle: The Civilians of Gettysburg, 1863," *Pennsylvania History* (Oct. 1988), 55: 166; Pennypacker, "Six Weeks in Uniform," 329. Richards, *Pennsylvania's Emergency Men at Gettysburg*, 9.

46 Richards, *Pennsylvania's Emergency Men at Gettysburg*, 7; *Encounter at Hanover: Prelude to Gettysburg* (Gettysburg: Historical Publication Committee of the Hanover Chamber of Commerce, Times and News Publishing Co., 1962), 217. Jenkins was killed in 1864 during the Siege of Petersburg.

locomotive, tender, and several cars derailed, sending startled soldiers sprawling. The accident tore up several yards of rails and considerably damaged the engine. Luckily, only two men suffered minor scratches. The militiamen camped near the wrecked tracks and awaited the arrival of the second section, which was several miles behind. On board it, Private Pennypacker noted, "We slowly approached as near as was safe, and there getting off the cars were marched to a wood on the right of the track where we found the other part of the regiment, and stacked our arms by companies in regular order. Leaving our traps by the muskets, all hastened over to see what had happened. It appeared that an old woman had been driving a cow along the top of a high embankment where the road crossed a deep gully and small creek. The old woman got out of the way when the cars came up, but the cow ran along the track, was caught about midway and thrown over the bank dead. The cars were forced from the track by the concussion but fortunately kept their course almost parallel with the rails, bumping over the sills until they got beyond the gully, and there all the track was torn up and badly broken were piled together."

He added, "I went down into the ravine to look at the cow which was very old and miserably poor. I pitied the old woman who was standing there crying, while a number of our fellows, among whom was Sergeant [William G.] Meigs, had out their knives and were already busily engaged cutting off steaks wherever any meat could be found. After he had finished Meigs offered me his knife which I declined, feeling a good bit of hesitation about making use of it in that way, when he told me I would be glad to get meat like that before a great while. It was then about 4 P. M."[47]

While the militia roasted the old cow, in Gettysburg Granville Haller continued to monitor Rebel movements to the west. About 8:30 p.m., Capt. Samuel Young at Cashtown sent courier to inform Haller, "I advanced two miles—saw rebel Cavalry." He relayed an unconfirmed report, which he deemed as reliable, that infantry and artillery were now also on the mountain, indicating that the Army of Northern Virginia had arrived in force. Haller received the note at 11 p.m. and immediately telegraphed the worrisome news to General Couch in Harrisburg. Couch replied, "It would be well if you could find out what the Rebels are doing. Can't you get some Riflemen on their flanks in the mountains?" At 2:00 a.m., the seemingly tireless Haller sent a courier

---

47 Pennypacker, "Six Weeks in Uniform," 330.

riding through the night to Jennings, ordering him to prepare the railcars if possible to return to Hanover. If not, the colonel was to impress horses and "be ready to fall back on a moment's notice. The enemy in force, Artillery, Infantry, and Cavalry, have already possession of the mountain pass and no doubt intend marching here, perhaps today."[48]

Watching for the Rebels

At dawn on Thursday, June 25, Jubal Early's division rose in their camps near Greenwood. Gordon Bradwell commented, "The captain sent me and a comrade ahead of the column to fill the canteens with water. We stopped in front of a beautiful residence, with a grassy lawn in front, and hailed. An old gentleman, dressed in blue overalls, with a wide straw hat on his head, came out, apparently very much frightened. We spoke to him respectfully and asked if we might fill the canteens at the pump just over the fence in the yard. But the old fellow's mind was so preoccupied with the apprehension that his factory on the other side of the street would be burned that he paid no attention to our request and would talk to us about nothing else. We assured him that it would not be molested, but this did not satisfy him, and we left him in a state of extreme doubt and fear. No doubt he judged us from his own standard of right and wrong."[49]

Perhaps the old man worried that these two insolated Rebels were from the roving bands of lawless deserters who terrorized the countryside. Colonel Clement Evans of the 31st Georgia penned, "The whole country is full of deserters. They form themselves into companies. Have camps and resist all attempts to take them. It is too bad and our army will soon be ruined if there is not a stop put to it soon." Desertion also plagued the Pennsylvania militia and home guard units, albeit to a lesser extent. At McCall's Ferry along the Susquehanna River in eastern York County, a Marietta newsman noted, "An inn-keeper . . . named Richardson has been arrested for assisting desertion. He was sent to Philadelphia for trial."[50]

---

48 Haller, *Dismissal of Major Granville O. Haller*, 66.

49 Isaac G. Bradwell, "Crossing the Potomac," *Confederate Veteran*, 30, No. 10, Oct. 1922, 370.

50 Stephens, *Intrepid Warrior*, 215. Evans' diary entry for June 25, 1863; Marietta (Pa.) *Mariettian*, June 27, 1863. *The Chambersburg Repository*, June 26, 1863, reported that Ewell ordered a court-martial near the Birch Church, north of Chambersburg, on June 25. Two deserters from

Meanwhile in Gettysburg, Maj. Granville Haller anxiously sought information on Early's intentions. At 6 a.m. he sent Samuel Randall's First City Troop beyond Cashtown to observe the enemy and determine their composition. The Philadelphians halted at the tollgate and constructed "a very weak barricade." Randall sent two advance patrols a mile up the mountain road to Newman's Gap. Earlier in the week, he had assigned the unruly bay which caused Edward White's broken leg to Pvt. Jones Wister as a replacement for his played-out gray mare. The 24-year-old Wister had finally tamed the steed. He now rode in Sgt. Edward Reakirt's patrol.[51]

After Reakirt halted, Wister volunteered to ride ahead a few hundred yards to feel for the enemy. He soon encountered three prone Rebels, who fired at him. Wister zigzagged his horse to disrupt their aim. "Fortunately for me, they were poor shots. Bullet after bullet whizzed through the branches over my head." He wheeled his horse, intending to ride back to and report his success in locating the enemy. However, Wister's saddle turned under him, pitching him to the ground. He assumed either he or his horse was hit, but, to his relief, he found no wounds. Desperately, he clutched the bridle and dashed for safety, running alongside "Count White." After scampering for a quarter of a mile, Wister considered it safe to halt and restrap his saddle into position. Mounting, he sheepishly returned to his comrades.[52]

While his patrols skirmished with the Yankee cavalry that morning, Jubal Early rode into Chambersburg and met General Ewell, who directed him to cross South Mountain to Gettysburg. From there, he was to proceed to York and cut the Northern Central Railway between Baltimore and Harrisburg. If he could, Early was to destroy the Columbia Bridge across the Susquehanna, thereby severing the railroad between York and Philadelphia. Early was then to pass through Dillsburg and rejoin Ewell at Carlisle.[53]

Rodes' 45th North Carolina (Daniel's Brigade) were stripped of three months' pay. Ewell ordered them branded with a two-inch "S" on the left hip.

51 *History of the First Troop*, 73; Wister, *Reminiscences*, 159. One of Wister's five brothers, Langhorne, was colonel of the 150th Pennsylvania at Gettysburg, in Col. Roy Stone's brigade. He was wounded July 1 near the Chambersburg Turnpike. Ironically, their parents were strong Quakers, and so opposed to the concept of war.

52 Wister, *Reminiscences*, 160.

53 *OR* 27, pt. 2, 464-65; Early, *War Memoirs*, 255. Early later wrote: "It will be seen that General Lee says in his Report, published, some time since, in the *Historical Magazine*, that orders were given to me to seize the bridge from Wrightsville to Columbia. The orders received by me were

Worried that the Rebels might thrust northward from Franklin County, farmers and residents of the small towns south of Harrisburg thronged its two major bridges. Desperation had driven many in the Cumberland Valley to strip their homes of valuables. Useless household "treasures" dotted the roadside where families had discarded items to lighten the burden on the horses, mules, and oxen yoked to their wagons. Once in Harrisburg, they herded droves of cattle, horses, sheep, and swine through city streets. The spectacle alarmed many residents, who made plans to leave town. Heavily laden with trunks, bundles, and huge amounts of baggage, they packed the train station. Some were frantic with fear, shouting and screaming as if the Confederates were ready to dash into town or shell it within moments. An estimated 900 trunks were stacked on the platform of the Pennsylvania Railroad, awaiting shipment to safer locations. A locomotive struck one end of the enormous pile, scattering luggage in all directions. Most were never shipped and instead were returned to their owners.[54]

That morning, while some of their neighbors also fled, several Gettysburg residents packed picnic baskets and headed east to Jennings' impromptu campsite at Swift Run. The boys from the town's Company A enjoyed pies, bread, and other delicacies. Men from other companies began intercepting the country wagons and lying that they too belonged to Company A. Other militiamen foraged the countryside and procured butter, bread, and other foodstuffs. Late in the cloudy and very windy afternoon, pickets brought in a

---

as stated in my Report, which was written very shortly after the close of the Campaign. This discrepancy may have arisen from a misapprehension, by General Ewell; but my recollection is very distinct, and I have now a memorandum, in pencil, made at the time, in General Ewell's presence, showing what was to be my march on each day, and the time of my probable junction with him, and also a note from him, from Carlisle, all of which rebuts the idea that I was to hold the bridge. However, afterwards, I determined to depart from my instructions and to secure the bridge, cross the river, and move up in rear of Harrisburg, as I found the condition of the country different from what was contemplated at the time the instructions were given. This discrepancy is a matter of very little moment, really, as the destruction of the bridge, by the enemy, settled the question without any agency of ours; and I have made this explanation simply from the fact that the statement, as contained in my original Report, is variant from that in General Lee's Report. I can well see how General Ewell may have misapprehended General Lee's direction, or how the latter, writing several months after the events had happened, may have fallen into the mistake, from the fact that I really attempted to seize the bridge and the enemy burnt it, to thwart my purpose." Jubal A. Early, "The Invasion of Pennsylvania, by the Confederate States Army, in June 1863," in *The Historical Magazine and Notes and Queries*, Vol. 1, Series 3, Morrisania, N.Y.: Henry B. Dawson, 1872-73), 232.

54 Wister, *Reminiscences*, 157.

prisoner suspected of being a spy. They escorted him to Colonel Jennings for disposition. Citizens spread rumors that the Rebels were "advancing in large force, and that considerable numbers of them were in the woods and hills about Cashtown." Most soldiers refused to believe the gossip.[55]

However, trouble indeed lurked just across the dark mountains west of Cashtown. That afternoon Jubal Early rode from Ewell's headquarters in Chambersburg back to Greenwood. He stripped his division of all excess encumbrances for hard and fast marching. He sent his supply trains and most noncombatants back to Chambersburg. Only one medical wagon, ordnance wagon, and wagon with cooking utensils could accompany each regiment. Early also retained the ambulances and fifteen empty wagons to fill with procured supplies. No officers, not even his headquarters staff, could keep any personal baggage except what they could carry on their backs or horses.[56]

Meanwhile, Major Knox's Pennsylvania cavalrymen had remained in the saddle all day monitoring the Rebels. One patrol encountered seven Confederate pickets two miles west of the Cashtown tollgate. They drove them back into their main force, which delivered a fruitless long-range volley at the Federals, who promptly retired to Cashtown. There, the 24-year-old Knox split his force into three detachments to explore a wider perimeter. He sent Captain Bell's Adams Countians three-and-a-half miles northwest to Arendtsville, where the enemy had been reported just a few hours beforehand. Bell's patrols scouted Hilltown and Mummasburg before heading southwest.

Leaving Sergeant Reakirt and Jones Wister's patrol in Cashtown to monitor the turnpike, Knox accompanied Captain Randall's remaining First City Troopers along South Mountain south toward Fairfield. Near Monterey Pass, he spotted what he believed was a "flanking brigade." Creeping within 200 yards of the crest, he dodged a couple of shots from enemy infantry pickets. He returned to Gettysburg and informed Haller, "I think it very suspicious I have not found their cavalry, and my opinion is the Rebels will move by another road than the turnpike and that their cavalry will precede them, hence I will scout all roads." To Haller, this important information indicated the Rebels were securing the passes in the direction the Army of Potomac would arrive, in order "to prevent their line of retreat" and to cut off their line of retreat.

55 Richards, *Pennsylvania's Emergency Men at Gettysburg*, 8; *Gettysburg Compiler*, June 29, 1863.

56 OR 27, pt. 2, 464-65; Early, *War Memoirs*, 255.

Haller wired Colonel Jennings at Swift Run Hill that he needed 100 men to fulfill Couch's request. He expected "reliable riflemen" with previous military experience. Instead, Jennings randomly selected ten recruits from each company and directed that this detail, under Lt. Lemuel Moyer of Company E, be equipped for a prolonged stay. However, the regiment's rations were on a different train, and about 8 p.m. the detachment marched away without any provisions. Subsequently, Haller ordered Jennings and the rest of the 26th PVM to "come up. The [rail]cars have been ordered to your camp, at 5:30 o'clock, a. m., to bring your command to this place (Gettysburg). Please be ready and hasten the loading…. The Regiment will encamp about three miles from town, towards the mountain, in supporting distance of the Sharp Shooters."[57]

Moyer's "sharpshooters" believed they were merely being sent out to picket the roads west of Swift Run. Private Samuel Pennypacker said they were "looking into every thicket for a picket station, and imagining that every wood in the distance must form part of the line, but one after another was passed, and still we did not stop. About two miles from camp, we halted at a tavern, but it was only to get some water in the canteens. We there saw some of the outer pickets, among them the 'one-eyed sergeant,' and after leaving them, we knew that picketing was not the object for which we were sent. It soon commenced to rain, but not very rapidly. That was my first experience in marching, and as the Lieutenant appeared to be in great haste, we moved very quickly, and it was not long before I began to feel exceedingly warm and disagreeable. Those seven miles seemed almost indefinitely prolonged. At last, however, Gettysburg was in sight, and before entering the town, the Lieutenant made us a short speech, saying that he wanted us to go through the streets quietly and in ranks, and that he had been informed, supper and comfortable quarters for the night were already provided for us, so we began to think we were more fortunate than those who were left in camp."[58]

After midnight, as rain fell harder, Gettysburg's Committee of Safety procured bread and hot coffee at a restaurant for Moyer's famished soldiers. Seeking instructions, the 25-year-old lieutenant entered Haller's headquarters in the Eagle Hotel. Haller wanted him to make a night march to a defensive

---

57 *History of the First Troop*, 73; Haller, *Dismissal of Major Granville O. Haller*, 66-68; Richards, *Pennsylvania's Emergency Men at Gettysburg*, 8-9. Richards refers to this officer as "Lieutenant Mowry," misspelled as Moiser in some records.

58 Pennypacker, "Six Weeks in Uniform," 336.

position on steep hill above Newman's Gap and then harass the enemy when they came into the narrow gorge near Munshower's tavern west of Cashtown. However, to Haller's dismay, Moyer announced that his men knew nothing about deploying as skirmishers. In fact, few even knew how to load a gun. The veterans had been left in camp. Upset at being ordered on the suicidal mission, Moyer departed, rented a horse, and rode back to Swift Run to protest to Colonel Jennings.

Meanwhile, Capt. Robert Bell's weary patrol finally halted near midnight several miles south of Gettysburg on the Emmitsburg Road. He returned to Gettysburg and informed Haller that Newman's Gap was already in Confederate hands. The unexpected announcements ruined Haller's plans, so he decided to await the arrival of Jennings' regiment in the morning. To verify Bell's report, Haller advanced a few pickets from Cashtown toward Chambersburg. Confederate patrols captured some, and the remainder sent word back that Rebels now were east of South Mountain, just a short march from Gettysburg. Very late at night, Moyer returned to his men, who slept outside on the platform of the train depot.[59]

As a torrential overnight downpour soaked Adams County, a clash loomed the next day between John Gordon's battle-hardened veterans and Granville Haller's untested Pennsylvania militia.

---

59 Richards, *Pennsylvania's Emergency Men at Gettysburg*, 9; Haller, *Dismissal of Major Granville O. Haller*, 68.

Chapter 5

Gunfire at Gettysburg

A Mountain March

Rumors ran rampant that rainy early summer, because no one knew exactly where the Rebels might strike. Opinions varied, especially in the press. The *New York Herald* speculated that General Lee was contemplating an advance on either Harrisburg or Baltimore. "In the one case, the trip would not pay expenses, as the broad, rocky Susquehanna river is in his way, and in the other case, his army, in getting into Baltimore, would get into a trap, from which Lee would never extricate it." Gettysburg became a critical defensive point because that hub offered the Southerners so many options, with York a secondary concern.[1]

A Richmond paper predicted a paralyzing strike on Pennsylvania's important anthracite coal industry, because several major mines lay only forty or fifty miles beyond Harrisburg. The Federal Navy, the countless workshops and factories throughout the North, and the locomotives of the U.S. Military Railroad all consumed enormous quantities of anthracite. The newsman speculated that Lee's first aim would be to cut all the railroad connections, grinding the transportation of coal stockpiles to a halt. A second goal might be the destruction of the "most costly and not easily replaced" machinery in the pits and mines. After that, Lee's mission was uncertain to the reporter. The general might set fire to the mines, leaving "the heart of Pennsylvania smoldering for years." The resulting underground conflagration would "never

---

1 *New York Herald*, June 26, 1863.

be quenched," unless a river was diverted into the pits or until the vast coal seams had been reduced to ashes. The editor opined, "Northern industry will thus be paralyzed at a single blow."[2]

John Gordon's Georgians would have been pleased with an editorial that ran in the *Macon Telegraph*:

> The Northern panic is getting to be gigantic—magnificent! . . . An invasion force of probably no more than thirty-five thousand men all told had thrown the great North into spasms of consternation. They are not used to this business as the South is. . . . But as violent as is the panic, it is only begun. When they have rallied their motley force of whipped veterans and militia men against Lee's ragged rebels, and have been thoroughly whipped in Bull Run fashion, there'll be a panic in good earnest and resting upon a solid substratum of reason." He added, "The turnout of volunteers in the North to meet the invasion shows very little war enthusiasm, and after they are once brought to face with the cannon's mouth we think they will show less. A battlefield in Pennsylvania will sicken the masses with the horrors of war.[3]

The invasion of the Keystone State drew international attention. In London, England, *The Times* opined, "If the Confederates can only make this invasion really effective, and can force on the Northern States the necessity of themselves fighting for desolated homes and wasted territories, they will do more to produce disgust and weariness of the war than any number of defeats in Virginia, or the slaughter of whole regiments of Irish and Germans would produce."[4]

Stories spread that the Rebels planned to burn or rob much of the state. The uncertainty as to their actual plans and objectives created a growing sense of anxiety among many Pennsylvanians. In Newberry in northern York County, G. K. Bratton, recently mustered out from the Union Army after Chancellorsville, was in an "agitated state of feelings at this time." He wrote, "We are in a most intense excitement on accounts of reports that the Rebels are in Penna. and some say they were at Carlisle today and some say even closer than that and that we may expect them here tomorrow. The citizens of

---

2 *Richmond Whig*, July 1, 1863.

3 *Macon (Ga.) Telegraph*, June 30, 1863.

4 *London Times*, July 13, 1863.

Cumberland Valley are in a wonderful commotion; hundreds of them are moving across the river in the direction of Reading and removing horses and cattle out of harm's way if possible." He added, "These are indeed squirrelly times."5

Gettysburg resident Sallie Broadhead was "filled with anxieties and apprehensions." In northwestern York County, farm wife Phebe Angeline Smith wrote her sister that, "What day the enemy may be here we don't know, but I hope this won't be their battleground. But, we can't tell where it will hit, but they say it will be soon. . . . We can't tell how soon our homes will be in danger." She added what may have been the opinion of most Pennsylvanians, "I hope this war will soon be over."6

On Friday morning, June 26, the cold northeast downpour delayed Maj. Gen. Jubal Early's departure for Adams County until 8 a.m. His division marched toward South Mountain with roughly 6,500 men, including infantry, artillery, Elijah White's cavalry battalion, and Col. William H. French's 17th Virginia Cavalry from Jenkins' Brigade. Behind the rowdy horsemen, Gordon's crack Georgia Brigade marched with eight men across on the wide turnpike. Brigadier General Harry Hays' brigade, the vaunted "Louisiana Tigers" that had created so much negative press in Waynesboro, strung out behind Gordon. Trailing the Tigers were two more veteran infantry brigades. Young Col. Isaac E. Avery commanded Brig. Gen. Robert F. Hoke's North Carolinians while that officer recuperated from severe wounds suffered at Chancellorsville, and Brig. Gen. William "Extra Billy" Smith, a veteran politician turned soldier, led what once was Early's Brigade of Virginians. He was the commonwealth's governor-elect and the oldest general in Lee's army. Lieutenant Colonel Hilary P. Jones' sixteen-gun artillery battalion, the remaining wagons and ambulances, and vast cattle herds brought up the rear of the winding column, which stretched for several miles.

Colonel Clement Evans, a pre-war lawyer and judge accustomed to decorum and manners, observed that the Pennsylvanians along the path of his dusty 31st Georgia "do not impress one favorably." They generally lived in

---

5   G. K. Bratton to My Dear Sir, June 16, 1863. Collection of Phillip Dodson. Used by permission.

6   Phebe Angeline Smith to Most Cherished Sister, June 26, 1863, from Washington Township, York County, Pa. Letter courtesy of James Brown; Broadhead diary entry for June 15, 1863, ACHS.

"pretty good style," but the majority was uneducated, apparently possessing little knowledge of the outside world. Some had never before seen artillery and expressed great anxiety to see the big guns. Evans and his men were considerably surprised at the profane language of the ladies. To those Rebels who had never heard a rough word escape the lips of a proper Southern belle, it was "very strange" to hear these rural Northern women cursing repeatedly. "In crossing the mountainous part of the country," observed Private Bradwell, "we found the few people we saw to be rough and ignorant, living in little log shacks; but the men were not at home; they had business somewhere else at that time."[7]

A dozen or more civilians were traveling north to Harrisburg to enlist in the Federal army. One of them, G. Frank Lidy of Waynesboro, had accidentally been trapped between Union and Rebel lines near Burnside's Bridge at Antietam. As an unarmed civilian, he "embraced the first opportunity to get to a place of safety." Now his luck ran out when Early's cavalry scouts captured the group near Caledonia Furnace. Through the personal influence of General Gordon, they were paroled on the promise they would not take up arms while the Confederates remained in Pennsylvania.[8]

Early paused at the Caledonia Furnace & Iron Works, owned by Pennsylvania abolitionist congressman Thaddeus Stevens. Early believed the Radical Republican advocated that Union soldiers use "the most vindictive measures of confiscation and devastation" in the occupied South. Notwithstanding Lee's General Orders No. 72, he decided to destroy Stevens' facilities "on my own responsibility, as neither General Lee nor General Ewell knew I would encounter these works." Superintendent John Sweeny tried vainly to parley with Early, explaining that the forge had been losing money and Stevens only kept it operational to provide employment for the poor of the region. Its destruction would actually benefit Stevens while harming the workers, who would lose their livelihood. "Yankees did not do business that way," Early shot back.

Unfazed by Sweeny's pleas, Early ordered French's 17th Virginia troopers to apply the torch. Squads burned Stevens' furnace, rolling mill, and two forges,

---

7 Bradwell, "Crossing the Potomac," 370.

8 Henry P. Moyer, *History of the Seventeenth Regiment Pennsylvania Volunteer Cavalry* (Lebanon, Pa.: Sowers Printing, 1911), 291. Lidy later enlisted in Company M of the 21st Pennsylvania, the regiment joined by Robert Bell and most of his Adams County Cavalry. He mustered out after seven months. In August 1864, Lidy joined Co. G of the 17th Pennsylvania Cavalry. He was among the 14-man escort for Gen. Philip Sheridan during his famous ride to Winchester.

as well as his office, sawmill and attached storehouse. They caused nearly $65,000 damage. However, when Sweeny pleaded that many other buildings were private residences, Early ordered his men not to disturb the ironworkers' houses and possessions. Other than a few broken windows, this order was obeyed. He discovered large quantities of provisions in one building and appropriated them for his command, including four thousand pounds of bacon. Rebels seized more than $10,000 in provisions and goods from company stores, along with large amounts of grain and corn in the grist mills and $4,000 in bar iron. Soldiers destroyed Stevens' wooden fences. French's and White's cavalry horses consumed or ruined eighty tons of grass. Nearby in Adams County, Rebels visited the Graeffenburg Inn, a large roadside tavern that J.E.B. Stuart's cavaliers raided of fifty-one gallons of whiskey the previous October.[9]

Throughout the Cumberland Valley and beyond into Gettysburg, lurid newspaper accounts for days had attributed atrocities to unruly Rebels. Several articles insisted that Lee's main goals were destruction and plunder. Correspondents reported that Ewell's force included a three-mile-long train of empty wagons specifically intended for confiscated Yankee goods. The burning of Congressman Stevens' private property reinforced the fear that the Confederates intended to create mischief. Some Pennsylvanians took up arms and hid in mountain passes or woods to waylay unsuspecting invaders. Some operated in the mountain passes along the Chambersburg-Gettysburg Turnpike as Early's division crossed South Mountain after burning Caledonia Furnace. Colonel Evans wrote to his wife, "The bushwhackers occasionally fire on our stragglers, but this helps us to keep them in camp and in ranks."[10]

Shortly after navigating the 1,900-foot high Cashtown Gap, scouts informed Early that felled trees partially obstructed the turnpike to Gettysburg,

---

9   Early, *War Memoirs*, 255-56; *The Chambersburg Repository*, July 15, 1863; Edwin B. Coddington, *The Gettysburg Campaign: A Study in Command* (New York: Charles Scribner's Sons, 1968), 166; *Gettysburg Times*, June 25, 1942. Stevens later sarcastically commended the Rebels for doing such a thorough job of destruction. Nearly 200 men worked at the complex; all were jobless. Three days later, when Robert E. Lee passed the ruins, he had his quartermaster tell overseer Sweeny that needy families could draw supplies from his army. Stevens provided for some of his workers and their families for up to three years. The facility's old bell, used to signal work shifts and call the workers for meetings or emergencies such as two 1860 fatalities, now hangs in Emmanuel Chapel in nearby Mont Alto. *The Gettysburg Compiler*, Aug. 3, 1863, placed the value of the destroyed iron works as $50,000.

10 Stephens, *Intrepid Warrior*, 218.

which was defended by a Yankee force of unknown size. Early decided to move Gordon's Brigade and White's cavalry along the pike to "skirmish with and amuse the enemy in front." He planned to get on the Yankees' flank and rear in order to capture the entire force. Accordingly, about a mile and a half west of Cashtown, the rest of the division and French's cavalry turned to the left on an old country road through Hilltown and Mummasburg. He allegedly paused at a nearby stone tavern. While conversing with some ladies who were drinking tea, Early noticed a large map of Adams County hanging on a wall. He took his knife, cut the center of the map from its frame, and stuck it in his coat pocket. He told the astonished ladies, "I need this more than you do," and then mounted his horse and rode off.[11]

The heavy overnight rains had diminished but the muddy Hilltown Road slowed Early's column to a crawl. Meanwhile, John Gordon's expeditionary force marched steadily eastward on the macadam turnpike. During mid-morning, the soldiers descended the mountain range. "When we reached the open country it was quite different," remembered Private Bradwell. "Our route lay through a lovely country of well tilled farms, nice towns, and villages. We, the infantry, were kept close in ranks, while the quartermasters and the small cavalry force with us were busy collecting horses, cattle, and sheep for the use of the army; but we were not allowed to appropriate anything to our own use." The Georgians tramped through Cashtown, New Salem (McKnightstown) and Seven Stars.

Private Bradwell continued with his description of what he saw along the march:

Passing in front of a lovely home, which reminded me, from its style of architecture and the grounds in front, of a Southern residence, I rushed in at the front gate, through which others were passing, and went into the spacious hall through the open front door, thinking to find hospitable people who would give me something to eat; all doors were wide open. I found a lady, trembling with fear, in a room to the left, with three little children clinging to her. I think I never saw anyone so badly frightened as this woman was at the

11 Early, *War Memoirs*, 256; OR 27, pt. 2, 465; Emmitsburg (Md.) Historical Society. The original Hilltown Road (about six miles east of Caledonia Furnace) was laid out in 1747. In 1813, crews constructed the Chambersburg-Gettysburg turnpike on the ridgeline, which bypassed the Hilltown Road. The tavern's wartime owner was Mary M. Bruch (also spelled Brough).

sight of our men coming into the house in a great hurry, all asking for bread and milk.

She excited my sympathy, and I stepped up to her, supposing a kind word would dismiss her fear, and told her not to be afraid, that the soldiers did not mean to do her any harm, but only wanted to get something to eat; but the poor creature was so overcome by her feelings that she did not seem to hear me. I was disposed to stand by her side until the whole army passed, but I knew that would not do, so I hastily snatched up from the dining room such as I found convenient and left her and her little ones there to themselves, knowing that they would not suffer any violence at the hands of our men, for there was not a one in our whole army mean enough to do such a thing.[12]

Skirmish at Marsh Creek

While Jubal Early marched his veteran division through western Adams County, refugees from the Cashtown vicinity hurried as fast as their feet and wagons could get them to Gettysburg. Once there, they claimed to have seen Rebels "in force," but few residents believed them. Soon afterward, Robert Bell's cavalrymen rode in from Emmitsburg. On the way they encountered several of Milroy's harried men, driven from Winchester by Early's Confederates. Scouts scurried about the hill country just west of Gettysburg sending messages back that they had spotted fifty to sixty enemy cavalrymen approaching in the dense morning fog. At first Maj. Granville Haller believed this was probably only a small enemy foraging party searching for supplies, horses, and of course information. He remained hopeful that Early's main infantry force would stay west of the mountains. Haller was soon disappointed.[13]

Before long other messengers reported that a large Confederate infantry column was approaching. Several more residents left town, taking their horses and wagons full of furniture, heirlooms, and any other transportable valuables to safety. In the hamlet of Round Hill, storeowner Ira Shipley filled his wagon with boxes of his inventory and dispatched it to York. Shipley asked that his goods be loaded into a railcar for transportation to Philadelphia by way of Wrightsville. Major Haller oversaw the safe removal of government supplies

---

12 Bradwell, "Crossing the Potomac," 370-71.

13 *Gettysburg Compiler*, June 29, 1863; Gibson, *History of York County*, 421; Haller, *Dismissal of Major Granville O. Haller*, 69.

stored in Gettysburg to Hanover in southwestern York County. Workers loaded railcars with "the Public Arms, and accoutrements, Brass gun, etc."[14]

Haller soon received much needed reinforcements. After breakfasting in local hotels, Lieutenant Moyer's detachment had waited for their comrades. Jennings' 26th Militia struck their tents early in the morning and boarded their re-railed train. They arrived in Gettysburg about 9 a.m. Most were drenched after riding in the open coal cars in the chilly northeast rain. Haller welcomed them as they disembarked and formed into companies. Just as Company I had received a hero's welcome in Hanover two days before, now the men of Company A received the adulation of their hometown. Friends and family turned out from all over the area to greet and "bountifully" feed them with pies, sandwiches, and hot coffee. The neatly uniformed and well-equipped men received the admiring attention of their college professors and the town's "pretty girls." The locomotive soon returned to Hanover, pulling the railcars that Haller's men had loaded with military stores. The train also carried revenue officers, clerks, government employees, and other people escaping the Rebels, including home guard officer Joseph Broadhead.[15]

Granville Haller was determined to defend the crossroads town. Protesting vigorously that it was sheer nonsense to fight the more experienced Confederates, William Jennings nonetheless obeyed a direct order to engage the enemy. Sam Pennypacker later opined, "It has always seemed to me that the situation had in it much of the heroic. Untrained, untried, and unused to war, they were sent to meet an overwhelming and disciplined force, not in some Grecian pass or mountain defile of the Swiss or Tyrol Alps, but in the open field with the certainty that they could make no effectual resistance. These young men, in their unsoiled uniforms, and flushed with enthusiasm, were to be thrown as a preliminary sacrifice to the Army of Northern Virginia for the accomplishment of a military end. The order setting before them this hopeless task has been criticized," he concluded, "but it was correct."[16]

---

14 RG-2, Records Relating to the Civil War Border Claims, Adams County Damage Claims, Records of the Department of the Adjutant General, ACHS; Broadhead diary entry for June 27, 1863, ACHS.

15 Samuel Gring Hefelbower, *The History of Gettysburg College: 1832-1932* (Gettysburg, Pa.: Gettysburg College, 1932).

16 Samuel W. Pennypacker, *Pennsylvania at Gettysburg: Ceremonies of the Dedication of the Monuments* (Harrisburg: W. Staley Ray, 1904), 2: 784.

Jennings retained Capt. C. Wilson Walker and forty men from various companies at the train station to serve as a commissary guard. The remaining soldiers paraded through town in front of a wet, but appreciative crowd. Leading the way, Colonel Jennings had a "serious look on his face," as did Capt. Robert Bell as they rode westward along Chambersburg Street. Next in line came the homegrown Company A and young Henry Richards, who wrote that "at 10 a.m. with drums beating, sweethearts, relatives and friends waving us farewell, we proudly stepped out and passed through town."[17]

Carried away with the excitement of the moment, two townspeople joined the ranks—a child who helped carry a bass drum for a mile before dropping out of the column, and a civilian who stayed with Company A throughout the day. A newspaperman, watching the infantrymen parade through town with their flags flying proudly, commented that, "All look like good fighting material, and will do their whole duty." Sallie Broadhead noted that Gettysburg was quiet after the militia departed.[18]

The military situation was growing desperate. There were not enough Union soldiers in Pennsylvania to hold back the oncoming Confederates. In Harrisburg, where "it had been raining for 18 hours, and the Susquehanna had risen 20 inches, but not too high to be forced by cattle," Governor Curtin issued a new call for sixty thousand volunteers to repel the growing threat. However, time was running out in Gettysburg. To First City Trooper Jones Wister, the excitement intensified because the question was no longer whether the Rebels would seize the town, but when? Haller wired York's Committee of Safety that Rebel infantry, artillery, and cavalry were approaching Gettysburg. Those civic leaders held a public meeting at noon and organized additional home defense companies.[19]

At 11:00 a.m., Capt. Samuel Randall's detachment returned to Gettysburg from their picket on the Fairfield Road. They reported that all was now quiet in that direction, although they earlier exchanged shots with a small body of

---

17 Jacobs, *Notes on the Rebel Invasion,* 14. The professor believed that Haller's orders, "contrary to the earnest remonstrances of Jennings," resulted in a "suicidal movement." He added, "The Rebels afterwards laughed at the folly of the order." Twenty-five-year-old Christopher Wilson Walker had been captain of Co. H of the 137th Pennsylvania, but was dishonorably discharged in Nov. 1862 after serving three months.

18 Richards, *Pennsylvania's Emergency Men at Gettysburg,* 9; *Gettysburg Compiler,* June 29, 1863.

19 *OR* 27, pt. 3, 347-48; *Richmond Daily Dispatch,* July 2, 1863; Wister, *Reminiscences,* 161; Gibson, *History of York County,* 175.

Rebels. After unsaddling their horses, the troopers had just sat down to dinner provided by local citizens when orders were received to saddle and report to Haller's headquarters immediately. The enemy reportedly was advancing rapidly on the same road the pickets had just traversed. Without a horse of his own, Major Haller was in the habit of requisitioning one from the First City Troop whenever he needed a mount. Stating that he wanting to ride to Hanover to secure the government property previously sent there, he borrowed his orderly Pvt. John Lowber Welsh's horse.[20]

Meanwhile, after marching three miles west of town along the Chambersburg Pike, Colonel Jennings halted his column, with Company A in the van. Private Dennis B. Shuey spotted three distant riders, likely Confederate officers in his opinion, who slowly approached the regiment before wheeling their horses and galloping off into the mist. The infantrymen filed off across a field some seventy-five yards to the north into some woods and a swampy meadow along the banks of Marsh Creek. Several soldiers, assuming this would be their new campsite, raided a nearby pile of shingles for a dry floor on which to pitch their tents. Jennings selected his forty "best" soldiers, veterans who knew how to fire their rifles, and sent them slogging westward through the fields. In fog and light drizzle, they advanced beyond Marsh Creek to a small hill. A few of Bell's cavalrymen picketed 200 yards beyond this skirmish line, straining to see the Rebels. Occasionally, pairs of scouts clattered in with fresh reports, their horses lathered from exertion. Captain Bell twice rode out in the fog to reconnoiter, both times seeing 500 to 100 enemy cavalrymen, but no infantry.[21]

Before Jennings' newly arrived men could unpack their baggage, an excited scout rode in and exclaimed that the enemy was "quite near." Because the Rebels were now at hand, Jennings knew this was no place for his green troops. He divided his command into three battalions in order to deceive the Rebels

20 Wister, *Reminiscences*, 161; *History of the First Troop*, 74. According to Wister, this event took place in York. Frazer's account (JMSIUS, 1908), Vol. 43, 283) disagrees with Wister: "Welsh not being able to procure a horse was taken prisoner and paroled" at Gettysburg on June 26, 1863.

21 Shuey, D. B., *History of the Shuey Family in America from 1732 to 1919* (Galion, Ohio: self-published, 1919), 106; Richards, *Pennsylvania's Emergency Men at Gettysburg*, 9; Diary & journal entries of Henry Wirt Shriver, 26th PA Militia from June 16 to Aug. 1, 1863, W. S. Nye Collection, GNMP; Nye, "The First Battle of Gettysburg," 14; Haller, *Dismissal of Major Granville O. Haller,* 69.

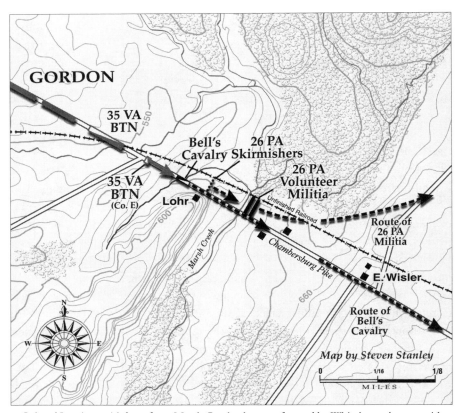

Colonel Jennings withdrew from Marsh Creek when confronted by White's cavalrymen with Gordon's long column of infantry in the distance.

into thinking he had a larger force. It may have been at this point that Lt. Col. Elijah White first spotted the distant Union regiment. He later wrote that as his cavalry approached Gettysburg, he "saw 700 to 900 of the enemy drawn in line of battle." He reported the news to General Gordon "and told him that if he wished to see the fight to come up, which he did." [22]

Accompanied by Robert Bell, Jennings rode to the brow of a nearby hill. From there he could see a column of Confederate cavalry, infantry, and artillery about three-quarters of a mile away. Bell asked the colonel what he proposed to

22 Broadhead diary entry for June 26, 1863, ACHS; Richards, *Pennsylvania's Emergency Men at Gettysburg*, 9; Shriver account, GNMP; John S. Mosby, *Stuart's Cavalry in the Gettysburg Campaign* (New York: Moffat, Yard & Co., 1908), 156.

do. Jennings, fearing that his men might soon be surrounded, concluded that the only route of escape was to get beyond the Mummasburg-Hunterstown Road before any Rebels could cut their line of retreat. He ordered his infantrymen, except the skirmishers and pickets, to withdraw. Orders were given to "Strike tents!" and "Fall in!" then almost immediately, "Forward!" No one in the ranks quite knew what was happening to cause all the sudden excitement. The regiment marched through the soggy grasslands along Marsh Creek and then tramped through muddy cultivated fields that led to a dirt farm lane running northward.[23]

According to Samuel Pennypacker, the regiment:

crossed three or four fields until we came to one of the numerous back roads, which we entered, and along which we proceeded in a rapid march. It is scarcely necessary to state, that in consequence of its muddy and slippery condition, traveling was laborious and tiresome. At first, we chose our path as much as possible, and avoided the mud puddles, but we had not gone a great way before we came to a running stream about knee deep. There was nothing to do but ford, and through we went. 'I guess that settles the question of wet feet,' said Lieutenant Richards, and we afterward continued straight forward, moving out of the direct line for nothing.

Pennypacker continued:

The first intimation of danger which we received through the officers, was from the Lieutenant-Colonel [Joseph H. Jenkins], who came riding back, and muttered as he passed, 'We'll go up here a little way, get a good position, and give 'em h__l before they do take us.' But we still kept marching, and the position was not taken. Indignation was the uppermost feeling in my mind. I believed we were running away from a lot of cavalry, because the Colonel was afraid to rely upon us, and that we would be everlastingly disgraced.[24]

Jennings left his pickets and skirmishers near the shallow creek as a rear guard, fronted by some of Bell's cavalrymen. About 2:00 p.m. on the dismal

---

23 Richards, *Pennsylvania's Emergency Men at Gettysburg*, 10; Nye, "The First Battle of Gettysburg,"15; Shriver account, GNMP. Some accounts suggest Jennings may have ridden two miles past the camp, spotted the Rebels near the McKnight farm, and returned to order a withdrawal. The 26th PVM likely turned north on Belmont Road after crossing the fields.

24 Pennypacker, "Six Weeks in Uniform," 340-41. This may have been Belmont Road.

gray afternoon they perceived shadowy forms in the distance: White's vanguard had arrived on the turnpike. Some of the Rebels dismounted, drew their arms, and began to slowly approach the Yankees. Confederate Capt. Frank Myers watched as some forty mounted soldiers of Company E under 19-year-old Methodist preacher Lt. Harrison M. Strickler charged with "barbarian yells and smoking pistols" in what he called a "desperate dash." Private Albert Bowers rode "boot to boot" with Strickler as the veterans boldly closed in on the defenders. Without firing a shot, Bell's frightened inexperienced troopers wheeled their horses and scattered as fast as they could toward Gettysburg and Harrisburg.[25]

Strickler's howling men regrouped and charged the terrified militia skirmishers. Myers noted that those who could not withdraw "threw down their bright, new muskets, and begged frantically for quarter." No Yankees were wounded except "one fat militia Captain who, in his exertion to be the first to surrender, managed to get himself run over by one of Company E's horses, and bruised somewhat." The Confederates captured nearly three dozen skirmishers, and the few remaining quick-thinking Pennsylvanians took to their heels. Most of them made they way toward Gettysburg, together with their supply wagons.[26]

According to Jubal Early, the militia "fled across the fields at the first sight of White's advance party without waiting to see what was in the rear." Their sudden withdraw enabled Gordon's infantry to proceed toward Gettysburg without further resistance. Strickler's company was more concerned with looting the abandoned tents and knapsacks than chasing Yankees. Lieutenant Strickler found a coat and rummaged through its pockets. Inside he discovered a combination knife that he kept with him for the balance of the war. According to Frank Myers, Strickler's company then vainly pursued Bell's fleeing cavalrymen, who were "finely mounted, but they had been on the run while the

25 Myers, *The Comanches,* 192; Jacobs, *Notes on the Rebel Invasion,* 14-15. After the war, H. M. Strickler became a prominent minister in the Methodist Episcopal Church South serving in Page County, Virginia, and in Greenbrier County, West Virginia. During the Gettysburg Campaign, Strickler was reunited with his older brother William Maberry Strickler, the assistant surgeon of the 5th Louisiana in Harry Hays' Louisiana Brigade. According to Strickler's brief postwar account, he had only ten to twelve men in his advance guard when he first charged the militia.

26 Myers was born Oct. 16, 1840, two miles from Waterford in Loudon County, Virginia. His father, a Republican, voted against Virginia's secession, as did two Democrat uncles.

other were losing time in the camps, and were, of course, too far gone to overtake."[27]

Meanwhile, Capt. Sam Randall and most of the men in the First City Troop had remained in Gettysburg while Major Knox sent four men, one in each cardinal direction, to reconnoiter the network of roads. A rumor spread at 2:00 p.m. that the Rebels were only two miles west of Gettysburg. According to Sallie Broadhead, few remaining townspeople believed the shocking news, for similar reports had been repeated for days and no Confederates had ever appeared. However, the militia's fleeing wagons thundering through Gettysburg's streets startled the citizens, as did the news shouted by the guards that Rebel cavalry had driven them back. Mrs. Broadhead and her fellow residents began to realize that this time the rumors were almost certainly true. By this time there was little left to do except stand in their doorways and watch for the enemy. When they learned the news, the girls attending Carrie Sheads' Oak Ridge Seminary on Chambersburg Pike rushed back into town, ignoring the mud that soiled their dresses.[28]

Scouts brought word that Captain Bell advised "a hasty retreat," and his cavalrymen should report in Harrisburg or Columbia. Thirty-three-year-old Sgt. William T. King, thrown from a horse a few days earlier, rested on a couch in his York Street home. His wife Sarah called, "The Rebels are here . . . get up and get your horse ready, for you will only have a few minutes in which to escape." King and a few others of the company hurriedly disappeared down the York Pike.[29]

Soon, Bell and several cavalrymen rode "pell-mell" into Gettysburg. He shocked onlookers with the news that Jennings had hastily retired before only "fifty to one hundred Rebels," without putting up any defense, and now Confederates filled the roads to the west, heading directly for Gettysburg. Major Haller would be furious to learn that Jennings hurried off without informing headquarters of his unexpected movement, and without giving any orders to Walker's detachment, which had been left in town to guard the railcars filled with the regiment's provisions.[30]

---

27 Myers, *The Comanches,* 192-93; Early, *War Memoirs,* 256-57.

28 *History of the First Troop,* 74; Broadhead diary entry for June 26, 1863, ACHS.

29 *Gettysburg Compiler,* July 6, 1906, ACHS. King was a master tailor. Three bullets pierced his advertising sign.

30 Haller, *Dismissal of Major Granville O. Haller,* 69.

Fleeing refugees using all kinds of improvised vehicles crowded the roads leading to the Susquehanna River. To one trooper, the terrified inhabitants were "truly a distressing sight" as they hastened out of town with their families, driving their remaining livestock before them. "The cry of terror on every tongue was 'they come, the rebels come!'" Postmaster David Buehler raced home and picked up a satchel of valuable government property and a valise of clothing packed by his wife Fannie. He and tax assessor Robert G. Harper high-tailed it in a wagon toward Hanover because it was rumored the Rebels intended to seize all Federal workers. Anna Gerlach later discovered a dropped a mail pouch laying on the ground in front of her house on Baltimore Street in Gettysburg.[31]

Meanwhile, Strickler's cavalrymen finished looting the militia camp, remounted, and continued eastward on the Chambersburg Pike. A local boy spotted cavalry descending Seminary Ridge and raced through Gettysburg's streets, screaming, "The Rebels are on the outskirts of town!" Fifteen-year-old Matilda "Tillie" Pierce, a student at Rebecca Eyster's Young Ladies Seminary on High Street, was in the midst of her regular Friday afternoon literary exercises when she heard the cry. Mrs. Eyster and her students raced to the front porch and looked northward, where they could make out "a dark, dense mass, moving toward town." Eyster quickly hustled the girls off to their homes.[32]

As the head of the Rebel column entered the western end of Gettysburg, Charles Knox reconnoitered the town "with four men and found the enemy entering it in as many directions in force." He quickly sent orders to Samuel Randall for the First City Troop to withdraw to York. The Philadelphia gentry headed out on the York Pike toward Hunterstown Road. Knox and his detachment galloped southeast toward Hanover. A reporter commented, "The gallant Major, seeing nothing but capture or death before his eyes, bade a hasty

31 *History of the First Troop*, 74; Buehler, *Recollections of the Rebel Raid*. David (a former attorney and editor of the *Adams County Sentinel*) and Fannie Buehler and their six children lived at 116 Baltimore Street. Fannie had for days urged her 42-year-old husband to hide outside of town, fearing the Rebels would capture him. He had refused to leave town. Now, with the Rebels finally arriving, Buehler heeded his wife's advice and quickly left town. After leaving Hanover the next day when Elijah White approached, Buehler made his way to Elizabeth, NJ, before returning home two weeks later. One of their black servants fled town to avoid capture, and the Buehlers never saw her again. Someone reported seeing her on the road to Philadelphia.

32 Alleman, *At Gettysburg*, 21.

adieu to personal friends and departed, Rebel cavalry pursuing him three miles unsuccessfully."[33]

Scarcely half an hour after Jennings' wagons left for Hanover, Confederate cavalrymen entered Gettysburg about 3 p.m. "with such horrid yells that it was enough to frighten us all to death," according to Sallie Broadhead. Photographer Charles J. Tyson and his wife Maria were putting down the last carpet on their front second-floor room when they heard unusual noises. Looking up the turnpike toward Seminary Ridge, they noted mounted men, "some with hats, some without; some in blue, some in gray." Soon, the horsemen galloped past Tyson's house into Gettysburg, yelling and discharging their carbines and pistols.[34]

Strickler's Company E galloped down Chambersburg Street toward the Diamond. He and a dozen men later claimed the distinction of being the first Confederates to enter Gettysburg. Almost simultaneously, the other five companies of Elijah White's "mounted guerillas" arrived on two other roads, surrounding the town. A Pennsylvania College professor named Michael Jacobs recalled how the Confederate cavalrymen dashed about, "yelling and shouting like so many savages from the wilds of the Rocky Mountains" as they galloped by his home on Middle Street. The grayclad Rebels fired their pistols into the air, recalled Jacobs, "not caring whether they killed or maimed man, woman, or child." Other Rebels raced south and east from the square, pursuing lingering Yankees.[35]

The Rev. Abraham Essick, presiding minister of the St. James Lutheran Church, "witnessed the charge down York Street, and it was truly terrific to one unaccustomed to such things," he later recollected. "They rode at the top of their speed and yelled like demons, their faces black with dirt and their hair streaming in the winds." Sarah King and her children stood on their porch watching as screaming Rebels chased Captain Bell, who "was perfectly at home on his horse and was not uneasy, keeping at a very tantalizing distance

33 *JMSIUS* (1908), Vol. 43, 287-88; *History of the First Troop*, 74; *New York Tribune*, July 2, 1863.

34 Broadhead diary entry for June 26, 1863, ACHS; Charles Tyson account, ACHS. Mrs. Broadhead states that the Rebel cavalry arrived at 4 p.m. The *Gettysburg Compiler* June 29, 1863, places the time of White's entry as 3 p.m., as does Myers, *The Comanches*, 193, and OR 27, pt. 3, 377.

35 *Gettysburg Star and Banner*, June 28, 1863; Jacobs, *Notes on the Rebel Invasion*, 15. Jacobs places the time of the Rebel cavalry's arrival in Gettysburg as 3:15 p.m.

seemingly."[36] Near the tollgate farther out on the York turnpike, Rebels surprised three militiamen who had been ordered by Jennings to rejoin the regiment in Gettysburg after completing detached duty. The cavalrymen charged the trio and capturing them after a brief, but spirited engagement in which one of the Federals allegedly bayoneted a Comanche.[37]

Schoolgirl Tillie Pierce had just reached her Baltimore Street home when she spotted oncoming horsemen heading southward. Scrambling into the house, she slammed the front door and peeped at the Rebels from between her sitting room shutters. "What a horrible sight! There they were—human beings clad almost in rags, covered with dust, riding wildly, pell-mell down the hill toward our home shouting, yelling almost unearthly, cursing, brandishing their revolvers, and firing left and right." Frightened residents peered out of shade-covered windows, others huddled in cellars and attics, and a few leaped on horses and galloped out of town with Rebels in hot pursuit. From a shuttered second floor window, nine-year-old Gates Fahnestock and his three brothers enjoyed the spectacle as much as a "wild west show."[38]

Youthful telegrapher Hugh D. Scott wired his counterparts in Hanover, Daniel E. Trone and George H. Grove, "The Johnnies were entering Gettysburg. . . . I will leave this place at once. This in my last message. A minute later I will have my instrument under my arm ready to drive down the turnpike to York, for I do not want to be captured." Because Confederate pickets were now only 200 yards from his office, Scott cut loose his instrument, tossed it into the back of his open spring wagon, and rushed off for York. Half a dozen cavalrymen chased him, but their worn horses were no match for his fleet steed. A few carbine bullets whizzed by the fleeing 17-year-old, but he eluded his

---

36 Abraham Essick, *Franklin County Diary of Abraham Essick (1849-1864, 1883, 1888)*, Virginia Center for Digital History, University of Virginia, Charlottesville. On-line at "The Valley of the Shadow" website; *Gettysburg Compiler*, July 6, 1906, ACHS. Sarah King had just watched her husband and some of Bell's men leave town. Her father, who had been indoors reading the newspaper, headed upstairs and watched from behind a high French bedpost as he peered out a window.

37 Richards, *Pennsylvania's Emergency Men at Gettysburg*, 12; Pennypacker, *Pennsylvania at Gettysburg*, 786. The three militiamen were Corp. Charles Macdonald, Pvt. George Steele, and Pvt. A. W. Shick of Company F. They had completed "special duty" and walked into the Rebel patrol as they entered Gettysburg. They fired their muskets at the Rebels, who fired several shots in return. Shick "endeavored to bayonet a horseman."

38 Alleman, *At Gettysburg*, 18; *Gettysburg Compiler*, June 29, 1863; Broadhead diary, ACHS; McCurdy account, GNMP.

pursuers. An exhausted Scott arrived in York a few hours later, spreading news of his close escape and further alarming the Committee of Safety.[39]

Alarmed by Scott's message, Trone conferred with Grove about the advisability of both of them skedaddling from Hanover in the same way that Scott left Gettysburg. Trone, dually employed by both the telegraph company and the Northern Central Railway, decided to stay at his post. However, Grove "packed up his traps, and took his instrument with him to York." There, he gave it Albert W. Barnitz, a friend who lived on Carlisle Street, for safekeeping. Grove and his father then boarded a train for Lancaster.[40]

Among the refugees also headed out of town was Gettysburg postmaster David Buehler, who had abandoned the wagon in which he was riding as the Rebels approached. He raced on foot through a patch of woods to a friend's farmhouse along the Hanover Road. The farmer, Eden Norris, had sent his good horses ahead to York, but had retained an old "raw-boned" nag. Buehler, realizing the danger of remaining there for very long, straddled it and started for Hanover. On his way, "it rained hard for awhile." Buehler had never ridden a horse before and, without the comfort of a saddle, he was wet, tired, and sore. Luckily, he encountered other refugees and asked them to have some sort of vehicle sent back for him when they arrived in Hanover. Just outside of that town, the exhausted Buehler was gratified when he met a man with a buggy who had been dispatched to convey him to the Central Hotel.

Upon arriving, Buehler sent for A. W. Eichelberger, the president of the Hanover Branch Railroad, an old friend whom he knew quite well. He explained the recent situation in Gettysburg and inquired whether Eichelberger was sending the rolling stock to York that night. If so, he would go on to York. If not, he would remain in Hanover overnight and get some dry clothes. The executive replied, "I think now, I shall wait until morning, but I will inform you in time should I change my mind." However, Eichelberger soon learned of the destruction of the railroad property in Gettysburg and decided to send the locomotives and railcars parked at Hanover to York at once. He sent a man to the hotel to fetch Buehler. The postmaster had just removed one of his water-logged boots when the messenger arrived. He grabbed the soggy boot

---

39 *Gettysburg Compiler*, Oct. 20, 1909. Scott lived with his parents in the first block of Chambersburg Street, across from Christ Lutheran Church.

40 *Ibid.* On Saturday, June 27, the Groves traveled to Philadelphia. In the evening they took the fast train to Baltimore, where the rest of their family had gone after fleeing Hanover.

and raced off with it in his hand to the depot, where he caught the last train leaving Hanover.[41]

Gettysburg under the Rebel Flag

While terrified refugees clogged the roads, Elijah White's cavalrymen rushed from stable to stable searching for horses. They found very few, because most had been forwarded to Hanover and York a few hours earlier. Southerners appropriated a group of horses near Evergreen Cemetery, including a "gentle and very pretty" mare belonging to Tillie Pierce's father. Several youths, including the Pierce's hired hand Samuel Wade, had been instructed by owners to move them toward Baltimore to safety if the Confederates approached. White's riders had entered town so quickly, however, that no warning could be relayed to the youths. The cavalrymen seized them and the horses. A weeping Tillie and her mother futilely pleaded for the return of their mare. One "impudent and coarse" Rebel ordered Tillie to go into the house and mind her own business. They finally released the boys, but kept all of the horses. White's cavalrymen fanned out of town for several miles along the main roads, pursuing fleeing Federals. They overtook several terrified citizens and escorted them back to Gettysburg, where they confiscated their horses before releasing them.[42]

Captain Bell had advised his cavalrymen to head to York or Harrisburg. Private William Lightner and fellow Gettysburg native George Washington Sandoe followed Rock Creek from the Hanover Road before cutting through fields along the Baltimore Pike. Earlier, they were west of Gettysburg, monitoring the Rebels as they marched from Cashtown. Now, in the late afternoon, they were the ones being sought. Bushes and trees blocked their view of the approaching Rebels as White's pickets fanned out south of town. The Confederates spotted the two mounted Yankees and ordered them to surrender. Lightner spurred his horse away to safety, jumping a fence and disappearing into the fields across from his namesake Nathaniel Lightner's farmhouse. Private Sandoe fired at the Rebels and then tried to make his escape.

41 Fannie Buehler, *Recollections of the Rebel Invasion and One Woman's Experience during the Battle of Gettysburg* (Gettysburg, Pa.: The Sentinel Press, 1900).

42 Alleman, *At Gettysburg*, 26. Mary Virginia "Ginnie" Wade helped secure her brother Sam's release from General Early. She would be killed during the battle of Gettysburg on July 3.

However, his horse balked at the same fence, and he took a bullet during the ensuing brief flurry of return fire. A member of Bell's Cavalry for only three days, the 20-year-old Sandoe had returned to die scarcely two miles from his home. Seventy-seven-year-old miller Peter McAllister witnessed the incident; he loudly complained that the Rebels shot the trooper in the back.[43]

Nearby, Elizabeth Thorn, acting as caretaker of Evergreen Cemetery while her husband Peter served in the 138th Pennsylvania, was walking back to her home in the gatehouse. She watched six cavalrymen ride up the Baltimore Pike and discharge their revolvers, chasing away several men who escaped capture only by leaping over nearby fences. Fearful that they had fired on her mother, Elizabeth hurried home. Rebels rode on the paved sidewalk around the gatehouse to a window and demanded bread, butter, and buttermilk. They reassured the women that they would not hurt them, unlike what the Yankees often did to Southern ladies. Elizabeth's mother, Catherine Masser, complied and the hungry soldiers dismounted to eat. Soon they noticed a rider coming up the pike leading a saddled horse. "Oh, you have another one," they said. The horseman replied, "Yes, the —— shot at me, but he did not hit me, and I shot him and blowed him down like nothing, and here I got his horse and he lays down the pike."[44]

Just east of town, Captain Walker's commissary guards skirmished briefly with White's cavalrymen near the arched stone bridge over Rock Creek. J. Howard Jacobs of Company F had been left in town with a squadron to guard the wagons; they captured a stray Rebel cavalryman before retiring. A few First City Troopers were fleeing on the York Road, intending to take the

---

43 *Gettysburg Compiler*, June 28, 1863; Slade, *Firestorm at Gettysburg*, 26. Some accounts say Wm. Lightner was Nathaniel Lightner's son. According to Tim Smith of ACHS, they were not closely related. It was coincidental that he died near the Lightner farmhouse. Sandoe had been married for only four months to Gettysburg resident Anna Caskey. For several years a museum displayed his uniform jacket. It had two holes, the left front breast and a corresponding hole in the rear, perhaps giving credence that Sandoe indeed was shot in the back. According to T. W. Burger, "First to Fall," *CWTI,* Aug. 2000, 32-38, Lightner rode to a nearby thorn thicket and hid his horse and accoutrements. He reached a nearby house and informed a Mrs. Conover that he believed his companion Sandoe had been killed. Peter McAllister, not recognizing the dead soldier lying in the road, placed the body in his wagon. A neighbor identified it as Sandoe's. G. W. Sandoe is buried in Mount Joy Cemetery.

44 Elizabeth Thorn account, GNMP. Following the battle of Gettysburg, David McConaughy, president of the Evergreen Cemetery Association, ordered her to bury more than 100 bodies. Her 63-year-old German immigrant father and a few hired hands helped her. Three months later, she gave birth to a baby girl.

Hunterstown Road eastward. They heard the firing, wheeled their horses, and galloped back toward Gettysburg. They quickly dismounted and pitched in with Walker, allegedly unhorsing a Rebel before withdrawing.[45]

Frightened refugees streamed along the turnpike. Most intended to cross the Susquehanna River at Wrightsville, some 45 miles to the east. One of Gettysburg's butchers had sent an employee, Charlie Supann, off with his horse just as the Rebels entered town. However cavalrymen caught him near the tollhouse gate and confiscated it. While Supann futilely negotiated with the Rebels, carriage maker David Troxel's boys dashed by with their family's horse and buggy, heading for York. Meanwhile, White's men explored Gettysburg, ransacking and looting barns, stores, and chicken coops. Frank Myers stated that a few found supplies of liquor, and soon drunken cavalrymen roamed the streets, in "a half-horse, half wild-cat condition." Each trooper "imagined himself to be the greatest hero of the war; in fact some were heard recounting to the horrified citizens of Gettysburg the immense execution they had done with the sabre in a hundred battles."[46]

Fifteen-year-old Albertus McCreary spotted a cavalryman wearing spurs on his bare feet. Other Rebels approached the Warren house on Railroad Street and loudly banged on the drawn shutters, demanding matches. A shocked Mrs. Warren inquired, "Oh, are you going to burn the old barn?" When the Rebels replied that they wanted to shoe their horses in the neighboring blacksmith shop, her young son Leander hastily gave them matches.[47]

Several cavalrymen asked Margaret Pierce for food. She chided them for returning after stealing the family's horse, but out of her inherent kindness she fed them anyway. Watching from a doorway, her daughter Tillie was shocked as the laughing and crude-joking cavalrymen "threw the apple butter in all directions while spreading their bread." When Margaret pleaded for the horse's return, they told her to go see Colonel White. Tillie was "heartily glad when they left, for they were a rude set." Her father accompanied them, but White refused

---

45 Richards, *Pennsylvania's Emergency Men at Gettysburg*, 10; Pennypacker, *Pennsylvania at Gettysburg*. 786. Walker's men claimed to have taken the captured Rebel with them to Wrightsville.

46 Clifton Johnson, ed., *Battleground Adventures: The Stories of the Dwellers on the Scenes of Conflict* (Boston and New York: Houghton Mifflin, 1915), 160; Myers, *The Comanches,* 193. The *Gettysburg Compiler* June 29, 1863, verified that the Rebels purchased "a number of barrels of whiskey."

47 Leander Warren recollections, ACHS.

to return the captured mount. He understood that James Pierce was a "black Abolitionist" whose two sons were in the Union army; men who he supposed had taken as much from the South as the Rebels were now taking from the North. Later, the Pierces saw the cavalrymen frequently riding past their house on the mare until it became lame. They never saw the animal again.[48]

Meanwhile, John Gordon approached Gettysburg from the west on the Chambersburg Pike. In a "raw, drizzling rain," he advanced Col. Clement Evans' 31st Georgia through the town as pickets. As I. G. Bradwell's company, the Decatur County Arnett Rifles, rose over "a little hill in the suburbs," they noticed "a fellow in his back yard waving his hat frantically and shouting at the top of his voice: 'Hurrah for Jeff Davis! Hurrah for Jeff Davis!' Our men looked upon him as a sneak and a coward who wanted to curry favor with us," remembered Bradwell long after the war, "and they replied to him in language too inelegant to print, but among other things told him where to go and get a gun and fight."[49]

Townspeople had laughed at the frequent reports that the Rebels were coming. Fannie Buehler penned, "We tried to make ourselves believe they would never come, and we made merry over the reports which continued to be circulated until they really came. When we saw them, we believed."[50]

As Gordon's rain-soaked soldiers began filing into downtown, residents who had stood in open doorways watching Knox's cavalrymen now shut and latched their doors. According to Sallie Broadhead, townspeople were afraid that the infantrymen would run into their houses and carry off everything they owned. She headed upstairs and peered from her window. The grimy Southerners marched by in an orderly manner, some pausing every now and then to ask residents how many Yankee soldiers were in town. When Sallie called from her window that she did not know the answer, a Rebel replied, "You are a funny woman; if I lived in town I would know that much." Nearly 2,000 Georgians quietly marched by her home.

---

48 Alleman, *At Gettysburg*, 26. James Pierce was a Gettysburg butcher, and owned a house at Baltimore and Breckinridge streets. One son was in the 1st Pennsylvania Reserves; another in the 15th Pennsylvania Cavalry. The Pierces suspected that their neighbor Mary Virginia ("Ginnie") Wade informed White about their abolitionist views.

49 Isaac G. Bradwell, "The Burning of Wrightsville, Pennsylvania," *Confederate Veteran* (1919), Vol. 27, 300-301. The "little hill" likely was Seminary Ridge.

50 Buehler, *Recollections of the Rebel Raid*, 6.

James M. Smith of the 31st Georgia's color guard related, "While passing through Gettysburg my dilapidated shoes gave completely out, and my feet, bruised, swollen and bleeding through tramping over the stone pike, were on the ground. I could have taken a pair of shoes from a store, but General Lee had enjoined us to take nothing; we were not there to plunder, but to fight. There was no alternative but to keep up as best as I could."[51]

"The day we marched into Gettysburg was cold and raw," according to Bradwell, "although it was June, and a drizzly rain falling. The brigade entered the town from the west and marched to the public square, where the head of the column turned down the main street to the south." On South Baltimore Street, Fannie Buehler took down the sign for her husband's post office and buried the keys in her yard. As Gordon's lead regiment marched past her home, she "never saw a more unsightly set of men, and as I looked at them in their dirty, torn garments, hatless, shoeless, and foot-sore, I pitied them from the depth of my heart. . . . I wondered what this coming meant; what they were going to do; and how long they were going to stay, so I sat myself down on the door step with my children, and Bruno, our faithful Newfoundland dog, to watch operations."[52]

Gordon allowed his men to stack arms and rest. Many lay down on the sidewalks and in the streets using their knapsacks as pillows. When residents tried engaging them in conversation, most of the Georgians remained silent. They were exhausted by the grueling hike across South Mountain.[53]

Bradwell mentioned, "Our military band took position on the principal corner and played 'Dixie' and many other selections; but none of the older citizens showed themselves. The younger set, however, of both sexes, considered it a holiday and turned out in force. They were anxious to know when we were going to burn the town. Crowds of these youngsters hung to us everywhere we went, asking this same question. Our only answer was that Southern soldiers didn't burn towns." The children "seemed to think that was our only reason for coming, and they were anxious to see the fun begin. This question was perhaps answered a thousand times, but never seemed to satisfy the kids."[54]

---

51 *The Sunny South*, Sept. 23, 1904.

52 Bradwell, "Crossing the Potomac," 371; Buehler, *Recollections of the Rebel Raid*, 10.

53 Bradwell, "Burning of Wrightsville," 300; *Gettysburg Compiler*, June 29, 1863.

54 *Ibid.*; Bradwell, "Crossing the Potomac," 371.

The last regiment stacked arms on both sides of Chambersburg Street in front of the Broadhead house, remaining there for an hour. To Sallie, the Rebels were "a miserable-looking set." Some were barefooted and they wore all kinds of hats and caps, including heavy fur ones. A regimental band played Southern tunes in the Diamond. Sallie wrote, "I cannot tell how bad I felt to hear them, and to see the traitors' flag floating overhead."[55]

Across the street, photographer Charles Tyson and his wife, Maria, remained hidden upstairs in their house. "We had taken the precaution to lock the front door and yard gate," he recounted, "and were looking out through the Venetian shutters—seeing but unseen." After several Georgians tried to open the door, Tyson invited them inside and offered some water. He added, "They came right along . . . and then they wanted bread and butter, but we told them we did not have enough to commence on, and they were satisfied far more easily than I expected; were very polite and gentlemanly."[56]

At one house, Pvt. George F. Agee and some comrades of the 26th Georgia were sitting on steps that led upstairs when a resident descended and politely greeted the Rebels. "Well," he said, "You seem to be a clever set of gentlemen; you are not bothering any and seem to behave so well." He related that a young lady upstairs had believed the Rebels "had great long horns on their heads." She was relieved when she looked out the window and saw they looked normal.[57]

A reporter noted that when the first Rebels appeared, the people were "greatly alarmed." However, when they saw that their homes were not being entered and private property was protected, "they gained confidence and courage, and circulated freely among the soldiers. Some of the boldest of the inhabitants even ventured on the experiment of uttering abolition sentiments in the presence of rebel officers, who did not resent the intended insult, but treated it as a very good joke and laughed at the exerted fanatics." Sallie Myers wrote, "We are not afraid, but it is exasperating that we are now under control of armed traitors."[58]

Most of the nearly 200 blacks who lived in Gettysburg fled prior to the Confederates' arrival. The ones that remained now hid as Gordon's men

55 Broadhead diary entry for June 26, 1863, ACHS.

56 Charles J. Tyson account, GNMP.

57 *The Sunny South*, July 20, 1901.

58 *Macon (Ga.) Weekly Telegram*, July 16, 1863; Salome Myers account, ACHS.

occupied the town. Catherine Foster noted, "The colored People feared the rebels more than death. They played hiding and peeping all this time." Several white residents, including Mary Fastnacht, hid their black neighbors. The wife and daughter of Abraham Cole, a black minister, "were alone and did not know what to do." According to Mary, "Mother told them to come to our house; that she would hide them in the loft over the kitchen, take the ladder away, and they would be safe."[59]

Professor Michael Jacobs observed that Gordon's men were "exceedingly dirty, some rugged, some without shoes, and some surrounded by the skeleton of what was once an entire hat." Wet from the rain and perspiring heavily after their long march, the Georgians filled the air with "filthy exhalations from their bodies" as they foraged through shoe, hat, and clothing stores. Ten-year-old Charles McCurdy dazed enviously at Phillip "Petey" Winter's sweet shop and was rewarded when a "big Rebel" emerged with a hat full of candy and shared his booty with the expectant lad.[60]

Jennings' three dozen skirmishers who had surrendered to Lt. Harrison Strickler near Marsh Creek made quite a stir as guards paraded them along Chambersburg Street. Sallie Broadhead's "humiliation was complete" as she watched them from her second floor window. A mounted Confederate officer trailed the captives, followed by "a Negro on as fine a horse as I ever saw." A guard noticed the woman's admiration and commented, "We captured this horse from General Milroy." Pointing toward Gordon's distant wagon park, he added, "Do you see the wagons up there? How we did whip the Yankees and we intend to do it again soon."[61]

The procession of prisoners amused Gordon's weary infantrymen, who lined the street from the Broadhead house eastward. One Georgian joked, "Not being as well trained and practiced in running as the soldiers of Hooker's army, some few of them could not make the time required for their escape and were consequently captured." Guards escorted the captives a few blocks to Christ

---

59 Mary Warren Fastnacht, *Memories of the Battle of Gettysburg, Year 1863* (New York: Princely Press, 1941), 3.

60 Jacobs, *Notes on the Rebel Invasion,* 15-16; Charles McCurdy account, ACHS. His father Robert was the president of the Gettysburg Railroad. The family lived at 26 Chambersburg Street on the town's west side.

61 Broadhead diary entry for June 28, 1863, ACHS. The wagons likely were on Seminary Ridge.

Lutheran Church where, seated on the steps out front, they conversed with young Henry Jacobs and other citizens. Several ladies took the boys their dinners. "The Confederates were very business-like in their attitude toward the townspeople," recalled Henry after the war, adding, "but were considerate enough."[62]

Never one to miss an opportunity to make a speech, Gordon formed his men and delivered one of his characteristic charismatic orations. According to one of the captives, the Georgian's fiery words resulted in "the wildest enthusiasm" from those in attendance. When the Confederate brigadier general told his men that their march through the heart of the enemy's country had been "marked with victory and plenty," his men responded with more lusty cheering.[63]

Skirmish at Witmer Farm

Jubal Early accompanied Col. William French's 17th Virginia Cavalry to Mummasburg, where a scout reported "a comparatively small force" of the enemy at Gettysburg. With that news he halted to wait for his infantry, which was slowed by the mud and dispatched a company of cavalry toward Gettysburg to reconnoiter. The patrol captured a few straggling militiamen. When a courier returned with the news that the main Yankee force was hastily retreating through the fields between Mummasburg and Gettysburg, Early sent the rest of French's regiment in pursuit. Soon afterward, the infantry began arriving in Mummasburg, with the Louisiana Tigers of Harry Hay's brigade marching in the lead. Early instructed Hays to move immediately toward Gettysburg, ordered the rest of the column to camp upon its arrival, and then rode off behind Hays' brigade. After another messenger announced that Gordon's men had taken possession of Gettysburg, Early ordered Hays to halt and camp on a large hill along Mummasburg Road about one mile northwest of Gettysburg. Early also dispatched two regiments to help French catch the

---

62 *Savannah Daily Republican*, Aug. 6, 1863; Slade, *Firestorm at Gettysburg*, 65; Henry Eyster Jacobs, *How an Eye Witness Watched the Great Battle* (Gettysburg, Pa.: s. n., undated, copy in ACHS). The president of Gettysburg College, Dr. Henry Baugher, pastored the church. Many of his students regularly attended his services. Baugher, having lost a son at Shiloh, had repeatedly discouraged them from enlisting. Now, some were held captive on his church's front steps.

63 *Philadelphia Press*, June 30, 1863.

fleeing Yankee militia but, slowed by the muddy roads, they trailed well behind the cavalry.[64]

Colonel William Jennings continued moving the main body of the 26th Militia away from the Chambersburg Pike. He feared that Confederates might be following him, intent on capturing his men. Preceded by a few of Bell's troopers, the regiment, with "more haste than military precision," hurried northward. According to Private Pennypacker, "The route pursued was an exceedingly crooked one, turning at nearly every corner." After reaching the Mummasburg-Hunterstown Road, Jennings intended to circumnavigate Gettysburg and press on to a rendezvous point in Hanover. Soldiers cursed that "the Colonel would not let us halt long enough for us to get our traps in good order and reach our place in line." Straggling began almost immediately as the untrained men, heavily loaded with knapsacks, blankets, and haversacks, struggled to keep pace in the mud, which in places was three to four inches deep.[65]

The tremendous pace and emotional strain, coupled with the miserable condition of the roads, had a telling effect. Pennypacker mentioned, "We had not marched many hours before a number began to flag, and a rest being absolutely necessary, we halted for a few minutes, but soon started on again. The effect of this was, that the companies became very much scattered and confused, the stronger men working forward to the front of the regiment, and the weaker gradually falling back to the rear. About the middle of the afternoon many tired out, commenced to drop off, and were passed sitting by the roadside, and all were fatigued enough to conclude that it was extremely hard work." Dozens of men straggled behind the column. Others took refuge in fields, hoping to avoid detection.[66]

After slogging to a point about four miles northeast of Gettysburg, Jennings halted the vanguard about 4:00 p.m. near the Henry Witmer

64 Early, *War Memoirs*, 257; Malone, *The Diary of Bartlett Y. Malone*, 36; Seymour account, GNMP. Avery's and Smith's brigades camped in the southwestern corner of the village, accompanied by Jones' artillery battalion. In the early evening, Hilary Jones dispatched Capt. William Tanner's battery to Gettysburg per Jubal Early's orders.

65 Pennypacker, "Six Weeks in Uniform," 341; Richards, *Pennsylvania's Emergency Men at Gettysburg*, 9; Shriver account, GNMP. From Pennypacker's description, the 26th may have turned right on Mummasburg-Gettysburg Rd. and then used the crooked, winding Russel Tavern Rd. to reach the Mummasburg-Hunterstown Road (now Goldenville).

66 Pennypacker, "Six Weeks in Uniform," 341.

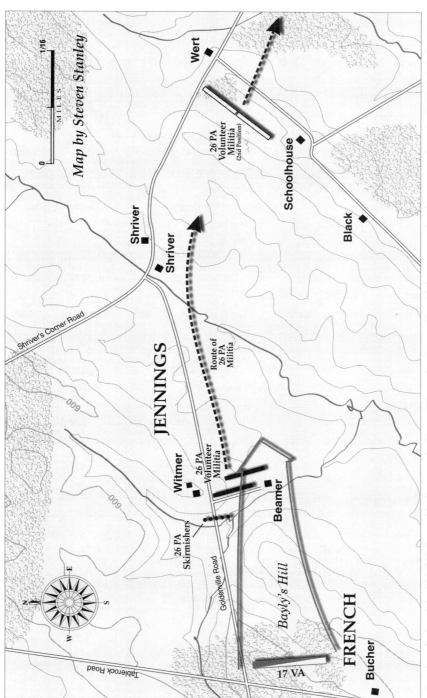

Jennings deployed the 26th PVM on a ridgeline near the Henry Witmer farmhouse. He withdrew eastward under pressure from the 17th Virginia Cavalry before reforming his scattered militia.

Map by Steven Stanley

farmhouse, which stood on a low ridge above a small stream in northwestern Straban Township. Meanwhile, his individual companies strung out well behind him to the west. Private D. B. Shuey placed the halt somewhat earlier, stating that the column marched "until about three o'clock in the afternoon, when many from fatigue could no longer march and straggled, and some climbed cherry trees to eat cherries."[67]

According to Pennypacker, "At four o'clock, I was near the centre of the regiment, and had just passed Web Davis and [Wm. P.] Buckley, a friend of Doc. [Cyrus] Nyce, who said they would go no further. I was ascending a small hill, to the right were fields, and at some little distance a wood. Upon the top of the hill on the left was a medium sized brick house. About opposite the house, a branch of the wood extended to within perhaps a hundred and fifty yards of the road."[68]

The Witmer homestead consisted of a modest two-story red brick house fronted by a roadside well, an imposing barn, and a square-hewn log storage house. On the hilltop, according to Henry Richards, Company A and other early arrivers "threw themselves down by the wayside to rest, while others visited the house in search of food." Their provisions were still on the supply train in Gettysburg, and the militiamen were hungry. Several climbed the 62-year-old Witmer's row of heavily laden cherry trees and passed fruit down to their waiting comrades. His 60-year-old wife Catherine and some of their daughters had been baking. They served steaming hot loaves of bread to the hungry but appreciative boys in the muddy blue uniforms. Thirsty soldiers threw down their rifles and packs and eagerly gulped cool well water, unaware that Rebel horsemen were closing in on them.[69]

French's cavalrymen swept across the area north of Gettysburg, collecting Jennings' stragglers and raiding farms for horses. The men of the Joseph Bayly family removed their horses from their large barn and hastened off to the east, intending to flee to Hanover. As they crossed one of the roads radiating from

67 Richards, *Pennsylvania's Emergency Men at Gettysburg*, 11; Pennypacker, *Pennsylvania at Gettysburg*, 786, Pennypacker, "Six Weeks in Uniform," 341, Shuey, *History of the Shuey Family in America,* 107. The name "Strabane" was also used until the 1870s when "Straban" (the current spelling) became commonplace.

68 Pennypacker, "Six Weeks in Uniform," 341.

69 Richards, *Pennsylvania's Emergency Men at Gettysburg*, 11; Nye, "The First Battle of Gettysburg," 16. Some accounts state that the Witmers had two sons and six daughters; others suggest seven daughters.

Gettysburg, 13-year-old Billy Bayly noticed a horse and rider coming over the hill toward him. Anxious for information about the enemy and confident in the fleetness of his mount, Bayly halted and allowed his party to go on. The horseman, covered with a rubber poncho splashed with mud, rode up to where Bayly's horse was standing. The youth, recognizing the trooper as a recruit in Bell's Cavalry, exclaimed, "Hello, Bill! What's up?"

The soldier replied, "If you don't get out of the here pretty quick you'll find out what's up. The Rebel Cavalry chased me out of town about fifteen minutes ago, and must now be close on my heels."

"But where is the rest of your company?" asked Bayly.

"Oh, h——," retorted the trooper, "I don't know; they ran long before I did. But you git or you'll be got." The soldier rode toward Harrisburg, and Bayly raced after his family.[70]

French's cavalrymen captured several more stragglers during the advance to Bayly's Hill, a low ridge running diagonally across the Mummasburg-Hunterstown Road. The colonel swung his Virginians off the road and deployed them for battle while Jennings' rearmost companies scrambled for safety. A bugle blared and the Rebels charged through the open fields in the valley between the ridgeline and Witmer's hilltop farmhouse. Near a small shallow stream, they overtook Jennings' rearmost unit, Company B under 23-year-old Capt. Warner H. Carnachan. The Federals leaped a wooden fence, rushed across an adjoining field, and formed behind another set of rails. Their powder was wet from the rain, so many could not get their guns to fire. They threw down their muskets and quickly raised their hands in surrender.[71]

"Seeing all of our men jumping over the fences on the right, I followed suit," explained Sam Pennypacker of Company F,

and found myself in a corn field. Nearly all were in the adjoining wheat field further on, so I directed my steps thither. Everyone knows the disadvantage of going through a wet corn field, and how the mud clinging to the feet, impedes every moment. If in addition, they remember that I carried a pretty heavy load upon my back, was wearied with the previous fast tramping, and

70 William Hamilton Bayly, *Stories of the Battle,* Files of the Library of Gettysburg National Military Park.

71 Samuel W. Pennypacker, "The Twenty-Sixth Pennsylvania Militia," in *Pennsylvania in History* (Philadelphia: W. J. Campbell, 1910), 391.

the 'rebs' not far behind, they can form a pretty good idea of an unpleasant situation. I thought to myself, 'Well, I wouldn't run across this field if the devil himself were after me,' and I do really believe, that if the whole rebel army had been within a few paces, I would have turned around to fight in a kind of determined desperation. So I walked slowly toward the rest.[72]

Confederate Pvt. James Hodam recalled, "Those on the side of our approach were captured before they had a chance to run. Those on the farther side including most of the officers fled as fast as their legs could carry them leaving everything behind except their arms and knapsacks. Such a sight is not often witnessed by three hundred cavalrymen charging and driving nearly a thousand men as if they were so many sheep." In reality, Jennings had only 700 men at this point, but they seemed more numerous to Hodam.[73]

Up at the Witmer farmhouse, young Henry Richards sought to rejoin his company. Scattered rifle fire crackled from the western-facing windows. Jennings tried to form his remaining men, feverishly issuing orders to his company commanders. Bugles blared and drums beat as subordinate officers tried to form the 26th Militia behind scrub-lined fences along a sunken farm lane leading south to the Beamer homestead. Officers barked inconsistent commands at the frightened militiamen. As the bulk of Company I plodded along the muddy road toward the farm "in rather bad order," 25-year-old Pvt. Henry Wirt Shriver noted a sudden movement in front and "all hands commenced scrambling over the fence. . . . Such confusion I never saw— everyone gave orders and nobody obeyed—we were all green and knew nothing about regular forming, and half the right was skedaddling already."[74]

D. B. Shuey recalled, "All was confusion and many men lost their places in their own company." Future governor Sam Pennypacker later provided a colorful glimpse of the panic and mass confusion among men who, just four days before had been farmers, college students, and shopkeepers. None had been in the army long enough to acquire a knowledge of military drill and

72 Pennypacker, "Six Weeks in Uniform," 342.

73 Kesterson, *Campaigning with the 17th Virginia Cavalry,* 288.

74 Richards, *Pennsylvania's Emergency Men at Gettysburg,* 11; Shriver account, GNMP; Nye, *Here Come the Rebels,* 276; David Shriver Lovelace, *The Shrivers: Under Two Flags* (Westminster, Md., Willow Bend Books, 2003), 40. Shriver, born at Union Mills in December 1837, enlisted June 17 at Hanover and became clerk of his company. Some sources place Carnachan's rear guard farther west on Goldenville Road (the wartime Mummasburg-Hunterstown Road).

decorum. "In the field, there was the greatest amount of confusion," wrote Pennypacker. Most enlisted men did not even know their officers, who were "running around waving their swords, shouting and swearing, but no one dreamed of obeying them." Men became separated from their companies, and "each fellow did as he thought proper. . . . The commands from half crazy Captains and Lieutenants were often unintelligible, and perfectly contradictory." Some confused men were streaking off over the fields, while others took cover behind nearby fences and tried to reform their ranks. Pennypacker added, "Collected together in little knots, or standing alone, they commenced firing off their pieces as rapidly as possible. Some were falling in behind the fences, and others streaking off over the fields. I believe every man was shouting or yelling. I did not see any of the regimental officers, and think they must have been further [sic] ahead."[75]

Virginian James Hodam recorded the scene as terrified Yankees ran away from the approaching Confederates: "Through lanes, over fields and fences we dashed after them leaving our infantry support far behind but the enemy could not sustain the unequal force long and soon the ground was strewn with guns and knapsacks, musical instruments, blankets, and clothing. . . . On every side the blue coated fellows could be seen waving their white handkerchiefs in token of surrender. All we did was to make them break their guns over a stump or fence and send them to the rear as prisoners."[76]

Finally, some of the militiamen realized that the shouts, drums, and bugles were calling them to form into lines of battle. From the sunken road, Colonel Jennings ordered a volley, which unhorsed some Rebels. For the vast majority of the Pennsylvanians, it was the first time that they discharged their weapons at a live enemy. Return fire crackled from Southern carbines, and a bullet grazed the forehead of Thomas H. Dailey of Company C. He toppled in a heap before righting himself. Farm wife Harriet Bayly heard the distant gunfire and feared that her husband and his party had been overtaken.[77]

---

75 Shuey, *History of the Shuey Family in America,* 107; Pennypacker, "Six Weeks," 342-43.

76 Kesterson, *Campaigning with the 17th Virginia Cavalry,* 288. The June 29, 1863, *Gettysburg Compiler* reported that "The rebel cavalry captured a number of them past Mr. Leer's, on the Mummasburg Road, and some more lower down."

77 Richards, *Pennsylvania's Emergency Men at Gettysburg,* 11; Pennypacker, *Pennsylvania at Gettysburg,* 786; Pennypacker, "Six Weeks in Uniform," 356; Bayly account, GNMP. French reported two men wounded, with six missing, at Gettysburg. Pennypacker claimed, "Several rebels were shot from their horses before they retired."

Scores of infantrymen were caught in between Jennings' partially reformed line and the Rebels. Pennypacker recounted, "After firing off one load and ramming down another, I began to look around for Co. F., but could not see any one of them. About half a company were drawn up behind the next fence, and thinking I might find some of them there, I went over to them. The great bulk of the regiment was much farther off, and the balls from their muskets and the rebel carbines whistled over our heads very rapidly. We were rather between the two there, and had the benefit of all the firing. I was not at all disturbed by it, though I once or twice involuntarily dodged my head, and momentarily expected to see someone drop, but the aim was entirely too high." D. B. Shuey was prone behind an old fence; two bullets struck the rail near his face.[78]

Confusion and fear struck with more fury than French's cavalrymen. According to Pvt. Frank Richards, Company A formed behind a fence and "fired away at the rascals. Our pieces were in a bad condition. Half of them didn't go off at first firing, they being so wet." Henry Richards, sitting on his drum behind the line, could not help but notice the difference in action between the two bodies of troops, "both thoroughly brave, but one also thoroughly disciplined by years of service, whilst the other was entirely undisciplined for lack of them." Young Richards believed that the Rebels were losing more heavily than the militia, yet they "sat firm and steady on their horses, in straight and compact lines." By contrast, the Pennsylvanians were "full of excitement, most of them yelling at the top of their voices." Some soldiers loaded and fired without any pretense of aiming, while others calmly charged their pieces and fired them "with most deliberate aim." Still others were "so thoroughly worked up" that they placed the powder on top of the Minié ball, rendering their Springfields useless. A few neglected to remove their ramrods and inadvertently sent them sailing at the Rebels.

Richards heard a sound similar to a hummingbird. He turned to his older brother Mathias, who being "thoroughly exhausted," was prostrate on the ground. He had given his musket to a civilian who joined Company A during the parade through town that morning. Henry asked him if he had heard the hummingbird, to which Frank scornfully replied, "You idiot! You will find out soon enough whether it is a humming bird if it hits you." The musician claimed that a Confederate color bearer, sitting calmly on his horse in front of the

---

78 Pennypacker, "Six Weeks in Uniform," 343; Shuey, *History of the Shuey Family in America,* 107.

regiment near an officer, fell from his horse. Another Rebel quickly picked up the fallen flag and displayed it.[79]

Henry Shriver of Hanover's Company I blew out his gun's wet firing mechanism to clear and dry it. By the time he was ready to shoot, his comrades already were blazing away at six mounted Rebels crossing a field a quarter of a mile to the west. Militia stragglers still lined the road, and Shriver reported they were "in as much danger from our shots as from the Rebs. I fired one shot, more to try whether my gun would go off than anything else." Although his men still outnumbered the Confederates by more than two-to-one, Jennings ordered a ceasefire and initiated a withdrawal to a woodlot on their right flank. Because of their lack of martial training, the bewildered militia did not form quickly enough and only about one-half of the regiment made it into the woods. According to Private Shriver, Jennings led the rest of the militia in a different direction, crossing the road and filing off into the fields to the south. A portion of Company I was captured as they retreated. Panic was everywhere as "the Rebs were reported to be after us 5,000 strong, mounted infantry." The Confederates fired a final time just as Shriver found cover, two bullets whistling over his head.[80]

Confederate trooper Hodam left an insightful account of the affair:

Some four or five hundred of the enemy managed to keep together with the Confederate charge upon them in some show of order. The Pennsylvania Militia after crossing a deep ravine, they halted behind a fence and fired a few shots at us. As the ground in our front was too rough and steep for horsemen, Companies D, E, and G were dismounted and charged them led by Colonel Tavenner. Major [Frederick F.] Smith with Companies A, B, and C deployed to the left to turn their flank but the enemy only waited long enough to divest themselves of knapsacks, haversacks, canteens, blankets, and everything that would impede their flight and away they went soon crossing a stream.[81]

Jennings reformed almost one-half mile east on higher ground between Good Intent School and the William Wert farm. "In the meantime," recalled

79 Vertical files, GNMP; Richards, *Pennsylvania's Emergency Men at Gettysburg*, 11.

80 Shriver account, GNMP; Lovelace, *The Shrivers: Under Two Flags*, 40; Richards, *Pennsylvania's Emergency Men at Gettysburg*, 11.

81 Kesterson, *Campaigning with the 17th Virginia Cavalry*, 288. The stream is a tributary of Rock Creek.

Samuel Pennypacker, "the 'rebs' had divided, some coming up the road as far as the brick house where they captured a few of our men who had gone inside, and the rest went over to the right, and were separated from us by the wood. . . . Our regiment were now nearly all collected together, and were drawn up in line, some two or three fields distant."[82]

The fifteen or so isolated militiamen still in the farmhouse managed to get off a few final shots, but, "being very few in number, were obliged eventually to surrender." A young infantryman escaped by quickly changing into one of Witmer's old suits. Another secreted himself in a meat tub, according to drummer Henry Richards. One hid under a barrel in the storage shed adjacent to the house. Jennings managed to calm his remaining soldiers and they waited for renewed hostilities. However, the pursuit was only cursory, as French was content to round up Union laggards. The entire fight had lasted only twenty to thirty minutes.[83]

Stragglers such as Sam Pennypacker soon rejoined the ranks, but many could not be located. Jennings called the roll and found he was missing more than 120 men from his original 743. He led what was left of his regiment to the Harrisburg Road, turning northeasterly toward the state capital. More missing men, including Dennis Shuey, caught up with the retreating column within the first mile of the desperate march. According to Virginia trooper James Hodam, "They took advantage of our scattered condition to tear up the bridge delaying us a short time and [with] a hard rain setting in, we gave up the chase and returned to the main road and camped in sight of Gettysburg."[84]

Confederate cavalrymen discovered several "poor fellows" hiding in the cherry trees and "pricked them with their sabres in that part of the body where a trooper generally half-soled his trousers," ordering them to climb down or be shot. Lieutenant Robert Gore's Company D captured nearly a hundred terrified militiamen, some bleeding from minor wounds. Sue King Black, who lived southwest of Good Intent School, noticed students she knew from Gettysburg

82 Richards, *Pennsylvania's Emergency Men at Gettysburg*, 11; Pennypacker, *Pennsylvania at Gettysburg*, 786; Bayly account, GNMP; Pennypacker, "Six Weeks in Uniform," 344, 356. Some period maps the name is spelled "Wirt." The farmhouse still stands along Shrivers Corner Rd.

83 Richards, *Pennsylvania's Emergency Men at Gettysburg*, 11; Nye, "The First Battle of Gettysburg," 17; Pennypacker, "26th Militia," 391.

84 Richards, *Pennsylvania's Emergency Men at Gettysburg*, 11; Shuey, *History of the Shuey Family in America*, 107; Kesterson, *Campaigning with the 17th Virginia Cavalry*, 288.

among the panicked militia. She related, "One of the boys hid under a bed where a Reb found him and asked if his mother knew he was out." In less than thirty minutes of skirmishing around the Witmer farm, Colonel French's Virginians cleared the roads north of Gettysburg of any organized militia presence.[85]

Major Haller had already decided that if Jennings' regiment retreated, its rallying point would be Hanover in neighboring York County. While Jennings battled French at Witmer Farm, Haller and a small escort galloped into Hanover to forward these supplies onward to York. They found the town in a state of "general confusion." Dozens of residents were worried about the advancing Rebels and had made hurried preparations to flee across the distant Susquehanna River. One citizen, in describing Haller's late-afternoon arrival, recalled that some of Bell's scouts and a few Philadelphians came "dashing into our unusually quiet borough in such a tremendous hurry, upon their foaming chargers and begrimed with mud as if all bedlam was on their heels. After these came the commanding officer of this district, in a more composed manner, and in greater military bearing."[86]

Haller entered the telegraph office and asked Trone to wire General Couch the disappointing news that the Confederate advance guard had driven Jennings from "a good position" along the ridges three miles west of Gettysburg. Now, Haller turned his attention to York. He had Trone send a telegram to its Committee of Safety that Rebels now occupied Gettysburg with infantry, cavalry, and artillery. York's citizens should arm themselves and perhaps the town could be saved.[87]

A *New York Tribune* reporter in downtown York wrote, "The dread of the approaching enemy has fallen like a blight upon the interests of this community, and fearful suspense has taken the place of that business life and activity which erstwhile prevailed. At first alarm of danger most of the merchants of the town hurried away many of their goods and valuables out of the reach of the thieving

---

85 Hodam manuscript; Jim Slade and John Alexander, *Firestorm at Gettysburg: Civilian Voices June-November 1863* (Atglen, Pa.: Schiffer, 1998), 28. Shuey, *History of the Shuey Family in America,* noted that "all the cherry eaters" were captured. Some secondary sources suggest that 26 militiamen were wounded, none seriously. Gore received a battlefield promotion to captain for his efforts at Witmer Farm.

86 Haller, *Dismissal of Major Granville O. Haller,* 70; *Hanover Spectator,* July 17, 1863.

87 All-day recruiting efforts in York yielded only one company of volunteers, under the command of John Hays.

enemy who is expected, and for two days their almost emptied stores and shops have been closed. In lieu of business, crowds of citizens stand around the market-place and at the bulletin boards anxiously awaiting the latest news." A fresh report suddenly caught his attention: "While I am writing, a dispatch comes from Major Haller, of Gen. Couch's staff, that the borough of Gettysburg has been entered by a large Rebel force of infantry and cavalry, accompanied by artillery, and that they are advancing toward this place." Many alarmed residents hastened home to prepare to leave York.

The newsman watched as an increasing number of refugees clogged Market Street in their effort to cross the Susquehanna before the Rebels marched eastward, and recorded the following:

> Since early morning there has been a continual ingress and egress of people from Adams and Cumberland counties, fleeing with all that is dear and valuable to them. The streets are lined with wagons, carriages, carts, drays, and vehicles of every shape and design. Some loaded with grain, farming machinery and tools; others with household goods, store goods, and in fact all that are valuable and movable. Following these come other vehicles filled with women and children, whose wan and timid faces it is pitiful to behold. Then come men and boys driving before them droves of horses or of cows and sheep. All are hurrying away, before the dreaded enemy, from their once peaceful homes; and many left rich farms with ripening crops to be trampled down by the foot of the invader who will probably find little else to destroy.[88]

Early Ransoms Gettysburg

As evening approached, Jubal Early and his escort rode into Gettysburg to confer with Gordon. According to a local reporter, "Early immediately set about with threats of atonement for a purported bushwhacking of some of his scouts near Cashtown. . . . He appeared gruff in demeanor and demanded to know the name or names of the scalawags who had fired upon the scouts of White's Cavalry in the mountain passes above the town." The reporter admitted it was "a mystery as to who the assailants may have been, but one Georgia soldier told us that he had seen the body of one of their men lying in the road in

---

88 *New York Tribune,* June 28, 1863, citing a report dated June 26, 1863. The newsman considered York to be "one of the most active and thriving business towns in the interior of Pennsylvania."

a most deplorable condition, having been struck and left in the dust 'like some dead animal.'"[89]

Early rode to the courthouse, where guards formed the captured militiamen. A few townspeople, including relatives of the men in Company A, watched as the general surveyed the demoralized prisoners. He remarked, "You boys ought to be home with your mothers and not out in the fields where it is dangerous and you might get hurt." Provosts then locked the shamed captives in the courthouse. Early's disdained for the state militia remained evident years later when he wrote that they "seemed to belong to that class of men who regard 'discretion as the better part of valor.'" He added, "It was well that the regiment took to its heels so quickly, or some of its members might have been hurt, and all would have been captured. The men and officers taken were paroled the next day and sent about their business, rejoicing at this termination of their campaign."[90]

Early called for the mayor, but Robert Martin was absent. Mrs. Martin directed Early to the house of borough council president David Kendlehart on the first block of Baltimore Street. Early, sitting idly on his saddle while his horse drank water from a sidewalk trough, wrote a list of supplies to be delivered to his quartermaster—60 barrels of flour, 7,000 pounds of bacon, 1,200 pounds of sugar, 60 pounds of coffee, 1,000 pounds of salt, 40 bushels of onions, 1,000 pairs of shoes, and 500 hats—amounting in value to $6,000. If these could not be procured, the council could instead hand over $5,000 in hard currency.[91]

Retiring to William Duncan's law office on the Diamond, Kendlehart convened the town council, which failed to reach consensus on responding to Early's demands. Kendlehart returned to Early with a written response, pleading poverty. Diplomatically, he proclaimed that what goods Gettysburg possessed had already been removed to safety, but the Rebels were welcome to

89 *Adams County Sentinel*, June 27, 1863.

90 Nye, "The First Battle of Gettysburg," 16; Early, *War Memoirs*, 258. William Alonzo Scott, *The Battle of Gettysburg* (Gettysburg, Pa.: s. n., 1905) suggests that Early's mood was lighter and, with a grin, he uttered, "Hi, you little boys must have slipped out of your mothers' band-boxes, you look so nice. Now be off home to your mothers. If I catch you again I'll spank you all."

91 Vertical files, GNMP; *Adams County Sentinel*, June 27, 1863. The paper reported, "It is a mystery as to who the assailants may have been, but one Georgia soldier told us that they had seen the body of one of their men lying by the road in a most deplorable condition, having been struck and left in the dust "like some dead animal."

inspect the shops to see what they could find. Early ordered Gordon's soldiers to search the town, but they discovered only a small quantity of goods suitable for the commissary. A squad of Georgians approached one home. The corporal in charge informed the lady of the house of their mission and apologized for the necessity of their visit. She replied that she had few provisions, barely enough to feed her own family for a short time. The corporal explained that his instructions were not to take all she had, but to divide the food supply in private houses, leaving something for the family. She escorted him into the kitchen and displayed her meager supply of meat—only about two pounds. The corporal looked at her with some incredulity and remarked that he did not want any of her meat. Likewise, her supplies of flour, meal, and vegetables were found to be equally scant. Laughing and joking over her "starving prospects," the Rebels retired without taking anything. They did not know she had hidden the bulk of her ample larder.[92]

Other less polite Confederates forced clerk Samuel Bushman to open the bank and prove that it was empty of cash. Then they threatened to send him and the treasurer to Richmond as prisoners. They seized a few black people and hauled them off, while others managed to escape detection. When Gordon's infantry arrived in Tillie Pierce's Baltimore Street neighborhood, "the searching and ransacking began in earnest." The Rebels sought horses, clothing, and anything of value they could carry away and were "not particular about asking" before taking their spoils. She added, "I have often thought what a laughable spectacle this wing of Southern chivalry would have presented on dress parade, had they obtained the variety of hats generally found upon the shelves of a village store. But they were reduced to extremity and doubtless were not particular." James Pierce deemed the Rebels a "filthy, dirty-looking set," so dust-covered that they were hard to distinguish from the street.[93]

About 5:00 p.m. Early ordered Elijah White's battalion to mount and follow the railroad eastward to see if they could snag more Yankees. Gordon's provost, Colonel Evans, assigned the Arnett Rifles to picket duty. They took turns patrolling the streets while keeping an eye out for stray Yankees, unruly civilians, and any other threats. Evans posted guards at the public buildings, stores, and a few private dwellings to prevent looting. All saloons were closed

---

92 *History of Cumberland and Adams County*, 153-158.

93 Slade, *Firestorm at Gettysburg*, 31; Alleman, *At Gettysburg*, 24-26. Several black families hid in the woods on Culp's Hill. Others went to the northern part of Adams County.

and pickets barred entry. Some women offered them food or water, but they declined, curtly replying, "I must obey orders." The biggest challenge for the provosts came from their fellow soldiers. Shortly after Gordon first entered Gettysburg, a few Irish soldiers from Hays' Louisiana Tigers stacked arms, strolled into town, and walked along Baltimore Street to the southern outskirts. There, they found residents, also of Gaelic descent, who sold them liquor. Soon, a brawl began as drunken Louisianans quarreled with townsmen. The Tigers were busy "beating up the old citizens" when the provosts arrived. No one was arrested after the melee.[94]

Meanwhile, Capt. Robert Bell, accompanied by three men from the First City Troop, combed the roads near Gettysburg hoping to collect scattered Union cavalrymen. Some had slogged through the mud toward York, and Major Knox assembled a few more men to the southeast on Hanover Road. Near one intersection southeast of Gettysburg, Knox's rear guard encountered some of White's cavalrymen and, in a brief exchange of close-range gunfire, claimed to have mortally wounded a Rebel.

After a long chase, White's troopers returned to Gettysburg with only one additional prisoner—First City Troop member John Lowber Welsh, the orderly who had given his fine horse to Major Haller earlier in the day. Welsh had exchanged his uniform for civilian clothes and hustled eastward to rejoin his company. After walking a couple of miles on a country road, Welsh rejoiced when a passing farmer in a buggy gave him a ride. They rode in comfort for three miles, but then heard hoof beats approaching from behind. Soon, a horse raced by carrying two lads, pursued by five Rebel cavalrymen. Shots rang out, and Welsh insisted that they all halt or they might be killed. Reigning in their horses, the civilians and Welsh stopped as the Rebels rode up. The Confederates sported "grotesque" straw bonnets confiscated from a Gettysburg store.

The cavalrymen seized the horses and questioned the detainees. The quick-thinking Welsh lied. He identified himself as "John Merryman," a son of a local farmer. He waved to a nearby house that he said was his father's. Satisfied, the Confederates decided to allow the civilians to depart on foot. As Welsh and his newfound acquaintances were leaving, a Rebel called out, "John, give me your hat, and you can have my bonnet." As Welsh removed his large hat, a trooper

---

94 Early, *War Memoirs*, 257; *History of Cumberland and Adams Counties*, 153-57; Bradwell, "Burning of Wrightsville," 300.

noted his fancy haircut and inquired, "Mr. Merryman, how long has it been since the farmers' sons have had their hair cut in that style?" They escorted Welsh to Gettysburg and presented him to Colonel Evans. In turn, Evans forwarded the captive to Jubal Early for questioning. Welsh confessed his true identity and mentioned that the cavalry at Gettysburg was the famed City Troop. Early laughed, "This is as good of a farce. I was informed that there was a regiment of cavalry here. If I had known who you fellows were, my men would have taken some of the starch out of you." Given the choice of parole or Libby Prison, Welsh chose parole; he soon was released and allowed to pick up his uniform and side arms. He headed to Baltimore, where he later took a train home to Philadelphia.[95]

White's troopers passed the evening scouting and gathering horses and food. They supposed from the fat and sleek appearance of the stolen horses that they were fit for cavalry service. However, as 22-year-old Capt. Frank Myers later discovered, "No greater mistake was ever committed." In his opinion, Southern cavalry horses, even played-out nags, could travel farther and better than those liberated from Pennsylvania stables. "Many a man bitterly repented of exchanging his poor old horse for a new one, even if he got a watch to boot," lamented the young captain. They seized "every [horse]shoe and nail they could find."[96]

Throughout the early evening troopers from French's 17th Virginia, many of whom were also riding pilfered horses, searched the roads north of town for any remaining Yankees from the Witmer Farm fight. Because of the muddy roads, Hays' two Louisiana regiments sent in support failed to connect with the cavalry. Hays' Adjutant William Seymour later exaggerated the Tigers' role in dispersing the militiamen, "who no doubt had previously resolved to die if need

---

95 *History of the First Troop*, 75; Oliver W. Davis, *The Life of David Bell Birney, Major-general, United States Volunteers* (Philadelphia: King & Baird, 1867), 170-73. Birney, then a division commander in the Third Corps of the Army of the Potomac, was a pre-war private in the First City Troop. He maintained close relationships with many of its gentry, including Welsh.

96 Myers, *The Comanches*, 194; OR 27, pt. 1, 923, 926. According to Union Brig. Gen. John Buford, the Rebels left the region in "a terrible state of excitement." He complained, 'The First and Second Brigades moved through Boonsborough, Cavetown, and Monterey Springs, and encamped near Fairfield, within a short distance of a considerable force of the enemy's infantry. The inhabitants knew of my arrival and the position of the enemy's camp, yet not one of them gave me a particle of information, nor even mentioned the fact of the enemy's presence. The whole community seemed stampeded, and afraid to speak or to act, often offering as excuses for not showing some little enterprise, 'the rebels will destroy our houses if we tell anything.'"

be in the defense of their homes and friends, changed their minds when they caught a glimpse of our two little regiments in the distance and most precipitately and ingloriously fled the field. Darkness coming on, our men returned to camp, weary from their long and useless march in the rain and mud."[97]

As the 26th PVM headed away from Gettysburg, they frequently left the road and passed through fields. At one point, Colonel Jennings quietly lifted his hand, and his men, in utmost silence, threw themselves to the ground to avoid detection by a squad of Rebel cavalry passing by on the road 200 feet away. To Sam Pennypacker, "There was something very thrilling and romantic to me then in the idea of our position, and the resemblance we had to hunted game endeavoring to elude their pursuers. A sense of danger gave intensity to the interest with which we watched the chances of being captured."[98]

According to another militiaman, "A party of eighty rebels, cavalry, hovered around the rear of our retreating troops and annoyed them by an occasional discharging of carbines, resulting however in no loss of life. Several captures of stragglers were, however, affected."[99]

Straggling Yankees sought refuge in fields, farm buildings, and orchards. Confederate trooper James Hodam captured six exhausted militiamen hiding among the branches of a large apple tree. Nearby, a portly Pennsylvania lieutenant tried to crawl under a corn crib, but became stuck. His head and shoulders were under the outbuilding, leaving his lower body exposed. Troopers Charlie Hyson and Morgan Feather dragged the terrified officer out by his feet. To Hodam, "the most fun came when we dragged from a family bake-oven a regimental officer who, in his gold-laced uniform, was covered in soot and ashes. He was a sight to behold." Hodam's comrades in Company F "found a soldier laying on his face as if shot dead. Some thought he was dead sure, but when Charlie Hyson tickled him a little with his saber, he jumped up alright." The Confederates collected as much bounty as they could carry from

97 Seymour account, GNMP. The Tigers marched that day fifteen miles, with twelve additional miles for the two regiments sent off on the fruitless chase of the 26th PVM. Hays' campsite was near Oak Hill.

98 Richards, *Pennsylvania's Emergency Men at Gettysburg*, 13; Pennypacker, "Six Weeks in Uniform," 347.

99 *Philadelphia Inquirer*, June 30, 1894.

the discarded militia possessions. A gleeful Hodam reported, "Clean shirts and white handkerchiefs were plenty in our command for sometime after."[100]

Hodam escorted a group of frightened captives to the rear. As he returned to his company, he encountered a bareheaded little drummer. The wet, muddy, and exhausted boy was struggling to keep up with another line of prisoners. Hodam advised the boy to pitch his drum behind a fence corner, remove his uniform coat, and hide behind some bushes until he could safely return to his mother's home. The lad did as he was told, leaving one less prisoner to be processed by the inspector general. The sullen prisoners included 29-year-old Capt. John S. Forrest and eighteen men of his Company I. Most of Captain Carnachan's Company B had been captured, including three of the four Gifford brothers from Tioga County. The youngest sibling, 16-year-old Hiram, managed to escape detection.[101]

Darkness fast approached. In Gettysburg, General Early ran out of time before he could enforce his ransom demands. "The day was cold and rainy and the roads were very muddy, and as it was late when I reached the place," he later wrote, and desired to move upon York early next day, I had no opportunity of compelling a compliance with my demands on the town or ascertaining its resources, which, however, I think were very limited." Early accordingly halted the canvassing for supplies. Whatever liquor remaining in the hotels and taverns was gathered up, and medicines and drugs confiscated with the promise of future payment. Some unruly Confederates forced open a clothing store and rifled it, taking everything they could carry off. A few even entered the merchant's private living quarters and walked away with the quilts from his beds and his personal clothing.[102]

Gordon's regiments reformed and began marching eastward to camp along the York turnpike, passing Sarah King's house as they did so. From her porch

100 Kesterson, *Campaigning with the 17th Virginia Cavalry,* 288; Wheeler, *Eyewitness to Gettysburg,* 82-83. According to Henry Richards (p. 12), two militiamen escaped detection and returned to Gettysburg on June 30. Pvt. A. Stanley Ulrich of Company E and Pvt. James K. Moore of Company C had been cut off from their commands. Refusing to surrender, they stayed hidden until it was safe to travel. On July 1 during the Battle of Gettysburg, they fought alongside Company K of the 121st Pennsylvania (Biddle's Brigade) and helped bury the dead afterwards. See also Pennypacker, *Pennsylvania at Gettysburg,* 786.

101 Lovelace, *The Shrivers: Under Two Flags,* 43; George R. Prowell, *History of York County, Pennsylvania,* 2 vols. (Chicago: J. H. Beers, 1907), 1, 404; Hiram H. Gifford, 1892 Declaration for an Original Disability Pension, NARA; OR 27, pt. 2, 465.

102 *SHSP* 10, 540; *Macon (Ga.) Weekly Telegram,* July 16, 1863.

Sarah observed that several soldiers wore piles of hats on their heads, and strings of muslin and other goods trailed on the ground. Horses were piled high with blankets, quilts, and shawls, "altogether a laughable sight . . . they were having a good time." She felt sympathy for them, "ragged and with a look of hunger in their eyes." Some had crownless or brimless hats, worn-out shoes, and one man was missing one entire leg of his pants. As they marched by, a Rebel asked her son, "Bub, would you like to shoot a Rebel?" A couple of stragglers stopped by and asked for bread and butter. They crossed the street and sat on another porch eating, when one Georgian offered the chilling remark, "I think the people of this place are very kind considering we came here to kill off their husbands and sons."[103]

Early dispatched a courier to David Kendlehart's house to summon the council president. However, his daughter Margaretta calmly told the aide that her father was not home, just as he slipped out the back door to safety. Kendlehart did not return until the Confederates had left town. "After matters had been satisfactorily arranged between our Burgess and the Rebel officers," recalled Fannie Buehler, "the men settled down and the citizens soon learned that no demands were to be made upon them and that all property would be protected. Some horses were stolen, some cellars broken open and robbed, but so far as could be done, the officers controlled their men. The 'Louisiana Tigers' were left and kept outside of town."[104]

However, the Tigers and the rest of Early's Division were not idle. Despite the drizzle, foragers scoured the countryside and sent wagonloads of corn, oats, hay, meat, and other supplies to Chambersburg. They also appropriated "every farm animal that walked." Some of Early's Rebels accosted William Starry at Erstweiler's general store in Mummasburg. They forced him and other residents to drive herds of captured cattle south into Virginia. Some cavalrymen near Gettysburg ransacked the empty Boyer house, abandoned by its owners. They carried window shades and pictures to the woods and used the dough tray to feed their horses. They poured a jar of black cherries down the stairs, cut open a chaff bed, and spread it over the sticky syrup. Finally, a Rebel wrote on the wall, "Done in retaliation for what was done in the south." They stole a three-bushel bag of flour and took it to a neighbor's house, where they had her

---

103 *Gettysburg Compiler*, July 6, 1906; Slade, *Firestorm at Gettysburg*, 31-32.

104 Buehler, *Recollections of the Rebel Raid*, 15.

make shortcake while they waited on the porch. One offered her a fifty-cent silver piece as payment.[105]

Pickets out on the Hanover Road arrested a mud-caked traveler whom they suspected was really a Federal recruit arriving in town after a lengthy march. He was escorted to the Eagle Hotel and placed under the guard of a lieutenant and a private, likely from Clement Evans' 31st Georgia. The man protested that he was a New York newspaper correspondent, but the Confederates locked him up anyway. When about two hours later they initiated a "scrutinizing examination" that convinced them he was indeed a reporter, they released the man and allowed him to roam freely amongst the Rebel troops, which had been his goal all along. To his delight, he managed to interview several leading officers. The newspaperman located Jubal Early just as the general handed a copy of Lee's orders respecting private property to a citizen. Early, he later wrote, was a "tall and well looking personage, very dignified and gentlemanly in his demeanor . . . a capacious brown felt hat, looped up at the right side, resting easily on his head."[106]

Haller Retreats to York

While the Rebels strengthened their grip on Gettysburg, Union Maj. Charles Knox assembled a motley group that had dodged French and White's patrols. A handful of First City Troopers, some supply wagons, and remnants of Bell's cavalry followed Knox to Hanover. From time to time more cavalrymen, including Bell and his contingent, caught up with the column. Bell sent a messenger on a swift horse ahead to Hanover, carrying the unwelcome news that Jennings' regiment had been "cut to pieces and scattered as chaff before the driving blast."[107]

It was nearly dark when the exhausted column arrived in Hanover and dismounted. Knox updated Haller on the day's events. A few men were given fresh mounts and ordered to patrol area roads. Any missing troopers encountered should be sent directly to York, the new assembly point. The first town that Haller planned to defend had fallen, and now Gettysburg was in John

---

105 Samuel Bushman and Sue Black King accounts, ACHS.

106 *Macon (Ga.) Weekly Telegram,* July 16, 1863.

107 *Hanover Spectator,* July 17, 1863.

Gordon's hands. At 8:00 p.m., Daniel Trone wired another terse message from Haller to Couch:

> Major Knox and Captain Bell have arrived. Rebels in Gettysburg. Ran our cavalry through town; fired on them; no casualties. Horses worn out. Ordered all troops to York, to rendezvous at Camp Franklin. Will be in York at midnight. Cavalry, officers and men, did well. Major Knox specially mentions Cpl. J. R. Wood, Private William A. Davis, and Private George W. Colkett.[108]

Haller sent a late-night telegram to York informing the Committee of Safety that Gettysburg had fallen and its defensive force retreated. He seethed with anger at Colonel Jennings for pulling out without authorization, raging that the "slow and cautious advance of the enemy" should have allowed the militia ample time to reach Hanover unmolested. As the forty-man commissary guard had not suffered any losses despite leaving Gettysburg later than he did, Haller firmly believed that Jennings' entire regiment should not have lost a single man.[109]

Haller accompanied Knox's horsemen as they trudged out of Hanover toward York. They did not arrive until well past midnight, when they entered a military camp on the fairgrounds for some welcome rest. The bulk of Randall's First City Troop had exchanged shots with some of White's cavalry "long after the middle point of the journey," but had countermarched and avoided capture. They arrived in York between 9 and 10 p.m. and received much better quarters. The rain had turned the soft country roads into a morass of mud, and the hooves of the forward platoons splattered muck into the faces of those who followed, making the troopers unrecognizable. One cavalryman, William Canby, grandson of flagmaker Betsy Ross, wore a military coat with a huge cape that he used to shield his face. However, mire covered all the rest of the troopers from head to heel. After bathing, they slept under clean sheets in the comfortable beds of a downtown York hotel. It had been a strange day for the Philadelphia gentry. That morning, they breakfasted in a fine hotel in Gettysburg and then dodged rain and Rebels for thirty miles; now, most of

---

108 *OR* 27, pt. 3, 344. J. R. Wood, William A. Davis, and George W. Colkett were First City Troopers who had accompanied Captain Bell to Hanover, Pennsylvania. Camp Franklin, established earlier in the war on the York fairgrounds, was named in honor of Maj. Gen. William B. Franklin.

109 Haller, *Dismissal of Major Granville O. Haller*, 69.

them rested in a comparable York establishment. Hostlers groomed and fed their jaded horses at a nearby public stable.[110]

Trooper Jones Wister received special treatment from Michael Schall, a prominent York businessman. Schall co-owned the Empire Car Works, a company that built railroad oil tank cars using iron purchased from Wister's Duncannon Iron Works. Wister wearily undressed in his friend's house and washed. Schall gave Wister a good breakfast while the trooper's uniform was scraped and cleaned. After "a couple hours of loving care and a much-needed nap," Wister was "fairly presentable."[111]

Meanwhile, while the First City Troopers and Bell's exhausted cavalrymen rode into York, dozens of foot-weary militiamen slogged along the turnpike. They somehow avoided Elijah White's patrols. Captain Walker's commissary train guards, "who had been entrusted with its care had no resource but to walk to Hanover. They ventured to go to bed (almost worn out) at the town of [New] Oxford, on the route, but were obliged to wake up and 'skedaddle' at midnight. They all reached Hanover in safety," according to a Philadelphia newsman covering the story. After a brief rest, they too headed on to the rendezvous point in York.[112]

Flames in the Gettysburg Night

In Gettysburg, Colonel Evans' band resumed playing patriotic Southern airs in the square. To 15-year-old resident Albertus McCreary, it was "very exasperating" to hear them "through the night." Several Georgians chopped down the municipal flagpole in the center of the Diamond. Rebels discovered two thousand rations in a railcar, food intended for Jennings' militiamen. Early ordered them seized and distributed to Gordon's Brigade. A couple cars contained private property such as mowing machines and leather; the Rebels removed the goods and set them aside to later be claimed by their owners. Early also ordered Gordon's men to protect a private car belonging to George Strickhouser, a boarder at the downtown Globe Inn. Innkeeper Charles Wills and his son John carried six barrels of whiskey, forty bushels of potatoes, three

---

110 *Philadelphia Press*, July 20, 1863

111 Wister, *Reminiscences*, 160-61.

112 *Philadelphia Inquirer*, June 30, 1863.

barrels of sugar, a barrel of syrup, and several hams and shoulders of cured meat back to their hotel.[113]

Meanwhile, other soldiers torched the railroad's covered bridge spanning Rock Creek. After stealing what was left of the militia's baggage, some Rebels came up with the idea to ignite much of the rolling stock and start it down the track toward the burning bridge with the hope that as it collapsed, the cars would tumble into the creek. To their dismay, the flaming rail cars passed safely across the span and were consumed just beyond it. Elizabeth Thorn watched from a window in the Evergreen Cemetery gatehouse as the blazing railcars descended the grade.[114]

Because Gettysburg had no railroad buildings of any consequence, Early spared the town from further destruction, other than telegraph lines and rails. All the same, apprehensive townspeople watched the glowing red sky, wondering if the entire borough would be put to the torch. Newspapers reported that Union forces had looted and burned the seaport of Darien, Georgia, on June 11. Because Gordon's Brigade was from that state and might want vengeance, many Gettysburg residents had trouble sleeping. Some kept loaded guns handy.[115]

Sallie Broadhead was uneasy throughout the long night. "I was left entirely alone, surrounded by thousands of ugly, rude, hostile soldiers, from whom violence might be expected," she wrote. "Even if the neighbors were at hand, it

113 Albertus McCreary, "Gettysburg: A Boy's Experience of the Battle," *McClure's Magazine* (July 1909), Vol. 33, 243-53; *Macon (Ga.) Weekly Telegram,* July 16, 1863: *Gettysburg Compiler,* April 24, 1907; Charles Wills account, GNMP. The McCreary house was at the southwest corner of Baltimore and High streets. James Gettys, founder of Gettysburg, opened the Globe Inn (10 York Street) in 1798. For weeks before the invasion, Charles Wills suspected that certain guests might be spies. His building was headquarters for the Adams County Democratic Party. On June 26, as Rebels occupied town, he recognized one of Early's aides as a former patron who, three weeks before, paid for his dinner with a silver quarter.

114 Thorn account, GNMP; Early, *War Memoirs,* 258; *Gettysburg Compiler,* June 29, 1863. The Rebels burned seventeen railcars, including a private car owned by Wm. E. Bittle, two belonging to Stein & Young, one of the Hanover Branch Railroad, two from the Northern Central, and the eleven cars of the Pennsylvania Railroad that had transported Jennings' regiment and supplies to Gettysburg. Other cars full of lime were spared the torch. One car was full of muskets, which the Rebels did not take as they "had enough already."

115 The 54th Massachusetts, the black regiment with eighteen men from Columbia, accompanied the 2nd South Carolina to burn Darien. The undefended town of 500 people was of little military importance, sparking immediate controversy. The glow from the fire could be seen 15 miles away on St. Simons Island, a Federal camp. Only one church and three small houses were salvageable, as well as one other structure (OR 28, pt. 2, 11).

was not pleasant, and I feared my husband would be taken prisoner before he could return, or whilst trying to reach me." Others, however, took comfort from the Rebel guards patrolling the streets to prevent looting or damage to private property. Like Granville Haller, some went to bed furious that the militia had not put up a stiffer fight. However, young Tillie Pierce expressed kind words for the inexperienced boys of the 26th Militia. "The stand they made, and the valor they displayed before an overwhelming force, cannot fail in placing the loyalty and bravery of her citizens in the foremost rank."[116]

Residents noted hundreds of campfires westward toward South Mountain, indicating the presence of thousands more Confederates. The Louisiana Tigers spent the night west of Gettysburg near Oak Hill and Willoughby Run, their fires fueled by rails taken from fences along Mummasburg Road. White's horsemen camped two miles east of town along the York Road, with picket outposts extending to New Oxford. Many groomed newly acquired mounts before retiring. Gordon's Brigade billeted on the nearby Wolf farm, with Capt. William A. Tanner's Courtney Artillery close by after rolling through Gettysburg during the evening. Charles C. Williams, a private in the 26th PVM held prisoner by the Georgians, noted that General Gordon made an impassioned speech to his men in the woods.[117]

Another militiaman alleged, "On Friday night, after their exploit, the enemy encamped on Wolf's farm, half a mile from Gettysburg. They told Wolf that their force was eight thousand cavalry and infantry. They were commanded by General _____, who gave Wolf a pass and sent him to Hanover to buy, beg, borrow, or steal a horse, threatening him that, unless he should return with the animal, he (Wolf) would find his house destroyed." The note bore the signature of Gordon's adjutant, Capt. George Robinson.[118]

---

116 Broadhead diary entry for June 27, 1863, ACHS; Alleman, *At Gettysburg*, 27. Joseph Broadhead had taken the train to Hanover Junction. Fellow railroaders told Sallie that he had been captured and paroled, and had gone to Harrisburg. On June 29, at 9 a.m., he started walking 36 miles home to Sallie, reaching Gettysburg at 1 a.m. on June 30.

117 Hodam manuscript; Washington (D.C.) *Evening Union*, June 27, 1863; *New York Herald*, June 29, 1863.Some authors place Early in a tent near the Louisiana Tigers east of Willoughby Run. However, Early in his memoirs (page 258) states, "With the rest of the command, I moved at light the next day (the 27th) from Mummasburg."

118 *Philadelphia Inquirer*, June 30, 1894. The newsman added, "The singular spectacle would therefore have been presented of a good Union man hunting in a good Union town (Hanover) for a horse for a rebel general. This spectacle was prevented by the Provost Guard of Hanover, to whom Mr. Wolf was handed, having been arrested while on one horse soliciting another."

Well after dark, a Georgia lieutenant and three privates entered the Globe Inn and compelled Charles Wills to roll three barrels of whiskey up from the cellar. The enlisted men carried off the alcohol. At 11:00 p.m., the officer returned and wrote out an order on the Confederate government. When Wills demanded good money, the Rebel curtly responded, "In two months our money will be better than yours as we may remain in your state an indefinite time." He left the draft and departed. In the middle of the night, Wills, his son, and their "colored help" removed the remaining supplies from the cellar and hid them in a loft above the rear of the building. They dug a trench in the garden and placed in it two barrels each of whiskey, brandy, and gin. After covering the casks with boards and a layer of dirt, they planted cabbage over the freshly turned earth.[119]

Gordon had assigned the 31st Georgia to safeguard Gettysburg. Later during that raw and cool evening the company of Arnett Rifles guarded the two Yankee officers and 36 militiamen locked in the courthouse. Exhausted from the day's wet twenty-mile march and his strenuous efforts to break up the Louisiana Tigers' brawl, Pvt. Gordon Bradwell collapsed on a bench in the courthouse in front of a red-hot stove. In just a few minutes, he "was oblivious to everything until at earliest dawn the rattle of the drum aroused us to resume our march." According to Col. Clement Evans, "The town was kept very orderly & quiet. The citizens expected us to revel & riot all night, burning & destroying property. They were therefore very much surprised at the quiet of the town."[120]

According to the *Adams Sentinel*, the Rebels' "deportment in general was civil. Many of them courted conversation, and were not disposed to interfere with anybody for exercising the largest liberty of speech. In capturing horses, etc., they made no distinction, Republicans and Democrats suffering alike." However, the political rivalries intensified the bitterness between the parties. The rival Democratic paper, *The Compiler*, would later castigate Republican

---

The pass which he carried was in the following words: Mr. George Wolf has gone to his place after a horse for me. The pickets will please pass him. June 26, 1863, George Robinson, Adjutant." Robinson was the captain of Company K of the 38th Georgia before becoming Gordon's adjutant.

119 *Gettysburg Compiler*, April 24, 1907; Charles Wills account, GNMP. The buried liquor became water-soaked in a July 4th rainstorm, ruining its value. Wills later "disposed of it by selling some off cheap, and giving it away and throwing some out."

120 Bradwell, "Burning of Wrightsville," 330; Stephens, *Intrepid Warrior*, 218.

David McConaughy for having "urged the Major in command . . . to send the 26th Regiment, P. M., into the jaws of the enemy."[121]

June 26, 1863, was a day to remember for Sallie Broadhead, Tillie Pierce, Elizabeth Thorn, and hundreds of other citizens. Many believed that Adams County had finally seen the war firsthand, and that it would now surely pass them by. Little did they know that within one week Gettysburg would be forever immortalized.

121 *Adams County Sentinel*, June 27, 1863; *Gettysburg Compiler*, July 13, 1863.

Chapter 6

Gordon Reaches York County

The Gray Shadow Stretches Eastward

After capturing Gettysburg, Maj. Gen. Jubal Early planned to occupy the prosperous town of York. Situated fewer than thirty miles from Lt. Gen. Richard S. Ewell's primary goal of Harrisburg, York was an important secondary target. The vital Northern Central Railway that connected Harrisburg to Baltimore (and extending by a short journey through Baltimore's harbor-side streets to the B&O terminal, southward to Washington, D.C.) ran through the town. Early wanted to sever this railroad and destroy any related manufacturing sites. His cavalry would burn railroad bridges, rolling stock, and warehouses. They were to cut telegraph wires, destroy transmitters, and inflict as much damage as possible to the infrastructure—culverts, tunnels, switches, and tracks.[1]

Ewell authorized Early to collect a duty from the citizens and secure any useful military supplies. Although Pennsylvania cities had been spared the torch so far, few doubted that a conflagration was a real possibility if Confederate demands were not met. Two weeks before, Union troops, including Pennsylvania-born blacks in the 54th Massachusetts, had indiscriminately set fire to Darien, Georgia. The previous fall, Federal artillery severely damaged Fredericksburg, Virginia. In rumor-crazed Pennsylvania, many believed the Rebels would eventually pick a town to level, extracting revenge for Northern

---

1   The NCR terminated at a station on President Street. Travelers walked or took public transportation to Camden Station, from which the B&O departed.

atrocities. York citizens grew anxious, including 34-year-old Cassandra Morris Small, daughter of wealthy businessman Philip Albright Small. When news came that an immense force of Rebels threatened York, the women and children were "dreadfully terrified."[2]

Early planned a three-pronged approach to York so his troops would cut the broadest swath to acquire fresh horses and supplies. He retained the infantry brigades of Brig. Gen. Harry Hays, Col. Isaac Avery, and Brig. Gen. William "Extra Billy" Smith. The bulk of Col. William French's 17th Virginia Cavalry would lead the way. Three batteries of Lt. Col. Hilary Jones' artillery battalion would follow the infantry. Early's column would use an east-west dirt road from Hunterstown to East Berlin. Shortly thereafter, his force would enter York County. After camping, they would continue eastward to Weigelstown and Emigsville the next day before turning south to enter York.[3]

Slightly to the south of Early, Brig. Gen. John Gordon's brigade and Capt. William Tanner's Courtney Artillery were to use the paved Gettysburg–York Turnpike. Screening them would be Capt. Thaddeus P. Waldo's Company C of the 17th Virginia Cavalry, which reported early in the morning to Gordon's headquarters in George Wolf's barn. Gordon asked whether the men had eaten breakfast and if they had full haversacks. Private James H. Hodam related, "Most of us had a big loaf of bread and several kinds of canned stuff captured the day before. But Frank Ryan somehow always could find room for a little more, and he soon found an empty haversack which the General's black waiter filled with sugar crackers and then filled our canteens with strong coffee." Waldo's company was to be scouts and couriers.[4]

Gordon's expeditionary force, unencumbered by baggage wagons, would pass through York and march to the Susquehanna River at Wrightsville. His

---

2   Cassandra Morris (Small) Blair to Lissie Latimer, June 30, 1863, YCHT (Reprinted as *Letters of '63*, Detroit: Stair-Jordan-Baker, 1988). Three letters from Cassandra to her cousin were discovered 65 years later in a wooden box in the Latimers' attic. In 1864, she married Dr. A. G. Blair of York's U.S. Army Hospital. He had studied under Dr. Theodore Haller, brother of Maj. Granville Haller.

3   Kesterson, Hodam manuscript. Hodam noted, "Gordon took the road leading to the city of York, his command consisted of his own Georgia Brigade and Ex Gov. Wm. Smith's Virginia Brigade, four pieces of artillery and our company of cavalry (in all about seven to eight hundred men)." Stiles (*Four Years Under Marse Robert*) placed Smith's Brigade at the head of Early's column as it entered York, followed by Avery's Brigade.

4   *Ibid.* Company C was from Lewis County, WV. It mustered into service on Aug. 25, 1862, at Hillsboro under Capt. William Caleb Tavenner.

more direct route meant that Gordon would physically enter York before Early, thereby avoiding a traffic snarl. If the Yankees demonstrated any signs of mounting an aggressive defense, this pincer movement might trap them. It was almost exactly the strategy that Early planned at Gettysburg to ensnare Jennings' regiment. Early assumed that there would be even more militia assigned to defend York, an important manufacturing center. He was upset that so few militiamen had been captured at Gettysburg, and this time, he wanted to snare all of them. Their shoes were useful, as well as their new weapons, blankets, knapsacks, tents, and ammunition.

A third force would operate farther to the south. Lt. Colonel Elijah White's cavalry was to destroy telegraph lines and burn railroad bridges around Hanover Junction, where the Northern Central intersected the railroad to Hanover and Gettysburg. White was to locate any Yankees in the vicinity and seize any horses that could be found. The battalion left town at daylight, "branching off in various directions." The main body headed out the turnpike for Abbottstown.[5]

About 6:00 a.m. on Saturday, June 27, drums shook Early's men awake after what the general described as a "most uncomfortable and dreary" night. Because they had left most of their tents at Greenwood, almost all of his men had slept on "the naked ground, and their covering the sky above them." Shortly thereafter they departed Mummasburg and headed eastward. By 7:00 a.m. the rain abated after nearly 1.3 inches had soaked the Pennsylvania soil. Hays' Louisiana Tigers rejoined Early, leaving an injured man in a barn along Mummasburg Road in the care of Dr. John O'Neal, a Southern sympathizer. Even though it was early morning, the effects of alcohol were still present and made for difficult marching. According to Capt. William Seymour, "many of the men were drunk and caused me much trouble to make them keep up with the column."[6]

5   *Gettysburg Compiler,* June 29, 1863; OR 27, pt. 3, 377. Other detachments followed the railroad through New Oxford before turning south to Hanover. Gibson, *History of York County,* 686. State damage claims suggest that some of White's men followed Hanover Road.

6   Early, "The Invasion of Pennsylvania," 232; Seymour account, GNMP. Professor Michael Jacobs of Pennsylvania College kept detailed notes on the local weather: "The entire period of the invasion is remarkable for being one of clouds, and, for that season of the year, of low temperature. From June 15th until July 22nd, 1863, there was not an entirely clear day. On the evening of June 25th at 8 p.m. a rain began. . . . This rain continued at intervals until Saturday June 27th, at 7:00 a.m., the perception being in inches 1.280."

The 17th Virginia Cavalry had camped overnight near the Witmer Farm west of Hunterstown. Early's inspector general, Maj. Samuel Hale, paroled most of the remaining prisoners from Jennings' ill-fated 26th Militia, and 126 of them marched as a group toward Shippensburg. However in downtown Gettysburg, Col. Clement Evans did not release the two militia officers locked in the courthouse. Presumably detained to serve as guides, they rode sullenly at the head of Gordon's column when it departed at daylight.[7]

Several captives had escaped during the night and hid in some woods near Hunterstown. They watched as Early's "large army" marched north of Gettysburg, followed by 150 supply wagons. From their hilltop vantage point, they also saw another force (Gordon's) in the distance marching along the turnpike in the direction of York. When it was safe, the escapees exited the woods and began walking north toward Harrisburg.[8]

By 8:00 a.m., the last Rebels were en route to Hanover and York. Learning of their departure, a *New York Herald* reporter scribbled, "The bird has flown." Three scouts from Cole's Maryland Cavalry dashed into Gettysburg at 9:30. They captured two of Ewell's couriers, one a chaplain, who were seeking General Early. Alice Powers wrote, "Considering all things we were well treated, but when Saturday noon found the Rebels gone every citizen felt satisfied to have them depart."[9]

Marching four abreast along the turnpike, Gordon's Georgians followed Waldo's cavalrymen through eastern Adams County. Despite persistent clouds, the rain had stopped and it was now a pleasant morning with temperatures in the low sixties. The old pike, constructed in 1819, had a pulverized stone surface, so the soldiers did not have to worry about the mud that marked the roads and farm lanes to either side. However, men and horses soon were covered with fine powdery dust ground by wheels on the macadam. Many of

---

7   Maj. Samuel Hale, Early's acting adjutant and inspector general, was his nephew. Early paroled a total of 175 militiamen in Gettysburg and Hunterstown; it is unclear how many others escaped or were freed without paroles. Later that day in Shippensburg, they encountered some of Rodes' men, who stripped them of their shoes. They later hiked barefooted to Carlisle, where other Rebels confined them for twelve hours under guard in the market house. They were again paroled and finally allowed to head to Harrisburg (after receiving new shoes from residents).

8   Early, *War Memoirs*, 258; *Philadelphia Press*, June 30, 1863. Early's wagons did not clear the Gettysburg area until Saturday afternoon. OR 27, pt. 3, 377. The escapees reached Union lines on the evening of June 29.

9   Jacobs, *Notes on the Rebel Invasion*, 19; *Gettysburg Compiler*, June 29, 1863, and June 24, 1903.

the Rebels were bareheaded, and Gordon commented "altogether it was the most forbidding looking set of men doubtless."[10]

An infantryman marveled at the "most beautiful and highly cultivated country" he had ever beheld. "Everything that science could furnish had been applied to a soil already fertile. The houses were neat and well built. Everything was in the most perfect order, and everything that man or beast could want abounded in the greatest plenty." However, the primarily German inhabitants were "intensely afraid," and, except in the management of their sprawling farms, were "the most ignorant people" he had ever encountered. He added, "It seemed as they felt that the Northern people deserved severe treatment at our hands, and expected, as a matter of course, to get their share of it."[11]

The Pennsylvania Germans had one redeeming value: they were good cooks. "Those people make the most delicious bread I ever tasted," wrote a grateful Georgian. The women usually devoted one day a week entirely to baking, making all the bread they expected to need in the ensuing week. Like clockwork, the brigade seemed to march past every farmhouse just after baking day. The astonished soldier sated his appetite on "such oceans of bread I never laid eyes on before. They supplied us with milk, butter, and cheese in the most extravagant abundance."

Another Georgia soldier marching through the region believed that part of Pennsylvania was distinguished for its immense fields of waving grain ripened for the harvest and "nice large cherries, Dutch farmers, and ugly females." He lamented that "handsome females were much more scarce than Copperheads." Along with pretty girls, horses also seemed in unusually low supply for such an agrarian region because thousands had been driven across the Susquehanna River to keep them away from Confederate raiders. That didn't stop the Rebels from ranging far and wide in search of any remaining horses and livestock. Their efforts paid off when horses were discovered in the most unusual places,

---

10 *Atlanta Journal*, Sept. 16, 1888. Early in the 19th century Scotsman John L. McAdam developed a process to construct sturdy paved roads. He crowned the roadbed to allow water to run off. After side ditches were dug, large limestone rocks, one to three inches in size, were placed close together to form a base layer. The holes between the large stones were "chinked" (driven into place using a maul) with medium-sized stones. The gaps between the medium stones were filled with fine gravel. The process was repeated until the road was 9 to 12 inches thick. A cast-iron roller was often used to compress the layers. The first macadam surface in the U.S. was used in 1823 for a turnpike between Hagerstown and Boonsboro, Maryland.

11 *Mobile Advertiser & Register*, Aug. 9, 1863.

including parlors, living rooms, spring houses, and other highly unlikely temporary stables.[12]

Farmers protested vigorously in broken English as Gordon's men confiscated their animals—the Rebels did not own them and had not paid for them, they complained. In response, the soldiers offered Confederate currency, which the farmers rejected "with great indignation." They demanded good money—gold or Federal greenbacks. Gordon, who refused to use greenbacks for horses, offered to give the Dutchmen "an order on the President of the United States to pay for so many horses at so much per head," adding, "I don't suppose my drafts were honored, but I have never heard of their being protested, nor have they been returned to me. Such incidents were common on the road."[13]

The *Gettysburg Compiler* mentioned, "There is no doubt that large numbers of horses were taken by the rebels in the lower part of this county, inflicting heavy losses upon the owners. It is hoped that the invaders will be overtaken, severely punished, and the property of our citizens again restored to them."

York countian Phebe Angeline Smith wrote to her sister, "Lewis Larue brought his paps horses down yesterday going on down to cross they river over into Lancaster is whare they are nearly all aiming for," she wrote, "as thare has bin a proclimation sent on I think by they govener that they men are to take thare stock across they river till he can send men on to clear they rebels out." Many residents, however, chose to ignore Curtin's proclamation, much to the delight of the oncoming Confederates.[14]

Lieutenant W. C. Matthews relished that as the 38th Georgia marched toward York, they were "living on the best that the country afforded and gobbling up all the horses, wagons, cattle and sheep for miles on either side of the line of march." Besides appropriating horses and food, Southerners ripped down telegraph lines along the railroad from Gettysburg. They paused near Goulden's Station to torch a large warehouse filled with nearly a thousand bushels of grain. Nearby, Rebels visited Hann's warehouse, but did not destroy it after an excited Hann pleaded that it contained nothing intended for the

---

12 *Savannah Daily Republican*, Aug. 6, 1863. The author referred to himself as "Veritas," Latin for truth.

13 *Atlanta Journal*, Sept. 16, 1888.

14 *Gettysburg Compiler*, June 29, 1863; Phebe Angeline Smith to "Most cherished sister," June 1863, James W. Brown collection. Used by permission.

government. Later, they burned a wooden railroad bridge over Conewago Creek near the crossroads community of New Oxford.[15]

An excited civilian horseman rode through that village screaming, "The Confederates are coming; the Confederates are coming!" Peter Diehl owned a tannery on High Street, as well as a freight line to Baltimore. One of his Conestoga cargo wagons had just lumbered into his large barn when Diehl heard the alarm. He quickly summoned his 23-year-old son Charles and instructed him and another family member, Amos Lough, to gather up all the horses and move them to Lancaster County, where he thought they would be out of reach of the approaching enemy.[16]

Captain Waldo's cavalry patrols reported sporadic contact with Union cavalry videttes (likely Bell's men), but no major threat from militia. Reassured, General Gordon maintained a rather leisurely march through the lush countryside. Behind the Courtney Artillery, drovers pushed along a small herd of purloined Adams County cattle. New Oxford resident Lewis Miller later learned that Rebels had appropriated one of his prized horses. Days later, by sheer luck, he recovered the same animal after the battle at Gettysburg. Several other farmers along the turnpike also reported stolen horses, mules, and livestock.

As word of the Rebels' imminent arrival spread, the throng of refugees increased. In East Berlin, merchant C. A. Raffensperger quickly decided to move much of his inventory to safety. He asked teenaged brothers Charlie and Joseph Harlacher to take charge of a two-horse team hitched to a cover wagon loaded with silks and other dry goods such as boots and shoes, the store's account books, and some of Mrs. Raffensperger's jewelry and silk dresses. The boys joined a large caravan of area residents who headed eastward through

---

15 *The Sunny South*, Jan. 10, 1891; *Gettysburg Compiler*, June 29, 1863; Skelly account, GNMP. A detachment of Rebel cavalry likely caused this destruction. Goulden's (spelled Gulden's on modern maps) Station was near today's intersection of U.S. 30 and Centennial Road.

16 Elanine King, William L. Zeigler, and H. Alvin Jones, *History of New Oxford: Looking at the Past, 1874-1974, 100th Anniversary* (New Oxford, Pa.: Privately printed, 1974), 128-29. Diehl hauled farm produce, tanned hides, and local products to Baltimore, and returned with merchandise and dry goods for area stores. Lough and Charley Diehl made it as far as Zeigler's Church near Seven Valleys in York County, where on June 30 they encountered some of Jeb Stuart's cavalrymen guarding a portion of a captured Union wagon train. The Confederates confiscated all of Diehl's horses, though they were gracious enough to exchange them for several worn out animals. Rebels ordered them to fetch water and help care for the wounded before they released the pair in the early evening.

York County, taking with them enough food and horse feed for a two-day absence.[17]

Protecting York

While Gordon headed eastward, Maj. Granville Haller planned his defense of York, despite the paucity of trained troops. Captain C. Wilson Walker's detachment of the 26th Militia had marched late into the night, and his exhausted soldiers rested in Camp Franklin (formerly Camp Scott) at the local fairgrounds. The Patapsco Guards quartered at the army hospital, with about 200 stewards, orderlies, and invalids still recuperating from their wounds. In addition, a few members of the 87th Pennsylvania had hastily returned home to York after Maj. Gen. Robert Milroy's failed attempt to hold Winchester. Most were willing to fight again, but their numbers were insignificant. Darius Couch had previously assigned Col. William B. Thomas's 971-man 20th PVM to York County, but they were deployed to defend vital railroad bridges south of the town. There were a few civilian volunteers and scouts, but Haller knew he that needed thousands more men if he truly wanted to defend York. He had no artillery, and knew that the advancing enemy force included several guns with trained, seasoned crews.[18]

Captain Robert Bell's few available cavalrymen had fanned out across western York County, searching for intelligence on Confederate movements. One scout on the Abbottstown Road spotted nearly a hundred Rebel horsemen rapidly approaching York, but he did not see any other troops. Throughout the morning, other scouts sporadically contacted Rebel patrols, at times exchanging gunfire. No casualties resulted from the desultory shooting, but it served notice to the Southern officers that the militia might aggressively defend York. More of Bell's men, who had impressed or bought fresh horses since fleeing

17 *East Berlin News Comet*, April 24, 1942. Stuart's cavalry detained the boys and confiscated the wagon, horses, and goods on July 1 as they rode through York County.

18 The civilians were from Capt. David Z. Seipe's volunteer company. They organized in June and united with the First Battalion on guard and provost duty around York. In March of 1864 they mustered into service as Co. B of the 187th Pennsylvania Infantry and were assigned to the Army of the Potomac's Fifth Corps. The Pennsylvanians fought at Cold Harbor and during the Petersburg siege under Gen. Joshua L. Chamberlain. The company served as an honor guard for President Lincoln's body during funeral ceremonies in Philadelphia. Gibson, *History of York County*, 176.

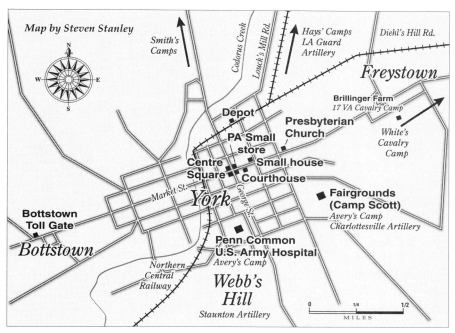

York, Pennsylvania, was a bustling commercial center with some 8,600 residents. Chief Burgess David Small was a prominent Democratic newspaperman.

Gettysburg, trickled into the fairgrounds on York's eastern outskirts. Major Knox sent them westward on additional scouting patrols.[19]

In a downtown hotel, Capt. Samuel Randall allowed his exhausted First City Troopers to rest until late in the morning. They quartered their horses in a nearby public stable, alongside those of private citizens. One Philadelphian had swapped his tired horse for a beautiful steed that he found some miles out after leaving Gettysburg. He boasted of this exchange and invited some of his comrades to inspect his good bargain. "Much to the smart Alec's chagrin," he found his own played-out horse in the same stall where he had left the pilfered steed. The troopers roared with laughter when it became apparent that "the countryman from whose field the horse had been taken quietly followed him to York, stabled his horse with the others, selected his own and rode away."[20]

19 Haller, *Dismissal of Major Granville O. Haller*, 72. Bell by now had sixty men in the Adams County Cavalry and Captain Randall counted about fifty First City Troopers.

20 Wister, *Reminiscences*, 161.

Reports filtered in about 1:00 p.m. that Rebel cavalry had occupied Hanover at ten o'clock that morning. Randall's men saddled up and rode out to the fairgrounds, increasing Knox's available cavalry to more than one hundred. They were kept standing for two hours, awaiting orders. Fortunately, the day was cool and overcast.

As the day wore on, Haller and his officers grew concerned about the fate of the 26th Volunteer Militia, which had not reported to York as expected, other than Captain Walker's contingent of commissary and supply wagon guards. At 1:00 p.m., York telegrapher Peter Bentz wired Major General Couch, "Nothing has been heard of Jennings' regiment. The attack on them commenced about three yesterday, by a large cavalry force, and continued to the last advices. The loss is not known, but it is reported that a number were taken prisoners."[21]

Inside the counting room of P. A. & S. Small's hardware store on the square, Haller conferred with York's Committee of Safety, which seemed to be "in a state of confusion." He advised the fifteen members that his force was inadequate to hold the town. However, he had orders to do so, and he advised them to prepare for battle. A few authorities concurred, but most urged Haller to abandon York. His men should either surrender or fall back to the river, where they could augment Wrightsville's defenses. Surrender was not an acceptable option to Haller. He argued that Couch had sent strict orders that the Confederates were not to cross the Susquehanna River under any circumstances. The long bridge at Wrightsville, where there was already a full regiment of militia in place behind earthworks, might be a good place to stop Early. Haller needed to defend York as long as possible in order to buy time for Wrightsville's defenders to strengthen their fortifications. He reminded the committee that he had asked them days ago to block the roads leading from Adams County. Their failure to do so had now taken on importance.

Some of the council restated their constituents' concerns that any armed resistance might lead to York being shelled or put to the torch. Haller pointed out that no such thing had occurred at Gettysburg. The leaders listened intently, but could not reach a consensus. They continued dithering, even as the enemy

---

21 Pennypacker, "Six Weeks in Uniform," 345. During the night, Jennings dispatched Lt. Col. Joseph Jenkins to York to locate Haller, but he could not reach it because of muddy roads and roving Rebel patrols. The 26th PVM made it to Dillsburg in northwestern York County, where a battalion of the 16th Virginia Cavalry threatened them.

drew closer. The frustrated major left the store and marched his men westward to the Bottstown tollgate. He ordered Knox's cavalry to leave the fairgrounds and move west of York "to attack the enemy." Haller wanted to ward off any marauding Southern cavalry patrols to buy enough time to remove the large quantities of hospital supplies and to send off the remaining rolling stock at the railroad yard. He dispatched the supply and baggage wagons of the 26th Militia and the First City Troop to Wrightsville, along with a few other wagons carrying supplies removed from York's warehouses. Railcars transported the rest of the military stores to Harrisburg. The committee members, still apprehensive that any resistance might cause the Rebels to take revenge on York, did not appreciate Haller's initiatives.[22]

Bell's scouts reported that more than a thousand horses were being shepherded toward York, heading for Columbia. Despite the hungry and thirsty throngs passing through town, all taverns and businesses were closed. Fleeing Adams Countians horrified listeners with tales of the ease with which Gettysburg had fallen and the speed of Haller's withdrawal. At York's railroad depot, workers feverishly loaded the few remaining freight cars with goods from private citizens and businesses. Adams County shopkeeper Ira Shipley arrived with a wagonload of merchandise from his store. Freight agent George Heckert packed the boxes in one of Wrightsville lumberman Henry Kauffelt's private railcars, sending it to the river town with the next train. Frederick Scott, in charge of York's machine shops, ordered his workmen to hide tools and supplies of oil in piles of cinders and in a freshly dug sewer trench.[23]

Farquhar Negotiates with General Gordon

That morning, young businessman Arthur Briggs Farquhar visited the Committee of Safety meeting. He was born September 28, 1838, in Sandy Spring in Montgomery County, Maryland, to Quaker parents. Farquhar was educated in Alexandria, Virginia, at the prestigious Hallowell School, where Robert E. Lee had studied. The self-confident entrepreneur had traveled to New York City to ask several leading millionaires and bankers how he too could earn his first million. Before the war, he joined a York manufacturing firm and

---

22 Gibson, *History of York County*, 421; *JMSIUS* (1908), Vol. 43, 287-88; Haller, *Dismissal of Major Granville O. Haller*, 72.

23 Adams County Damage Claims, Reel 9, ACHS; Gibson, *History of York County*, 209.

traveled throughout the South selling seed planters, plows, and machinery to plantation owners, including many who later became Confederate officers. He purchased the farm implement company after a devastating fire and rebuilt its factory, renaming it the Pennsylvania Agricultural Works.[24]

Farquhar listened to the vigorous debate in Small's counting room on York's course of action. He was intensely interested in protecting his fledgling business. He proposed that civic leaders negotiate directly with the enemy before they took any military action. Several in the room found Farquhar's suggestion to be preposterous. However, during the 1862 invasion of Maryland, he had crossed enemy lines to meet with Brig. Gen. Fitzhugh Lee and discuss the Rebels' intentions regarding York. Lee had assured him that the town was not a military target. Farquhar was certain that the Confederates would grant him another audience to discuss their present intentions.[25]

Fifty-year-old Republican attorney Thomas E. Cochrane, a former state senator, was skeptical about Farquhar's audacious idea. He bombarded him with questions: Who would make up the delegation that would meet with the Rebels? How many men should go? What ransom might the enemy ask for? Could York comply with their demands? Would the Confederates honor their part of any negotiated settlement? Travelers from Gettysburg had brought news that the Rebels had burned their railroad bridge, rolling stock, and other private property. Thaddeus Stevens' ironworks was now smoldering ruins. Would York fall prey to this type of wanton destruction, or did the important center of commerce face an even worse fate? Could the invaders be trusted? After all, they were traitors, observed another committee member.

Farquhar volunteered to be an emissary to the Rebels again. He was certain that if he headed west on the Gettysburg Pike, he would run into them. Few members of the Committee of Safety supported his proposal or offered to go with him. Alone, and without authority to speak for the council, he rode off in the early afternoon, driving his horse and carriage against the incoming flow of

---

24 Prof. Benjamin Hallowell (1799-1887) built a boarding school in 1824 at 609 Oronoco Street next door to the Lee family home. Despite his Quaker background, he prepared students such as young Robert E. Lee for admission to West Point, emphasizing mathematics. He sold the school in 1858.

25 Arthur B. Farquhar and Samuel Crowther, *The First Million: The Hardest: An Autobiography of A. B. Farquhar* (Garden City, NY: Doubleday, Page & Co., 1922), 69-73. Farquhar, a schoolmate in Virginia of W. H. "Rooney" Lee, asked for that officer. He instead met with Lee's cousin, Brig. Gen. Fitzhugh Lee.

refugees and livestock. Soon Farquhar was free of the congestion, and he proceeded at a brisk pace.

About fifteen miles west of York, he found the Confederates just inside the Adams County line. Gordon had paused for a midday break near Abbottstown. This village of log houses was normally a day's journey by horse or buggy from the Wrightsville crossing over the Susquehanna River. It had gained a reputation as a convenient stop for travelers in pursuit of a hot meal, liquid refreshment, and a warm bed. However, its famed hospitality did not extend to Gordon's invaders. Several Southerners crowded around Sara Steffan's water pump on the town square. After they quenched their thirst, she angrily buried the fouled tin cup in her yard. A provost squad of Evans' 31st Georgia sought out John M. Wolf, a Federal army recruiting agent and vocal opponent of the secret Copperhead organizations. Informants asked the Rebels to take him prisoner, but Wolf had received sufficient warning to escape before Gordon's arrival.

The general quizzed locals in the square as to the whereabouts of the Yankee militia. Aged immigrant Georges Jordy, a 66-year-old native of the Alsace region of France, insisted that the Unionists planned to defend York. Gordon tried to impress upon Jordy the size of the advancing Confederate army. However Jordy retorted that he had seen much bigger, and better, armies during Napoleon's Russian Campaign. Gordon suppressed a smile at the old man's insolence.[26]

Gordon instructed his pioneers to dig shallow earthworks for Tanner's artillery on a hill just north of Abbottstown. He gave his pickets strict orders to watch for approaching cavalry or militia. None were seen, but during the early afternoon, pickets near Beaver Creek spotted a carriage approaching on the turnpike. The driver identified himself as A. B. Farquhar and asked to see the commanding officer. Soldiers escorted him into the Confederate lines, where several officers denied him an interview with Gordon. Undaunted, the York businessman spotted a college friend from Maryland, Lieutenant Redik, and asked for help in accessing General Gordon.[27]

---

26 Files of the New Oxford library. Jordy had been a leader in an anti-temperance counter movement in the 1840s.

27 There is a Lt. William R. Redding, Jr. listed in the roster of the 13th Georgia; it is uncertain if this is "Lieutenant Redik." There were two men named Reddick in the 61st GA, but neither was an officer.

After Farquhar explained his intentions, Redik climbed into the buggy and escorted him to meet Gordon. Farquhar and the general had never met, but soon discovered they had mutual acquaintances. Their small talk over, Gordon demanded to know what business brought him to the Confederate camp. Farquhar professed to represent the "terribly frightened" women and children of York, and he wanted to buy them time to escape should Gordon intend to attack the militia or perhaps burn the town. Seeking reassurance that the Rebels' intentions regarding York were honorable, he intoned, "General Gordon, unless you have entirely changed from the character you used to have, you are neither a horse thief nor a bank robber, and fighting is more in your line than sacking a town."[28]

Although young, Farquhar was already an experienced negotiator and shrewd businessman. However, he had misjudged both his bargaining position and the extent of the knowledge that Gordon possessed regarding his target. The general, a pre-war lawyer, peppered Farquhar with questions about the force that guarded York. Farquhar answered the best he could, but Gordon soon cut him off, stating that he already knew their size and composition. A shocked Farquhar sat in silence as Gordon rattled off how many men were in the defenses at York and Harrisburg and who commanded them. Gordon further amazed his young adversary by mentioning the names of York's important persons, where they lived, and even their political leanings. He started describing the local road structure and then "took a little map of York County out of his pocket which had everything on it." Having seized the initiative, Gordon pressed home his requirements. York must not put up any opposition. In return, he would spare the town the kind of destruction that the Federal army had brought to Southern towns. The Confederates would not take any private property or molest anyone, but they would requisition necessary supplies. York would have to comply in full. Gordon made it clear that there would be no further discussion of this point.[29]

Some of Gordon's staff suspected that the smooth-talking businessman might actually be a spy sent to count the number of troops. Farquhar gave his word of honor that he would reveal nothing of what he had seen. If Haller's

---

28 Farquhar, *The First Million*, 75.

29 Cassandra Small to Lissie Latimer, June 30, 1863, YCHT. Farquhar had married an "intimate friend" of Cassandra's. Mrs. Farquhar apparently relayed to Miss Small the details of his meeting with Gordon.

men put up a fight, Farquhar agreed to return to Confederate lines to be hanged as a spy. Finally, the parties agreed upon the remaining terms, and Farquhar chronicled the points of agreement. He informed Gordon that having the general's signature on the meeting notes would give Farquhar credibility with the Committee of Safety, and would ease the minds of York's terrified women and children. Gordon complied, and after exchanging a few more pleasantries, Farquhar mounted his buggy and headed back to York County.

Unfortunately, Farquhar had not obtained the correct password, which would allow him to proceed readily through Confederate lines. Spurring his horse to a gallop, he raced through a gauntlet of Gordon's pickets before they could react. He was about 100 yards past the last picket line when a couple of bullets whizzed by his speeding buggy. Farquhar finally slowed the horse to a trot once he was satisfied that he was clear of any further Rebels. He saw a fair amount of debris lying alongside the pike, apparently cast aside by the crowds of refugees. Every now and then, he maneuvered around a broken carriage or abandoned wagon. After giving his horse a respite, Farquhar picked up the pace, riding "furiously" back toward York.[30]

Reaching town a little before 3:00 p.m., Farquhar met Granville Haller at his post on West Market Street and introduced himself. He detailed his dialogue with John Gordon and the negotiated terms by which the Rebels would peaceably enter York. Because Farquhar was a stranger to him, Haller suggested they find some reliable person to verify his story. Farquhar knew that Philip and Samuel Small trusted him, so he asked Haller accompany him into downtown.[31]

Together, they entered the Smalls' hardware store on Centre Square and showed Gordon's signature to the Committee of Safety. After Samuel Small vouched for Farquhar's honesty, Haller questioned the transplanted Marylander about the size and composition of Gordon's forces, as well as their intentions. Remembering his oath at the point of death, Farquhar refused to answer other than to say the enemy force was "immense," and contained infantry, artillery, and cavalry. Attorney Thomas Cochrane fretted that Farquhar had acted on his own, without any official sanction. Farquhar realized that he needed to act quickly, so he urged the committee to assign a small

30 Gibson, *History of York County*, 207. Farquhar commented that the last picket line was two miles east of Farmers, where Gordon's men encamped for the night.

31 Before the Civil War, Farquhar borrowed money from the Smalls to finance the acquisition of his employer's company.

delegation to ride back out to parlay with Gordon for more formal, legally binding terms. As a lawyer, Cochrane could help prepare such a document. Chief Burgess David Small and others agreed, moving the committee toward consensus.[32]

Those assembled in the closed store made two decisions. The defensive forces would withdraw to the Susquehanna, while a contingent of leading citizens would meet with General Gordon to ensure that the town would be spared. Haller protested again, but his arguments were in vain. He realized that he had insufficient troops to stop a determined Confederate advance, so he started making preparations to leave. He had telegrapher Peter Bentz wire General Couch that he was off toward Wrightsville and Columbia. The enemy was approaching York with their Gettysburg force, about four thousand men. The Rebels would respect private property if there was no military resistance, and the borough authorities had complied.[33]

While the officials deliberated, Northern Central engineer George Small's train steamed into York's depot shortly before 3:30 p.m. A larger train was preparing to leave later that afternoon. A reporter from the *Philadelphia Inquirer* climbed onto the roof of a railcar sitting on a siding. He hastily scribbled his notes about the "strange appearance" of the vicinity of the rail yard. "The streets leading to it from the town are full of women and children, hastening to obtain seats in the LAST train which will leave York until affairs are more quiet," he wrote. "This train is a medley of passenger, freight, cattle, and dirt cars and, in order to accommodate the ladies, soldiers have been stationed with muskets at the doors of the passenger cars, with instructions to allow no man to enter. The number of infants is astonishing, as [is] the number of colored persons."

The reporter continued:

> The latter conduct themselves with propriety, but the former are evidently angry at being torn from their homes, and join their infantile chorus to the shrill screams of the locomotives, the earnest words of railroad employees,

---

32 In 1836 David Small began a 49-year tenure as owner of the *York Gazette*, a Democratic mouthpiece and town newspaper. Politically and socially active, Small also served a stint as the borough's postmaster and the county's director of the poor. By 1863, he was among York's most prominent citizens and was highly influential particularly among fellow Democrat leaders, some of whom served on the Committee of Safety.

33 *OR* 27, pt. 3, 367.

and the commands of military officers who are loading the military and hospital stores on the cars. It is not long before a few wounded men are also carried along, and close behind them, with steps that totter, is an old colored woman, whose age is, apparently, so great that might have been the original one who fondled George Washington. The cars fill up rapidly and more climb upon the open trucks and into recesses intended only for freight. There is no undue haste, but an evident anxiety to leave the place as quickly as convenient, and in a manner as decorous as possible. A despatch received by the agent of Adams' Express Company, telling him to quit, does not lessen the bustle. The military forces, who are guarding the bridges near the town on the railroad, show no desire to follow their baggage and stores.

In addition, hundreds of residents had come to the depot to bid their friends good-bye. The massed throng was soon sprinkled with a cloud of dust.[34]

York was generally calm, but there was a growing sense of urgency. About 5:00 p.m., in accordance with the civic leaders' controversial deal with the Confederate commanders, Major Haller withdrew his men from their outposts west of town. His orders frustrated them. They had marched for an hour to a point four miles west of York, according to a wounded Fredericksburg veteran in the invalid battalion. Several soldiers were upset at the pointlessness of being ordered out to meet the enemy, and then being recalled. Nineteen-year-old Persifor Frazer, Jr. of the First City Troop complained, "Like that celebrated emperor, we walked to the top of the hill and came down again."[35]

Another Philadelphian sarcastically wrote, "The company of infantry that was in the town marched to the front, and they and the Troop drew up to await the enemy for purposes only known to the higher authorities; but after some time delaying in this way, they wended their way slowly back, through the crowds of able-bodied young men (who, it must be said to their credit, did look very anxious at the prospect of an Early occupation of their homes by the rebels) to the railroad depot, the Troop bringing up the rear."[36]

Major Haller's men had marched more than thirty miles since leaving Gettysburg and were about to abandon another town to John Gordon. With

34 *Philadelphia Inquirer,* June 30, 1863.

35 Wray, *History of the Twenty-third Pennsylvania,* 151-52; *JMSIUS* (1908), Vol. 43, 288.

36 *Philadelphia Press,* July 20, 1863.

great resignation, Haller informed them of their new destination. The bulk of the First City Troop and Bell's Cavalry would fall back on the turnpike to Wrightsville, some ten miles away. Major Charles Knox would retain a few horsemen to scout the roads west of York in case of a sudden Confederate advance during the night.[37]

The York battalion grudgingly headed back downtown, marching along Market Street past Cassandra Small's home. While her family sat drinking tea, they suddenly heard the strains of martial music. From their windows, they could see the town's "little force retreating—all of whom we knew." She recognized several local soldiers from Milroy's scattered 87th Pennsylvania, as well as some of the men from the military hospital. "Oh, how do you think we felt—and they, too," she wrote, "for they were leaving us to the mercy of the Rebels, but of course it was all right."[38]

Haller managed to scrounge up one last train for part of his force. Engineer George Small visited the railcar factories and "added a number of new and half-built cars to his train, on which a company of Union soldiers were also to be transported to Wrightsville." He coupled them to his locomotive, the "Susquehanna," and prepared to steam out of York. A few First City Troopers watched as Haller hurried much of his infantry into the railcars and departed. A *New York Tribune* reporter noted, "Major Haller, learning that he was likely to be outflanked, and that the enemy were in overpowering numbers, at 6 p.m. Saturday retreated to Wrightsville, Major Knox protecting his rear." There was some last minute excitement according to one of the invalids from the 23rd Pennsylvania, "We returned hastily and took the last train for Wrightsville, none too soon, for the mounted infantry [17th Virginia] of Early's Corps [division] appeared on all the hills and formed a cordon around the town. After an exchange of shots at very long range, we arrived at Wrightsville."[39]

York was now defenseless.

---

37 Gibson, *History of York County*, 206.

38 Cassandra Small to Lissie Latimer, June 30, 1863, YCHT.

39 George Small, 1905 *York Dispatch*; *History of the First Troop*, 75; Gibson, *History of York County*, 175; *New York Tribune*, July 2, 1863; Wray, *History of the Twenty-third Pennsylvania*, 152. Many of the railcars came from the Billmeyer & Small Company, proprietor of the York Car Works.

Chapter 7

White Raids Hanover Junction

Comanches on the Warpath

A Pennsylvania newspaper accused Rebel cavalry of raising the "gentlemanly" art of war to a new level of terror: "It was no unusual thing to see a fine quilt as a horse blanket, and while these demons were devastating the country, and robbing your house, you were subject to . . . vile abuse, such as 'you d__n abolitionist, if we would do as your men done in our country, we would burn your house and barn, and turn you to the woods. Now d__n you, we are in the Union again, and we intend to make it the hottest Union this side of h —, etc.'"[1]

As Confederate horsemen traversed eastern Adams County on Saturday morning, June 27, squads raided farms and spread fear among the nervous populace. The same Rebel yell heard at Gettysburg the previous afternoon rang out again as Lt. Col. Elijah White's battalion and Col. William French's Virginia "wildcats" rode from village to village. Many farmers heard the rattle of accouterments and the clatter of hooves as detachments of cavalrymen sought information, provisions, and most importantly, fresh horses and mules.

To the Pennsylvania German farmers, White's troopers were "Teufeln," or devils. Joseph H. Trundle, one of Company B's Marylanders, bragged, "We gave the old dutch in Penn. fits. Our army left a mark everywhere it went. Horses, cattle, sheep, hogs, chickens, spring houses suffered alike. They cried peace, peace most beautifully everywhere we went." In some cases, when told the horses already had been sent away to safety, the Rebels forced the farmers to

1 *Lancaster Daily Express*, July 8, 1863.

pay them the net value of the missing steeds. In one village, the thirsty Elijah White asked a young boy for cool milk. The lad complied, but the colonel, fearing the drink might be laced with poison, asked him to take the first sip.[2]

Cavalrymen visited the Rev. Benjamin Albert of Reading Township (near New Oxford) and took a gold American lever watch. Nearby, Joseph A. Smith had his bay mare stolen, and John Cashman and Daniel Sheely also lost horses. Reaching southeastern Adams County, the marauders appropriated two of Union Township farmer Daniel Geiselman's horses. After raiding several more farms for horses and food, White's six companies headed toward Hanover, an important stop on the railroad connecting Gettysburg and Hanover Junction. However, nearly all of the locomotives and rolling stock previously had been sent across the Susquehanna to Columbia, and the military stores had been loaded onto wagons or trains and sent to York by Maj. Granville Haller.[3]

Several Confederates expressed surprise at seeing so many able-bodied young men in the region, having expected the majority to be in the army. The reasons were many. Considerable numbers of local regiments had mustered out of the service, and many of the veterans had not re-enlisted. The area also boasted a large population of Mennonites, Dunkards (Brethren), and other Anabaptist pacifist sects, as well as Quakers. More than 100 congregations in Adams and York counties were denominations that did not condone war. However, the Civil War came to them as the Rebels arrived and systematically searched the district for horses and livestock.[4]

About 10:00 a.m., Lige White led his booty-laden troopers along the railroad tracks into McSherrystown. The village, just west of predominantly German-speaking Hanover, was an Irish-Catholic enclave. Several Rebels entered a dry goods store, after threatening to break in if co-owner Vincent Sneeringer did not open the locked door. They walked out with more than 400

---

2 Joseph H. Trundle, *Gettysburg Described in Two Letters from a Maryland Confederate* (Montgomery County, Md.: Montgomery County Historical Society, 1959), 211-12; James McClure, *East of Gettysburg: A Gray Shadow Crosses York County, Pa.* (York, Pa.: York County Heritage Trust, York Daily Record, 2003), 44.

3 Adams County Damage Claims, ACHS; *New York Tribune*, July 2, 1863.

4 James O. Lehman and Stephen M. Nolt, *Mennonites, Amish, and the American Civil War* (Baltimore: The Johns Hopkins University Press, 2007). According to Jonathan Stayer of the Pennsylvania State Archives, "156 York Countians sought exemption from military service on grounds of conscience in 1862, the sixth highest number in the counties of Pennsylvania. Even tiny Adams County was home to at least 129 conscientious objectors."

dollars worth of clothing and merchandise, as well as ten gallons of liquor. As White quizzed residents about the whereabouts of Yankees, a farmer slipped out of town and galloped to Hanover, where he cried, "The enemy will soon be here! They are now in McSherrystown!" Shortly thereafter, a Hanover clergyman verified the report. He had been traveling west on the McSherrystown Pike when he spotted Rebel cavalrymen in the distance. Wheeling his horse, he raced back to Hanover with the warning.[5]

One Hanoverian claimed that many citizens tarried to see the Rebels' entrance. Some of them "wistfully" peered down Carlisle Street, hoping to catch the first glimpse of the cavalry, which was now cautiously feeling its way into town in compact columns of fours. The witness added, "Their longing eyes were soon greeted with the sight of one, and then another horseman, with cocked pistols in their hands, moving slowly and steadily up the avenue and commanding all who attempted to flee to halt."[6]

Many of the 1,600 residents shuttered their windows, bolted doors, and huddled together for comfort. Few were eager to meet White, whose reputation as a raider preceded him. He sent a four-man patrol down Carlisle Street toward the center of town. Still clutching their pistols, the videttes could see eyes peering at them from half-shuttered windows. They were leery because reports were filtering in about enemy cavalry patrols operating in the region, and they worried about falling into a potential trap. Behind them, more than 150 cavalrymen slowly rode toward Hanover. Details fanned out around the outskirts to guard every road. They were to watch for Yankees and prevent residents from leaving town with their wagons and horses.[7]

In the public square, a group of well-dressed citizens waited anxiously near the market shed. They included 37-year-old Dr. William K. Zieber, the influential minister of Emmanuel's German Reformed Church. A talented bilingual speaker, Zieber was chairman of Hanover's Committee of Safety, which planned to surrender the town. At his side stood the Rev. Julius C. Kurtz,

5   Adams County Damage Claims, ACHS, Reily & Sneeringer claim; Prowell, *History of York County*, 1: 495. Among the items taken were 60 hats, 10 caps, 20 pairs of boots, 12 pairs of shoes, 100 yards of sheeting, as well as drawers, socks, pen knives, and handkerchiefs.

6   *Hanover Spectator*, July 17, 1863.

7   The 1860 Census has 1,632 people in Hanover. The June 19 *Hanover Spectator* wrote, "Our town has been in an intense state of excitement during the last few days. A thousand and one rumors are circulated in the course of the day."

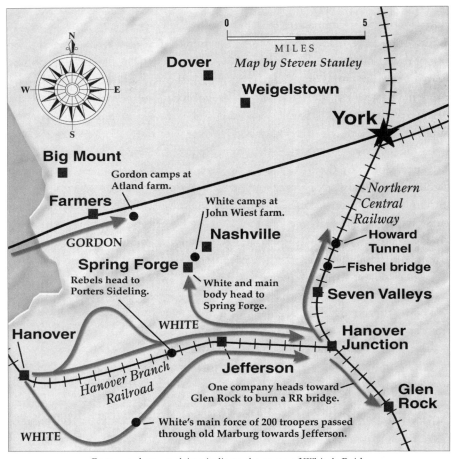

Post-war damage claims indicate the route of White's Raid.

who first spotted two advance videttes riding toward them. "There they come!" exclaimed Rev. Kurtz. When one of the Confederates commented on the many able- bodied men present who had not joined the Union Army, Zieber replied, "We will soon all join the Union Army." The soldier retorted, "The devil you say!"[8]

8 William Anthony, *Battle of Hanover* (Hanover, Pa.: s. n., 1945), 58. Dr. Zieber helped Hanover change from speaking German to English. By the end of his pastorate in 1882, he was conducting one sermon a month in German, reflecting the overall cultural shift toward English. Kurtz was associated with Zieber's church, having studied under the doctor. He pastored the West Manheim Reformed Church, also known as Sherman's Church or St. David's Church.

About 100 yards behind the advance pair rode the vanguard of thirty to fifty grimy cavalrymen, guided by a McSherrystown resident. They slowly approached Center Square. Their commander rode in the middle on a dark horse, probably procured from a Pennsylvania farm. A bugle blared, and the column halted in front of the Central Hotel. The leader introduced himself as Lieutenant Colonel White, sending a murmur through the gathering. They had not expected him to look like a Southern gentleman, albeit one in a well-worn and very dirty gray suit. To one observer, he "seemed to be an excitable, impetuous sort of personage, of large build and auburn complexion." White assembled his soldiers in the square, allowing them to dismount and water their horses. Sensing "wonderment mingled with fear," he decided to make a brief speech. In language "more forcible than elegant," he informed the gathering that his men were all true Southern gentlemen fighting for a cause that they believed was right. As such, they would do no harm to the town or its people. The small crowd breathed an audible sigh of relief.[9]

To the north, a large group of Rebels rode about the rail yard. An officer called out, "Where is the telegraph office?" Inside, operator Daniel Trone wired Hanover Junction, "The Confederates are here and I guess I will pull up." He started dismantling his equipment and slid the sounder into his pocket. Trone and his assistant left the station house through the front door just before a few cavalrymen entered the back. Trone "skipped across town" to his Frederick Street home. He dashed upstairs and grabbed sufficient cash to assist in his flight to a place of safety. The intruders failed to find the new transmitter, battery, and sounder the quick-thinking Trone hid in a wooden box in the loft. They ransacked the office and smashed a pair of old transmitters on a table, not realizing they were inoperable. In another room, freight agent Joseph Leib and another man heard the commotion. They also escaped, desperately pumping a handcar down the tracks toward Hanover Junction while Rebels fired at them.[10]

Confederates cut the telegraph lines that Haller used the previous night to announce the fall of Gettysburg. In nearby Hanover Junction, the alarmed operator wired at 1:00 p.m., "Telegraphic communication with Hanover stopped half an hour since. The inference is that the Rebels are there. There is no station between here and there to ascertain the fact." While operators

9   John Gibson, *History of York County*, 213.

10 *Gettysburg Compiler*, Oct. 20, 1909; Prowell, *History of York County*, 1, 406; Anthony, *History of the Battle of Hanover*, 68.

relayed the dire warning to other nearby towns, White's men busily destroyed rails and switches at Hanover. A few cavalrymen entered the express office and rummaged through the parcels. Eighteen-year-old Daniel Skelly worked for Gettysburg's Fahnestock Brothers dry goods store. He watched Rebels open a large package addressed to his employer and appropriate its contents, a shipment of gloves. A dozen howling cavalrymen chased Abdiel Gitt and another resident through a street near the station house. They fired a dozen shots in the air, but the two men escaped.[11]

Fleeing telegrapher Daniel Trone, after walking about a mile out Westminster Road, noticed a horse and rider approaching him. He called out, "Don't go into town! The Rebels will capture your horse!" The farmer calmly replied, "Well, I must go to Hanover, but I will lend you my horse and you can ride to Westminster." Trone rode sixteen miles to the Maryland town. After putting the borrowed horse in a stable, he spread the news of the Confederate raid, boarded a train, and made for Baltimore.[12]

Unlike the excited telegrapher, Elijah White felt relieved. His men had not encountered any resistance in Hanover and they had seen no Yankees since Jennings withdrew from Gettysburg the previous day. He ordered a short rest break. Pairs of pickets positioned at the ends of streets stopped incoming and outgoing traffic, whether Copperhead or Unionist. Rebels accosted carriage maker A. N. Michael and commandeered his nine-year-old roan and his saddle and bridle. He dejectedly walked home.[13]

Virginians and Marylanders entered shops and warehouses, searching for supplies, food, cutlery, and clothing. They often paid with Confederate scrip.

---

11 *Albany Evening Journal*, June 29, 1863; Daniel A Skelly, "A Boy's Experiences in the Battle of Gettysburg" (Gettysburg, Pa.: s. n., 1932). During previous rumored incursions, Skelly helped pack the Fahnestocks' inventory in a chartered railcar bound for Philadelphia. Hanover had two glove manufacturers, Henry Winebrenner (whose tannery figured prominently in the June 30 battle of Hanover) and Wolf Brothers. Skelly used a handcar the next day to try to get home, but walked from New Oxford because Gordon had burned the railroad bridge over Conewago Creek. His brother Johnston, 87th Pennsylvania, was mortally wounded at Second Winchester.

12 *Gettysburg Compiler*, Oct. 20, 1909. Trone reached Baltimore safely that evening. On June 28 he met George Grove and several other Hanover refugees. They stayed in contact throughout the week and heard about the battle at Hanover. They arrived via omnibus in Hanover on July 3 while artillery at Gettysburg thundered in the distance. Three Trones fought on June 26 at Witmer Farm in Hanover's Company I of the 26th PVM.

13 RG-2, Records Relating to the Civil War Border Claims, York County Damage Claims #6177-89, Records of the Department of the Adjutant General, Pennsylvania State Archives, Harrisburg, Microfilm reels 19-31.

They stuffed their saddlebags, but most of the apparel and dry goods had been sent out of town. However, gleeful soldiers pillaged Heiman's Clothing, where full shelves indicated the owner had not followed suit. Other Confederates noticed a telegraph pole in front of the Grove Brothers store, but no wires were attached. George Grove had hidden them, along with an auxiliary transmitter, before he skedaddled to York. Other cavalrymen ransacked Wintrode's Hotel, breaking open cabinets and forcing the safe. The nearby Hanover Savings Bank was empty, having sent off its assets.[14]

Shoes and leather goods were particular targets because Hanover had three tanneries. Several Southerners approached Joseph C. Holland's shoe store on Baltimore Street. Holland had sent most of his inventory away, and his store was closed. Waving pistols, Rebels demanded that he unlock the door. "I don't like that," Holland defiantly declared, "and you are cowards if you continue it. If you want to go in my store, I will open it." Angry troopers ransacked his nearly empty shop, stealing the few remaining pairs of men's shoes.[15]

A thirsty officer entered A. G. Schmidt's drug store, hung his sword belt over a desk post, and demanded whiskey. Schmidt did not sell liquor, but he took an empty medicine bottle across the street to John Irving's hotel and bought some for the shocked Rebel. Other troopers came in later to buy soap, brushes, and combs for themselves, and several acquired fine-toothed ladies' combs to send home. The officer, still sitting in a chair savoring his whiskey, told the druggist that he should only accept greenbacks. Schmidt declared that the soldiers could take whatever they really needed and not worry about payment. He did accept a few Confederate bills, keeping them as souvenirs.[16]

Another Rebel handed a draft on the Confederacy to a merchant, intending to pay a hefty bill for a stack of merchandise he had on the counter. The skeptical shopkeeper asked if he could redeem this certificate if he visited the South. The trooper admitted "It would not be worth a darn," and walked away with the goods leaving the dismayed owner with the worthless document. A resident later complained the Rebels were "common robbers" because they knew their money and bank drafts were valueless. He also grumbled Hanover's

---

14 Grove Brothers, on Frederick Street near the Central Hotel, were candy manufacturers and dealers in watches and jewelry. George Grove maintained a telegraph station in the store.

15 McClure, *East of Gettysburg*, 45.

16 Gibson, *History of York County*, 54. A. G. Schmidt became Hanover's Chief Burgess in 1878. The drugstore was at the northeast corner of the town square.

Copperheads openly had welcomed the Rebels, "As the carrion crows will collect around their stinking feast, so our sympathizers flocked around these vagrant thieves to . . . ingratiate themselves into their good graces."[17]

Several Confederates traded played-out horses for fresh mounts, at times using dire threats to get their way. Others exchanged Confederate currency for new horses. A staff officer wanted his lame horse re-shoed. Locating a blacksmith shop on Baltimore Street, he asked a group of townsmen standing across the street where the owner was. Blacksmith Peter Frank identified himself and said that he wasn't working; it was a holiday. When asked why it was a day off, he replied, "The Johnnies are in town," and he was not open for business with Rebels. However, he complied when the officer reached for his pistol. Entering his shop, Frank fanned the fire with his bellows and went to work. The Southerner pulled out a large wad of Federal greenbacks and left two dollars for Frank's trouble and the horseshoes. A surprised Frank told him that if there were more Rebels with that kind of good money who also needed blacksmith services, the officer should send them his way.[18]

After spending an hour filling their saddlebags, pockets, and bellies, the cavalrymen prepared to leave. Elijah White did not ransom Hanover nor demand its surrender. A bugle sounded and the 35th Battalion remounted, many on newly acquired horses. Cheering loudly, they headed out of town on York Street. White paused briefly to dispatch patrols throughout the vicinity. Cavalrymen occasionally fired at curious citizens who lingered near Hanover to gawk at the invaders.

Unseen by White, a few troopers stayed behind. They were either tired of the war or perhaps too drunk to continue. The next day, Hanoverians discovered some of these stragglers still in town. Because there were no Union soldiers nearby and no policemen present to arrest them, the Confederates were "impudent and boastful in their manner." Dr. Zieber, the chairman of the Committee of Safety, walked up to them and demanded to know why they were still in Hanover. Assisted by others, he arrested the Rebels and took them to the Central Hotel. There, guards placed them on a wagon and conveyed them to Westminster, where they turned the captives over to military authorities.[19]

---

17 *Hanover Spectator*, July 17, 1863; McClure, *East of Gettysburg*, 46.

18 Anthony, *History of the Battle of Hanover*, 68; Prowell, *History of York County*, 1, 405-406.

19 *Encounter at Hanover*, 107.

Jewelry retailer William Boadenhamer, after a late start, was leaving Hanover on the York Road. Gun-toting cavalrymen overtook his carriage about a mile from the town and stole a large box of retail goods. Resting in the shade of a tree near Samuel Mumma's mill along Oil Creek, the Rebels opened the chest and found to their delight that it contained nearly a hundred watches and jewelry. Boadenhamer later estimated his loss at $200.00.[20]

At least one company followed the Hanover Branch Railroad to the hamlet of Porters Sideling, where foragers stole a roan from Jonas Becker's stable. Others headed for the general store and startled young storekeeper Aaron Rudisill, who fell into a large cracker barrel he was using as a seat. He was stuck inside, with only his head and feet showing. An officer tilted the barrel onto its side and Rudisill, still trapped, watched while the soldiers cleaned out his father's store. They left a few Confederate bills. Nearby, two Rebels rode up to Isaac Rennoll's farm and asked him where his horses were. He replied that one was in the stable. One of the cavalrymen entered it and emerged leading the horse. Rennoll tried to stop him, but he drew a pistol. Leveling it, the soldier told the farmer that if he did not desist, he would shoot him. Rennoll reluctantly watched as Southerners rode away leading his 10-year- old bay.[21]

White's men ripped down telegraph wires and burned three wooden bridges along the tracks to Hanover Junction, 12.5 miles northeast of Hanover. As a squad of soldiers arrived at the wooden railroad bridge at the Walter farm, young Levina Walter and her mother had just finished baking a large batch of cherry pies. Hungry soldiers soon arrived at the farmhouse and appropriated all of the pies before resuming the toil of tearing up the railroad.[22]

Rebel riders seemed to be everywhere, seizing any horses not yet sent away to safety. The battalion was "passing through a land of plenty. The grass had been cut, the hay had been placed in stacks or in barns, and the harvesting of wheat and rye had just begun. This was a busy season to the York County

---

20 Skelly, "A Boy's Experiences in the Battle of Gettysburg," GNMP; Mosby, *Stuart's Cavalry in the Gettysburg Campaign*, 156. In 1906 White wrote to former cavalry officer John S. Mosby that "Nothing occurred on the way of any consequence, except I captured a wagon load of jewelry. After supplying ourselves, we buried the balance." Boadenhamer became Hanover's Chief Burgess in 1883. His jewelry, watch, and clock shop on Broadway flourished after the war.

21 Prowell, *History of York County*, 1, 406; York County Damage Claims, various reels.

22 Armand Gladfelter, *Das Siebenthal Revisited: The People of Seven Valleys, York County, PA* (York, Pa.: Mehl Ad Associates, 1988), 153; Pennsylvania State Auditors' Office, *Reports of the Railroad Companies of Pennsylvania for 1862* (Harrisburg: Singerly & Myers, 1863), 83.

farmers, and some venturesome countrymen had kept their horses at home. Many of them had been made to believe that by joining a secret league, their horses and cattle would be protected from capture by the enemy. Colonel White and his men . . . exchanged many of their worn out horses for those found in barns and stables of the well-to-do farmers south and east of Hanover."[23]

York resident Cassandra Small related that city slickers had duped the countrymen into paying a dollar for a printed ticket and a special hand signal that supposedly would protect their property when the Rebels visited. The shysters purported that these tickets came from the Knights of the Golden Circle, a secret society rumored to be filled with Southern-sympathizers who would rise up to aid the Confederate army. The gullible Copperhead farmers suffered even greater losses than their Unionist neighbors. They made the designated hand gestures to the Southern raiders, and then, to their shock, the Rebels struck the tickets from their hands and declared, "We don't care for that now." Laughing soldiers forced the farmers to give them whatever they wanted. Crowds of these "poor ignorant people" later came into York and accosted the swindlers. Small added, "They brought them their worthless tickets and asked that their dollars be refunded, but to no avail."[24]

A squadron accosted farmer George Bowman at gunpoint and took his mare. Some of them entered his barn and emerged with another horse. While Henry Miller was sick in bed, his friend Charles Smith heard that "several hundred" Rebels were in Hanover. He hurried to Miller's stable and was leading out his dark roan mare to take it to safety when cavalrymen arrived. Family members peered out of their windows and saw the soldiers seize the horse.

Near Jefferson, a trio of cavalrymen visited John Schnyder's Manheim Township farm. While the terrified Schnyder watched from his window, they entered his stable and appropriated two roan mares. His son Levi had been helping with a barn-raising at a neighbor's farm since early morning. In the early afternoon, Levi walked home. About a half-mile away from his destination, he spotted a squad of Rebels making their way through a nearby field. He was near

---

23 Prowell, *History of York County*, 1, 406.

24 Cassandra Small to Lissie Latimer, July 8, 1863, YCHT. Jubal Early mentioned in his memoirs (p. 265), "As we moved through the country, a number of people made mysterious signs to us, and on inquiring we ascertained that some enterprising Yankees had passed along a short time before, initiating the people into certain signs, for a consideration, which they were told would prevent the 'rebels' from molesting them or their property, when they appeared. These things were all new to us, and the purchasers of the mysteries had been badly sold."

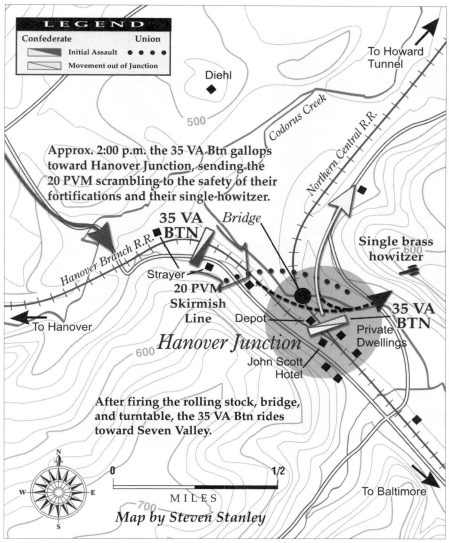

LEGEND

Confederate   Union

Initial Assault   ● ● ● ●
Movement out of Junction

Diehl

500

Codorus Creek

Northern Central R.R.

To Howard
Tunnel

Approx. 2:00 p.m. the 35 VA Btn gallops
toward Hanover Junction, sending the
20 PVM scrambling to the safety of their
fortifications and their single howitzer.

35 VA
BTN   *Bridge*

Hanover Branch R.R.

Strayer
20 PVM
Skirmish
Line   Depot

To Hanover

600

Hanover Junction

John Scott
Hotel

Single brass
howitzer   600

35 VA
BTN

Private
Dwellings

After firing the rolling stock, bridge,
and turntable, the 35 VA Btn rides
toward Seven Valley.

N
W   E
S

0   1/2

MILES

700

Map by Steven Stanley

To Baltimore

Hanover Junction was an important railroad and communications hub that included a
telegraph school and relay station. Elijah White's Rebel cavalry sacked it on June 27, 1863.

enough to them to recognize his father's horses; one led by a Confederate, the
other being ridden.[25]

25 York County Damage Claims, reel 30.

The John Scott Hotel is at the left, with the Hanover Junction depot in the center. Photo taken in November 1863. *Library of Congress*

Rebels stopped at George Bair's stable and left with his chestnut bay stallion. Some residents tried bartering with them to keep prized horses or mules. One group of farmers, hoping to save their livestock, told White they had seen a column of graycoats marching on the turnpike. This implied to White that Gordon had not met real resistance thus far. However, scouts brought news that militia was in the cavalry's path guarding Hanover Junction.[26]

White Sacks Hanover Junction

At the small hamlet, the Northern Central Railway intersected the Hanover Branch Railroad. This latter line covered 30 miles, running east-west through Jefferson Station to Hanover, where it intersected the Gettysburg Railroad and the Littlestown Railroad. The Northern Central connected Baltimore (46 miles south of Hanover Junction) with Wrightsville and Columbia. Other tracks led to the busy community of York (11 miles north of the depot) and on to

26 York County Damage Claims, reel 23. Bair lived in Codorus Township.

Harrisburg (47 miles away). The depot housed an important relay station for Federal telegraph lines linking Baltimore and Washington with the North.[27]

In 1863, Hanover Junction consisted of the stationhouse and its outbuildings, a hotel, and a few modest brick homes. The Hanover Branch Railroad had built the three-story wooden depot in 1851. The first floor had office space for employees, a small ticket booth, and a passenger waiting area with a wood-burning stove. The second floor held sleeping rooms for travelers awaiting morning trains. In its early days, the building also housed a telegraphy school, and the apprentices used a dormitory on the third floor. As passenger business increased, the need for additional lodging led to the construction of the nearby Scott Hotel. This three-story brick building contained a bar, full service restaurant, small general store, and a few nicely appointed upstairs guestrooms. John Scott's staff included family members and friends.[28]

A low mountain known to the local Pennsylvania Germans as der Hundsrueck ("the dog's back") guarded the approach to Hanover Junction. The South Branch of the Codorus Creek, a shallow steep-banked stream, meandered among nearby hills. The surrounding terrain was mostly open pastureland and cultivated fields, dotted by small farmsteads, orchards, and woodlots. Cattle grazed in the lush valley between the depot and the commanding ridge to the east. Most residents still primarily spoke the Pfälzisch dialect of the German language, although the coming of the railroad had begun opening up the somewhat isolated agrarian region to a more general usage of English for business and commerce.

Despite its prominence as a potential military target, Hanover Junction was only lightly defended. Days earlier, General Couch hastily dispatched the 971-man 20th Pennsylvania Volunteer Militia to York in response to Granville Haller's urgent plea for troops. Organized in Philadelphia on June 17, it was one of the first emergency regiments raised after Governor Curtin called for volunteers. The commander, 52-year-old Col. William B. Thomas, was a prominent businessman and abolitionist who had helped organize the Republican Party in Pennsylvania. President Lincoln rewarded Thomas in 1861

---

27 A. W. Eichelberger was elected president of the HBRR in 1853, mainly because of his excellent administrative and executive abilities. At his retirement, he was the longest serving railroad president in American history.

28 Codorus Valley Historical Society. The HBRR charged seven cents per mile for a round trip first class ticket to Hanover and four cents per mile for one way.

by appointing him as customs collector for the port of Philadelphia, after considering him for a cabinet position. Many of his militiamen worked in the Customs House. A few were veterans of the bloody fighting at Antietam, but most had not seen combat.[29]

The Pennsylvania soldiers tried to reassure the terrified citizens of York County, but just as often they angered them by causing damage and inciting ill will. The soldiers established a series of camps on June 20, including one on a farm in eastern Manchester Township near the railroad. Owner Samuel Bair later filed claims for eight days' worth of milk and butter from his seven cows, as well as eight bushels of potatoes, two barrels of flour, entire fields of oats and rye, barrels of hams, and "one new chopping axe." Hungry soldiers appropriated two sheep for dinner, and Colonel Thomas impressed four horses for his scouts.[30]

Thomas assigned nearly 400 men to defend the Howard Tunnel, a single-tracked 300-foot-long passageway on the Northern Central five miles north of Hanover Junction. Authorities heard that the Confederates planned to damage the tunnel, which would effectively shut down the shortest route from Harrisburg to Baltimore and Washington. Thomas issued orders to shoot any Rebel on sight.[31]

Thomas also assigned a battalion of three companies (B, F, and H), about 200 men under the command of 40-year-old Lt. Col. William H. Sickles, to defend Hanover Junction. Arriving at Hanover Junction on June 22, Sickles surveyed the landscape and selected a modest hill less than a mile from the stationhouse as his base of operations. He sketched out a line of entrenchments, and his men constructed light fortifications along the crest. Some accounts suggest that he secured a six-pound howitzer for the bastion. Sickles established several small camps in the vicinity, including one near the

---

29 Bates, *History of Pennsylvania Volunteers*, 1226. In 1856, Montgomery County native William B. Thomas unsuccessfully ran for mayor of Philadelphia. A wealthy flour miller, he was a delegate to the 1860 Republican National Convention. He raised the 20th Militia for the Emergency of 1862 and reconstituted the unit in June 1863. In October, he wrote Lincoln and offered to raise 100,000 men to defend Washington. The president declined the offer. Thomas later raised the 192nd Pennsylvania, a 100-day regiment that served in Maryland and Ohio.

30 York County Damage Claims, reel 23.

31 The York & Maryland Line Railroad constructed the tunnel in 1838 (the Baltimore & Susquehanna / Northern Central later purchased the Y&MLRR). A second track was laid in 1868 after the Civil War when the tunnel was widened. Today, the Howard Tunnel is part of the York County Heritage Rail Trail, a bicycle path paralleling the old railroad.

hamlet of Larue. There his men burned more than 600 chestnut fence rails as firewood.[32]

On Wednesday, June 24, Colonel Thomas received a chilling message from Couch that a party of Confederate cavalry might attack the railroad bridges at any time. Couch warned him to hold them "at all hazard," and keep provisions and water in his defenses. Now on Saturday afternoon, Elijah White's main force rode toward them through Jefferson and Cold Springs. Other companies took alternate routes, collecting horses, food, and supplies. They would rendezvous near Hanover Junction.[33]

Mounted pickets reported Rebels' impending arrival, and Sickles formed a thin skirmish line fronting the railroad depot and bridge. His inexperienced militia soon heard wild yells from the approaching grayclad troopers. "Looking toward Seven Valleys and Hanover Junction from our home," wrote 12-year-old Harry I. Gladfelter, " we could see men galloping their horses along the highway, over the creek and Rail Road." At the same time, a northbound Northern Central train was passing through the junction toward York. The engineer, George Small, had been sent earlier that day from York down to a siding near the Mason-Dixon Line. His task was to pick up some boxcars for transport back to York for safekeeping and eventual transfer to Columbia. Now, he was on the return leg of this seemingly uneventful assignment.

Off to his left Small spotted Rebel cavalrymen galloping along the roadbed of the intersecting Hanover Branch Railroad. They seemed to be trying to head off his engine, the "Susquehanna." Small opened the throttle to the limit. Calling to the fireman to follow him, he abandoned the unprotected cab for the sheltering side of the tender. Hurriedly dismounting, White's cavalrymen fired several shots at the fleeing train but none struck home. Small and his fireman narrowly escaped to York, where they arrived shortly before 3:30 p.m.[34]

Some accounts suggest a second train also left about this time. The army had ordered the railroad to leave one locomotive, the "Heidelberg," at the

---

32 Armand Gladfelter, *The Flowering of the Codorus Palantine: A History of North Codorus Township PA 1838-1988* (York, Pa.: s. n., 1988), 267-68; York County Damage Claims, J. Bowman claim. Gettysburg had a small brass howitzer in its military stores. Haller had moved it via rail to Hanover. Perhaps it ended up in Hanover Junction.

33 *OR* 27, pt. 3, 297.

34 Harry I. Gladfelter typed manuscript, The Casper Glattfelder Association of America, 21; George Small, 1905 *York Dispatch*; Philadelphia *Inquirer*, June 30, 1863.

junction in case it was needed. The locomotive was apparently fired up and ready to move before the Confederates arrived. Conductor John Eckert ordered the engineer to head to Baltimore, telling him to put on more steam and hurry away as fast as possible. They "needed no more pressing orders to leave than the approach of the enemy cavalry." The 33-year-old Eckert exclaimed that the Rebels "shall not have the train if we can help it." The telegrapher, an elderly man who lived on the station's third floor, jumped on board as the train roared south toward Glen Rock. The engine, tender, and coach disappeared around a curve while a few howling troopers gave chase, their pistols barking.[35]

Meanwhile, across the valley in the hilltop defenses, volunteers manning the howitzer may have fired a single errant shot at the approaching Rebels. Undeterred, Lige White led his cheering horsemen forward along the tracks. Fearful residents scurried to their cellars, scattered small arms fire broke out, and Lieutenant Colonel Sickles' resolve to defend the junction evaporated. Confederate Capt. Frank Myers noted that, rather than resisting, the Yankees retired to their fortifications "about a mile off." White did not deem it prudent to attack, so after a short skirmish he allowed the militia to withdraw. Some of his men wanted to pursue them, but White was against charging across the valley and up the slope. Such an attack might prove too costly, and the goal was not to kill Yankees, but to destroy the usefulness of the junction and cut off its communications linkages.[36]

Sickles' militiamen watched the drama unfold in the valley below them. Confederate commanders, riding recently procured Pennsylvania horses around the rail yard, barked orders. Inside the depot, a telegrapher, likely 16-year-old apprentice John Hinkle Shearer, tapped out a final message warning authorities that Confederates were riding around the station and destroying the Northern Central Railway. That unhappy news triggered a flurry of messages among Federal commanders in the region. One telegram was relayed from

---

35 *Encounter at Hanover*, 121. In November 1863, Eckert was the conductor when Lincoln traveled on the Hanover Branch Railroad to Gettysburg to deliver his speech. Upon completion of his trip, the president reportedly gave him a silver watch as a gesture of thanks. The telegraph operator likely was Howard Scott, who resigned as telegrapher in 1867 to become the freight and passenger agent for the Northern Central at Hanover Junction. See Western Union Telegraph Company, *Journal of the Telegraph*, Vol. 2, No. 15 (July 1869), 185.

36 Gladfelter, *The Flowering of the Codorus Palatinate*, 260; Myers, *The Comanches*, 194.

Hanover Junction in November 1863 looking toward the west-northwest. In June, Elijah
White's cavalry rode around the rail yard and destroyed cars and a turntable. *Library of Congress*

Baltimore to army high command in Washington to inform them the enemy
was unknown, but supposedly a small cavalry force.[37]

Dismounted men started fires with kindling and wood stored for the trains.
Acrid black smoke soon filled the mid-afternoon sky as Rebels pushed railcars
of coal into the bridge, poured on coal oil, and then ignited it. Others climbed
telegraph poles and cut the wires connecting Hanover Junction with the outside
world. Still others burned the large wooden turntable used to change the
direction of locomotives. A small cluster of cavalrymen tried to burn a large coal
pile, but it failed to ignite. Several soldiers crushed a couple of culverts and
destroyed railroad switches. Fires erupted in rolling stock parked on a siding,
including an eight-wheeled house car owned by a private Hanover company,
two railcars owned by Joseph Wible of Adams County, and one other car.
Occasionally gleeful cavalrymen discharged their pistols into the air.[38]

37 OR 27, pt. 3, 360.

38 *Gettysburg Compiler*, June 29, 1863; Adams and York County Damage Claims. Wible asked
for $1,100 for two railcars burned at Hanover Junction. Hanover's Klinefelter, Slagle & Co.

Elijah White galloped up to the stationhouse and demanded the surrender of the telegraph equipment. The Confederates took apprentice John Shearer into custody and robbed him of his pocket watch and coins at gunpoint. Shearer was the younger of two sons of a York cobbler, and Rebels seized his fine custom-made leather shoes. They forced him to sit astride a nearby rail fence and watch while they looted the depot. Rebels hurtled loose items out the stationhouse windows, and the sound of their laughter mixed with the tinkling of breaking glass.

The Spoils of War

The sport was finally over late in the afternoon. White freed Shearer before departing Hanover Junction. The youth and a few citizens entered the looted depot to see what might be salvageable. Shearer, to his relief, found that the telegraph battery was undamaged. He searched for the key for nearly an hour before finally discovering it in some high weeds outside a broken window. A cavalryman, not recognizing its significance, had tossed it aside. With telegraph wires down throughout the region, all Shearer could do was tidy up the stationhouse and await help. Local women brought him dinner.

Meanwhile, Elijah White sent a detachment into Seven Valleys (its rail depot was known as Smyser's Station). Most residents had fled earlier that afternoon when news spread that Rebels were in Hanover. Thirty wagonloads of people and valuables were en route to Cross Roads, fifteen miles to the southeast. A "company of more than fifty Rebel cavalry" entered Henry Bott's post office and general store, one of the few buildings still occupied. He lost almost his entire inventory of calico, muslin, gingham, dress goods, cassimere cloth, hats, shoes, boots, socks, and handkerchiefs. The Rebels, "not having any wagons, could not take large quantities of groceries." However, some of them took an axe and damaged his fire-proof safe, but failed to get it to open. Luckily one of his staff had taken the key away when the Rebels approached.

An honest cavalryman picked up a small item and offered Sarah Bott a Confederate dollar bill. When she protested that Rebel money was worthless and instead demanded Federal-issued cash, the soldier insisted she accept the note, saying it would soon be worth more than her Yankee greenbacks. He bragged that they were going to York and would soon cross the Susquehanna

---

claimed $215 for the loss of a car. Coal oil, a flammable distillate of cannel coal, was often used for lamps and torches.

before moving on Philadelphia. In parting, he stated the war was nearly over, and the South would surely win. Later when Henry Bott returned home, he discovered that raiders had stolen two of his horses.[39]

The unwelcome visitors remained in the Seven Valleys region about an hour before rejoining White's main force. A detachment stopped at the Henry Fishel farm to confiscate a large supply of homemade rye whiskey. Breaking open the locked door of Fishel's distillery room, soldiers drank their fill before an officer intervened. They destroyed the remaining 42 barrels of spirits by smashing in the barrelheads. An estimated $1,200 worth of alcohol poured onto the floor. A few Confederates burned the nearby railroad bridge over Fishel Creek.[40]

Patrols stole more horses and then relayed news to Elijah White that Yankees guarded the Howard Tunnel and a small railroad bridge near Reynolds Mill. They also reported a much larger force north of Brillhart Station. White decided not to attack these objectives. He ordered his men to return to Jefferson, while sending one company four miles south to destroy a 50-foot-long Northern Central bridge near Glen Rock. This detachment appropriated more mules and horses along the way back, including farmer Jeremiah Krebs' prize gray stallion. Luckily for the Federals, the Rebels did not enter Glen Rock nor damage the telegraph lines leading from there. Hanover Junction's telegrapher hopped off the southbound train and wired the authorities about the raid.[41]

As soon as the Rebels were well away from the area, Lt. Col. William Sickles and the badly embarrassed battalion of the 20th Militia abandoned their hillside fortification. They trudged up the tracks past Smyser's Station, but found that Colonel Thomas had recalled the companies assigned to guard the tunnel and Northern Central bridges. Sickles' men tramped northward. They eventually learned that Haller had withdrawn to Wrightsville, so they wearily headed there.

Meanwhile, White's remaining companies trotted toward the crossroads village of Jefferson. They paused to garner more food and supplies, and stole "a fine horse" from Daniel Shue's farm. One squad encountered sixteen-year-old Jacob Hamm, who was riding a beautiful mare on his way home to his father's

---

39 Prowell, *History of York County*, 1, 906; York County Damage Claims, reel 19.

40 York County Damage Claims, reel 30.

41 *Boston Daily Advertiser*, June 29, 1863.

farm. The soldiers forced Hamm to accompany them to Jefferson, where they released the teenager but kept his horse. They gave the lad a "worn-out plug" so he could ride back to his home.[42]

The jubilant Virginians and Marylanders rode into Jefferson's square from the northeast via York Street. A Confederate approached a small girl and traded a brooch stolen from jeweler Boadenhamer for a glass of cool water. A squad of dusty cavalrymen carrying cornmeal and flour knocked on the door of a residence and asked the occupants to bake them some bread. The ladies, pitying the young soldiers so far from home, complied. She noted that they looked like "typical farm boys," and most had no uniforms. Those that did were "well dressed." A messenger found Lt. Colonel White and informed him that General Gordon planned to halt for the evening near Farmers Post Office on the Gettysburg-York Pike. White was to camp nearby, and they would enter York together in the morning.[43]

White's raid exacerbated the refugee situation in York County as news spread that Rebels had occupied Hanover. According to a reporter, "Information was received at about 5 o'clock this afternoon from Glen Rock that the rebels were then at Hanover Junction, tearing up the railroad tracks. The operator there left as they approached and came down to Glen Rock, from which he communicated these facts." The quiet village of Shrewsbury, eight miles southeast, "was thrown into a state of intense excitement" about 5:00 p.m. when a "cavalcade of people, with their horses and stock, wagons and such things as they could gather, passed through and announced the approach of the Confederates toward Hanover." The residents grabbed their horses and followed the exodus. Most were determined to push eastward until they crossed the Susquehanna, although a few headed south toward Baltimore.[44]

---

42 Gladfelter, *Das Siebenthal Revisited*, 153. Jacob Hamm would later marry Levina Walter, another of White's victims, who had lost the cherry pies she and her mother had just baked earlier that afternoon. His father, George Hamm, would lose two other horses to J.E.B. Stuart's column on June 30 (York County Damage Claims).

43 Gregory C. White, *This Most Bloody and Cruel Drama: A History of the 31st Georgia Volunteer Infantry* (Baltimore: Butternut and Blue, 1997), 34; Prowell, *History of York County*, 1, 886; York County Damage Claims, reel 30, John E. Divine, *35th Battalion, Virginia Cavalry* (Lynchburg, Va.: Virginia Regimental Series, H. E. Howard, Inc., 1985). 34. In 1863, Jefferson had 50 houses and 234 residents according to York County tax records. Three days after White's raid, J.E.B. Stuart's cavalrymen visited Shue's Codorus Township farm. They stole a sorrel mare, riding saddle, 16 bushels of oats, a ton of hay, six cotton shirts, and three large bushel grain bags.

44 *Boston Daily Advertiser*, June 29, 1863; *Baltimore Sun*, June 29, 1863.

In the early evening, Lige White led his jubilant cavalrymen through the now deserted countryside to Jefferson Station. On a rail siding, they discovered several carloads of tanbark owned by businessman Henry Rebert. The Confederates torched the cars, sending plumes of dense black smoke high into the sky. Near the depot sat a small cluster of modest structures, including a post office and store co-owned and managed by 51-year-old Jacob Rebert. He had abandoned his small building when word came of the Confederate incursion. Entering the shop, delighted soldiers discovered two barrels of fine aged whiskey. White's thirsty cavaliers cracked open the wooden kegs and refreshed themselves.[45]

After leaving Jefferson Station, the battalion passed through the countryside toward the small paper mill village of Spring Forge. Anxious farmers in the region spread rumors that the Rebels intended to impress the able-bodied men of Codorus and Jackson townships into the infantry. As a result, they gave them anything they asked for—especially horses—in exchange for a guarantee of freedom. Few of the draft animals were suitable as cavalry mounts, but many found utility as teams for the artillery limbers and caissons. Major Robert Stiles, a Virginia cannoneer accompanying Jubal Early, believed that the quartermasters were "common horse thieves," although they did offer to pay in Confederate currency. Occasionally the farmers accepted the money, grousing that it was "better than nothing." Stiles felt sorry for them. Those determined to accept neither thievery nor Southern money attempted to conceal their horses in dwellings. The Rebels had become "veritable sleuth-hounds" in tracking down hidden horses, having learned all the tricks and dodges devised by the farmers to throw them off track.

Stiles believed the artillery gained little from this thievery. The impressed animals were often "great, clumsy, flabby Percherons or Conestogas" requiring more than twice the feed as the compact hard-muscled smaller Virginia horses. Despite their immense size, the Pennsylvania farm horses could not deliver half the work of their Southern counterparts, nor could they stand half the hardship and exposure of a standard military campaign. Stiles found it pitiful to watch these great brutes suffer when compelled to dash off at full gallop while dragging a cannon. Upon the army's return to Virginia, these stolen horses pastured on dry broom sedge and a small portion of weevil-eaten corn. They

---

45 Prowell, *History of York County*, 1: 887.

seemed to pine for the full rations and slow work pace of their former Pennsylvania homes.[46]

The scattered cavalry patrols regrouped and spent Saturday night on John Wiest's farm between Spring Forge and Nashville. They were two miles southeast of Gordon's camp at Farmers. Quartermaster Capt. John J. White purchased a large supply of oats from Wiest to feed the horses. The troopers swapped tales of how they had frightened off the Yankee militia and would surely do so again tomorrow at York. So far, the expedition was a rousing success. Captain Frank Myers stated "no people were ever in finer spirits than those who had followed the stars and bars to Pennsylvania." Other troopers trickled in throughout the night, bringing supplies, additional horses, and livestock.[47]

Several cavalrymen paused at the sprawling Jackson Township farm of Andrew J. Menges, where his wife Caroline and teenage daughters Agnes and Magdalena served them food and fresh-baked pie. The commander promised they would not take their horses because Menges and his two sons were using them in the fields. Some Confederates bivouacked on a nearby wooded hill, near the Revolutionary War camp of "Mad" Anthony Wayne's brigade. About 11:00 p.m. in bright moonlight, a few Rebels spotted a horse grazing in a nearby pasture. They forced farmer Samuel Roth to draw the gelding into his barnyard in order to halter him. Then they led away the seven-year-old bay, much to the farmer's consternation.[48]

Many other southwestern York Countians went to bed wondering how they would recover financially and emotionally from the Rebel raid.

46 Robert Stiles, *Four Years Under Marse Robert* (New York: Neale Publishing, 1904), 200-201. Spring Forge is now Spring Grove.

47 Prowell, *History of York County*, 1, 997-98; Myers, *The Comanches,* 195. Wiest's grandson William presented the Rebel note to the Historical Society of York County. The Wiest house, at the intersection of the roads to Spring Forge and Hanover, was a popular hotel in colonial days. George Washington stopped there in 1791 to meet a delegation that would escort him to York.

48 Howard A. Overmiller, *York, Pennsylvania, In the Hands of the Confederates* (York, Pa.: s. n., undated), 2-4, YCHT; Gibson, *History of York County*, 695; York County Damage Claims, reel 30. The Menges farm was on the road leading to Gordon's camp and a short distance from the Wiest farm. The family claimed it entertained General Gordon, who shared his impressions of York County versus the South. When the officer and his staff were ready to leave, Andrew Menges, a 59-year-old devout Christian, led them in prayer. Standing in a circle, they doffed their hats and bowed. One officer left his personal New Testament with the family. Among the Revolutionary War soldiers who camped at Menges Mills was the 5th Pennsylvania's Lt. Col. Persifor Frazer, great-grandfather and namesake of Persifor Frazer, Jr. of the First City Troop.

Chapter 8

Gordon Parades through York

To Surrender or Not

In the late afternoon of Saturday, June 27, while Elijah White's cavalrymen raided the vicinity of Hanover Junction, Brig. Gen. John Gordon's infantry brigade and Tanner's Battery left Abbottstown and entered York County. Gordon's meeting with businessman A. B. Farquhar offered promise, and, if York's Committee of Safety agreed, his command would peacefully enter the town the next morning. There was no longer any need to hurry to surprise its defenders. The column proceeded at a relaxed pace, a welcome change for foot-weary soldiers. Some rode bareback on huge farm horses appropriated in Adams County. The vanguard, Captain Waldo's cavalry company, reached Thomasville, about eight miles east of Abbottstown, in the early evening. They found few horses along the way, because most residents had taken their livestock and horses to safety. Among the victims who had stayed home was Abraham Straley, who lost a black mule to the Georgia infantrymen.[1]

After marching nearly twenty miles since leaving Gettysburg, Gordon halted near the hamlet of Farmers. Colonel Clement Evans described the nondescript place as "a little town of two stores." For his headquarters, Gordon selected the homestead of Jacob S. Altland along the turnpike. His staff officers pitched a canvas tent in the yard. Several adjacent farms, including that of Absalom Menges, offered broad, rolling pastures for the regimental camps, and Paradise Creek provided fresh water. Soldiers chatted while confiscated

---

1   Federal Damage Claims, Gettysburg Campaign, NARA.

Pennsylvania beef roasted in iron pots and skillets. Rebels raided the nearby farm of Jacob Baker, taking $150 in groceries, a "big horse" worth $150, $100 worth of hats and caps, assorted calicoes, woolens, delicacies, and all of his dishes.[2]

A few Georgians scouted for more horses. A staff officer stopped at the home of Samuel L. Roth, who pastored a Mennonite church between the Confederate campsites at Farmers and Spring Forge. Soldiers had previously pilfered a pair of the preacher's horses, but had left behind "Fox," the family's gentle gray mare. Claiming it in the name of General Gordon, the lieutenant informed the family that Pennsylvanians had to provide both food and horses for the Confederates. One of Roth's daughters begged the officer not to take the last remaining horse of a minister, because he needed it to visit members of his congregation. Roth said that he would personally see the general and get his horse back. Unconcerned, the lieutenant seized the mare and took it to Gordon.[3]

Meanwhile, the infantrymen spent a pleasant evening in their rolling pastoral campsite. Some wondered whether tomorrow they would see the broad Susquehanna. Others talked about the "Melish" and how they would surely send them running again if any were audacious enough to guard York. After finishing their evening meals, many soldiers settled down to listen to a pair of regimental bands play "Dixie" and other patriotic Southern airs. In some companies, jubilant soldiers broke into song and loudly accompanied the musicians. Spirits ran high. To youthful Pvt. Gordon Bradwell, the trip from Virginia had so far been a "picnic."[4]

As Gordon's and White's Confederates celebrated in their camps and Granville Haller's train steamed toward Wrightsville, Chief Burgess David Small convened York's Committee of Safety. They met in the Small brothers' hardware store to plan final details of their upcoming meeting with General Gordon. Committee members reached consensus on the central points. The final topic was the fate of the town's 18-by-35 feet handmade flag, which fluttered from a 110-foot high pine flagpole in Centre Square. Several

2 Stephens, *Intrepid Warrior*, 226; York County Damage Claims, reel 19.

3 Prowell, *History of York County*, 1, 1047. The *Philadelphia Public Ledger*, July 2, 1922, places the story at the home of the Rev. John Roth, who pastored a nearby church, and indentified the Rebel as a staff sergeant.

4 Bradwell, "Burning of Wrightsville," 301.

committee members wanted to haul it down and hide it. Others objected and argued that the Rebels should see the national colors proudly waving as they entered York. The committee finally rendered its decision—the banner would continue to wave. They passed a resolution declaring "That, finding our town defenseless, we request the Chief Burgess to surrender the town peaceably." Having settled on a course of action, the leaders chose the delegation to meet with Gordon—A. B. Farquhar, David Small, committee president George Hay, and members W. Latimer Small and Thomas White.[5]

Cassandra Small wrote to her cousin, "About 6 o'clock our beautiful flag was raised in the Square; many objected, but others said, 'let them come in seeing our colors flying,' and Lat helped to raise it. Oh, Lissie, imagine the whole excitement." After further deliberation in the public square, her brother Latimer Small and the rest of the delegation entered a carriage and left York. They rode west on the turnpike to find the Rebels. A reporter recalled the ceremony differently. "While Major Knox still occupied York, the cowardly Chief Burgess went out in search of the Rebels for the purpose of surrendering the town, and had to go six miles before he could find then, to consummate his disagreeable surrender," he wrote. "Major K., learning the fact remained till 8 p.m., ordered the stars and stripes run up the flagstaff, and demanded three rousing cheers for the old flag, which were given with a will, then casting the dust off his feet against the copperhead town, he retired to Wrightsville, reaching there at 10 o'clock."[6]

The remaining townspeople dispersed to their homes to prepare for the Confederate occupation. Eager to prevent looting, families stashed valuables in chimneys and cellars. Others found more exotic hiding places. Francis Polack and his son packed jewelry and silver from their South George Street store in coffins, planning to bury them temporarily in the nearby Christ Lutheran Church graveyard. Shoemaker Jacob Emmitt made several trips next door to cabinet maker George Hay's shop, hiding his stock of leather goods in empty caskets. Attorney James Latimer wrote, "Our Post Office skedaddled Saturday

---

5   Civil War files, YCHT; Gibson, *History of York County*, 175.

6   *New York Tribune*, July 2, 1863; Cassandra Small to Lissie Latimer, July 8, 1863, YCHT. William Latimer Small was the son of hardware store co-owner Philip Small. George Hay, undertaker and cabinetmaker, had been colonel of the 87th Pennsylvania since 1861. He had been discharged due to medical reasons, thereby missing the Milroy debacle at Winchester. Thomas White was a businessman with extensive property holdings in York. He was widely rumored to be a Copperhead.

night and won't resume for some time probably." Cassandra Small reported that her sister's husband, his father, and his two brothers fled. She deemed their decision as "disgraceful." The town's bakers and butchers were put to work preparing food for the unwelcome guests. Guards were stationed at the saloons and other places where liquor could be obtained. One jeweler near the courthouse placed a scribbled sign in his door, "Small-pox within," hoping to deter any potential thieves.[7]

Telegraph wires hummed with messages being relayed to Union high command, as well as Governor Curtin and other political leaders. Crews fixed the wires near Gettysburg, and David McConaughy notified authorities, "About 200 cavalry, one battery, and 2,000 infantry occupied Gettysburg last night, and moved this morning toward Hanover Junction, on the Northern Central Railroad. They were part of Ewell's Corps, under General Early; the cavalry under White. Another column is reported as moving 5 miles north of Gettysburg, in the direction of York, and the rebels told the country people that another column would come from Carlisle and meet them at York."[8]

Meanwhile, the four companies of the 20th Militia that had guarded the Howard Tunnel region retired to York Haven along the river. There they joined Colonel Thomas's camp on the large farm of Col. John Hoff. Despite Haller's abandonment of York, Thomas intended to protect the Northern Central bridges over Conewago Creek. One of his men, Pvt. Joseph Kaucher of Company G, later wrote his mother, "We had to leave little York in a great hurry as the rebels were right behind us."[9]

Negotiating York's future

John Gordon relaxed in the Altland house and studied his maps of York County, some of which detailed individual farms and houses. His brigade was now only ten miles from his next objective, York. On Sunday morning, he

7   James Latimer to Bartow Latimer, July 8, 1863; Cassandra Small to Lissie Latimer, June 30, 1863, YCHT. Emmitt's son, Jacob, Jr., was the adjutant of Hay's 87th Pennsylvania.

8   *OR* 27, pt. 3, 370. Scouts R. G. McCreary and T. J. Carson joined McConaughy in signing the report, which at 9 p.m. reached Brig. Gen. Julius Stahel of the Army of the Potomac's cavalry. McConaughy's wife gave birth to their third child, a son named Samuel, on Friday, June 26, as White's men entered the town.

9   Joseph E. Kaucher to Mother, June 27, 1863, Historical Society of Berks County, Reading, Pa.

would attack the town if he found it defended, and then search out A. B. Farquhar and hang him for breaking his word. So far, his expedition was going quite well, and he had no reason to think that it would not continue to do so. The key was York's willingness to avoid a fight. He was reclining on a featherbed when an aide brought welcome news. A delegation from York had arrived, carrying a flag of truce. They sought out Lieutenant Redik, but he was under arrest for allowing Farquhar to pass through the picket lines at Abbottstown without the proper password.

Gordon, his manner more formal than during his afternoon session with Farquhar, met the emissaries in Altland's farmhouse. A staff member recognized pre-war acquaintance George Hay as a Union officer and suspected him of being a spy. Hay, recently medically discharged as colonel of the 87th Pennsylvania, replied that he now was a civilian whose sole interest was York's safety. The delegates informed Gordon that they had tried to raise enough of a force to resist the Confederate advance. However, with so few men at their disposal, any attempt to defend the town would result only in useless bloodshed. They asked for protection for the people of York and their private property.

The general reiterated his position. He did not intend to pursue the Union army's style of warfare. Private property would be respected, and the townspeople would not suffer any indignities. However, any manufacturing centers or supplies intended for the government would be destroyed, and it was up to Jubal Early to define the details for requisitioning provisions once his troops occupied the town. An anxious Latimer Small mentioned his family's flour mills and asked Gordon to protect them. Gordon replied that he already knew about the Smalls, and his men would not harm their mills. Small later surmised that Gordon had learned these facts from Confederate generals Ewell or Trimble, who he believed were familiar with York from antebellum railroad work. When the delegation expressed a desire to leave, Gordon initially balked, but rafter further dialogue he allowed them to return to York.[10]

John Gordon tried to rest again, but soon another visitor interrupted his slumber. Jubal Early and his escort rode to Farmers from their billet at the

10 Cassandra Small to Lissie Latimer, June 30, 1863, YCHT. Although other contemporary accounts also mention Richard Ewell's antebellum familiarity with Pennsylvania railroads, it was his older brother Benjamin who was an assistant engineer with the Baltimore & Susquehanna in York. Dick Ewell remained in the army. They bore a striking resemblance, according to biographer Donald Pfanz, despite an age gap of seven years.

Widow Zinn's house near Big Mount, approximately four miles northwest of Gordon's camp. Early wanted "to arrange with him the means of moving against the town next day in the event that it should be defended. The information which Gordon had received was that there were no troops in York, and I directed him, in the event the town should be unoccupied, to move on through to the Wrightsville and Columbia bridge and get possession of it at both ends and hold it until I came up." They conferred with for an hour. Gordon and his staff were convinced that York's Committee of Safety intended to honor its agreement and would not interfere with Confederate operations.[11]

Early later described his intentions this way:

> Notwithstanding my orders to destroy the bridge, I had found the country so defenseless, and the militia which Curtin had called into service so utterly inefficient, that I determined to cross the Susquehanna, levy a contribution on the rich town of Lancaster, cut the Central Railroad, and then move up in rear of Harrisburg while General Ewell was advancing against that city from the other side, relying upon being able, in any event that might happen, to mount my division on the horses which had been accumulated in large numbers on the east side of the river, by the farmers who had fled before us, and make my escape by moving to the west of the army, after damaging the railroads and canals on my route as much as possible.[12]

The division leader granted his subordinate a degree of freedom to react to the circumstances. Gordon interpreted his discretionary orders as giving him the option to "pass rapidly through Lancaster in the direction of Philadelphia" which might "compel General Meade to send a portion of his army to the defence of that city." After watching Jubal Early and his escort ride off, Gordon retired for the night, settling again into Jacob Altland's fine featherbed.[13]

As the delegation rode back to York in the moonlight, telegraph wires already buzzed. Peter Bentz, York's telegrapher, "believing that the Chief Burgess had been captured, telegraphed that the Rebels were coming into the town, and then left." At 11:30 p.m., well before the negotiating team reentered

---

11 Prowell, *History of York County*, 1, 408, 1046-47.

12 Early, *War Memoirs*, 259, 261; *SHSP*, Vol. 10, 540.

13 Gordon, *Reminiscences*, 147.

York, rumors already ran wild in Baltimore. City officials surmised that the Rebels would send a force from York to capture Wrightsville and Columbia, clearly intending to destroy the Pennsylvania Railroad and then burn the long bridge over the Susquehanna. Somehow, they correctly guessed Ewell's original plan.[14]

About 1:30 on Sunday morning the delegation arrived at the hardware store, where concerned citizens awaited news of the meeting with Gordon. David Small informed them that a sizeable enemy force would occupy the town sometime after daybreak. Any armed resistance would be madness and would result in the town being reduced to ashes. "We felt so relieved that all was settled," recalled Cassandra Small. York's residents finally went to bed.[15]

Although no one could have known it then, York would be the largest Northern town Confederate troops would occupy during the entire Civil War. Residents expressed decidedly mixed views on the conflict. Many such as Farquhar enjoyed strong business ties with the South before the war, and several townspeople had long-time family and social connections. The county leaned heavily toward the Democratic Party in past presidential elections, and many questioned Republican Abraham Lincoln's policies. However, army recruitment consistently met or exceeded government quotas in many parts of the county.[16]

Unionists in the region created immediate controversy. They claimed that Chief Burgess David Small had timidly surrendered York, although that term did not appear in the final negotiated settlement. Darius Couch wired Lincoln that York had surrendered. A contemporary historian characterized it as "one of the most shameful, cowardly exhibitions of this groveling spirit." New York author Benson J. Lossing agreed: "When Early's corps [division] approached York, the meek mayor, sympathizing, it was reported, with the Peace Faction, took the trouble to go several miles in the direction of the approaching invaders, to meet Early and surrender the borough to him, which, because of this mark of submission, was promised special immunity from harm."[17]

---

14 *New York Herald*, June 29, 1863; *Philadelphia Press*, June 29, 1863.

15 Cassandra Small to Lissie Latimer, July 8, 1863, YCHT.

16 Gibson, *History of York County*, 315. The 1860 York County vote for governor was 5,631 for Democrat Henry B. Foster and 5,322 for Andrew Curtin. The differential was greater in 1863 (8,069 for Democrat George W. Woodward to Curtin's 5,510). Curtin won reelection.

17 Lossing, *Pictorial Field Book of the Civil War*, 3, 54.

Newspaper reports reached the Army of the Potomac, which was still marching northward toward Lee. The 14th Connecticut's Capt. Samuel Fiske was upset by what he read. "I sincerely hope that the scare up in Pennsylvania isn't going to drive all the people's wits away and prevent them from making a brave defense of homes, altars, and hearths. When I read in a paper today of the chief burgess of York pushing eight or ten miles into the country to find somebody to surrender to, I owned to have entertained some doubts as to the worthiness and valor of that representative of the dignity of the city," Fiske admonished, "It would be well for the citizens of Pennsylvania to remember that Lee's soldiers are only men, after all, and that their number is not limitless."[18]

To supporters, David Small's skillful negotiations had saved York from the torch without the need of a formal capitulation. Small repeatedly insisted that the delegation had not offered to surrender the town or its military force to Gordon. For many years afterward, however, the Democrat had to justify his actions to local firebrands and Radical Republicans. He often stated that he sought to protect private property from destruction and prevent citizens from being injured in a battle. However, attorney James Latimer believed that borough authorities had behaved "so sheepishly."[19]

A Sunday Stroll

After spending the night in the rolling fields near Farmers, Gordon's men arose at 5:00 a.m. and ate their morning meals. Many attended religious services. All was peaceful on this gray, overcast Sabbath, although the skies threatened additional rain as the Rebels prepared to break camp. The general accepted an invitation to breakfast from Jacob Altland, "a staid and laborious farmer of German descent." According to Gordon, the farmer had built his dining room immediately over a spring gushing from a cleft in an underlying rock. Gordon

---

18 Urban, *Battlefield and Prison Pen*, 186; Samuel Fiske, *Mr. Dunn Browne's Experiences in the Army* (Boston: Nichols & Noyes, 1866).

19 James Latimer to Bartow Latimer, July 8, 1863, YCHT. Latimer wrote, "Early established his headquarters in the Court House; and in a few hours made the demands for money & supplies. Had the demand been refused, I don't believe they would have done any damage. In Gettysburg they made similar demands which were not complied with & no evil consequence followed. I do not believe such large requisitions would have been made had not the Boro' Authorities behaved so sheepishly in regard to the surrender."

entered the "quaint room, one half floored with smooth limestone, and the other half covered with limpid water bubbling clear and pure from the bosom of Mother Earth." He was amazed at the sensation of rest it produced after days of marching on the dusty turnpikes under a broiling sun. The general ate his hot breakfast on one side of the room, while "from the other the frugal housewife dipped cold milk and cream from immense jars standing neck-deep in water."[20]

Two days earlier, when his division first occupied Gettysburg, Jubal Early had assigned the Courtney Artillery to accompany Gordon to provide long-range firepower for the expedition. Now, Captain Tanner's artillerymen harnessed their teams of draft horses, which included many of Lige White's recent acquisitions from York County farmers. They attached the heavy iron guns to their respective limbers and inspected the caissons to ensure that they contained a full complement of artillery rounds. The Virginians freed a few broken-down nags to roam the pastures.

After breaking camp Gordon resumed the eastward march. Detachments of soldiers appropriated more horses from farmers along the turnpike. Peter F. Maul reported losing three horses to Gordon's infantrymen. Nearby, farmer George Sunday watched as Rebels marched by his house leading his neighbor George Smyser's horse. In the village of LaBott, Amanda Smyser watched out the window while Rebels led "one good mare" away from her stable. Near Thomasville, a squad overtook Jacob Stambaugh and confiscated his bay, harness, and spring wagon. When a patrol of cavalrymen encountered Eve Loucks and Jacob Bare in West Manchester Township, they had something more sinister in mind: they seized Bare at gunpoint and threatened to kill him. After taking sixty dollars in cash from his pocketbook they allowed the couple to go on their way. Others accosted Daniel Kauffman along the turnpike and took his horse, a mare he was leading, and his expensive silver hunting case watch.[21]

William Smyser lived on a prosperous farm at Five-Mile House, a popular tavern along the busy turnpike west of York. As news spread that the Rebels were approaching, he asked his hired hand, 15-year-old Charles W. Kline, to

---

20 Gordon, *Reminiscences*, 141-42. While Gordon does not specifically identify Altland in his account, this house has an old spring in its basement, according to York County author James McClure.

21 York County Damage Claims, reels 31 and 22. A hunting case (or hunter case) watch has a front cover, as opposed to an open face watch.

Colonel Clement A. Evans was a devout Methodist who kept tight rein on his 31st Georgia Infantry, which often operated as the provost regiment for John B. Gordon's Brigade during the Gettysburg Campaign.

Author's Collection

take his five horses and $650 in cash to safety. The youth strapped the money around his waist and hitched a pair of horses to a wagon and tied the others behind it. The youngster also loaded fifteen bags of corn into the wagon bed and headed as quickly as he could toward York. He did not stop until he had crossed the toll bridge into Columbia. He finally rested at Chickies Rock, a high bluff overlooking the Susquehanna.[22]

While his foragers terrorized local farmers, Gordon ordered Col. Clement Evans' provost of the 31st Georgia to take possession of York and establish guards to secure the passage of the rest of the brigade. As the vanguard approached the town, the army hospital's chief surgeon, Maj. Henry Palmer, wired Darius Couch: "This city was formally surrendered to General Gordon's command of rebel forces last evening—9 miles toward Gettysburg. They are 4,000 to 6,000 strong, and sent a force last evening to destroy bridge at Glen Rock. All the forces left last evening for Columbia, taking most of the Government stores. The rebels will occupy the town today; they will not destroy private property." News continued to trickle in about the Hanover Junction raid. Some of it proudly proclaimed the affair was a Union victory. The *New York Tribune* was one of the sources that reported the incorrect news: "Two

22 *Gettysburg Times*, December 12, 1940. In 1864, young Kline enrolled in the 200th Pennsylvania Infantry. He participated in the Siege of Petersburg and survived the battle of Fort Steadman where several comrades fell.

rebel companies of cavalry attacked four companies of the Twentieth Pennsylvania regiment last night below York, but were driven off badly whipped. Our loss was insignificant."[23]

"Sunday morning, June 28, the sun rose high in the clear sky over our peaceful borough," recalled York teenager M. L. Baman. "Groups of persons could be seen in eager and anxious discussion in and around Centre Square, while many others were on their way to the various churches and the church bells were ringing in the accustomed manner." The bells might be ringing as usual, but most residents realized the Confederates could do whatever they desired in York County. Mary Fisher, the wife of a prominent judge, summed up the community's general feeling of general helplessness. "Inasmuch as we were utterly without means of defense," Fisher lamented, "there was not much danger of opposition."

A "Sabbath stillness" reigned over York, broken only by clanging bells calling residents to worship. Churchgoers and people out for a morning stroll filled the sidewalks. Faint bugle calls were followed by a distant dust cloud rising west of town along the turnpike. An excited rider dashed along Market Street shouting that the Confederates were at the Bottstown Gate, less than two miles from downtown York. The anonymous rider vanished down the pike at a full gallop to carry the alarm to Wrightsville and on to Columbia. A moment later, Mrs. Fisher spotted a line of bayonets, flashing in the morning sun, on the distant hills. Soon, Gordon's "superbly mounted" cavalry rode into town and halted in Centre Square under the massive flag. To Mrs. Fisher, it proclaimed to the Rebels that York was indeed a loyal community.[24]

Meanwhile, Dr. Palmer's nurses debated how best to save the U.S. flag waving from the hospital's flag pole. The medical staff were determined not to allow the colors to fall into enemy hands. Hearing the alarm that the Rebels were near, some of the nurses lowered the banner and rolled it up. The hospital's matron, Mary "Mammy" Ruggles, volunteered to take it to her home. The women folded the flag around her waist and hid it in the folds of her

23 OR 27, pt. 3, 389; *New York Tribune*, June 29, 1863.

24 Mary C. Fisher typescript, YCHT. Judge Robert Fisher was a key liaison to Jubal Early during the occupation of York. His daughter Anne Helen married attorney James W. Latimer. The Bottstown gate was at the intersection of the Carlisle Pike and the Gettysburg Pike (now routes 74 and 462, respectively). The tollhouse was the first structure on the north side of Carlisle Road. In 1863, Bottstown contained about 200 people, some living in antiquated log homes.

petticoat. Mammy calmly walked six blocks to her home near the Codorus Creek.[25]

While York's residents scurried about, bright red Confederate battle flags fluttered in the morning breeze. The long infantry column passed the area west of town where Haller had posted his militia the day before. Industrialist A. B. Farquhar and his brother-in-law Alfred Jessop spent the morning on Webb's Hill south of town watching the distant parade of Rebels. Gordon's six regiments entered York on three parallel streets, with Waldo's cavalrymen leading the pioneers and Clement Evans' 31st Georgia in the center column up Market Street. Tanner's Battery, the ammunition and commissary wagons, and the ambulances brought up the rear. Just as Gordon's first troops entered downtown, Dr. Henry Palmer and the few remaining attendants at York's army hospital finished loading wagons with "very fine" rifles stored in the barracks. Having previously sent off their horses, they hastily pushed the vehicles downhill to an outbuilding, where they hid them.[26]

The 31st's Capt. William Henry "Tip" Harrison recalled the moment when Southern troops entered town. "The citizens of York, who witnessed the entry of the first Confederate regiment, will probably remember a small squad of cavalry, followed by one of infantry of perhaps sixty, stationing a sentinel at each cross street in the town," explained the Rebel captain. "As we marched into the town of York, a lady was heard to say, 'I am ashamed of York, to quietly surrender to forty or fifty nasty, dirty rebels, when there are hundreds of able-bodied men here to fight them.'" In reply, Harrison assured her there were several thousand just behind.[27]

Evans' provosts quickly dispersed throughout York, securing sidewalks and alleyways. Cassandra Small and the ladies of her family had dressed for church, while the men stayed home. Just as the church bells rang, the Smalls heard shouts that the Rebels were coming. She later informed her cousin that she felt "humiliated and disgraced." Men who did not often cry now openly

---

25 Mary Ruggles (1805-1874) lived on Washington Street with her daughter Agnes and son-in-law George Geiselman. She endeared herself to the hospital's patients through her frequent cheery visits. She often brought homemade bread, cakes, and other delicacies to the expectant soldiers. After the Rebels departed York, Mammy brought the flag out of hiding. On July 4, it was again raised over the Army Hospital.

26 Gibson, *History of York County*, 207.

27 *Columbia Spy*, Jan. 16, 1886.

wept as Rebels marched into York with loud music and their flags fluttering in the morning breeze. Miss Small noticed a Confederate picket standing in front of the door of her home and wondered how he got there because he had arrived so suddenly and quietly. Soon other sentries lined Market Street. When she spoke to the guard, he informed her that they were only there to keep the infantrymen in line when they passed through town.[28]

Soon, Cassandra spotted "the first ones to appear—an immense number with shovels, spades, pickaxes, hoes and all sorts of tools—carried them like guns. One lady told us she thought that she would see first officers on prancing horses with handsome uniforms, but when she saw these frightful creatures, she raised her hands and exclaimed, 'Oh, my Heavenly Father, protect us; they are coming to dig our graves.'"[29]

Mrs. L. M. Hartman sat in church listening to the sermon when the back door opened and an excited messenger hurried to the front of the sanctuary to tell the pastor that Rebels were entering town. The preacher folded his sermon notes upon his pulpit, bowed his anguished head over the papers, and wept. Many of his congregants filed onto the church's broad porch, where they could hear the loud strains of "Dixie" coming from an enemy band. Some parishioners rushed to Centre Square to watch the Rebel procession.[30]

Marching behind the pioneers, Colonel Evans termed his regiment's arrival a "triumphal entry" as Capt. W. H. "Tip" Harrison led the color guard and Company E into town. The band played a popular lively tune, "Who stole a ham, Johnny stole a ham." Gordon Bradwell noted the strong contrast between their sullen hosts in Gettysburg and the more curious residents of York, who "seemed animated by a different spirit." As this was Sunday, everyone, young and old, male and female, was "rigged out in his or her best." The crowd was so thick that the regiment passed through the throng with great difficulty, marching two by two instead of the customary four by four. The townspeople exhibited "the greatest anxiety" to converse with the Confederate soldiers, but officers hurried their men along at the quickstep, determined that they should not pause or break ranks.[31]

---

28 Cassandra Small to Lissie Latimer, June 30, 1863, YCHT.

29 *Ibid.*, July 20, 1863, YCHT.

30 Hartman account, YCHT; Prowell, *History of York County*, 1, 407-408.

31 Stephens, *Intrepid Warrior*, 226; Bradwell, "Burning of Wrightsville," 330-31.

As the 31st Georgia approached Centre Square, an elderly resident implored town leaders to take down the American flag. John L. Evans was a well-regarded attorney who lived in a small apartment at the corner of the square. In a voice choked with emotion, he cried, "Is it possible to have lived to this day to see the flag torn down and trampled in the dirt?" Several citizens gathered around Evans and joined him in urging the Committee of Safety to haul down the flag to prevent the Confederates from confiscating it. Committee member Latimer Small defiantly exclaimed, "Let them take the flag, and I will replace it."[32]

Not wanting his soldiers to march directly under the massive Union flag, Colonel Evans ordered it hauled down. "A courier of General Gordon's escort, assisted by [Pvt. Augustus E.] Choate, pulled down the flag and placed it upon the sidewalk," remembered "Tip" Harrison. "Afterward a young man picked it up and folded it in his arms, and later it was placed in an ambulance and carried into Virginia to be kept as a souvenir of the first Confederate invasion of Pennsylvania."[33]

York's beauty impressed Clement Evans. His men marveled at the towering flagpole, flanked by two small open-sided sheds used by farmers to market their produce. A pair of imposing buildings dominated the scene. John Hartman's six-story edifice, a local landmark, elicited admiration. William C. Goodridge owned the other eye-catching multi-story structure on the square. The son of a Maryland slave, the free black businessman had for several years reportedly shipped escaped slaves across the Columbia Bridge hidden in his freight cars. Some Yorkers speculated that Goodridge's emporium and his Philadelphia Street house actually were hiding places for runaway slaves passing through town.[34]

Arriving in town shortly afterward with his main force, John Gordon noticed the stark contrast between his marching infantrymen and the

---

32 Fisher account, YCHT; Gibson, *History of York County*, 436. Sixty-three-year-old John Evans had read law with Thaddeus Stevens, and future President Buchanan served on the board when Evans passed his bar exam in 1822.

33 *Columbia Spy*, Jan. 16, 1886. The fate of the flag is uncertain. Years later, in response to a letter from a York editor to Governor Gordon, Tip Harrison, then of the executive staff, replied that he did not know its whereabouts. Another account from the *York True Democrat* suggests that Gordon hauled the flag down himself with some of his men's help, and rode off with it draped across his horse.

34 The house still stands at 123 E. Philadelphia Street.

churchgoers in their Sunday best. His men, horses, and wagons were begrimed from "head to foot with the impalpable gray powder" from long days of marching on the turnpike. It was "no wonder that many of York's inhabitants were terror-stricken as they looked upon us." Jubal Early had left the brigade's baggage wagons at Greenwood in order to speed its marches. There was now no possibility for the dirty soldiers to change their clothing nor did they have time to brush their uniforms or wash the dust from their faces, hair, and beards. All the Confederates were of the same hideous hue. "Barefooted men mounted double upon huge horses with shaggy manes and long fetlocks" speckled the grotesque-appearing column.[35]

Gordon and his staff entered Centre Square about the same time as A. B. Farquhar, who galloped into town from the south after leaving his vantage post on Webb's Hill. Gordon noted the vast gathering in the heart of York. The faces of the men expressed their apprehension, and many of the women were clearly alarmed. Small children appeared to be terrified at the spectacle of more than a thousand Confederate soldiers and cavalrymen who marched along the three parallel streets. Anxious to reassure the crowd, Gordon halted his column and delivered a brief speech from horseback:

Ladies and gentlemen of York: It is doubtless a painful sight to you to see a hostile army in your midst. I beg you to remember, however, that you have been accustoming our eyes to such sights for several years past. I wish to assure you, however, that General Lee and the Confederate soldiers have entered your state in no spirit of retaliation. We are here simply to fight the armies which are invading our soil and destroying our houses. The men who are before you in dusty gray uniforms, barefooted many of them and ragged, are gentlemen and the sons of gentlemen. They are actuated by no mean spirit, but by the loftiest conception of duty that ever moved men in any war—that of self-defense.

I beg to assure you that no private property will be disturbed, and if one woman in this city is insulted by one of these soldiers, I promise you the head of such a man. They have just read in the *Philadelphia Inquirer* of this morning of the destruction, by order of Federal commanders, of the town of Buford, South Carolina, and of Darien, Georgia. Some of these men were citizens of Darien, and naturally feel some indignation at the destruction of their homes,

35 Gordon, *Reminiscences*, 142.

but as I have already stated, there is in their hearts no spirit of retaliation, and they fight only the men with arms in their hands.[36]

After Gordon's remarks quieted the throng, Farquhar implored him not to replace the confiscated flag with a Confederate banner. Gordon generously agreed, and his column continued its parade through York. Several Georgians spotted another prominent flag flying from a 20-foot pole on E. Main Street in front of Pierce's bookstore, just past Centre Square. Assisted by local Copperhead Kirk White, a Rebel officer quickly hauled down the flag and carried it away.[37]

Nearby, Gordon again paused to address a large group of citizens packing the sidewalks. A bevy of young ladies recoiled at his dust-begrimed appearance, but a few words from the general quieted them. He assured them that his ill-clad and travel-stained soldiers were actually good, brave men and that beneath their rough exterior appearance beat hearts as loyal toward women as any honorable man's. Many of his soldiers and their mothers, wives, and sisters at home had experienced a hostile army occupying their towns. His men were under the strict orders of the Confederate commander-in-chief, and both private property and non-combatants were safe. His dust-covered, "knightly men" had no place in their bosoms for revenge and rapine. He closed by pledging that he would have the head of any soldier who destroyed any private property, disturbed family homes, or insulted a woman.[38]

Cassandra Small related that Gordon stopped his horse at her door and walked up to the paved sidewalk. "Ladies, I have a word to say," announced the officer. "I suppose you think me a pretty rough looking man, but when I am shaved and dressed, my wife considers me a very good-looking fellow. I want to say to you we have not come among you to pursue the same warfare your men did in our country. You need not have any fear of us, whilst we are in your midst. You are just as safe as though we were a thousand miles away. That is all I have to say." Gordon bowed, wheeled his horse, and rode away.[39]

---

36 *Atlanta Journal*, Sept. 16, 1888.

37 Prowell, *History of York County*, 1, 408; James Latimer to Bartow Latimer, July 8, 1863, YCHT.

38 Gordon, *Reminiscences*, 142-43.

39 Cassandra Small to Lissie Latimer, July 8, 1863, YCHT.

Republican attorney James Latimer questioned the propriety of women conversing with an enemy general. Most of the ladies of York had the sense to stay home, including those of his own household. He had shuttered the parlor windows, and his family stayed hidden. Latimer thought that the conduct of the people that crowded the streets to gawk at the Confederates was disgraceful. "Even Philip Small, who should have known better," he wrote, "allowed his family to stand on his porch to gaze at them."[40]

As they marched through York, Gordon's soldiers had time to form judgments about the townspeople. Not surprisingly, they paid close attention to the ladies lining the sidewalks and balconies. During the entire time ordnance officer William Lyon was in Pennsylvania he never encountered a single female who appeared delicate and refined. While he saw many well-dressed ones in York and other towns, even these women "showed unmistakable signs of lowness and vulgarity."[41]

In return, York residents drew mixed opinions about the dirty, foul-smelling Southern troops marching through their principal streets. In some cases, bareheaded Confederates lifted hats from the heads of bystanders, including 17-year-old David Landis. A few terrified inhabitants withdrew into their homes, shutters and curtains drawn tight. By contrast, some Copperheads openly demonstrated support for the invaders. Handkerchiefs waved from two leading hotels and a few nearby residences. Other citizens were merely curious, expressing no opinion regarding these dirt-caked men from Dixie. A few Rebels carried knapsacks confiscated from the 87th Pennsylvania after Milroy's debacle at Winchester, causing anxious family members to wonder about loved ones still missing from that regiment.[42]

Among the enemy soldiers was Cassandra Small's cousin, George Latimer. She was happy that she did not see him, because she absolutely did not want to speak to him, nor he her. When some of Latimer's Copperhead friends spotted him and shook his hand, he begged them not to tell Cassandra and her family. However, they could not keep the secret. "We all respect him a great deal more than we do them," admitted Miss Small.

40 James Latimer to Bartow Latimer, July 8, 1863, YCHT.

41 *Mobile Advertiser & Register*, Aug. 9, 1863.

42 James Latimer to Bartow Latimer, July 8, 1863, YCHT. One of the Copperheads waving flags was the wife of prominent physician Dr. Charles M. Nes, the son of a former U. S. congressman.

Some ladies encouraged the passing Rebels by waving handkerchiefs and red streamers. Others stopped soldiers and obtained uniform buttons as souvenirs. Small wrote disgustedly that these traitorous women "will never be recognized again" in York society. She marveled that the Rebels marched with such order and strict discipline, remaining "all perfectly quiet, making no noise at all." Townspeople did not insult the enemy soldiers, fire upon them from the windows, or even wave small flags in their faces, as "our poor fellows had wherever they went" in the South. Other residents opened their hearts and pantries. Sarah Ann Bayler noticed some Rebels resting near her house. Pitying the youths so far from their homes, she brought them food.[43]

"York was much larger than Gettysburg, and the inhabitants did not shut themselves up in their houses through fear of us, but were so anxious to see us and converse with us that we had some difficulty in forcing our way through the city," Private I. G. Bradwell recalled, who went on to explain,

It was Sunday morning, and everybody was dressed in his very best. So great was the pressure that our officers marched us through the town in single column of twos. Handsomely dressed women extended their hands from each side, anxious to have a word with us; but our officers hurried us along as rapidly as possible. Among the men I saw several who were suffering from wounds, but these kept themselves well to the rear and did not seek to come in contact with us. The people of York were the most refined and intelligent folk we met in the State and reminded us of our friends at home, both in manners and personal appearance. They did not seem to be a bit reserved, and if we had not known where we were, we might, from their conduct, have supposed ourselves in Dixie.[44]

One Confederate officer, whose identify is lost to history, rode slowly along Market Street and picked up Mary C. Fisher's daughter (also named Mary). "I have a little daughter at home with eyes just as blue as yours," he told her. The officer gently set her down and continued riding east. Private George F. Agee of

---

43 Cassandra Small to Lissie Latimer, July 8, 1863, YCHT. George S. Latimer and his brother Thomas were footsoldiers in Company C of the 1st Maryland in Brig. Gen. George Steuart's brigade, also of Ewell's Corps. They likely were guides for Gordon because they were York residents before the war. They had traveled to Baltimore to enlist in the Confederate army.

44 Bradwell, "Crossing the Potomac," 371.

the 26th Georgia recalled, "In passing through York, and when about midway, the street was lined from end to end with citizens, both men and women, as though there was no war going on. A gentleman stepped up to me and asked what troops we were. I told him we were Stonewall Jackson's foot cavalry." James J. M. Smith's shoes had given out the day before as the 31st Georgia marched into Gettysburg. "In York," he recalled, "an old lady came out to the sidewalk and gave me a pair of coarse woolen socks with some kind of words— bless her. There were many soldiers in the same pitiable plight."[45]

Gordon and his staff quietly passed by the Presbyterian Church and its old graveyard, which contained the remains of James Smith, a signer of the Declaration of Independence. Now Gordon's Georgia was seeking her independence from the United States as part of a new confederation and, ironically, riding near colonial hero James Smith's grave was Col. James Smith, commander of the 13th Georgia. He would resign his commission in 1864 to become a Confederate congressman.[46]

Gordon later claimed that as he rode his horse along the main street, a young girl slipped out of the crowd and handed him a bouquet of fresh red roses. Much to his surprise, hidden inside was a handwritten note. Quickly scanning it, he learned that only militia defended the crucial bridge leading to Lancaster County. The unsigned letter did not express any sympathy for the Southern cause, and was so terse and explicit that he believed its authenticity. He carefully reread it to make sure he comprehended its contents.[47]

The authorship of this intriguing note, written in a woman's flowery handwriting, has long been debated. It could have come from a Southern sympathizer or spy in Wrightsville. Perhaps she (or he, disguising his writing style) had described the Federal defenses from firsthand observations. The spy may have entrusted the vital communication to a neighbor girl or family member for personal delivery to Gordon, who was widely known to be entering York that Sunday morning. Devoid of any distinctive military markings or

---

45 McClure, York Towne Square blog entry, May 7, 2007, citing James Rudisill's interview with Mary Fisher; *The Sunny South*, July 20, 1901, and Sept. 23, 1904.

46 The Articles of Confederation were adopted in York in the colonial courthouse.

47 Gordon, *Reminiscences*, 143. Gordon stated that the girl was twelve. In an interview with the *Atlanta Journal* on Sept. 16, 1888, Gordon related that the girl was "about ten years old." Research by the York County Heritage Trust suggests this girl was 12-year-old Margaret Ann Small, the daughter of York butcher William Small. *York Sunday News*, Jan. 21, 2007.

signature, it is unlikely that the letter came from one of the many Virginia cavalry patrols roaming the area.

Locals suspected that the Confederates for months had secretly scouted possible targets in the region. Townspeople thought to be in league with slave traders and bounty hunters were suspected of spying; strangers even more so. For weeks, rumors circulated regarding a certain Bible salesman hanging about the Federal positions, watching the comings and goings of the soldiers and taking notes. According to one story, he now rode beside General Gordon. Another resident recalled meeting an individual in a downtown bar who expressed unusual interest in what went on in Wrightsville, days before Gordon's expedition.[48]

Some citizens likely recalled a well publicized incident from the previous invasion scare in September 1862. Authorities then had arrested a man and four women at Hanover Junction "under very suspicious circumstances." At the time, according to newspaper accounts, "there is evidence to believe that the whole party has been scouting through the country as spies. The women were intelligent, and when taken into custody persistently refused to give any account of themselves." The arrest served to heighten the region's sensitivity to inquisitive strangers.[49]

On July 2, Union guards at Harrisburg would capture a man in a rowboat measuring the depth of the Susquehanna River near the Cumberland Valley Bridge. He had hidden horses on a nearby island. Apparently he intended to report to the Rebels with information on the fords and the number of Federal troops in the vicinity. It is possible this spy penned the Wrightsville note days earlier. If not this particular agent, there were undoubtedly other scouts who had reason and opportunity to take notes on Yankee positions and relay them to Confederate commanders.[50]

---

48 According to a Reading newspaper, shortly before the battle of Gettysburg, authorities arrested six alleged Confederate spies in Pottsville and sent them in irons to Philadelphia. One of them possessed sketches of Schuylkill County and all of its collieries.

49 *Philadelphia Inquirer*, Sept. 12, 1862.

50 Bates, *History of Pennsylvania Volunteers*, 5, 1227-28. On June 29 in Gettysburg, Pvt. Thomas Smith of the 7th Michigan Cavalry captured 35-year-old Will Talbott, who was dressed in civilian clothing and asking school children for information regarding Union troops. Talbott admitted that he was a member of White's battalion, but insisted he was a scout, not a spy. When his captor found documents hidden in a boot, Talbott was locked in the county jail. Later he was turned over to Brig. Gen. John Buford, who executed him in Frederick. Buford left the

Gordon, with the mysterious note allegedly in his pocket, supervised the lengthy march through York. His three parallel columns converged near the town limits and took the turnpike east toward Wrightsville. A dozen ambulance wagons followed them. Most had been captured earlier in the war and still bore the markings of the U.S. Army. With flags flying and bands playing, Gordon's Brigade marched away from what they assumed would be their only visit to York. The general and his escort remained behind to await the arrival of Jubal Early. About noon, Col. Isaac Avery's North Carolinians, moving by way of Weigelstown to the Harrisburg-York turnpike, entered York and quartered at the fairgrounds and the military hospital. There, Early met with Gordon and again instructed him to proceed to the Susquehanna and secure the Columbia Bridge, if possible.[51]

As Gordon leisurely rode eastward to rejoin his command, Early established headquarters in the courthouse and laid York under tribute. Commissary officer Capt. William Thornton requisitioned 165 barrels of flour or 28,000 pounds of baked bread; 3,500 pounds of sugar; 1,650 pounds of coffee; 300 gallons of molasses; 1,200 pounds of salt; 32,000 pounds of fresh beef or 21,000 pounds of bacon or pork. All were to be delivered at the market house on Main Street at 4 p.m. Early's chief quartermaster, Maj. C. E. Snodgrass, demanded 2,000 pairs of shoes or boots, 1,000 pairs of socks, 1,000 felt hats and $100,000 in greenbacks.[52]

Unlike in Gettysburg, this time the Pennsylvanians fulfilled most of Early's demands. However, Chief Burgess David Small informed him that the town's banks had already sent off their assets and could not raise that amount of cash. One Rebel wrote, "As there is no money in the bank, there has been a committee of the citizens appointed to raise it, which I think can be done, as they are terribly scared." Authorities went door to door throughout York's wards soliciting cash to meet Early's demands. Attorney James W. Latimer, as

---

corpse hanging for three days with a note that a similar fate awaited anyone who cut it down. Perhaps Talbott was Gordon's informer, having returned to Gettysburg after dropping off the note on Wrightsville's defenses to the little girl in York. He would have known that White's battalion and Gordon were passing through York that Sunday. He also associated with children.

51 OR 27, pt. 2, 466; Early, *War Memoirs*, 259; Stiles, *Four Years Under Marse Robert*, 210-12. Most of these ambulances were captured from Milroy near Winchester. The old Harrisburg Road today is N. George Street.

52 Prowell, *History of York County*, 1: 410.

he later rued, "very foolishly gave them one hundred dollars." Aged John Evans donated $50, W. Latimer Small $25, and the firm of P.A. & S. Small contributed $752. Major Snodgrass eventually wrote a receipt for $28,610, well below Early's goal of $100,000. Gettysburg resident Sallie Broadhead penned in her diary that the people of York were "dunce-like" in paying this ransom to the Rebels, "which they pocketed." Early thought differently when he wrote, "I was satisfied that they had made an honest effort to raise the amount called for." On another occasion, he penned, "The people of York were wise in 'accepting the situation.'"[53]

The Reverend Samuel L. Roth sought an audience with General Early. The Mennonite pastor complained that one of the Rebels had taken his prized horse: "It was the best animal I ever owned. My wife and daughter can drive him. He was our family horse and I want him back. Will you let me have him?" Early informed him that Gordon's men had probably taken the horse. If he talked to that general, he would probably get his mare back.[54]

Telegraph wires buzzed with the news that Confederates occupied York. Earlier in the war, Col. Thomas A. Scott had been assistant secretary of war, supervising all government railroads and transportation lines. In June 1862, the 39-year-old resigned and returned to Philadelphia to resume his position as vice-president of the Pennsylvania Railroad. Now in Harrisburg serving as an adviser to Governor Curtin, Scott wired railroader J. H. Black that Rebels had taken possession of York and that all engines and trains should be sent across the Wrightsville bridge which, he added, had to be defended to the very last. "The rebels must not get a footing on this side of the Susquehanna," he admonished. "Can you keep them off? I hope every man will place as musket to his shoulder, and never surrender the town."[55]

53 Files of YCHT; Broadhead diary, ACHS; *SHSP*, Vol. 10, 540; Jubal A. Early, "The Invasion of Pennsylvania, by the Confederate States Army, in June 1863," in *The Historical Magazine and Notes and Queries*, Vol. 1, Series 3 (Morrisania, N.Y.: Henry B. Dawson, 1872-3), 233. Early's headquarters were in the sheriff's office in the County Courthouse on E. Market Street.

54 Prowell, *History of York County*, 1, 412.

55 OR 27, pt. 3, 367; *History of Franklin County, Pennsylvania* (Chicago: Warner, Beers & Co., 1887), 425. In his early adulthood, Scott collected tolls for the Pennsylvania (North Branch) Canal in Columbia before moving to Altoona to become a railroader.

Chapter 9

Wrightsville Prepares

A War Hero Returns to Duty

While refugees thronged eastward toward the Columbia Bridge and perceived safety beyond the Susquehanna River, military preparations were well under way to defend the structure. Major General Darius Couch, commanding the Department of the Susquehanna, assigned 38-year-old Col. Jacob G. Frick of Pottsville and his 27th Pennsylvania Volunteer Militia to the task. Six feet, two inches tall and powerfully built, Frick was a career regular army soldier who immediately impressed those who met him. The stern-looking veteran of the Mexican War had faced Confederate bullets at Fredericksburg and Chancellorsville. On June 7, 1892, long after the Civil War, Frick would receive a Medal of Honor for his efforts at those fights.[1]

Jacob Frick was born in Northumberland County on January 23, 1825, the ninth of sixteen children. They were fourth-generation descendants of a Swiss immigrant who had settled in Pennsylvania in the 1700s. As a youth, instead of joining his family's boat-building business, Frick went to Canton, Ohio, to learn printing. In June 1846, he was commissioned as a third lieutenant in the 3rd Ohio Volunteer Infantry with the outbreak of the Mexican War and served with gallantry in several engagements. After the war, Frick was commissioned as a second lieutenant in the 11th U.S. Infantry. He married in 1850 and garrisoned at several army bases across the country throughout the decade. Later, he served as assistant instructor of infantry tactics at Fort McHenry in Baltimore

---

1 Bates, *Martial Deeds*, 834.

Colonel Jacob G. Frick after the Civil War received the Medal of Honor for his valor at Fredericksburg and Chancellorsville while commanding the 129th Pennsylvania. During the Gettysburg Campaign, his 27th Pennsylvania Volunteer Militia guarded the Columbia Bridge. *Schuylkill County Historical Society*

before returning home to Pottsville and civilian life. Frick was a delegate to the 1860 Republican National Convention, where Abraham Lincoln received the presidential nomination.[2]

When the Civil War erupted, Frick became lieutenant colonel of the 96th Pennsylvania and subsequently fought in the Peninsula Campaign. On July 29, 1862, he became colonel of the 129th Pennsylvania, again serving with distinction. Major General Joseph Hooker ordered Frick to lead the last charge at Fredericksburg in December, and he bravely guided his regiment toward the celebrated stonewall on Marye's Heights. His flag bearer and most of the color guard went down as the battle line advanced. Frick quickly seized and raised the fallen flag, but almost instantly, a Minié ball passed close to his head and sheared the wooden staff in two. The banner drooped over his shoulders. Undaunted, Frick continued at the head of his cheering command until he was wounded near the stone wall. Like most other Federal efforts on the fateful day, Frick's charge failed. His regiment held its ground briefly, but in the face of the excellent Confederate position, it had no chance. More and more Pennsylvanians were shot down. Frick, holding his flag aloft, finally led his remaining men from the field.[3]

A dispute with division headquarters over dress coats for his men led Frick to be cashiered by a court-martial on January 25, 1863, but the War Department quickly recommissioned him. At Chancellorsville in May, Frick's precision in handling his regiment impressed his brigadier, who declared that "no man ever saw cooler work" than that of the 129th Pennsylvania. Their firing was "grand—by rank, by company, and by wings; all in perfect order." His embattled soldiers clearly heard Colonel Frick's stentorian voice above the roar of musketry, and his regiment "did its duty well." He even managed to recapture their lost flag in hand-to-hand combat with several Rebels.[4]

The 129th mustered out in May when its term of enlistment expired and Frick returned to Pottsville. When Robert E. Lee's invasion threatened the

2 *Albany (NY) Evening Journal*, May 14, 1860. Other delegates to the 1860 Republican convention included abolitionist Thaddeus Stevens; Gettysburg attorney David McConaughy; Samuel Schoch, cashier of the Columbia Bank which owned the Columbia Bridge; and William B. Thomas of Philadelphia, later colonel of the 20th PVM.

3 See: www.pacivilwar.com/cwmohd

4 *OR* 25, pt. 1, 551; Pennsylvania Civil War Veterans' Card File, State Archives; Bates, *History of Pennsylvania Volunteers*, 4, 186. Gen. A. A. Humphreys pressed the charges against Colonel Frick.

Keystone State, he hurried to Harrisburg to assume command of the 807-man 27th Pennsylvania Volunteer Militia. It was raised primarily in Frick's native Schuylkill County in north-central Pennsylvania, as well as in nearby Northampton, Huntingdon, and Berks counties. Several recruits from this mountainous region were anthracite coal miners, used to hard labor with the pick and shovel. That skill later would prove handy.

Upon receiving a telegraph from Governor Curtin that Confederates threatened Pennsylvania, Schuylkill County officials had called a mass meeting of their citizens and exhorted them to prepare to resist the invaders. When a second telegram soon arrived confirming that the Rebels now had entered the state, the county leaders passed a resolution to close all places of business, and "let the whole population devote itself to the organization of companies to march at once."

In the county seat of Pottsville, Capt. David A. Smith called out the local 113-man militia group, the "Washington Artillerists." They departed for Harrisburg at noon on Wednesday, June 17, along with seventy-three men raised in Donaldson through the exertions of wealthy coal merchant Theodore Garretson and the local Union League. Ten Pottsville newspaper employees, including associate editor and military veteran Francis B. Wallace, left their office and enlisted. Their impulsive act, however, left only three men to produce the paper's next editions. The 34-year-old Lieutenant Wallace would send frontline reports back to his newspaper.[5]

Patriotism and emotions ran high. As Daniel Dillman and fellow volunteer Jesse Hawley said goodbye to Hawley's father, the elderly Quaker instructed his son, "If thee doesn't get a chance to shoot a rebel, don't forget to kill a 'copperhead' before thee comes home." On Thursday morning, a company of seventy men under Capt. Levi C. Leib left for Harrisburg. Leib was badly wounded at Fredericksburg the previous year and still supported his arm in a sling. However, he felt that his state was in danger and needed his services. He would be turned down, but his most of his men joined the 27th Militia.[6]

---

5   Francis B. Wallace, *Memorial of the Patriotism of Schuylkill County in the American Slaveholders Rebellion* (Pottsville, Pa.: Benjamin Bannan, 1865), 256. Wallace was the second lieutenant of Co. F of the 2nd Militia during the Emergency of 1862, serving under Capt. David A. Smith, his commander in the new 27th Militia.

6   *Pottsville Journal,* July 17, 1913. Hawley would return home from the 27th Militia's camp in Chambersburg on a ten-day furlough just prior to his father's death on July 26 after a brief illness.

One eager volunteer ended up missing his train to the state capital. A young Irishman enlisted in one of the companies from Ashland. At the station, his father dragged him from a railcar against his protests. His mother also tried to force him to return home, but the young man broke free and was trying to re-board the train when his parents again grabbed him. He struck his father and once more attempted to enter the car. While they struggled, the train departed without him.[7]

A former soldier in Frick's 129th Pennsylvania had better luck. Nineteen-year-old Elias Hoppes enlisted on June 18, but Tamaqua recruiting officers turned down his 56-year-old father Solomon because of his advanced age. The older man, a prosperous farmer, declared that he would follow the army with a shotgun in order to help suppress the Rebels. His determination convinced Capt. Jacob Martz to enroll him as a private in what would become Company E. That same afternoon, 65 employees from a Pottsville rolling mill also enlisted in a move that effectively shut down entrepreneur Benjamin Haywood's facility.[8]

After arriving at Harrisburg's sprawling Camp Curtin, the excited volunteers were soon mustered into the new 27th Militia and given Springfield muskets, tents, and accouterments. Frick and his staff began cursory military drills after establishing camp on June 22 on the heights near Bridgeport, across the river from the capital. Jacob Frick's personal courage and bravery were unquestioned, and he expected no less from his subordinates. All of his field officers and most of the line officers were veterans of the Army of the Potomac. One subaltern, newspaperman Wallace, reported that the regiment's field and staff officers are all "gentlemen of ability, and much beloved already by our men." He rated Frick as a "tip-top Colonel, thoroughly understanding his business." Wallace also had high regard for 31-year-old Lt. Col. David B. Green, Frick's former adjutant in the 129th Pennsylvania. Wallace thought it would "be difficult to scare up a superior quartermaster" than Lt. William F. Patterson, also from Frick's old regiment. These officers commanded "a

7 Wallace, *Memorial of the Patriotism of Schuylkill County*, 256.

8 *Reading Eagle*, Jan. 17, 1909. Twenty-two-year-old Jacob H. Martz had been a sergeant in Elias Hoppes' Company E of the 129th Pennsylvania. Hoppes' pension affidavit states, "When I came home [from the 129th] I was Lame in Back and legs and by rest and a good bed I came able again for the Emergency of our state Enrolled June 4 1863 had a Battle at Wrightville Pa had to burn the Bridge at Columbia to safe Harrisburg all the time I was not able to sleep on the ground always on board . . ." Elias S. Hoppes Pension File WC–698-748, NARA.

Regiment of which Schuylkill may be proud." Private John O. Beck of Company B proclaimed that Frick's reputation was "so firmly established as one of the very best officers in the service, that anything I might say of him, could not add anything to it."[9]

On to Columbia and Wrightsville

Colonel Frick issued marching orders during the afternoon on Monday, June 22. His men packed their knapsacks and struck tents, and at 4:30 p.m. tramped from Camp Curtin through the capital and across the bridge to Camp Susquehanna near the fortifications being built to defend Harrisburg. The boys were in such high spirits that soldiering was voted "a decided institution." They pitched tents and established a camp guard. "Lights were ordered out at 'taps,' 9 o'clock," wrote Lieutenant Wallace, "and our first guard was unmarked by any episode more startling than the firing by one of the guard of his piece at 3 o'clock in the morning, at an imaginary rebel stealing upon him through the wheat of a neighboring field."[10]

On Wednesday the 24th, General Couch issued Special Order No. 14 which instructed Frick to proceed to Columbia to "effectively secure all bridges and fords in Lancaster County along the Susquehanna." The commanding general called upon the loyal citizens to render Frick "all assistance" for this purpose. The assignment of Frick, a seasoned veteran of the regular army, relieved volunteer officers Col. Emlen Franklin and Maj. Charles Haldeman, the region's previous commanders. Couch ordered them to turn over to Frick any instructions that had been previously received from District headquarters. Frick and his hastily trained regiment departed Harrisburg at 9:00 a.m. in freight cars owned by the Pennsylvania Railroad. Much to the soldiers' delight, the small towns along the Susquehanna welcomed them with enthusiasm. Francis Wallace informed his newspaper readers that as the regiment rolled along a fourteen- mile stretch near Marietta, they were "cheered heartily by the entire

9 *Pottsville Miners' Journal,* June 27, 1863, and Oct. 24, 1863. The regiment mustered into state service at 2:00 p.m. on Friday, June 19, at Camp Curtin. Patterson and Green served under Frick in the 129th Pennsylvania, a 90-day regiment. Green was Frick's adjutant and Patterson his quartermaster. Frick recruited other former officers and staff to serve with him during the emergency, including Surgeon Otto Schittler.

10 *Pottsville Miners' Journal,* Oct. 24, 1863.

population which thronged the avenue. The people were badly frightened last week, but are now more calm."[11]

Arriving in Columbia about noon, the militia elicited praise from the residents. Local newspaperman Samuel Wright opined, "The entire regiment is made up of splendid material, and as the men are uniformed and equipped by the government, they present a very different appearance from the motley militia of 1862." The 27th marched through town and camped in a ravine near Lockard's Meadow. Frick, following military protocol, met with Franklin and Haldeman to inform them that he was officially assuming command. Haldeman, home in Columbia after mustering out of the 23rd Pennsylvania, volunteered his services as an unofficial aide, an offer that Frick eagerly accepted. Haldeman soon became the liaison between the colonel and civic authorities, many of which were acquainted with the veteran major. Frick also accepted the services of Capt. Matthew M. Strickler's company of local civilians as informal cavalry scouts.[12]

Colonel Frick instructed Lt. Colonel Green to take four companies to man the rifle-pits one-half mile west of Wrightsville. Clad in their crisp new uniforms, the soldiers paraded across the old bridge and followed Hellam Street up a steep hill. Frick's old 129th Pennsylvania silk flag fluttered above them. The detachment camped in the fields of the Joseph Detwiler farm, just east of the rifle-pits. Frick ordered Green to send out pickets to watch for Confederate cavalry rumored to be operating in eastern York County. Several other companies remained in Columbia at Lockard's Meadow, a short distance from the railroad station. Fort Case, still manned by several Lancaster County volunteers, was just to the south. Another detachment of home guards patrolled the crescent-shaped earthworks dotting Grubb's Ridge. Frick wired Harrisburg asking that field artillery be dispatched to Columbia for this new fortification. Suitable guns soon arrived fairly quickly on flatcars from Philadelphia, though without ammunition or crewmen. The guns sat idle on a rail siding.[13]

11 OR 27, pt. 3, 297-98; *Pottsville Miners' Journal*, June 27, 1863.

12 *Columbia Spy*, June 27, 1863. Haldeman had been captain of Company I of the 23rd Pennsylvania before resigning on New Year's Day, 1863. Strickler, Columbia's internal revenue tax collector, owned several limestone quarries. He was a sergeant in the 2nd PVM in the Emergency of 1862.

13 *Pottsville Miners' Journal*, Oct. 24, 1863; *Columbia Spy*, June 27, 1863.

The next morning, June 25, Frick dispatched four more companies across the bridge to Green for duty in the rifle-pits. One infantryman remembered, "On Thursday we left camp in the meadow which was the property of a Mennonite family who were 'Conscientious' in everything except charging us full price for everything we got, except for some cream which was 'confiscated' by some of our men." Another soldier recalled a visit to the J. H. Huber farmhouse "where some of us appropriated a quantity of cream and milk from a spring house."[14]

Frick relieved most of the civilian volunteers, including Professor Wickersham's home defense company from the Millersville Normal School and Capt. William Atlee's Franklin & Marshall contingent. The collegians marched back to Lancaster the next day and stacked their muskets in Center Square, ending their brief service as amateur soldiers. A year later, student J. R. Shallenberger wrote, "We were at Wrightsville one week and from that I experienced that a soldier is not the life for me, and yet I know that it would be my duty to go and fight for my country." Frick's two militia companies in Columbia found comfortable new quarters in the Columbia Bridge Company's old tobacco warehouse. Captain David Smith's Company A and Capt. Frank Pott's Company B rotated shifts as bridge guards. Newspaperman Francis Wallace commanded one group of sentinels.[15]

Colonel Frick spent most of Thursday in downtown Columbia, tending to the dismissal of several more home guard companies and to other military matters. He detailed Lt. Delaplaine J. Ridgway and a detachment of the 27th Militia to man the fieldpieces. Two of these guns protected Fort Case, while a third guarded the eastern entrance to the bridge. Frick relieved Capt. E. K. Smith, the previous volunteer artillery commander, but Smith and some of his civilian crew volunteered to help the soldiers with the guns. Frick and Haldeman met with Chief Burgess Peter Frailey and other Columbia authorities to make sure lines of communication were open and clear. Frick was introduced to W. Robert Crane, the superintendent of the Reading & Columbia Railroad

14   Spicer, John E., *The Columbia Civil War Centennial* (Middletown, Pa.: Wert Binding, 1976), 30; *Pottsville Miners' Journal*, Sept. 23, 1875. The second soldier visited the area 25 years later with his family. He noted, "We plead the statute of limitations and war's demoralization—the lacteal fluid would have soured before the family returned, or been gobbled up by the Rebs anyhow, and besides it was our only depredation during the whole campaign."

15 J. R. Shallenberger to his uncle, Daniel Rohrer, May 7, 1864, courtesy of Rodger Hornberger.

Terrified residents often hid their horses or livestock in remote woodlots in rural York County. This photo was taken by Marion Post Wolcott in June 1939 for the Farm Security Administration. *Library of Congress*

and a civic leader. They discussed logistics and what the railroads could provide to help supply the militia. The colonel dispatched regimental quartermaster Lt. William Patterson and Sgt. Norman Willetts to accompany Crane in order to take an inventory of any usable materials stored in the warehouses lining the canal.[16]

Frick and Haldeman inspected Fort Case and the Grubb's Ridge lunette, and examined the terrain just outside of Columbia. He noted where to place troops in case of an attack. Frick learned the location of nearby fords where Rebels cross the river. He sent Strickler's scouts to watch them, although recent heavy rains had swollen the river. Frick noted some empty canalboats tied

16 Ridgway served in the 2nd Militia during the Emergency of 1862 as a sergeant in Company F, comprised of several members of Pottsville's "Washington Artillery." The Reading & Columbia Railroad only began service in January 1863, but Crane was already well known in the community from various business ventures and his strong Democratic politics.

alongside the North Branch Canal; these might come in handy if he needed to ship troops up to the Marietta ford.[17]

Finally satisfied with the military preparations unfolding on the eastern riverbank, Frick turned his attention to Wrightsville. About 5:00 p.m. on Friday, June 26, he and his adjutant, William L. Whitney, rode across the bridge into York County. When they reached the makeshift camp at the Joseph Detwiler farm, Frick dismounted and surveyed nearby terrain the Rebels would surely use to their advantage. In particular, the colonel took note of a sharp ravine to south of the farm and the Hellam Heights rising north of the turnpike. With sufficient troops these would positions would make excellent defensive strongpoints, but Frick only had his regiment and the remaining civilian volunteers—far fewer than the thousands of soldiers he needed to properly defend such an extended line.

Frick ordered Adjutant Whitney to return to the Columbia telegraph station to await further instructions from General Couch. Throughout Friday and into Saturday, Frick, still hoping to occupy Hellam Heights, sought more troops to reinforce his position. He briefly considered repositioning the guns from Columbia to a small knoll on the J. H. Huber farm, between the heights and his lines. However, lacking confidence in this position as well as in his untested militia, the veteran officer prudently decided to leave the artillery on the other side of the river, which was "rapidly rising and the fords will be impassable."[18]

Frick's aides briefed local officials that more than a thousand Rebels were reportedly passing through eastern York County. Lancaster leaders braced for what they expected would be a full-fledged invasion of their county. Sidney Josephine Myer recorded in her diary that many horses and carriages with refugees passed through the county, creating "great excitement" by reporting that Rebels were advancing on Hanover Junction. The Rev. E. V. Gerhart, President of Franklin & Marshall College, dismissed the school year on Saturday and sent all students home in the face of the advancing armies. Earlier, many of the collegians and educators had dug the first rifle-pits at Wrightsville. Instead of heading home, several students headed for Columbia to watch the enemy's approach. In nearby Marietta, "Saturday capped the climax in our

17 A lunette is a temporary fortification or detached bastion and usually shaped like a crescent. These were common during the Civil War as short-term artillery positions.

18 *Albany Evening Journal*, June 27, 1863.

borough—confusion worse confounded—the stores having packed up nearly everything and windows and doors closed, making everything look like a thanks-giving day "away down east."[19]

The chaplain of the 27th Militia, Richard H. Austin, placed an advertisement in the *Columbia Spy* soliciting contributions of religious books, tracts, magazines or papers to be left at Colonel Frick's headquarters. Samuel Wright, the editor, operated the paper from the second floor of the old Baltimore & Susquehanna Railroad depot. He had company in covering the war news. At least eight correspondents, including some from rival papers in New York City and Philadelphia, were sending dispatches from Columbia's telegraph office by nightfall.[20]

Throughout the day, a steady stream of refugees passed through Frick's position on the turnpike. They shared graphic descriptions of the Rebel advance through Adams and York counties. Lieutenant Francis Wallace reported that excitement that morning was high, despite the persistent drizzle. The fleeing throng included large numbers of black men, women, and children from the upper valley, as well as hordes of livestock. Wallace observed, "The negroes are especially anxious to elude the rebels as they fear they would be made slaves if captured. . . ." He complained that the people of York County were "alive to the perilous state of affairs but are slow in organizing to resist the invasion. To me, their apathy is incomprehensible."[21]

Columbian Annie Welsh's husband, Brig. Gen. Thomas Welsh, was serving under Ulysses S. Grant near Vicksburg, Mississippi. She informed him, "I guess there never was a time when Columbia was in such a state of excitement as the last ten days. Last week, all week, droves of horses, mules and cattle, and teams of all descriptions kept passing through the town coming from Franklin, Adams and York Counties going, a great many of them, they know not where. On Saturday last, it was distressing to witness old and young, black and white, with all that they were able to move, and a great many with nothing but what they had on, come crowding through and into our town." [22]

---

19 Sidney Josephine Myers, 1863 Diary, LCHS; *Marietta (Pa.) Mariettian*, July 4, 1863.

20 *Columbia Spy*, June 27, 1863, and Dec. 28, 1889.

21 *Pottsville Miners' Journal*, July 4, 1863.

22 Annie Welsh to Thomas Welsh, July 1, 1863. Courtesy of Richard C. Wiggin. Private collection.

A few refugees learned that the immediate threat to their animals was not the Rebels, but the state militia. Wallace commented, "This morning, we are pressing horses for general purposes." Gettysburg carriage maker David Troxel's sons, having eluded Elijah White's raiders in Gettysburg, were taking their father's horse and buggy to Columbia. After a ride of more than forty-five miles, they "got to the big covered bridge at Columbia over the Susquehanna, and . . . people were going through there with their horses just like a cavalcade—chasing through one after the other all the time. At the far end were some Union officials stopping every one that had a good horse, and if the horse suited 'em they'd take it and give in return a slip of paper entitling the owner to pay from the government." The boys managed to convince the officer that it was not a good riding horse, so they were allowed to pass. Several other civilians were not so lucky.[23]

Even the local Columbia home guards became involved in the search for fresh horseflesh. Privates Albert C. Hippey and John C. Clark of Captain M. M. Strickler's scouts were detailed in Columbia to impress more horses. They found one in Bank Alley and forced the owner to surrender it. Clark took charge of the horse, while young Hippey, a veteran of the 135th Pennsylvania, walked up Locust Street to Lancaster Avenue. There he overtook a farmer driving a pair of horses. He halted the wagon and unhitched one of the steeds. The dumbfounded farmer demanded to know what the soldier was doing. Hippey responded that "the general down at the bridge wanted horses for immediate service, and had sent him out to get him one." Furious, the farmer reached for his horse-whip, climbed down from the wagon, and charged the soldier. A stunned Hippey "was compelled to fall back in disorder and wait for reinforcements, which didn't come until the farmer was far out in the country."[24]

Many of Frick's militiamen had little respect for the refugees or townspeople. Corporal Daniel Dillman wrote that the soldiers were "very indignant" at the cowardice of the farmers and the apathy of those citizens who should be the first to defend their homes. He believed that the people of Columbia "exhibited little military spirit," although everyone seemed fully

---

23 Johnson, *Battleground Adventure*, 161; Slade, *Firestorm at Gettysburg*, 33. The Troxel boys temporarily took a job helping a Lancaster farmer with his harvest until they could return to Gettysburg.

24 *Columbia Spy*, Jan. 23, 1886.

aware that they should immediately organize to protect their town. Frustrated editor Samuel Wright agreed, "We are glad to see a force such as the 27th sent to this point. If this place is to be defended—not tamely surrendered—we need a respectable force." However, the response from the citizens was "a feeling of secure indifference," and the editor believed "we are not doing our duty." The present danger has "paralyzed us completely." He urged, "Columbia can do well, and must do well. She is losing her credit by her supineness." He followed through on his own rhetoric. The 34-year-old Wright would sell the paper in August after he joined the army.[25]

Frick, hearing reports that Rebels were near York, ordered his last two companies in Columbia to report to Lt. Colonel Green, "that we might be prepared to resist any sudden attempt by the enemy to get possession of the bridge." About 4:00 p.m. on Saturday (while White's cavalrymen were leaving Jefferson Station and workers loaded military stores into railcars at York), Frick's Companies A and B marched westward through Wrightsville. They manned the trenches just north of the turnpike. Frick sent a small contingent back to the bridge to ensure that none of the refugees were "spies looking to create mischief." He realized the bridge was the militia's lifeline to Columbia and must be kept clear and open. His provosts detained several civilians lingering on the waterfront and forced them to state their intentions. The guards arrested a few loiterers but soon released them, except for a man arrested near the canal lock. After reciting several conflicting stories, he finally declared that he was a Rebel deserter. He subsequently took the oath of allegiance and mustered into one of the 27th PVM's companies.[26]

A Philadelphia reporter arrived on the late afternoon train from York. He wrote at 6:00 p.m., "A trip of about an hour brings the refugees to this place. The turnpike, which is frequently in sight along the route, is dotted at very short intervals with wagons, horses, and foot passengers. There are thousands of people leaving their homes and making for the bridge over the Susquehanna. On arriving at this bridge and crossing into Columbia, the crowd is found almost equal to that which has so recently been left at York. It is composed of

25 *Pottsville Journal*, July 18, 1913; *Columbia Spy*, June 27, 1863. Wright was busily trying to find a buyer for his paper, writing that "the circulation of the paper is small, but may be readily doubled with little effort."

26 *OR 27*, pt. 2, 277; *Pottsville Journal*, Oct. 24, 1863; *Columbia Spy*, June 28, 1863.

even more heterogeneous elements, for it is a grand melee of white men and women, negroes, donkeys, cows, and horses."[27]

In the early evening, the thunder of horses' hooves echoing in the bridge caused panic. A New York correspondent captured the chaos:

> A man arrived from York on Saturday afternoon with a premature dispatch of the capture of that place. Everyone expected the immediate approach of the enemy on the spot. This was amusingly illustrated by a circumstance that occurred a few hours later. A party of our own cavalry dashed over the bridge at rather a quick pace, and terrified everyone by the suddenness of their approach, who, without stopping to inquire, concluded they were a party of the enemy. 'The rebels,' 'The rebels are coming' ran through the streets. Women fled to fourth stories and basements, and men wherever they could find a shelter. There was a general alarm and no show of fighting. The old and the young were terrified alike, and all were equally relieved and delighted when they perceived the cavalry were friends instead of foes. Some, however, could not believe it a reality that the rebels were not yet among them for a considerable time.[28]

Throughout the day, the jittery civilians and toiling soldiers could hear the whistles of multiple trains passing through Wrightsville and Columbia. Railroader Thomas Scott had ordered all rolling stock in York and Adams counties to be transferred to the eastern bank of the Susquehanna for greater safety. Dozens of trains had since passed by, but now traffic was backing up. The engineers had to wait for each locomotive and railcar to be uncoupled, and for teams of mules and horses to pull the cars across the bridge and then return for the next group. The laborious and time-consuming process frustrated the crews.

As Frick watched the seemingly endless parade of trains and terrified civilians, Whitney handed him a terse telegraph from Darius Couch: "York has surrendered. Our troops will fall back from there to Wrightsville to-night. If Major Haller is with them, he is my aide-de-camp. Have reliable men sent down to the Conowingo Bridge. Impress horses, and send good officers or

---

27 *Philadelphia Inquirer,* June 30, 1863.

28 *New York Herald,* June 30, 1863.

volunteers. The commanding officer will take up planks, and in no event should that bridge fall into enemy's hands, or any fords. Tell the people of Lancaster that the time has come for action. Have all boats and rafts along the river brought on this side."[29]

Frick and Haller Join Forces

There could be little doubt that the Southerners would press on toward Columbia. At 7:00 p.m., the Philadelphia reporter who arrived on the afternoon train observed that "The news has thrown a firebrand into the dwellers of Columbia, and the soldiers who guard the works at the eastern end of the Susquehanna bridge begin to understand that the work they may be called upon to perform may be no child's play." He went on to add, "It is interesting at this time to recall a telegraphic despatch, fished from one's pocket, and dated Hanover, 1 p.m., stating that 'everything is safe, and that it would be advisable to send a train up for two deserters who had been captured.' The Rebels must have entered the delightful little town of Hanover about thirty minutes after the despatch was sent, and any train which might have been sent would have met an untimely fate."[30]

However, there was still one more train steaming through York County. Posted at Wrightsville's depot, Corp. Daniel Dillman watched Granville Haller's train arrive about 7:30, bringing some 200 men who had evacuated York to avoid capture. Telegraph operator Peter Bentz also disembarked from the cars, toting his instruments. "York," he exclaimed, "has surrendered!" The news frightened several residents, who soon joined the throngs waiting to cross into Columbia.[31]

"Wrightsville presented a melancholy spectacle," wrote Haller, "a scene that could hardly be exaggerated." Hundreds of loaded wagons filled the streets while refugees waited to pay the bridge toll. One wagon carried two of York's prominent citizens, who were escorting postmaster Alexander Frey and his mailbags to Lancaster. Angry refugees lined toll collector William McConkey's

29 *OR* 27, pt. 3, 367.

30 *Philadelphia Inquirer*, June 30, 1863.

31 *Pottsville Journal*, July 18, 1913. According to the 1856 and 1863 York directories at YCHT, Peter Bentz was the operator at the American Telegraph Office and a member of the town's Republican Party.

office, pressuring him to speed up the process. "Locomotives, tenders, and cars of all descriptions" lined the nearby tracks. Rolling stock from several different companies crowded together, waiting transport across the Susquehanna. Each engineer felt he had the right of way and should be allowed to go first. The transportation agents had done nothing to secure additional mule teams to haul the railcars across the bridge.[32]

Haller resolved the impasse by taking personal action, after obtaining suitable quarters for his men and arranging for their suppers. He sought out 63-year-old Dr. Barton Evans, the president of Columbia Bank, and pointed out the lengthy queue at the bridge. Haller urged the retired Wrightsville physician to suspend collecting tolls because the crowds were fleeing the Rebels, not crossing on business. Evans immediately ordered McConkey to open the gate, thereby allowing free passage. In Major General Couch's name, Haller authorized the harried transportation agents to impress teams from local residents and farmers to remove the rolling stock. That tiring work continued all night, with a constant stream of mule teams pulling the railcars to Columbia.[33]

Captain Samuel Randall and his First City Troop arrived about 8:30 p.m., clattering across the long bridge into Columbia. The troopers verified earlier reports that York had surrendered without firing a shot. Church bells clanged, calling out the town to hear the latest news. Rumors quickly spread that more than 35,000 Confederates had sacked York and were now heading for Columbia. Several residents buried or hid their silverware, gold watches, and other valuables. One reporter observed, "Black's Bridge Hotel . . . was the headquarters of the Troop, where the cavalrymen assembled to arrange their toilets and have their boots blacked." Eager to join the campaign, later that evening eleven more First City Troopers arrived on the late train out of Philadelphia. The cavalrymen entered the hotel and rendezvoused with their comrades.[34]

---

32 OR 27, pt. 3, 995; Gibson, *History of York County*, 206, 421. These businessmen were John F. Small and David E. Small, who owned a railroad manufacturing company. The latter was not closely related to Chief Burgess David Small, and ran for the office after the war against the latter Small. David E. Small was a member of the Committee of Safety from York's Second Ward.

33 OR 27, pt. 3, 995.

34 *Columbia Spy*, Jan. 16, 1886.

Across the river, Major Haller napped before heading out to introduce himself to Colonel Frick "at a very late hour." As Couch's aide-de-camp, Haller assumed overall command of the situation although Frick held a superior brevet rank. Frick was confident in the courage of his troops and prepared to resist any Confederate efforts to destroy the bridge. The two officers discussed the need to expand the rifle-pits farther toward the river and agreed to use every precaution to preserve the bridge for long as possible. Frick sent Adjutant Whitney scurrying out from headquarters in the middle of the night in search of more entrenching tools.

Four home guard companies totaling 175 Columbians, including 53 blacks, marched into Wrightsville about midnight. Many of these men had helped erect Fort Case. "They presented a motley appearance, attired as they were in every description of citizens' dress," wrote Lieutenant Wallace, who commanded the sentinels at the bridge. "They were armed with the old musket altered to the percussion lock."[35]

While the gentry of the First Troop, Philadelphia City Cavalry slumbered in Columbia hotel beds, Jacob Frick ordered his militiamen to sleep in their rifle-pits, with muskets at their sides. They suffered through several false alarms from nervous pickets who saw Rebels in every passing shadow. With his military preparations completed for the moment, Frick retired after ordering that he be awakened if scouts arrived with any urgent messages regarding Confederate movement through York. Like his soldiers, he did not sleep well. The local newspaper reported, "During Saturday night there were many sleepless eyes in Columbia."[36]

Annie Welsh wrote about the constant stream of refugees crossing into Columbia. "And so they kept coming all of Saturday night. Those who came in in the evening brought the news that York had surrendered at five o'clock that evening, so then we knew what to expect by the next evening," she concluded. "Indeed a great many expected that they would be in Columbia by midnight but I thought I knew enough about war to be pretty sure that they would not try it until the next day. So I made sure of another good night's sleep."[37]

---

35 *Columbia Spy*, July 11, 1863; *Pottsville Miners' Journal*, Oct. 24, 1863.

36 *Columbia Spy*, July 11, 1863.

37 Annie Welsh to Thomas Welsh, July 1, 1863. Courtesy of Richard C. Wiggin. Private collection.

A Restless Sabbath in Wrightsville

Sunday, June 28, dawned clear and pleasant just before 5 a.m. Whitney woke Frick a short time later. The colonel breakfasted and prepared for an uncertain day. Major Charles Knox and Capt. Robert Bell arrived and reported that the Rebels had not entered York the previous evening, refuting the rumors. Very early in the morning, Frick, Haller, and Major Haldeman examined the potential avenues of approach for the Confederates. Frick ordered the 27th Militia and the Columbia volunteers to widen and extend the earthworks in their front. Following Frick's instructions from the night before, Whitney and railroad executive Robert Crane had borrowed a considerable quantity of entrenching tools from the Pennsylvania Railroad. They also procured some from local merchants. A reporter later noted, "Mr. J. B. Bachman, acting on a patriotic impulse, gave an order on Cottrell's hardware store for a large lot of entrenching tools."[38]

A dismayed Frick and his officers watched the three companies of white civilians head toward the bridge instead of constructing more earthworks. A reporter later recalled, "These companies were never attached to any regimental organization, and were not included in the commissary's requisitions for rations. Accordingly Colonel Frick had no supplies for them, and they were obliged to go home for dinner! The colored company was fed by the citizens of Wrightsville."[39]

"Sunday morning's sun saw us still undisturbed, and witnessed the departure to Columbia of the white companies of citizens to get their breakfasts," wrote a disgusted Lieutenant Francis Wallace. "They must have become entirely absorbed in that interesting duty, for they forgot to return. The company of colored men remained with us, their palates either being smaller or their courage greater than that of the good burghers of Columbia." The blacks formed a line to receive entrenching tools from Quartermaster Patterson and, with the implements in hand, began digging. Frick was "pleasantly surprised" by their willingness to assist. Several men of the 27th Militia had left coal mines to become soldiers, and now once more wielded picks and shovels working alongside black civilians. "No men on that day worked more faithfully or

---

38 U.S. Naval Observatory records; *JMSIUS* (1908), Vol. 43, 283; *Columbia Spy*, Jan. 16, 1886.

39 *Columbia Spy*, Jan. 9, 1886.

zealously, than the colored company—their conduct elicited the admiration of all who saw them," explained Wallace.[40]

Frick ordered his men to extend the earthworks toward the Susquehanna, hoping to protect against a Rebel flanking movement. He knew that he could never hold the 2,800-foot-long, horseshoe-shaped line with his small force, but he had to try. Many of the veterans, including Corp. Daniel Dillman, understood the enormity of the task. They expected "warm work," while others argued that the enemy would not advance as far as Wrightsville. Dillman realized the militia was not large enough to withstand a heavy enemy force. He opined, "The real move will be made toward Columbia; the bridge destroyed at the west and being sufficient to prevent the advance of the enemy." He believed the earthworks were "a mere sham, to show that something has been done to repulse the foe."[41]

Haller noted with satisfaction that during the night nearly all of the cars at the railroad station had been removed to Columbia. Only one remained. Despite his repeated calls for it to be taken across the bridge, it seemed to be purposely left in Wrightsville. This boxcar, belonging to wealthy businessman Henry Kauffelt, contained Adams County shopkeeper Ira Shipley's inventory, which had been transferred from a car sent from York to a different one for reshipment to Philadelphia. It remained stationary at Kauffelt's lumberyard near the western end of the bridge. Haller retained "two engines and a train of passenger cars" in Columbia "to meet any emergency." Locomotives pulled the rest of the rolling stock to Philadelphia.[42]

During the early morning, according to a correspondent in Columbia, "The officials connected with the military hospital at York, accompanied by the Assistant Postmaster, have just arrived here, bringing advices from York up to 9 o'clock this morning." They confirmed the story that the chief burgess "offered

---

40 *Pottsville Miners' Journal,* Oct. 24, 1863. The three white companies were Capt. William Case's Rolling Mill Guards, the Silver Grays militia company, and the Susquehanna Guards, according to the *Philadelphia Press,* June 30, 1863. The *Columbia Spy,* Jan. 9, 1886, sheds additional light: "These companies were never attached to any regimental organization, and were not included in the commissary's requisitions for rations. Accordingly Colonel Frick had no supplies for them, and they were obliged to go home for dinner! The colored company was fed by the citizens of Columbia."

41 *Pottsville Journal,* July 18, 1913.

42 OR 27, pt. 3, 995; Adams County Damage Claims, reel 9, ACHS; *Philadelphia Inquirer,* June 29, 1863.

to surrender the place… without the sanction or authority of the military authorities holding the lower end of the town, who would have fired on the rebels had they advanced." Also arriving that morning was another shipment of artillery, still without any ammunition.[43]

Columbian Annie Welsh later informed her husband, Brig. Gen. Thomas Welsh near Vicksburg, "On Sunday morning things seemed pretty quiet. We went to church, the children went to Sunday School in the afternoon, but it seemed to me everybody else was spending the time packing up. People seemed surprised at me that I did not seem frightened but I thought it best to keep cool. The children begged me to pack up but I said I would not till I heard the guns, but would not leave home unless they shelled the town. Then I would have sent the children out to Aunt Mary's till it was over but would have stood my ground myself. But I did not believe they could do much harm for I supposed they had nothing with them but light artillery, but I could not persuade many to think so with me. People were leaving in all directions."[44]

That same morning Major Haller's motley York battalion of convalescent soldiers, civilian volunteers, fifty men from Milroy's 87th Pennsylvania, and the Patapsco Guards joined Frick. The invalids, some with wounds still bandaged, must have offered an unusual sight to his trained eye. They marched slowly behind their leader, a one-armed boyish-looking lieutenant from a Pennsylvania regiment. Looks can be deceiving, however, for these veterans knew how to handle their rifled-muskets. Frick had already concluded that the Confederates would probably try to launch a flanking attack against his left, so he posted the new arrivals near the ravine to better defend against such maneuver. He assigned Lt. Colonel Green to command that sector, with the Patapsco Guards in reserve. Soon, Captain McGowan's Marylanders were busy lengthening the flank trenches near "old Joe Detwiler's" farm.[45]

While military preparations continued briskly, Northern Central engineer George Small worked to safeguard the bevy of locomotives left in Wrightsville. They could not be taken through the cavernous bridge because their ponderous funnel-shaped smokestacks were too tall to fit. Small and his fireman laboriously uncoupled the heavy iron stack from the "Susquehanna." They ran

43 *Philadelphia Inquirer*, June 29, 1863; *Columbia Spy*, July 11, 1863.

44 Annie Welsh to Thomas Welsh, July 1, 1863. Courtesy of Richard C. Wiggin, private collection.

45 OR 27, pt. 2, 278; Wray, *History of the Twenty-third Pennsylvania*, 152.

a small gondola car up to the cow-catcher and unceremoniously dumped the stack onto it. A team of ten mules slowly hauled the locomotive up the curve toward the bridge entrance. However, the front wheels left the tracks, causing a "sulphurous atmosphere to emanate from the mule driver's mouth. He had objected strenuously from the beginning to this innovation and unusual proceeding, and the derailing of the engine only added to his vocabulary of choice anathemas." Small's ingenuity solved the issue. He used jacks and tackle to re-rail the locomotive, which was then successfully pulled to Columbia. To anyone's remembrance, it was the first engine to cross the bridge. Small returned to help the other engineers similarly take their locomotives across the river to safety, one at a time. The protracted process took the better part of the day. Once they were all on the Columbia side, the dismantled engines were coupled to waiting trains and pulled to Philadelphia.[46]

Intelligence regarding the timing of the enemy advance was critical. Captain M. M. Strickler's civilian scouts rode along the turnpike two miles west of Wrightsville to collect information and watch for the Rebels. "The rebels occupy York in force with cavalry and infantry," they penned in a note to railroader Robert Crane in Columbia, though they misidentified them as "General Rhodes' [sic] division of Ewell's troops." The scout added, "All the Union cavalry and infantry from York have passed this outpost for Columbia. I judge from the rebel train of wagons that their force is very heavy." To guard the southern approach to Wrightsville, Maj. Charles Knox dispatched most of Bell's Adams County Cavalry south on the Old Baltimore Road. Major Haller left strict instructions that at the first sign of Rebels, Crane was to supervise the boring of holes in key timbers of the fourth span out from Wrightsville.[47]

Similar preparations were occurring in Harrisburg as Ewell's column approached. In mid-morning, Darius Couch sent a confidential message to Capt. E. C. Wilson, his assistant quartermaster, directing him to have combustible materials taken to the western end of the Camelback Bridge. He ordered Maj. Gen. William F. "Baldy" Smith to supervise the placement of these flammable materials so that the bridge could be fired at a moment's notice. "Combustible materials of any kind could be used," but in Couch's opinion, "turpentine, tar, and wood shavings would be the best. There must not

46 George Small, 1905 *York Dispatch*.

47 *Philadelphia Inquirer*, June 29, 1863. The infantry was likely Sickles' battalion, 20th PVM.

be any delay in executing his orders." Workers punched holes in the roofs and walls to vent the flames.[48]

Couch sent similar orders to his other commanders along the Susquehanna, including Granville Haller. If the major deemed it necessary to withdraw Colonel Frick's soldiers from Wrightsville and Conowingo, he was to leave a sufficient number on the other side to destroy the bridges. Haller could use his own discretion in ordering their destruction, but he was to "keep them open as long as possible with prudence." An anxious Abraham Lincoln telegraphed Couch about the status of the Confederate incursion. In return, the major general sent a series of messages informing the president that the Rebels had "not up to this point made any show of an attack in force." They were burning the Northern Central Railway's bridges, and Couch wired that he might have lost 400 men near Gettysburg and York. He did not quite know what had happened to the fragmented 20th Militia, because five companies had not reported their whereabouts after leaving the vicinity of the Howard Tunnel. He estimated that the Rebels had "probably 15,000 men within a short distance of my front."[49]

The pace quickened in the forenoon as nearly 1,000 men worked feverishly to expand the defensive works surrounding Wrightsville on three sides. The overcast sky kept the heat from becoming oppressive. The 27th's chaplain, Richard H. Austin, stopped periodically along the earthworks to encourage the men in their labors. Wrightsville's church services were cancelled; nearly half the populace had crossed the bridge into Lancaster County. James Kerr Smith, secretary of the Presbyterian Sabbath School, noted the following in the institution's minute book:

> Owing to the sense of excitement occasioned by the invasion of our county by the rebel army under General Lee, no religious services were held in the church this day, except morning prayer meeting. No meeting of the Sunday School. At an early hour of the day martial law was proclaimed in town by Major Haller . . . and the male citizens were called upon to erect barricades in the streets, and the women to cook provisions.[50]

---

48 *OR* 27, pt. 3, 388; *Philadelphia Inquirer*, June 30, 1863.

49 *OR* 27, pt. 3, 385.

50 Nye, *Farthest East*, 26.

Many of Wrightsville's men were gone, having removed their horses and household valuables to safety. Provost Marshal Samuel H. Mann organized the remaining men and barricaded the east-west streets with logs and planks taken from the lumberyards and other suitable materials scrounged from residents and shops. Captain Walker's company of the 26th Militia overturned iron ore hoppers from the railroad tracks leading into the bridge, leaving just enough room for a soldier to pass if a sudden withdrawal became necessary.[51]

Despite martial law, the relationship between the townspeople and the soldiers had improved dramatically. F. L. Baker, the editor of the *Mariettian*, wrote, "Everything went on in a gay picnic style—ladies falling in love with the fine looking officers—until Sunday afternoon." Editor Samuel Wright of the *Columbia Spy* had taken sympathy on the convalescing patients moved from York's army hospital to; he sent young Thomas Wright through the temporary wards in the Columbia Classical Institute and gave every soldier a copy of the paper.[52]

Later that morning, Frick and Haller received additional reinforcements. Lieutenant Colonel William H. Sickles and his three companies of the 20th Militia completed their long trek from Hanover Junction. Frick posted them on his right flank, facing north toward the wooded Hellam Heights. They hastily started digging rifle-pits.

Alongside the 27th Militia, the free blacks, including 15-year-old John Aquilla Wilson of York County, continued entrenching. They came primarily from the Maltby & Case Rolling Mill and most were accustomed to hard labor. A few must have questioned their fate should they fall into Confederate hands while serving under Federal officers. As non-uniformed civilians, they might not be treated as prisoners of war. They likely would receive shackles and a trip into slavery. Blacks toting guns were not common sights in the South, and none of them knew what a vengeful Rebel might do to them if captured. They kept their muskets and ammunition stacked nearby.[53]

---

51 The June 30, 1863, *Philadelphia Inquirer*, identified them as coal cars, not iron ore hoppers.

52 *Marietta (Pa.) Mariettian*, July 4, 1863; *Columbia Spy*, Jan. 16, 1886.

53 Lori Myer, "12 for the Record," *Central PA Magazine*, Feb. 2001. Wilson, the teenage son of Nathaniel and Louisa Harris Wilson, was among a group of parishioners from the Fawn African Methodist Church (near Gatchelville in rural eastern York County) to volunteer for the Columbia company. He was later drafted into the Union Army (*York Daily Record* website, www.ydr.com).

About noon, rumors spread that Maj. Gen. John A. Dix had departed Philadelphia with 1,000 soldiers to reinforce the militia. Several residents anxiously scanned the eastern horizon for signs of an incoming troop train or marching column. However, the excitement soon waned when telegraphic messages refuted the encouraging rumor.[54]

After a hasty lunch, Haller and Frick inspected the new, longer defense and planned where to place any additional reinforcements. The original north-south line stretched for 400 yards, bisected by the macadamized turnpike. The arms of the horseshoe ran east on either side of the older earthworks for 1,200 yards to the Susquehanna. Riding around the lengthy perimeter, Frick debriefed Haller on the current situation and how his limited force could best delay the Rebels. He had less than 1,500 soldiers, stationed every two yards or so, to guard the perimeter. He realized this disposition greatly reduced his defensive abilities, but he had no choice. According to standard tactics, a force of this size normally would defend an area four to five hundred yards wide. By conventional military wisdom, Frick needed at least 6,000 more men to defend the earthworks.[55]

Frick and Haller spoke with each subordinate officer to make sure each understood his specific routes of withdrawal if the Rebels appeared in force. Roughly 580 soldiers of the 27th Militia remained in place just east of the Old Baltimore Road, digging dirt and piling it onto the works. Alongside them were the 53 blacks. Frick sent Capt. Joseph Oliver, a veteran officer wounded and captured at Fredericksburg, together with 70 skirmishers of Company D forward into the fields west of the road, and deployed Maj. George L. Fried in charge of the left of the 27th's line (south of the turnpike). Frick retained personal command of Companies A and B, which were posted north of the pike. In the center near the tollgate was Company E (the color company) from Tamaqua under the command of veteran officer Capt. Jacob Martz. Frick next turned his attention to his vulnerable flanks.[56]

William Sickles, still smarting from White's raid on Hanover Junction, manned the northern flank with roughly 200 men. Frick was particularly concerned with the southern flank, where a sudden attack could come up from

---

54 *Columbia Spy*, July 11, 1863.

55 OR 27, pt. 2, 278.

56 *Columbia Spy*, Apr. 10, 1886. Oliver and Fried served in Frick's 129th Pennsylvania. Oliver, then a lieutenant, was wounded and captured at Fredericksburg. He enrolled in the 27th Militia on June 19 in Easton in Northampton County.

the Kreutz Creek ravine. Here he positioned the York battalion, with the Patapsco Guards in reserve to the east, the veterans of the 87th Pennsylvania in the middle, and the hospital invalids to the west. Lt. Colonel David Green of the 27th Militia, commanding this left wing, counted only 238 men to hold his 1,200-yard line. This forced him to leave great gaps between the companies. Because the ground in front of these earthworks sloped out of effective musket range toward the ravine, Green moved skirmishers well forward into the fields. Just to the east, the ravine narrowed and doglegged north where the railroad tracks entered town.

Haller assumed overall tactical control from a position on Hellam Street, while Frick rode over to his regiment's line. They believed they could hold the bridge if the Rebels sent only a small raiding party. A reporter examined the defenses in the late afternoon wrote, "should an attack be made by the enemy, every inch of ground would be contested and we believe successfully against the attack of any Cavalry force which would undertake to assail them."[57]

Haller recalled the Philadelphia cavalrymen from Columbia and detailed them as provost guards. They arrived in the late afternoon and dismounted along Hellam Street, where Haller detached several troopers as orderlies and messengers. Sergeant Edward Reakirt selected six volunteers for the hazardous duty. Captain Randall repositioned the remaining First City Troopers on the invalids' left flank and picketed the streets and railroad in Wrightsville's southeastern corner. Captain Walker and about fifty members of the 26th Militia marched to the overturned ore cars and fanned out behind them to defend the bridge entrance. A small contingent of the 27th Militia guarded the eastern end of the viaduct.

About 5:00 p.m. Haller detailed several soldiers, including Corp. Daniel Dillman, to crew Columbia's two bronze 12-pound Napoleons and the Supplee Foundry's iron rifled piece. He ordered Lieutenant Ridgway to rake the bridge in case the enemy attempted a crossing. One of Captain Strickler's scouts, John C. Clark, later wrote that the gunners "experimented from some point above Columbia. A barrel was anchored in the rapids, opposite the [Pennsylvania Railroad] tunnel, and used as a target, and the boys fired at it." However, no corroboration is known.[58]

57 *Lancaster Daily Express*, June 29, 1863.

58 *Columbia Spy*, Jan. 22, 1887.

Earlier that cloudy Sabbath, Jubal Early's Southerners fanned out through York County. Colonel William French impressed Manchester Township farmer Benjamin Miller as a guide for the 17th Virginia Cavalry. They rode through Liverpool and Mount Wolf, stealing horses and pausing to buy shoes and merchandise. Some soldiers bragged that they were heading for Philadelphia before going on to New York. One party ransacked George H. Wolf's store and cut down nearby telegraph poles. Another group stole four mules, two horses, a colt, and several harnesses and halters from Samuel Rutter's farm.[59]

About noon, the cavalrymen used coal oil to burn two railroad spans over Conewago Creek. They found them undefended because the 400 guards from the 20th Militia had "skedaddled" via rowboat across the Susquehanna to Bainbridge. The Virginians fired a few shots at a skiff with three of Colonel Thomas's scouts who had rowed back to check for Rebel presence. A militiaman later called the dense plume of oily smoke from the burning bridges a "sorrowful and humiliating spectacle." Their mission accomplished, the 17th Virginia returned to York and destroyed the sturdy Black Bridge with several powder charges. General Early ordered French to destroy the bridges and trestles near Hanover Junction that Elijah White skipped the day before.[60]

Miles to the west, Lt. Gen. A. P. Hill's Third Corps rested at Fayetteville, east of Chambersburg. Colonel Walter Taylor of Lee's staff sent orders directing Hill to move to York and "cross the Susquehanna, menacing the communications of Harrisburg with Philadelphia, and to cooperate with General Ewell." The situation in York County grew more precarious by the hour. Darius Couch had vowed that no Rebel would cross the Susquehanna, and now his men prepared to destroy the bridge that Jubal Early and John Gordon wanted left intact.[61]

---

59 York County Damage Claims, reel 30. In his 1884 book, Jacob Hoke reported that a white Chambersburg resident, D. M. Eiken, was held in a southern prison camp along with other Pennsylvanians. Eiken told him, "A little colored boy from York, Pa., captured during the invasion, was in Castle Thunder, but was allowed to come and go at his pleasure" (see Ted Alexander's article in *Blue & Gray*, Sept. 2001, 88).

60 *OR* 27, pt. 2, 467; Prowell, *History of York County*, 1, 995; Gibson, *History of York County*, 616; Philadelphia *North American*, July 2, 1863. French's route can be approximated from the border claims for June 28.

61 *OR* 27, pt. 2, 606.

Chapter 10

Gordon Attacks Wrightsville

Seize the Bridge!

While Union Maj. Granville Haller worked feverishly to strengthen Wrightsville's defenses on the overcast afternoon of Sunday, June 28, Brig. Gen. John Gordon's Confederate brigade paused along the turnpike three miles east of York. The Georgians ate their midday meal near a colonial-era stone house that once served as a tavern visited by the Marquis de Lafayette and George Washington. A mile west, Gordon and his staff finished dining at a different farmhouse called "The Cedars." When he rose from the table and thanked ther Widow Smyser for her hospitality, she asked him to safeguard her property as payment. After Gordon's entourage departed, Mrs. Smyser's 18-year-old son Albert discovered his black riding horse missing. He mounted a plow horse, rode off in pursuit of the Rebels, overtook them east of the farm, and obtained an audience with Gordon. Perhaps recalling the widow's request, the general ordered that the horse be returned. Albert rode home, the reins of his prized horse in one hand, and the reins of the plow horse held tightly in the other.[1]

Gordon's Georgians actively sought horses, food, and supplies throughout the region. Spring Garden Township farmer John Miller spotted a squad of Rebels leading a horse along an alley where Michael Dietz had a stable; Dietz later filed a claim asking for $180 for a missing eight-year-old horse. Daniel Gotwalt, Charles Diehl, and several other farmers reported losing horses that

---

1 *York Daily Record*, Aug. 16, 1947. Her husband, Daniel Smyser, died in 1862.

day. Nearby, hungry Rebels picked clean Jacob Holtzinger's well manicured apple orchard.[2]

Elijah White's 35th Battalion, Virginia Cavalry camped on the John H. Small farm along the turnpike near Freystown. When a trooper's horse broke down en route to the site, the cavalryman entered a nearby stable in search of a new mount. All he found was an ancient mare, which he mounted and rode away upon. Surprisingly, a fellow Virginian riding nearby recognized it. Ten years earlier he had taken horses from Loudoun County up to Pennsylvania to sell in Lancaster. His companion's pilfered mare was one of them. The former owner knew the aged horse would not survive the rigors of the current campaign. The trooper dismounted and removed his bridle and saddle and carried them to camp, where he secured another horse that was more suitable for the rigorous campaign ahead.[3]

White divided his command once he had established his bivouac. Some elements, including Capt. Marcellus French and Company F, would accompany Gordon to Wrightsville. They were to sever telegraph lines and burn bridges along the 13-mile-long Wrightsville, York & Gettysburg Railroad. The rest fanned out across the network of roads leading from York. Captain Frank Myers and Company A rode several miles to the north to picket and scout. White dispatched a patrol to the Susquehanna to determine whether the fords were usable in case the Columbia Bridge was heavily defended. Other squadrons ranged as far south as McCall's Ferry, about ten miles below Wrightsville. Along the way, they confiscated more horses and mules.[4]

Gordon broke camp about 2:00 p.m. When his mile-long column marched eastward toward Hallam, a village along the turnpike about midway between York and Wrightsville. Gordon Bradwell anticipated more adventure, for it seemed as though the brigade was heading toward Philadelphia. Beyond the Susquehanna River was the "Wheatland" estate of former president of the United States James Buchanan. Bradwell and his comrades were "eager to visit the old gentleman in his home and shake hands with him."[5]

2 York County Damage Claims, Diehl, Dietz, and Gotwalt claims.

3 McClure, *East of Gettysburg*, 56.

4 Myers, *The Comanches*, 195; *Richmond Times-Dispatch*, June 19, 1910; York County Damage Claims. The Northern Central Railway operated the WY&GRR. York businessman P.A. Small and Columbia Bank official Samuel Schoch were among its officers.

5 Bradwell, "Burning of Wrightsville," 301.

Leading the way for the jovial infantrymen, Capt. Thaddeus Waldo's Company C of the 17th Virginia Cavalry rode through the lush valley. Gordon ordered the troopers to screen his advance and provide intelligence on the location and strength of any nearby Yankees. The Rebels saw very few horses, because most had been taken across the river. A few enterprising farmers tied strings tightly around a particular muscle in their horses' legs, making them appear lame to Confederate raiders. Hellam Township farmer Jacob Rudy had failed to move his animals to Lancaster County. Now, he paid dearly for his mistake as Rebels robbed his stable, taking his family's riding horse as well as a bay, large roan, and small colt. Christian Seiple had taken his horses and his neighbor John Emig's four mules and young horse into the Codorus Hills in Hellam Township to hide them. A roving Rebel patrol found the animals and led them away, as well as four other hidden horses belonging to Henry Smyser.

In mid-afternoon, cavalry foragers stopped at Alexander J. Blessing's general store and post office in Hallam. They walked away with 200 dozen eggs, 20 pairs of boots, 20 pairs of shoes, 25 yards of calico cloth, six new tin buckets, two sacks of salt, and 10 barrels of pickled mackerel. Blessing quoted his loss at $242 in his postwar damage claim he filed with the state.[6]

Unlike the destruction often left in the wake of armies, houses and farms between Gettysburg and Wrightsville escaped significant damage. Gordon regularly reminded his men about Lee's strict orders to respect private property and civilians. Guided by these instructions and by his own instincts, Gordon resolved to "leave no ruins along the line of my march through Pennsylvania; no marks of a more enduring character than the tracks of my soldiers along its superb pikes." He was sure the citizens living along these highways would support his claim that his brigade marched through "that delightful region . . . without leaving any scars to mar its beauty or lessen its value."[7]

Between 4:30 and 5:00 p.m., Gordon's Brigade arrived just outside Wrightsville after an unhurried three-hour march. Some of Waldo's scouts reported that enemy horsemen had been seen "skedaddling" in the distance. Morale ran high within the Confederate ranks as reports circulated that the Yankees were running. The only militia the Georgians had encountered had

6 York County Damage Claims, S. Rudy, J. Emig, H. Smyser and A. Blessing claims. Several horses were secreted on the wooded estate of the Grubb heirs in Codorus Hills. Unfortunately for the claimants, the Rebels correctly suspected the area contained a trove of hidden horses.

7 Gordon, *Reminiscences*, 144.

The Schultz house in Hallam, Pa., is typical of the old German architecture so prevalent in York County during the early 19th century. At times residents hid horses in cellars to avoid roving Confederate foraging patrols. *Library of Congress*

been the three-dozen prisoners paraded through Gettysburg. Gordon Bradwell and his comrades saw no evidence that the enemy was anywhere near. They had not glimpsed an armed enemy soldier since they had arrived in Pennsylvania. That would change as they approached within a mile of Wrightsville. Waldo's scouts reported that considerable Yankees now blocked the way.[8]

Once he halted his column in the road's undulating terrain just out of sight of the enemy, Gordon guided his horse through the fields up a high ridge to observe the Yankee dispositions. Reining in just below the crest, Gordon dismounted and raised his field glasses. In the distance were freshly turned dirt fortifications filled with infantry. To his relief, there was no artillery supporting the defenses. Gordan watched as a handful of riders left, apparently carrying messages into town. Small flags waved along the lines of entrenchments, indicating the presence of a several separate commands. According to the handwritten message delivered by the girl a few hours earlier in York, only

8   Bradwell, "Burning of Wrightsville," 300-301.

militia held the works, and these untrained soldiers could be easily turned aside or captured. "Not an inaccurate detail in that note could be discovered," recalled Gordon after the war. With his reconnaissance complete, Gordon adopted the note's suggestion that he move down the ravine in order to position his command "on the flank, or possibly in the rear, of the Union troops and force them to a rapid retreat or surrender."[9]

After informing his regimental officers of their deployment and tactical objectives, Gordon ordered Capt. William Tanner to deploy move the Courtney Artillery on a long low ridge fronting the Strickler farm. Once pioneers chopped down a portion of the post and rail fence lining either side of the road, Tanner's artillerists guided the limbered guns through the gaps. One section headed north of the pike and the other unlimbered to the south atop Strickler's Hill. Waldo's company of horsemen remained in reserve on the pike.[10]

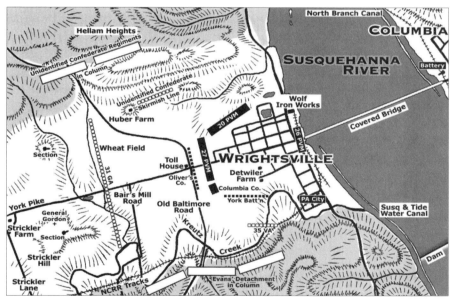

Jacob Frick and Granville Haller did not have sufficient manpower to defend the entrenchments and rifle pits that surrounded Wrightsville. Their best hope was to delay the Rebels for as long as possible and then withdraw across the Columbia Bridge. *Tom Poston*

9 *Lancaster Herald and Examiner*, July 1, 1863; Gordon, *Reminiscences*, 143-44.

10 Kesterson, Hodam Manuscript.

By now it was just after 5:30 p.m. Gordon Bradwell watched as the regiment in front of the 31st Georgia deployed at right angles to the road "across a field of rye . . . up to their shoulders." Gordon envisioned a classic "double envelopment" movement, hoping to bag the entire lot of Yankees. He ordered White's cavalrymen to follow the railroad east through the Kreutz Creek ravine. Colonel Evans would support them with three regiments of infantry, swinging in behind the Yankee position from the south. Two other regiments would march across the heights and surround Wrightsville from the north.[11]

It is unclear whether Gordon really knew his enemy's strength. No staff officers or other eyewitness ever corroborated the general's claim of a handwritten note elaborating the militia's position and numbers. Gordon's deployment of his six regiments, however, does suggest a solid grasp of the terrain and the layout of the militia's entrenchments. More than a week later on July 4, Clement Evans wrote to his wife about the degree of uncertainty he and his men had faced at Wrightsville. They had encountered some militia formed in line, he explained, protected by "rudely constructed trenches. Not knowing their strength, we cautiously advanced upon them from two directions, dividing the Brigade. I was sent along the railroad in command of a portion of the Brigade to attack their flank."[12]

The Skirmish of Wrightsville

Earlier that afternoon while Gordon's Brigade marched leisurely toward Wrightsville, Pennsylvania militiamen and black civilians worked feverishly to extend the trenches and rifle-pits. Couriers from Bell's Cavalry and Captain Strickler's civilian volunteers occasionally reported to Maj. Charles Knox. By 3 p.m., they had not spotted any Rebels within a two-mile patrol radius. A few riders sent eastward into Lancaster County came back with news that there were no Union troops on those roads, dashing any remaining hope that reinforcements had been dispatched from Philadelphia.

About 4:30 p.m., as the darkening skies threatened rain, a dozen of Strickler's scouts galloped in. They had been driven back by the Confederate cavalry screen without ascertaining the enemy's strength or whether they had

11 Bradwell, "Burning of Wrightsville," 300-301.

12 Stephens, *Intrepid Warrior*, 221.

artillery. Haller continued to hope that they might save the bridge if the Rebels were only a small raiding party. However, those hopes soon were dashed. A well known local music instructor, Professor James Brown Harry, had been visiting students in Wrightsville that day. As he drove his buggy west on the turnpike toward York he spotted a long column of Rebels in the distance, coming directly toward him. He hastily reversed course and sped back to Wrightsville. There, he notified the residents and soldiers of the approaching enemy, a message soon confirmed by scouts. He was escorted to Frick and Haller, who interviewed him as to the nature of the approaching column and then telegraphed the news to General Couch.[13]

Concern increased in Harrisburg with each passing hour. When John Wister, the Pennsylvania Railroad agent in Duncannon, wired Thomas Scott asking about how matters stood, Scott responded, "Matters look blue. Enemy are massing their forces within 2 ¼ miles of our works on the west bank of the Susquehanna." Waynesboro, Chambersburg, Gettysburg, Hanover, York, and Carlisle had fallen to the rapidly marching Rebels. Officials questioned 200 Confederate stragglers collected as prisoners regarding Ewell's destination. One Rebel, John Keyser, a former Harrisburg resident and an engineer on the Pennsylvania Railroad, was found carrying maps of the city and surrounding vicinity. Was the state capital the target of the next enemy thrust? It seemed likely. Officials removed valuables from the statehouse, including John Hancock's chair and the table upon which the Declaration of Independence had been signed.[14]

About 5:30 p.m. at Wrightsville, militia officers gazing westward through their field glasses discerned the Rebel movements. Lieutenant Francis Wallace watched as Confederate infantry "moved down on our left for the purpose of flanking us," while a section of artillery moved toward the Union right flank to "take position on a hill that commanded us." Jacob Frick knew that it was time to render the bridge useless to the Confederates. Frick had written a pass the day before in anticipation of the moment. "Robert Crane and E. K. Smith have permission to go upon the bridge with a party of carpenters, and bridge

---

13 OR 27, pt. 2, 996; *Gettysburg Star and Sentinel*, November 2, 1918.

14 *Philadelphia Inquirer*, June 30, 1863. A home guard company from Lewiston captured 23 Rebels at Shade Gap, including Keyser. Roster sheets of the 53rd North Carolina of Daniel's Brigade list a Pvt. John H. Keyser, and the 2nd North Carolina of Ramseur's Brigade lists a John L. Keyser. Both were in Rodes' Division.

builders, there to await the orders of Colonel Frick in writing or in person. Guards will pass them."[15]

Frick ordered Crane to prepare to demolish the fourth span from the Wrightsville end, some 800 feet from land. The railroad executive entered Black's Hotel in Columbia and asked John Q. Denney to join his group of carpenters. When the Rebels arrived within sight of the earthworks, Crane's party "commenced sawing off the arches and heavy timbers preparatory to blowing it up with powder, which they had arranged for that purpose." They also began removing the roof and sidewalls, weakening the span so that the charges would drop it into the river. Denney later testified, "I with the others went on to the bridge with R. Crane, tore up the planking on one of the spans near the West End, cut off all the timbers that we thought of would have been safe to cut without destroying the possibility of our troops to hop over, bored and charged the arches with powder ready for the match if acceptable." Crane believed these actions would render the bridge useless to the Rebels yet still permit it to be rebuilt quickly once the threat ended.[16]

Major Haller suspected the militia would retreat across the bridge, and he wanted to ensure that none of them set off the charges prematurely. While the carpenters labored, Haller ordered Captain Randall to detail men from the First City Troop to guard the mined section. Sergeant E. L. Reakirt chose six men from among many volunteers. When Randall arrived at the bridge, Crane asked for confirmation that Randall would be the officer to deliver the orders from Haller to light the fuse. Randall knew nothing of that sort, so Crane borrowed the captain's horse and rode out to the rifle-pits to see Haller.[17]

---

15 *Pottsville Miners' Journal*, Oct. 24, 1863; John E. Spicer, *The Columbia Civil War Centennial* (Middletown, Pa.: Wert Binding, 1976), 37.

16 Robert Crane deposition, July 20, 1863, John Q. Denney deposition, July 24, 1863, Columbia (Pa.) Historic Preservation Society; JMSIUS (1908), Vol. 43, 189; *OR* 27, pt. 2, 278. Jacob Hoke in *The Great Invasion of 1863*, reported, "The duty of superintending this work was laid upon Mr. Robert Crane, who was assisted by Messrs. E. K. Smith, William Faesig, Isaac Ruel, Henry Berger, John Gilbert, Frederick Bost, H. P. Moore, W. Green, Michael Libhart, J. B. Bachman, Davis Murphy, W. W. Upp, Michael Shuman, Henry Ruck, and I. C. Turner." Other accounts state that Crane had 19 carpenters at his disposal.

17 JMSIUS (1908), Vol. 43, 189. The six soldiers were P. A. Brown, Robert E. Gray, Henry Ashhurst, Thomas C. Oakman, George W. Colket, and Persifor Frazer, Jr. When the bridge guard was detailed, the firing had been going on for "some considerable time." Colket was one of the men specifically singled out by Haller in his message to Darius Couch regarding his performance at Gettysburg.

Meanwhile, dismounted Southern cavalrymen followed the railroad along the creek on the militia's left flank, occasionally sending scouts up the steep bank to their left to guide them. White's cavalrymen had fired the first Confederate shots at Gettysburg and Hanover Junction. Now, the honor was again theirs. About 6 p.m., fifty troopers encountered a small squad of Yankees guarding the railroad, and gunfire echoed through the ravine. Major Charles Knox narrowly escaped being hit, and his detachment "fell back to the entrenchments fighting." Colonel Evans' infantry skirmishers soon emerged from the ravine into a tall wheatfield. They initiated a long-range musketry duel with the 87th Pennsylvania and the York Invalids.[18]

As Pvt. Gordon Bradwell crossed the low ground that stretched for some distance in front of the regiment, he could see a line of "excellent earthworks" ahead of him on the rising ground. After Captain Warren G. Wood and Company F (the Pulaski Blues) advanced in skirmish formation about 150 yards, "the fun— the old-time familiar crack of rifles—began. This was instantly responded to by the popping of muskets and the whiz of balls over our heads. Everyone exclaimed: 'Musket balls! Melish!'"[19]

One of the Pulaski Blues, Pvt. Samuel Jackson, was a full-blooded Native American, now fighting the Federal military much as his Cherokee ancestors had done. Crouching in the wheatfield, the 24-year-old veteran soldier occasionally rose to fire at the Yankees, perhaps noting that their return musketry was sporadic and inaccurate. Jackson had just three more days to live. He would be killed just north of Gettysburg on July 1.[20]

Within thirty minutes the skirmishers drove in the untried Yankee pickets. Further extending their battle line, the 31st Georgia pressured the left-center of the main Union line. As the firing intensified, Haller received an alarming telegram from Colonel Thomas of the 20th Militia. A scout, having just arrived in Bainbridge from York, reported that the enemy was advancing on Columbia with three brigades of infantry and a full regiment of cavalry.[21]

---

18 *York Gazette*, June 29, 1863; *Lancaster Examiner and Herald*, July 1, 1863.

19 Bradwell, "Burning of Wrightsville," 300-301.

20 White, *A History of the 31st Georgia*, 215. Jackson hailed from Pulaski County, an area once inhabited by the Creek Confederacy and Cherokees. He died attacking Blocher's Knoll.

21 *Columbia Spy*, July 11, 1863. The scout likely saw Early's column of three brigades and a regiment of cavalry that had earlier in the day advanced on York.

With this intelligence that the Rebel force was much larger than a mere raiding party, Haller realized that any determined defense would result in senseless slaughter. He deemed it his duty to show this important message to Jacob Frick. He rode to the earthworks where he quickly located the colonel, who advised an immediate retreat. Dreading the inevitable confusion inherent in withdrawing inexperienced militia, Haller proposed the immediate destruction of the bridge. This would cut off that retreat route and force the infantrymen to "hold their ground as long as practicable." The two officers previously had decided that if they chose this option, they would retire along the hills bordering the Susquehanna and head to a ford above Wrightsville. After crossing the river, they would march back to Columbia. Frick, however, believed that their men could retreat across the bridge without being hard pressed by the enemy. After agreeing that this was the best option, they began informing their subordinates. To avoid confusion during the planned passage across the bridge, Haller detailed Major Knox and a few soldiers to deliver his orders to Robert Crane to destroy the bridge, when he so instructed.[22]

Meanwhile, Gordon ordered the Courtney Artillery on Strickler's Hill to provide long-range harassing fire. The 3-inch Ordnance Rifles could hurl a shell slightly more than a mile at a five-degree elevation of the iron barrel. At Gordon's command, Captain Tanner opened fire and a shell whizzed past the 27th Militia. According to resident James Kerr Smith, it "decapitated" a locust post in front of the rifle pit at the turnpike gatehouse. The shell ricocheted and exploded near the northeast corner of Fourth and Hellam streets. A fragment smashed into the eastern wall of Smith's house. He left it embedded there for a considerable length of time as "a memento of the occasion." Smith reported that the artillery opened fire at exactly 6:57 p.m.; although several other witnesses placed Tanner's first shot an hour earlier. Annie Welsh wrote, "Late in the afternoon we heard that they (the Rebs) were in the neighbourhood of Wrightsville and a fight was expected every moment. So about six o'clock we heard the booming of the cannon. Then we knew that the Ball had commenced."[23]

22 Robert Crane deposition, July 20, 1863, CHPS.

23 Nye, *Farthest East*, 26-27; Annie Welsh to Thomas Welsh, July 1, 1863. Courtesy of Richard C. Wiggin. The house later was occupied by Smith's relative, Jacob Levergood, who removed the artillery fragment. The house was razed in the 1900s after it had fallen into a state of disrepair.

Across the river in Columbia, militia Cpl. Daniel Dillman helped crew Ridgway's guns. "About six o'clock," the artilleryman heard the reports of cannons from the direction of Wrightsville and correctly perceived that the Rebels were "shelling our forces in the trenches." Resident Joseph H. Black noted, "They were shelling the town but not the bridge; they did not want that burned." A reporter penned, "The smoke was visible from Columbia, as well as the falling shells." Another witness related, "The residents of Second street came to their front gates after they had noticed the round puffs of smoke in the air, over the river, and inquiring of a veteran who had served in the 135th Penn'a Regiment. . . . if the rebels were shelling the town. His answer to everyone was—'Yes'um them's shells. I saw lots like that at Fredericksburg, and I know what they look like.'"[24]

When no return fire was forthcoming, Gordon ordered Tanner to limber and move closer. One section opened from a rise in front of the earthworks at a distance of 500 yards, just out of effective musket range. The other section galloped to a slight elevation on Gordon's left, a hill occupied by the Huber farmhouse, where they could readily fire on the Yankee center and northern trenches. As dense clouds of white smoke from Tanner's cannons filled the valley, it became increasingly difficult to track the Confederate movements.[25]

According to Private Bradwell, early on, two guns were firing from behind his position before the 31st Georgia advanced. One member of the 26th Georgia wrote that after the artillery had fired "not more than a dozen shots," Col. Edmund Atkinson ordered his battle line to move forward behind a screen of skirmishers. He used a field of "luxuriant grain" and some light woods as cover to approach the enemy line, while Frick's 27th Militia huddled in rifle-pits and entrenchments. The resulting musketry exchange did little harm to either side. Two other Georgia regiments circled to the north of the 27th Militia, turning east when they reached Hellam Heights. They slowly felt their way toward the river, bypassing a direct attack on Sickles' line.[26]

---

24 *Pottsville Journal*, July 18, 1913; Joseph H. Black deposition, Aug. 19, 1904, CHPS; *Philadelphia Inquirer*, June 29, 1863; *Columbia Spy*, Jan. 23, 1886. Dillman had served in the Washington Artillery, a Schuylkill County home guard organization. Many of these men were now in Company A of the 27th Militia, including Lt. Delaplaine Ridgway. Frick reconstituted the Washington Artillery to man the field pieces.

25 This rise is east of Bair's Mill Road on today's Cool Creek golf course.

26 *Savannah Daily Republican*, Aug. 6, 1863. Bradwell mistakenly called them 20-pound Parrott Rifles. They were 3-inch Ordnance Rifles.

Sporadic volleys erupted from the Union line along the Old Baltimore Road, but no Rebels went down. The fire was ineffective because of poor visibility through the tall wheat and the fear and excitement of the untested militia, many of whom had never fired their rifles. Granville Haller moved frequently among Frick's 27th Emergency Militia and the adjoining black company from Columbia. He traversed the entire length of the entrenchments, trying to calm down the jittery militia as bullets whistled by his borrowed horse.

Widely scattered musketry rang out to the north. Tanner's left section near J. H. Huber's farmhouse finally opened, hurling shells at Sickles' demoralized 20th Militia battalion. From his position above the turnpike, Jacob Frick saw a column of enemy infantry flanking Sickles, advancing under the cover of a high hill on his right to within a few hundred yards of the river. Only Confederate skirmishers had approached within range of the guns of the militiamen occupying the forward rifle-pits, and these remained hidden in a field of grain, obscured from Federal view, except when they rose to fire. Frick reported, "It was difficult to do them much harm or dislodge them. They depended exclusively upon their artillery to drive us from our position here."[27]

A reporter noted, "As the Rebels advanced, our skirmishers fell back, and the firing, which was pretty constant with an occasional volley, extended from our right to the rear of our left flank. After the skirmish had progressed some ten or fifteen minutes, Major Haller ordered the drum corps to the bridge, and directed the citizens of Wrightsville to take refuge within the brick walls, as a retreat and fight through the streets was quite probable."[28]

Captain David Smith, commanding Company A just north of the turnpike, narrowly escaped being struck by a shell. Many of the militiamen had never experienced incoming artillery fire and pressed their heads into the dirt. A *New York Herald* reporter wrote, "Our men gave them a volley or two from their rifle-pits, knocking six or eight over and losing two themselves, one of whom belonged to a colored company organized in the town. His head was shattered by a fragment from one of the enemy shells. It is noticeable here that while the cannonading was going on the church bells of Columbia were ringing to assemble the citizens to the ordinary divine worship of the Sabbath day." The Rebels later found a mangled body behind the earthworks. The unknown man

27 OR 27, pt. 2, 278.

28 *Columbia Spy*, July 11, 1863.

was the first Yankee fatality since George Washington Sandoe fell in Gettysburg.[29]

Jacob Frick was powerless to reply to the guns raking his position. He had left Lieutenant Ridgway and three cannons in Columbia, and several other guns were still sitting useless on flatcars on the railroad siding. Constant musketry and sporadic artillery fire had continued for about twenty minutes when Haller instructed all remaining citizens to take refuge behind the brick and stone walls of houses and churches. He ordered his drum corps back to the bridge, out of harm's way. He and Frick soon concluded that further resistance was useless. One of the militia officers ordered the remaining boats along the river to be cut loose from their moorings and set adrift to prevent the Confederates from using them. Gently bobbing in the current, the craft drifted under the bridge and passed out of sight.

Retreat to Columbia

By now, Colonel Frick had retained his tenuous position for about an hour and fifteen minutes. He lacked sufficient men to parry the persistent Rebel thrusts toward the river on both flanks. If he stayed much longer, the Rebels would sweep in behind him and gain the bridge, cutting off his retreat. Now was the time to withdraw. Fully exposed to bullets from Confederate sharpshooters, Frick quietly passed from left to right along his line, whispering to the company captains to fall back to the bridge. The 27th Militia fired one final heavy volley. Time was becoming critical. A Columbia reporter noted, "Shortly after the cavalry (Gettysburg and City Troop) slowly withdrew toward the bridge and as the firing indicated that the rebels were advancing along the railroad, it was thought the movement was intended to checkmate any advance from that quarter."[30]

Frick most likely ordered his men to retire between 6:45 and 7 p.m. The Rebel commanders later were uncertain as to exactly when the Yankees started withdrawing to Columbia. Jubal Early wrote that the militia "took to its heels

29 *Lancaster Weekly Express*, July 4, 1863; *New York Herald*, June 30, 1863. According to the *Weekly Express*, "One of the killed was a negro—whose head was taken off by a shell." *The Reading Daily Times*, June 29, 1863, mentioned, "Only one man, a negro, was killed, who had his head taken off by a shell in one of the streets of Wrightsville."

30 *OR* 27, pt. 2, 278; *Columbia Spy*, July 11, 1863.

after a few shots from the artillery," outrunning Gordon's weary men, who had marched a little more than twenty miles from Farmers. Colonel Evans thought that the "timid Militia" had fled at the first shell burst. Although Evans estimated that the Yankees equaled the Rebels in numbers, the inexperienced militia "believed that the shelling was terrible, although only two pieces were fired." According to Pottsville reporter Wallace, the retreat was "affected in excellent order by the command, although exposed during the movement to a heavy fire of shell and to a galling one of sharpshooters." Confederate Lt. William Lyon recalled that the Yankees' withdrawal was much less orderly, "We pitched into them and after a brisk little battle of about a half-hour duration, routed them."[31]

One militiaman agreed. "The retreat was hasty and precipitate," he wrote. "Every company except one—Company E, of Tamaqua, which was commanded by a veteran soldier, Captain Jacob Martz—fled in utter confusion from Wrightsville to the bridge. This company carried the colors, B. T. Hughes being the color bearer. The company was stationed at the gate or centre of the rifle-pits, where the rebels made their entrance into town. When the order to retreat was given, the companies to the left and right of Company E dropped almost everything except their arms and "skedaddled" through the town in confusion." As another soldier put it, "When we reached our dog tents in order that we might 'pull up stakes' as well as gather up our knapsacks, canteens, haversacks, &c., the rebel batteries on an adjoining elevation opened an unmerciful fire upon us, and in a moment all was confusion, and the retreat began in good earnest. . . . the route all along that back street was covered with blankets, knapsacks, &c., dropped by the men."[32]

Apparently the order to withdraw never reached the York Invalids. One later wrote, "A cloud of dust then going toward the river, indicated that the militia were being withdrawn across the bridge and the battalion left to get all the glory. We hadn't long to wait as the skirmishers appeared and we had it quite

31 Early, *War Memoirs*, 259-60; Stephens, *Intrepid Warrior*, 221; *Pottsville Miners' Journal*, July 4, 1863; William Lyon to George Lyon, July 18, 1863. *The Columbia Spy*, July 11, 1863, states the retreat commenced at "ten minutes before 7 o'clock."

32 *Columbia Spy*, Apr. 10, 1886; *Pottsville Miners' Journal*, Sept. 23, 1875. The latter writer used the pen name "Lantana." He and his family vacationed in Columbia and Wrightsville. He reported that no trace of the rifle-pits remained, although the editor of *Columbia Spy* showed him an unexploded conical shell that had recently been dug up. He reported that the Wrightsville of 1875 was a "rather dull and quiet town."

lively for some time. Our captain thought it was about time to end the fun, else we might have become boarders at Libby, Andersonville, etc., and word was passed along the line to rally on the centre, which was in an open field, in full view of the Johns. As soon as we were all in, he gave the command left face, and we marched steadily by the flank, until we reached a deep road along the river, from where it was every man for himself to reach the bridge."[33]

Haller hurried down to the bridge to check whether Robert Crane was ready to demolish the selected span. Satisfied with the preparations, Haller rode into Columbia to ensure that Lieutenant Ridgway's artillery was prepared. His hasty departure left some to question his moral fiber. One of the bridge guards from Jennings' 26th Militia, Pvt. John Ralston "Rolly" Caswell, later cursed Haller for being an "arrant coward." He claimed that as the Rebels were approaching the town, the major drew up the small knot of militiamen and told them that if they wanted him, they would have to send for him. Then he "scampered across the bridge as fast as he could travel."[34]

Confederate shells occasionally arced overhead while the remaining militia filed from the entrenchments. Several rounds exploded over the Locust Street neighborhood. Most inflicted no real damage but terrified the townspeople and sent them scurrying for shelter in cellars and attics. One round entered the brick Heppenstall house, near James Kerr Smith's house. Another shell struck the south side of the Presbyterian Church. Yet another one bounded on the pavement in front of Jacob Bahn's nearby residence, and then demolished the step in front of Michael Minnich's front door before striking the door jam. It bounced back into the street, but failed to explode.[35]

A shot passed through the Thomas Harris house on Locust Street above Third Street. It tore a large hole in the eastern brick wall before lodging in the ground without exploding. A shell considerably damaged the Ferry House (or "Big Brick Hotel") at Second and Walnut streets when it exploded in a first floor room. Another one later struck the upper story, where it was found intact on the floor of what had been the Sons of Temperance meeting hall. Locals later

33 Wray, *History of the Twenty-third Pennsylvania*, 152.

34 According to Pennypacker, "Six Weeks in Uniform," 361, "Rolly was about five feet eight inches high, and weighed two hundred and fifty pounds, so that he was not capable of much exertion, at least it was very fatiguing to him."

35 Nye, *Farthest East*, 27.

wagged that it would have been better if the Rebels had destroyed the teetotalers' venue.

Mrs. Amanda Beaverson was leading her two small children across Third Street when a shell burst nearby, thoroughly startling them. Neighbors helped her reach the cellar of Jacob Freet's house, where she comforted her terrified offspring. Another shot damaged the attic, adding to their fright. As Lieutenant Wallace's Company A marched toward the bridge, exploding shells rained fragments about them. He believed that, had the regiment delayed leaving its rifle-pits by just five minutes, their line of retreat would have been cut off.[36]

Shell fragments wounded a handful of retiring militiamen in other companies. A few soldiers ignored the incoming artillery rounds and paused at street barricades to squeeze off scattered shots at their pursuers. The York Invalids and the veteran 87th Pennsylvania "retired deliberately" with rifles blazing. Most of the First City Troop rode across the bridge into Columbia, where several citizens derided the Philadelphians for their apparent eagerness to precede the infantry to safety. Nearly fifteen minutes later, the first foot-soldier emerged from the covered bridge.

As he made his way through the tall wheatfields southwest of town, Gordon Bradwell of the 31st Georgia heard "a buzzing and confused noise" rising from the Yankee position "as if some event were taking place over there." In a moment, officers ordered their men to advance on the enemy's works, which they found to have been abandoned. From "there to the town, the enemy had divested themselves of their equipment in their hasty flight." Twenty-year-old Sgt. Francis L. Hudgins of the 38th Georgia simply wrote, "We drove them pell-mell through the streets of Wrightsville." Dozens of Yankees threw aside their new Springfield rifles and any accouterments that impeded their flight, and exhausted Georgians paused to collect the hastily discarded property, including knapsacks loaded with personal items. A few lucky Rebels discovered spare socks, welcome relief for feet worn by weeks of marching.[37]

Persifor Frazer of the First City Troop watched as a multitude of civilians and militiamen raced downhill, heading for the overturned ore cars at the

36 *Pottsville Miners' Journal,* July 4, 1863.

37 Bradwell, "Burning of Wrightsville," 301; Vertical files, GNMP; JMSIUS (1908), Vol. 43, 290; Hudgins, "With the 38th Georgia," *Confederate Veteran,* Vol. 26 (1918). Hudgins survived several severe wounds and became the regimental historian after the war.

western bridgehead. Colonel Frick had previously positioned troopers Henry Ashhurst and P. A. Brown at these obstructions with orders to notify the officers at the mined span whenever the Confederates approached. The two men stayed at their posts as the swarm of soldiers and civilians streamed around the temporary tete-du-pont. Robert Crane's workers had removed the planking on either side of the pier to prevent the passage of cavalry, artillery, or wagons. Knox and Frick stood on the footway on the downstream side of the bridge, supervising the retreat, with their horses picketed to the aged beams. Old Jacob Miller and the other three men assigned to light the fuses stayed ready for the signal. The teenaged Frazer observed Miller's calmness and wrote, "One old negro to whom was entrusted the duty of igniting the fuse sat very coolly on the edge of the pier, smoking a cigar."[38]

A portion of the Frick's regiment remained intact during the withdrawal. A reporter wrote, "Company E, 27th Regiment, P. V., covered the retreat in magnificent style." One of the soldiers later remembered the chaos of the rest of the regiment, but added, "We are proud, however, of the cool and quiet way in which Company E came marching down the main street with the colors of the regiment." The head of the column emerged from the bridge in fine military order, following the old battleflag of the 129th Pennsylvania. One of the cavalry scouts, possibly Captain M. M. Strickler, sent a courier across the bridge into Columbia with the alarming news, "The rebels have driven us in on the front, and flanked us on the left. I have lost four men who are certainly captured, unless they can escape by the lower river route. One of them is Lieutenant Souders."[39]

In some cases, groups of Rebels closely pursued the militia. They paused occasionally to fire their muskets at Yankees who sought refuge in yards and behind the barricades. Luckily, none of the civilians were hit, but several narrowly escaped Confederate bullets. Straggling militiamen engaged in footraces with pursuing Rebels who, after marching twenty miles, had little energy left to bag their opponents. Company E of the 27th Militia, the color guard, was among the last to leave Wrightsville. Several Georgians seized Sgt.

38 *JMSIUS* (1908), Vol. 43, 289. The "old negro" was a Columbian named Jacob Miller who is believed to have been a carpenter by profession; research by Chris Vera of the Columbia Historic Preservation Society.

39 Gossler, Jacob L., *An Old Turnpike-road* (New York: Baker & Taylor, 1888), 67; *Pottsville Miners' Journal*, Sept. 23, 1875; *Philadelphia Inquirer*, June 29, 1863.

Charles E. Steadman and demanded his surrender. Steadman wrestled himself free of their grasp and raced to the bridgehead to the cheers of his comrades. A Georgia infantryman sarcastically remarked that they had "arrived too late to catch the game, for when a Yankee does run, he can outrun anybody, and there is no use in trying to catch him by a stern chase, you have either to head him off or give it up as a hopeless case."[40]

Across the river in Columbia, fellow trooper Jones Wister noted that Major Haller was "thoroughly alarmed at the shells and balls, which were being thrown into the river." There was a sense of impending doom in the streets. Haller and borough officials struggled to maintain order as mobs of civilians dashed across the bridge, intermixed with retreating militia. "Panic seemed to have seized the authorities and common sense was in abeyance," wrote Wister.[41]

Haller ordered Wister and a delegation of First City Troopers already in Columbia to recross the bridge against the flow of traffic to collect any remaining troopers still in Wrightsville. They encountered the fleeing remnant of Sickles' 20th Militia battalion, crossing one way while they crossed the other. These raw recruits "came in broken ranks, presenting bayonets attached to their muskets in a dangerous fashion, rendering travel most precarious. By dint of constant yelling and shouting, I managed to notify the flying militia that I did not need to be bayoneted." Wister's detachment finally reached Wrightsville uninjured, found their videttes in the multitude, and escorted them back to Columbia.

Trooper Frazer recorded that some of the militia was disorderly during the retreat, especially from the mined span to the Columbia egress. Randall had stationed First City Troopers Colket, Gray, Oakman, and Frazer "to prevent any panic-stricken soldier from prematurely exploding the mine." Frazer recognized fellow Philadelphians from Sickles' command, who were "marching with broken step in orderly line amid the confused crowds of citizens and soldiers." Covering the rear, the 27th Militia also crossed in good order. A sergeant proudly waved their national flag to the cheers of the men as they moved off the bridge into Columbia. Major Haldeman assumed command and marched them to Lockard's Meadow, where they reformed and gave three rousing cheers for Colonel Frick. Lieutenant Ridgway secured horses for his

40 Nye, *Farthest East*, 27; *Savannah Daily Republican*, Aug. 6, 1863.

41 Wister, *Reminiscences*, 162.

guns in case they needed to be withdrawn, but for now, they stayed put, aimed at the hillsides above Wrightsville.[42]

Haller appointed Captain Randall as provost marshal. His First City Troop rode throughout Columbia's streets, where they discouraged looting and occasionally cajoled reluctant volunteers back into service at gunpoint. Most of the militia reformed and assumed new defensive positions. A few, however, simply melted away after reaching Columbia, including almost two full companies of the now-terrified 20th Militia. Some eventually ran as far as Lancaster and Millersville, carrying the alarming news that the Rebels had taken Wrightsville and were surely headed their way. Many civilians joined the panic-stricken flight, and "at seven o'clock, on that Sunday evening, it was impossible to hire a team of any kind for 'love or money.'"[43]

The black volunteers were still intact, surprisingly considering their lack of combat experience. A Philadelphia correspondent scribbled, "Two companies of colored troops remained in the intrenchments until ordered to retreat. They were volunteers, and behaved very well, except in the retreat, which was accomplished rather hastily." The majority camped on a hill along Third Street, behind Columbia. Haller detached one group to guard a ford. They marched out to their new post, "bearing themselves like veteran soldiers" according to a witness.[44]

Haller and Haldeman soon managed to restore order among the militia, with the exception of some of Sickles' men who "scattered throughout the county." Despite the chaos of the withdrawal, a Lancaster newsman noted that "Nothing was lost except a few tents, rations, and entrenching tools." One Philadelphia reporter declared, "Nothing of importance was captured at the intrenchments except about five hundred rations, which have been replaced."[45]

Knowing the Rebels would soon arrive, Frick and Knox remained just inside the bridgehead and directed the retreat of remaining Federals. Unknown to them, other than one squadron accounted for in Columbia, Bell's Cavalry was missing. The Adams County scouts had encountered the Confederate rear guard while riding up the Old Baltimore Road. Tanner's gunners adjusted their

42 *JMSIUS* (1908), Vol. 43, 290.

43 *Columbia Spy*, Jan. 23, 1886.

44 *Philadelphia Inquirer*, June 29, 1863.

45 *Lancaster Examiner and Herald*, July 1, 1863; *Philadelphia Inquirer*, June 30, 1863.

3-inch Ordnance Rifles and hurled a pair of shells at the distant Federal cavalry. A few Rebel infantrymen leveled their rifles and blazed away. Two horses dropped, and a detachment of Georgians quickly captured one injured cavalryman. The second fallen rider escaped detection by dashing into a nearby house, where the startled residents successfully hid him. Captain Bell quickly ordered his bugler to sound the recall, and the company galloped south to Safe Harbor. Because the Susquehanna was too swollen to cross on horseback, the cavalrymen commandeered a nearby raft to ferry their horses to Lancaster County. They eventually rejoined their comrades in Columbia.[46]

Meanwhile, four First City Troopers, including Persifor Frazer, remained at the mined span to keep careless militiamen from detonating the charges. After the first "noisy and excited mob" rushed by, there was a significant lull. At last the four pickets that Haller had left at the Wrightsville entrance rode by the guards, reporting that the Rebels were rapidly approaching. They picked their way across the partly dismantled carriage track on the span selected for destruction. Another short lull ensued, broken only by a few enemy artillery shells and rifle shots. Suddenly, a few daring Confederate cavalrymen dashed around the overturned ore cars and entered the covered bridge. They discharged their revolvers before disappearing back into the shadows.[47]

Confusion reigned. One of the York Invalids took the bridge's footpath, "and after running one quarter-mile, discovered his retreat was cut off, as the bridge on that side had been cut, and not knowing how to swim, he took his chances of going back to the mouth of the bridge." Fortunately, he found a window, crawled through it, and escaped using the towpath. The remaining invalids fired from behind the bridge's uprights, temporarily slowing the Confederates. By now the Rebels were swarming along the western riverbank. Frick knew he could wait no longer. He ordered the First City Troop guards to follow their companions to Columbia. The last of the quartet, Persifor Frazer, led away Colonel Frick's horse. That left only Frick, Knox, and Robert Crane's four volunteers, including cigar-smoking old Jacob Miller, still at the pier. Major Knox moved 400 feet to the west where he could clearly see Wrightsville's business district.[48]

---

46 *York Gazette*, June 30, 1863; OR 27, pt. 2, 999.

47 *JMSIUS* (1908), Vol. 43, 290.

48 Wray, *History of the Twenty-third Pennsylvania*, 152.

Not all of the retreating Federals made it to safety. Rebels cut off Lt. Colonel Sickles and eighteen of his 20th Pennsylvania Volunteer Militia who dawdled in leaving their position. Frick later accused Sickles of cowardice, incompetence, and disobedience of orders. Once the battalion did get moving, Capt. Robert G. March took bullets in an arm and his left leg. A few men from his Company B carried the wounded officer into the nearby house of Joshua Isaac. Francis Wallace later wrote that if Sickles' 20th Militia had "moved with half the celerity of the negro who as he rushed by me, exclaimed, 'Gorra, massa, we'll all be murdered!' not a man of them would have been captured." Clement Evans wrote, "They fled so rapidly that we captured only about thirty."[49]

One of Sickles' men later defended his much maligned regiment's honor in a Philadelphia newspaper. Signing the letter as "JUSTICE," he claimed, "It is said that the troops which were guarding the Northern Central railroad retreated to the Columbia bridge on the approach of the enemy, and all crossed the river except Colonel Frick's regiment, which remained at Wrightsville to guard the bridge. Those brave men of Col. William B. Thomas's regiment— Companies H, B, and F—remained on the ground in the face of the enemy till all the other troops had left the field. When they took up their retreat, the bridge on the Wrightsville side was on fire, which cut off the retreat of a part or portion of Companies H and F, who made their escape by crossing the Susquehanna in boats, and reported to their companies this morning."[50]

With the militia finally out of the way, victorious Rebels streamed into downtown Wrightsville from three directions. Many noted a large "white flag" fluttering above a large house on Hellam Street. Iron merchant Samuel Kauffelt had climbed onto his roof to secure a makeshift wooden flagpole to one of his brick chimneys to indicate the town's surrender, and to appeal to Gordon to prevent any further shelling of the borough. By now it was nearly sundown (7:39 p.m.), some ninety minutes after the Rebels had begun their deliberate assault on the works. John Gordon had chased Granville Haller out of yet another Pennsylvania town, and his Georgians controlled Wrightsville.

49 *Pottsville Miners' Journal*, Oct. 24, 1863; Stephens, *Intrepid Warrior*, 221. Some early newspapers erroneously reported that March perished from his wounds. He died Feb. 1, 1875, after working for several years as an internal revenue agent.

50 *Philadelphia Press*, July 1, 1863.

Chapter 11

A Scene of Confusion and Excitement*

Burning the Bridge Behind Them

Major Granville Haller believed that he had made every necessary arrangement to blow up one 200-foot span of the lengthy Columbia Bridge. Lieutenant Delaplaine Ridgway, volunteer Capt. E. K. Smith, and their militia artillery crew had moved two fieldpieces into position in Columbia to fire exploding shells at the huge bridge. Haller instructed Ridgway to stay ready to shell Wrightsville if necessary. Major Charles Knox soon reported that enemy infantry was forming to cross the bridge. A few more Confederate cavalrymen rode around the overturned railroad cars and dashed into the viaduct for an instant, firing their revolvers at Knox before disappearing from view.

Seeing Rebels bringing artillery into Wrightsville, Jacob Frick knew that time was running out. About 7:30 p.m., supposing that all of his men were safely across the river, Frick gave Knox the order to light the fuse. Knox signaled demolition supervisor Robert Crane, who had previously positioned four men, John Q. Denney, Jacob Rich, John Lockard, and an old black man named Jacob Miller, at the mined span on the western end. They applied matches to the fuses and ran back toward Columbia, out of the blast area. Crane reported that "every charge was perfect and effective." The 33-year-old Denney had been a lieutenant in the 2nd Militia during the Emergency of 1862, serving under Capt. William G. Case, the constructor of "Fort Case." He operated the Henry Clay Furnace near Chickies Rock just upriver from Columbia and had considerable

---

* This chapter was co-written with Professor Scott L. Mingus, Jr.

experience in blasting. The efforts to topple the span failed, however, as the charge "simply splintered the arch. It scarcely shook the bridge."[1]

A *Harper's Weekly* correspondent in Columbia reported, "But when the period of destruction arrived, three reports were heard in quick succession, followed by a cloud of smoke, which led us to believe that some of the cannon guarding the entrance at Columbia had been taken to this part of the bridge and fired at the entering rebels." West of Wrightsville, Gordon Bradwell heard the explosion, and "looking toward town, we saw the timbers of the bridge rising high into the blue sky." The detonation did have one benefit for the defenders—according to Lt. W. C. Mathews, it chased Company G of the 38th Georgia out of the bridge. Years later he wrote, "That company, the advance guard in the attack, thus accomplished the honorable exploit of penetrating farther north [east] than any company in the Army of Northern Virginia, of which fact the survivors are to this day justly proud."[2]

Meanwhile, a few Confederate artillery rounds howled into the river, with a couple landing dangerously close to the bridge. F. X. Ziegler had spent Sunday working in Columbia's telegraph station. The 46-year-old left the building and stood in Front Street near Gay Street. He had a good view of Tanner's errant shells splashing into the Susquehanna "about half way across."[3]

Having failed to topple one of the spans with explosives, Frick felt that it was his duty to set a portion of the bridge on fire. He again turned to railroader Robert Crane, who ordered the civilian volunteers to attempt this dangerous task. Former artillery commander, Capt. E. K. Smith, a civil engineer by trade, helped supervise the workers. A few men had previously rolled large barrels of coal oil and kerosene from a small Columbia refinery onto the bridge. Now they dragged the fuel, boards, and wood shavings to the specified location, where they knocked in the barrelheads and soaked the kindling and the oak floor with the volatile liquids. In search of more fuel, Crane sent a man back to Front Street in Columbia's mercantile district. He procured additional coal oil from the shop of Anthony J. Hindermeyer.[4]

1   *OR* 27, pt. 2, 278; pt. 3, 411; John Q. Denney deposition to Judge David E. Brundy, July 24, 1863, CHPS.

2   *Harpers Weekly*, July 18, 1863; Bradwell, "Burning of Wrightsville," 301; *The Sunny South*, Jan. 10, 1891.

3   F. X. Ziegler, diary entry for June 28, 1863, LCHS.

4   Columbia file, LCHS.

WRIGHTSVILLE AND COLUMBIA

Scene of the Burning of the Bridge Across the Susquehanna.

The New York *Herald* of June 30, 1863, depicted the river crossing between Wrightsville in York County and Columbia in Lancaster County. *Author's Collection*

Shortly before 8:00 p.m. Colonel Frick gave the order. John Denney and his three companions threw torches onto the oil-soaked floor and timbers. Persifor Frazer, still leading Frick's horse, was just then emerging from the eastern end. He "saw a curl of smoke rising from the pier where the mine had been placed, and shortly afterward a column of flame mounted high in the sky." Soon the span was fully engulfed, filling the evening sky with glowing cinders. Colonel Clement Evans' Georgians rushed into the "splendid bridge," but they lacked anything to fight the fire except their hands and coats. Evans opined, "Two or three pieces of artillery judiciously placed on the opposite side" could have saved the bridge. He surely did not know that the Federals had cannons in Columbia.[5]

Not wanting to bring artillery fire on the town and lacking ammunition, Ridgway's gunners merely stared at the disordered mobs of Rebels now crowding Wrightsville's riverbank. Colonel Frick emerged from the bridge and immediately headed for Columbia's telegraph station to have F. X. Zeigler wire an update to General Couch. Some local patriotic firebrands implored him to "man the gun; man the gun!" Frick replied, "No, let the gun alone; do you want to draw the fire of the enemy on a defenseless town?"[6]

In downtown Columbia, Annie Welsh worried about the success of the operation. "My only fear was that they would not succeed in retreating and getting the torch applied to the bridge in time," she admitted, "but they succeeded well. Some of the Rebels rushed in and tried to extinguish the fire but they could not succeed. Persons that come over from Wrightsville said that they were very much disappointed. They thought we would not have spunk enough to burn the bridge. They tried to flank our little force and capture them, and fifteen minutes more would have done it."[7]

The last remaining militiamen to make it onto the bridge raced through the blazing structure to reach safety, although nearly two dozen would be trapped in Wrightsville. Wm. Albert Myton of Company F "rather than be taken prisoner. . . . ventured through the flames in order to join his comrades on the opposite side." He likely was the last man to cross the bridge. As he emerged in Columbia, "Confederate soldiers could be seen on the York County shore swarming the banks and hills," according to his comrade Pvt. W. S. Halleman. Across the river in Wrightsville, Southerners discovered a locked boxcar sitting at a nearby lumberyard. They broke it open, ransacked its contents, and began carrying away boxes of dry goods, muslin, calicoes, cutlery, jewelry, silks, lace, and clothes. Adams County merchant Ira Shipley had days before sent these

5   *JMSIUS* (1908), Vol. 43, 290; Stephens, *Intrepid Warrior*, 222.

6   *Columbia Spy*, Jan. 22, 1887.

7   Annie Welsh to Thomas Welsh, July 1, 1863. Courtesy of Richard C. Wiggin.

from his Round Hill store to avoid their seizure, and unbeknownst to him, Rebels now possessed his inventory.[8]

Despite light rain, the flames grew higher and hotter. The wind from the east intensified as a rainstorm approached, and soon the entire western end of the bridge was on fire. Sparks filled the skies over Wrightsville. Cavalryman James Hodam, still in reserve on the turnpike, saw "dense smoke arising from the town," which he first supposed was caused by Rebel shells setting fire to buildings. However, "our signal Corps informed us that the enemy were retreating across the river and burning the bridge."[9]

John Gordon later explained that his men labored "with great energy" in their initial frantic efforts to save the bridge he was tasked with capturing. He called on Wrightsville's residents for buckets and pails, but none were to be found. "The bridge might burn," he added with a dollop of dry humor, "for that incommoded, at the time, only the impatient Confederates, and these Pennsylvanians were not in sympathy with my expedition, not anxious to facilitate the movement of such unwelcome visitors."[10]

Gordon sat on his horse along the riverbank at dusk watching as the flaming span collapsed into the river. Along with it went Confederate hopes of traversing Lancaster County to attack Harrisburg from the rear. No long after the bridge fell an unexpected visitor in the form of an anxious Jubal Early arrived. The general had led his staff and colorguard toward Wrightsville in the early evening and rode forward to ascertain the results of Gordon's expedition. The party of Confederates had not ridden very far when they noticed "immense smoke rising in the direction of the Susquehanna."

Spurring his horse, Early arrived in Wrightsville and found General Gordon on the riverbank. Gordon relayed the evening's events, including his battle plan to sweep around the enemy earthworks, cutting them off from the river. He estimated that his brigade had chased some 1,200 militiamen across the bridge after the "bursting of the third shell" from Tanner's Battery. Exhausted after marching more than twenty miles, Gordon's soldiers had failed to snare the Yankees, who had fled across the bridge. When the head of his column "got half way over," they found it was "on fire in the middle." Gordon

8   *Huntingdon* (Pa.) *Daily News*, July 3, 1923. Adams County Damage Claims, Reel 9, Shipley claim, ACHS; York County Damage Claims, Kauffelt claim.

9   Kesterson, Hodam Manuscript.

10 Gordon, *Reminiscences*, 147.

added that, as his men had nothing but muskets and rifles to fight the flames, he had sent back for buckets. However, before they arrived, the fire had progressed so far that it was impossible to arrest it. He had ordered his men off the bridge, leaving it to its fate.[11]

Early, disappointed in the premature end to his expedition, concluded his brief conference with Gordon. He had wanted to bag all of the militia and secure the bridge. Now, other than a handful of prisoners, the militia was gone and so was his chance to cross into Lancaster County. Frustrated, he spurred his horse into the twilight and returned to York. There, he dined with an aged Copperhead, retired dry goods dealer Robert Barry, before lodging in the Metzel House, a W. Main Street hotel.[12]

Saving Wrightsville

The conflagration—fueled by the dry, well-aged timbers of the bridge's superstructure—grew more intense. Between 9:30 and 10:00 p.m., fire engulfed the entire western end and wind-blown embers spread to the roof of the Kauffelt & Lanius lumber mill near the canal dam. The sky danced with flames and pillars of smoke as more riverside buildings caught fire. Before long, Henry Kauffelt's coal yard structures and small foundry were beyond salvage. The spreading inferno consumed his scales and a few empty railcars nearby, including the one ransacked by the Rebels when they stole Ira Shipley's merchandise. Rebels pushed Kauffelt's blazing railcar over an abutment and into the canal. Fire also destroyed the post office and millinery that shared a Front Street building. Nearby, a confectionery store and the office, engine house, foundry, and warehouse of W. H. Harris's lumberyard were ablaze. Embers threatened Wolf's Iron Works and warehouse, and dozens of homes.[13]

While her husband was away serving in the Union army, Catherine J. Albright had rented the ground floor of two-story frame house owned by George Harris. It soon caught fire. She dashed from the house with her children

---

11 OR 27, pt. 2, 467.

12 Prowell, *History of York County*, 1: 801; Latimer letters, YCHT. Hannah Metzel kept her husband Thomas's hotel open for several years after his death. For many years, the establishment was known as "The Turk's Head."

13 York County Damage Claims, various reels.

Artist Bradley Schmehl depicts the burning of the Columbia Bridge in this painting.

her household goods and furniture. The tenant in the upper story, Thomas Dasher, also escaped injury, but he too lost all his possessions.[14]

Frustrated in their failed efforts save the bridge, the Confederates now turned their energy toward waging a more humanitarian—and unexpected— fight. Evans' men of the 31st Georgia were marching into the Wrightsville business district when they spotted merchants rolling their goods into the street in an effort to avoid the oncoming firestorm. Private Bradwell watched "greedy flames eating their way from house to house up the street on the north side." Without orders, Georgians began assisting the shopkeepers in their effort to save their merchandise. Other soldiers helped citizens in their efforts to subdue the raging fire. Despite their joint labor, the conflagration continued to gain momentum.[15]

An astonished Gordon watched as the residents, so reluctant to help save their bridge, now frantically rushed to the riverbank as flames raced through the lumberyards. "Buckets and tubs and pails and pans innumerable came from their hiding places, until it seemed that, had the whole of Lee's army been present, I could have armed them with these implements to fight the rapidly spreading flames." Gordon's anger at the citizens for not helping his men fight the bridge fire turned to compassion as he saw their anguished faces. He ordered two regiments to form "around the burning district, with the flank resting on the river's edge, and pass rapidly from hand to hand the pails of water." Lacking fire engines or similar appliances, Gordon's sweating soldiers "labored as earnestly and bravely to save the town as they did to save the bridge."[16]

To Clement Evans and likely many other soldiers as well, Wrightsville was "a scene of confusion and excitement." Flames threatened the old Wrightsville House, a 20-room stone structure on N. Front Street that was once a popular hotel. Samuel Kauffelt's house caught fire. Perhaps the white flag tied to the wooden staff on the chimney caught a spark, or a flaming ember had blown

14 Federal Civil War Damage Claims, NARA, Washington, D.C. The state commissioners decided that Mrs. Albright was entitled to $200 to cover her losses, but a Federal agent intervened to reject her claim. His reason was clear: The claim was "not shown the United States took or used any of the stores claimed for or that the original fire was lighted by United States authority."

15 Bradwell, "Burning of Wrightsville," 301.

16 OR 27, pt. 2, 467; Gordon, *Reminiscences*, 148.

onto the roof and ignited there. Gordon personally detailed twelve men to Kauffelt's home, and the party was able to extinguish this fire.[17]

The Heppenstall & Gohn general store along the river caught fire, threatening the Heppenstall family's home immediately across Front Street. Quick action by Georgians saved both of the buildings, as well as toll collector William McConkey's nearby house and the railroad depot. They also saved a large barn used to house the canal's tow mules. The noise of the inferno was almost deafening, and the air was thick with pungent smoke. At one point, Gordon's men expended "immense energy" combating the fire, and with great difficulty saved an attractive Hellam Street house, the home of Mrs. Luther Rewalt, one of "the most superb women" that Gordon had the fortune to meet during the war.[18]

Private George W. O'Neal of the 31st Georgia commented that "by our heroic work we saved the residence and stopped the fire." However, not all of Gordon's men were as eager to pitch in. Ordnance officer William Lyon joined in the "most strenuous efforts" to save the town, but he "did not fully approve of our exerting ourselves to any considerable extent." Lyon could not help but recall that in a similar situation in Georgia, a Yankee army had not exerted themselves to save Southern towns from destruction.[19]

Private Bradwell noted that Gordon tried an unusual tactic. Pioneers arrived with kegs of powder, and placed them under the buildings most exposed to the fire. Officers ordered provost guardsmen to affix their bayonets and force the toiling soldiers back up the street out of the danger zone. The ensuing explosion "knocked the houses to pieces," collapsing the structures.

17 Stephens, *Intrepid Warrior*, 220. The building, erected sometime between 1806 and 1812, was a hotel until 1855 when owner John Kauffelt died. His widow closed the hotel, which had nine fireplaces, twenty guestrooms, and a large lobby. Georgians repeatedly extinguished flaming embers that landed on the roof. Later the house was subdivided into two private residences (127/129 N. Front Street). Sam Kauffelt's house was at 114 Hellam Street, uphill from the bridge.

18 Gordon, *Reminiscences*, 148. Chief Burgess James F. Magee owned a three-story brick house at 274 Hellam Street. His daughter, Mary Jane, stayed there while her young husband Dr. L. L. Rewalt served as the assistant surgeon of the 25th Pennsylvania. He married Mary Jane Magee on April 6, 1863. In January 1865, Rewalt became the asst. surgeon of the 21st Pennsylvania Cavalry (Company B included Bell's Adams County Cavalry). One of the Rewalts' direct descendants is author Gore Vidal.

19 Mamie Yeary, *Reminiscences of the Boys in Gray, 1861-1865* (Dayton, Ohio: Morningside Books, 1986), 579; *Mobile Advertiser & Register*, Aug. 29, 1863; letter written by an anonymous "Alabamian in Lee's army."

A sketch from *Frank Leslie's Illustrated* incorrectly depicts the Baltimore & Susquehanna rail station on the Columbia side of the Susquehanna River. Flames race eastward across the Columbia Bridge. *Frank Leslie's Illustrated*

Colonel Evans confirmed that his regiment stacked their arms and worked until nearly midnight to arrest the blaze. The 31st Georgia finally succeeded by "tearing down a few houses" and moving piles of lumber to safer locations. He added, "It was a singular sight to see those marching Rebels work so eagerly to save a Yankee town which the scamps had themselves set on fire."[20]

Evans accidentally kicked up a stray piece of a newspaper that the wind had blown to his feet. By the light of the flames, he paused to read an account of the Yankee raid of Darien, Georgia, and the resultant fire set by black regiments from Massachusetts. "Like gallant Southerners," wrote Evans, his boys from Darien battled flames in a Northern town even though the invaders of Georgia had pillaged and burned theirs. To Evans, this irony demonstrated the "noble spirit of Confederate men."[21]

20 Bradwell, "Burning of Wrightsville," 301; Stephens, *Intrepid Warrior*, 222. The *Columbia Spy*, Jan. 16, 1886, confirms that a house was indeed blown up as a fire break.

21 Stephens, *Intrepid Warrior*, 222.

English-born Lt. Joseph Hilton of the 26th Georgia resided in McIntosh County near Darien. His father established a lumber business and sawmill there during the 1850s. As with many other Georgians, Hilton had decided misgivings about saving Wrightsville. If the Rebels were ever again to invade Pennsylvania, a vengeful Hilton declared that "the next time we will be apt to apply the torch instead of putting out the fire." Gordon's bucket brigade continued its strenuous efforts for two more hours, well past midnight, saving a large warehouse along the canal. Dozens of buildings suffered some damage, but most were salvageable.[22]

However, time would heal the wounds. Twenty-five years later, a reporter noted, "The loyal people of Wrightsville have not, to this day, forgotten Early's rebel troops for their valuable assistance in trying to stay the flames."[23]

Saving Columbia

Meanwhile, fire was consuming the bridge east toward Columbia, advancing surprisingly well against strong gusts of wind and intermittent rainfall. Some of the York Invalids were still on the bridge. One commented, "We lounged around, until the smoke and flames made it a race for life to reach the other end, a mile away." Shortly before 9:00 p.m., authorities began fearing for the town's safety. Someone proposed that the First City Troop should try to save the remaining half of the bridge. The cavalrymen fell in and marched onto it. They removed floor planks and dismantled the supporting beams with axes in a vain effort to check the fire. Lacking sufficient manpower, Samuel Randall called for volunteers to assist his struggling men. According to Persifor Frazer, "The citizens positively refused to do anything until compelled, with drawn pistols, to go to work, but such forced labor was found to be of no avail." Refusing to give up their fight against the flames, the cavalrymen worked "as industriously as possible" for two hours. However, "the fire advanced with such rapid strides that it was necessary to abandon the structure to the flames. The men returned to quarters quite exhausted."[24]

---

22 Joseph Hilton to Lizzie Lachison, July 18, 1863, Georgia Historical Society. According to author Gregory C. White, Hilton (1842-1920) and his parents immigrated to Darien from England in 1855. No Darien businesses survived the fires set by the Union forces.

23 *Columbia Spy*, Jan. 16, 1886.

24 Wray, *History of the Twenty-third Pennsylvania*, 152; *JMSIUS* (1908), Vol. 43, 290.

Chaos reigned on the riverfront. Families separated in the chaotic final rush to the bridge now feverishly searched for one another. A reporter recalled, "A gentleman from Wrightsville. . . . was seen hurrying along Second street, fairly panic stricken, and without a hat, inquiring of everyone he met whether they had seen his wife." The newsman quipped, "Quite a number of wives were noticed on the street, but whether any of them was his wife was more than they could possibly say."[25]

With all the excitement, Annie Welsh's children "did not want to go to bed on Sunday night at all." She finally sent her two daughters to her aunts' house for the night, while her home filled with boarders. She "was not afraid of anything but my money, and think I put it in a safe place against thieves or fire." Annie and her neighbor Mrs. Hook were the only residents left on their street, because the rest had fled for safer locales. The two women walked down to Front Street to see the fire. "It was a Magnificent," she later wrote to her husband, "but awful sight." She added, "Mrs. Hook would have much rather seen the Rebels come into town than to see the bridge burnt. She made fun of our soldiers, calling them cowards for retreating. I believe she would have been pleased if they had been captured. She was very anxious that Columbia should be surrendered."[26]

Fire lit the rainy night sky as span after span fell into the water, floating away "like so many burning ships." During the frightening evening, many Columbians grabbed their valuables and fled the borough, "dreading a fire from the lumber or a shelling from the Rebs." Others stayed behind to gawk at the fire. A few continued ministering to the soldiers. According to artilleryman Daniel Dillman, "The disaster of the day opened the heart and pantries of the people of Columbia. Everyone was anxious to feed the soldiers. I had an excellent supper at Dr. [W. S.] McCorkle's."[27]

Frazer noted that twenty minutes elapsed from the time the western end of a span combusted until that entire section collapsed into the river. This process was repeated for each of the eighteen spans between where the blaze had

25 *Columbia Spy*, Jan. 23, 1886.

26 Annie Welsh to Thomas Welsh, July 1, 1863. Courtesy of Richard C. Wiggin.

27 *Columbia Spy*, July 11, 1863; *Pottsville Journal*, July 18, 1913. According to Dillman, Dr. McCorkle had served as surgeon of the 2nd Militia during the Emergency of 1862, although his name does not appear in its roster lists. Dillman was a private in Company F of the same regiment.

started and the Columbia egress. He estimated that it would therefore take six hours for the entire bridge to be consumed. A reporter for *Harper's Weekly* noted that the skeletal arches and frame-work of each section stood burning long after its roof and weather-boarding had disappeared.[28]

Residents of nearby Marietta could clearly see the flames and dense billowing clouds of black smoke. In Harrisburg, Governor Curtin and state and city officials spent anxious hours watching the glowing evening sky to the southeast and reading dispatches from Columbia. Hundreds of ladies lined a park along the eastern riverbank, watching the glowing night sky to the southeast. Among them were several volunteer nurses from Lancaster County who had been tending to the crowds of refugees and Milroy's soldiers from the fight at Second Winchester. "The bridge at Columbia was fired early in the evening, and though ten miles distant, we saw it distinctly," recalled one woman. "No lovelier evening can be imagined. The moon was shining in the clear and cloudless sky, and the lurid flashes from the burning bridge gave everything an almost supernatural appearance. During the still hours of that summer night, we watched and waited, not knowing what the morrow would bring forth."[29]

Millersville and Lancaster citizens also could see the reddish cast to the west. In Hanover, Mrs. Daniel Stair observed that, "Just after dark on Sunday night, the whole horizon in the northeast was lit up by a lurid glow." The vivid red sky prompted the rapid spread of rumors throughout Hanover that the Rebels were destroying York. Few realized that the massive fire was actually miles away at Wrightsville. Similarly in Gettysburg, "a large fire could be seen in the direction of York. . . . resulting probably from the burning of the barracks, machine shops, cars, etc. there."[30]

As they occupied Dillsburg, members of Albert Jenkins' 16th Virginia Cavalry took note of the strange red glare lighting up the southeastern sky. "An arrogant soldier" informed some citizens in a store that the light was doubtless caused by the Federal army's destruction of property between York and Wrightsville. As he paid for his provisions with Confederate script, he added, "We are marching to Philadelphia and New York. We will capture both these

28 *JMSIUS* (1908), Vol. 43, 290; *Harpers Weekly*, July 18, 1863.

29 *Philadelphia Inquirer*, June 30, 1863; "The Patriot Daughters of Lancaster," *Hospital Scenes after the Battle of Gettysburg* (Lancaster, Pa.: Daily Inquirer, 1864), 5.

30 *Encounter*, 67-68; *Gettysburg Compiler*, June 29, 1863.

cities. Then the war will soon be at an end and our money will be as good as gold."[31]

Still on the York Turnpike, Waldo's company of the 17th Virginia Cavalry witnessed the amazing aerial display. They finally filed into Wrightsville late in the night. According to Pvt. James Hodam, "We entered the town where all was confusion and dismay, many large buildings, mills and a lumber yard had taken fire from the bridge and a great conflagration was only prevented by timely exertions of the citizens and our soldiers. The great bridge was a vast sheet of flame from end to end and in the darkness was a sight not soon forgotten by friend and foe."[32]

Thousands of citizens, refugees, and soldiers lined the riverbanks and nearby hills, watching the fire steadily progress toward Columbia. Some sat on the roofs of homes and businesses. Borough officials and leading citizens watched from the high front porch of the Pennsylvania Railroad's Washington House. Sidney Josephine Myer described the scene simply as "awful." Among the fascinated observers was Gettysburg postmaster David Buehler. He and tax assessor Robert G. Harper had reached Columbia after narrowly escaping capture when Elijah White's cavalrymen thundered into Gettysburg on Friday afternoon. McSherrystown farmer and schoolteacher George W. Wortz also watched the bridge burn; he had taken his horses across it the previous day to evade Elijah White's raiders. In nearby Marietta, Mennonite minister Peter Nissley wrote, "We heard the cannon plain & saw the Fire of the burning bridge from my house. . . . They tried to shell Columbia but could not reach it. Our few men resisted them, retreated to, and Fired that magnificent Bridge." Well to the east in Coatesville, Northern Central engineer George Small noticed the brightly lit sky behind him as he steamed toward Philadelphia.[33]

A few journalists were among the swarm of spellbound onlookers. A *New York Herald* reporter penned, "A vast sheet of flame, at one time half a mile in length, crept slowly from Wrightsville to Columbia, illuminating the waters of the Susquehanna for miles each way, and lighting everything up as clear as

31 Prowell, *History of York County*, 1, 869.

32 Kesterson, Hodam Manuscript.

33 Hugh M. North deposition, Aug. 19, 1904, CHPS; Sidney Myer diary, entry for June 28, 1863, LCHS; Buehler, "Recollections of the Rebel Raid," *Gettysburg Times*, Sept. 3, 1923; Peter Nissley to John F. Funk, Aug. 6, 1863, Mennonite Church USA Archives, Goshen, Indiana; George Small, 1905 *York Dispatch*.

gaslight illuminates a room. The crackling noise produced by the burning bridge, and the shouts and confusion of the people, all made up such a scene such as is seldom witnessed." A Philadelphian described the scene as "magnificent." Some of the bridge's sturdy arches had remained intact even when their timbers were all in flames, reflecting on the dark water and giving the appearance of "a fiery skeleton bridge." One reporter waxed poetically when he described how burning wood floated downstream "like infernal ferry boats of the regions pictured by Dante."[34]

Jones Wister was among the First City Troopers patrolling Columbia's waterfront streets. He was mesmerized by "the great wall of fire" slowly approaching the eastern end. Its timbers well seasoned by three decades of exposure, the bridge burned "with a vigor and intensity that I have never seen equaled. For more than two hours the flames shot heavenward, lighting the surrounding hills and valleys for miles in all directions. It was a beautiful and never-to-be-forgotten exhibition."[35]

A Lancaster correspondent called the conflagration a "sublime sight." According to the *New York Times*, "The great bridge over the Susquehanna near Columbia is at this moment in flames. The firmament is illuminated by it even at this distance. It was fired by our own people to prevent the enemy from crossing. A skirmish occurred in Wrightsville, opposite Columbia, three hours ago," continued the paper. "Col. Frick's men fought the enemy is their rifle-pits gallantly, till surrounded and overpowered. Over one hundred [sic] were captured, and the rest retreated across the bridge, which was then fired. The bridge was one mile and a quarter long, and worth a million. The excitement here now amounts to a panic. Everything is leaving."[36]

Shortly before midnight the raging inferno finally engulfed the easternmost span. Columbia's fire department had already rolled its two fire engines into position. Haller or Frick may have sent Wrightsville's pumper over to Columbia that Sunday afternoon, or the firemen may have concealed it. In any event, it was not available to Gordon's Confederates. Columbia firefighters lost one Front Street house to the flames, but they rejoiced in saving the remaining homes and businesses.

34 *New York Herald*, June 30, 1863; *Philadelphia Inquirer*, June 30, 1863.

35 Wister, *Reminiscences*, 163.

36 *Lancaster Examiner and Herald*, July 1, 1863; *New York Times*, June 29, 1863.

Flying sparks threatened Lieutenant Ridgway's guns, so he ordered his artillerymen to move them to safety. As the cannoneers trudged through town pulling the heavy fieldpieces, Daniel Dillman noticed "a great stir" in one house on Locust Street. Through the window, he spied Pvt. Charles H. Voute of Company B prostrate on a sofa, "seriously ill with an attack of palpitation of the heart. Poor fellow, it is feared that he cannot recover." Voute lived, although his soldiering days were over.[37]

Jacob Frick later wrote that the entire bridge was lost despite his soldiers' "vigorous attempt" to save a portion of it. Exhausted First City Troopers exchanged opinions on the wisdom of setting the bridge ablaze in the first place. Captain Randall felt that it was a "mistaken policy." Jones Wister thought that Frick's order was "a wholly unnecessary act. . . . Everyone who witnessed it regretted what seemed like wanton waste and never again wished to see a similar catastrophe." A Harrisburg reporter complained, "The destruction of the bridge would seem to have been rash and unnecessary, as the tearing up of the planks at the southern end would have been sufficient to prevent any crossing by the enemy. The government is responsible for whatever losses may ensue from the burning of the structure."[38]

Some questioned why the militia retreated instead of fighting harder to protect the bridge. One of Frick's defenders wrote, "There were shot and shell enough at Wrightsville to satisfy the most blood-thirsty warrior, and there probably would have been much more of it had the 27th remained on the Wrightsville side of the bridge, as an inducement to the rebels to keep up the firing. . . . As to the destruction of the Columbia bridge, it is difficult to comprehend how anybody having a knowledge of the situation at the time, and the rapid advance of the enemy towards Harrisburg, can question its wisdom."[39]

U.S. Congressman and Lancaster newsman John A. Hiestand later challenged the assumption that the bridge needed to be burned to prevent Gordon from entering Lancaster County: "This bridge was a covered wooden bridge, more than a mile long, and no commander of troops would ever have undertaken to march across it until he had both ends of the bridge. The end of

37 *Pottsville Journal*, July 18, 1913. The heart attack victim, 22-year-old Charles B. Voute of Schuylkill Haven, recovered and mustered out in Harrisburg on July 31.

38 OR 27, pt. 2, 279; Wister, *Reminiscences*, 162-63; *Harrisburg Patriot and Union*, July 9, 1863.

39 *Columbia Spy*, Apr. 10, 1886.

the bridge on the east side of the river was guarded by loyal Union troops, under the command of competent and able officers, and any attempt of the rebels to march over or across it would have been suicidal and a most hazardous experiment. It was therefore a mistake or blunder, to say the least."[40]

Instead of second guessing his decision, Frick pondered potential enemy threats. He ordered militiamen to the fords and dam to contest any Confederate attempts to cross the Susquehanna. By the light of the burning bridge, the soldiers and civilians in Fort Case could clearly see the low dam, as well as Rebels milling about the Wrightsville riverfront. John Q. Denney later asserted that some Confederates attempted to cross over the breast, but they turned back when they "saw some cannon mounted in a brownstone fort below the old flint mill."[41]

Concern remained that the Confederates might still try to force a passage over the dam, especially when the river receded. J. Houston Mifflin wrote that Columbia was safe for a week, because crossing the dam was "a big job-ugly work getting over." However, many other Columbians, still worried about a Confederate attack, fled the borough. A Lancaster newsman reported that the retreat of the troops, the bridge fire, and the shells hurtling into the river created a panic, and "the skedaddle continued during the night as the shelling of the town was anticipated."[42]

As the fire began to die, Ridgway's artillerymen camped near Columbia in a field of oats. Near midnight, the lieutenant roused Corporal Dillman and his men and ordered them to impress horses to draw the heavy artillery. They scattered in several directions to gather all the horses that they could find in the darkness.[43]

Calm Returns to Wrightsville

By 1:00 a.m., the once imposing Columbia Bridge was gone and the danger abated. Weary Wrightsville residents began returning to their homes or seeking alternative lodging. Many retrieved their water buckets, tubs, and pails.

---

40 *Ibid.*, Feb. 20, 1886.

41 *York Sunday News*, June 26, 1983.

42 J. Houston Mifflin to Lloyd Mifflin, July 8, 1863, LCHS; *Lancaster Examiner and Herald*, July 1, 1863.

43 *Pottsville Journal*, July 18, 1913.

Confederate Lieutenant Lyon pitied "the poor women of Wrightsville," who were "left almost alone. The men ran to the opposite side of the river on the approach of our troops, and left the women to shift for themselves. They were of course dreadfully frightened, and could not be consoled."[44]

However, several grateful townspeople thanked the Rebels for their heroic efforts to save Wrightsville. Very late in the evening, Mary Jane Rewalt and her attendant found General Gordon in the throng. She had witnessed the furious efforts of his men when flames threatened her father's house, and she wanted to express her gratitude. Gordon informed her that his brigade had orders to leave Wrightsville in the morning. Mary Jane responded that she did not want them to depart without some token of her appreciation. Because she was not wealthy, she could not entertain his entire command, but in the morning, he could bring to her house as many men as she could fit around the dining room table for a home-cooked breakfast. A grateful Gordon thought that she was "blessed with an abundance of those far nobler riches of brain and heart, which are the essential glories of exalted womanhood."[45]

After receiving additional thanks, Gordon's men settled in for the night. Several regiments marched back to camp on the Detwiler farm, which offered fence rails, woodpiles, and small trees for campfires. Others camped on the Dellinger property. Kreutz Creek provided plenty of fresh water for the men and horses. Many fatigued soldiers finally ate dinner, more than twelve hours after their lunch break. Tanner's gunners, who played no active role in fighting the fires, camped nearby. Soldiers recounted the day. "Here the militia made a stand and threw up a strong breastwork," wrote Pvt. George F. Agee of the 26th Georgia. "They exchanged a few shots with the sharpshooters, but three shots from our little cannon put them to rapid flight, and we were in possession of the yankees, setting the bridge on fire as they crossed over. We spent the night at this little town."[46]

The 31st Georgia remained in Wrightsville as provosts. For the first time in several evenings the instruments of the regimental band remained silent. No

---

44 *Mobile Advertiser & Register*, Aug. 9, 1863.

45 Gordon, *Reminiscences*, 148.

46 *The Sunny South*, July 20, 1901. Wrightsville oral tradition suggests that a schoolteacher named Ella Lloyd served dinner late that evening to Gordon and his staff. She topped it off with brandied peaches, all the while sharing her frank opinions about the state of the country, the war, and the South. Later, Gordon allegedly sent her a thank you note that closed with, "We thank you for your brandied peaches, but do abhor your Union speeches."

one felt like celebrating. Soldiers ignored the rain and collapsed in lawns and gardens, too weary to seek shelter. Others slept on the streets or walkways, covered only by thin blankets or bedrolls. Some Confederates lodged in unlocked buildings. In cases where they entered occupied homes, the Rebels respected the property and its occupants. However, several houses abandoned by fleeing residents were ransacked or otherwise damaged.[47]

An exhausted Gordon Bradwell decided to slip away from the teeming riverbank to some quiet place and lie down for a few hours' rest. He and a comrade headed for the "suburbs." Coming upon "a neat-looking residence," they spread their blankets in the piazza to escape the falling rain. After taking seats on a nearby bench, they heard a multitude of voices speaking in low tones inside the darkened house. Several women had congregated there for mutual safety and reassurance. Hearing footsteps on the porch, one lady mustered up courage enough to open the door a few inches. She timidly asked, "When are the Rebels going to burn the town?" Bradwell replied that Confederates did not burn towns; Yankee soldiers did. The disbelieving women repeated the same question about a dozen times, each time receiving the same assurances. A frustrated Bradwell finally suggested to his friend that they would not get any sleep at that house, so they went back down the steps and spread their blankets on the wet pavement. They spent the rest of the night "oblivious to all the trying scenes of war until the rattle of the reveille roused us from our slumbers at first dawn."[48]

Before retiring for the evening, Bradwell's regimental commander, Clement Evans, recorded his impressions of the long day:

Marched through [York] toward Wrightsville. Reached the enemy's position. In attempting to get his position we frightened them off. All militia, who ran as fast as possible & burned the Bridge. Town on fire. Rebel Regiments which had marched 25 miles that day work to stop the fire. Tear down houses & at last the fire stops, after burning six or eight houses. Wrightsville was a scene of confusion and excitement. But the splendid behavior of Rebel troops soon restored quiet—I again guarded the town.[49]

47 Gibson, *History of York County*, 597.

48 Bradwell, "Burning of Wrightsville," 301.

49 Stephens, *Intrepid Warrior*, 222.

Evans' provosts guarded Lieutenant Colonel Sickles, his demoralized militiamen, and the injured Adams County cavalryman thrown from his horse earlier in the evening. Although happy to have routed the militia, the Georgians knew they had not accomplished their goal. To some, the perceived victory was much greater than reality. Private G. W. Nichols of the 61st Georgia later exaggerated the number of captives in the "little combat with the Pennsylvania militia." He claimed that Gordon "captured and paroled about 5,000 of them, and ran the rest through Waynesboro [Wrightsville] and across the Susquehanna river at Columbia."[50]

Several Wrightsville and Columbia residents went to bed that night full of recrimination. Telegrapher F. X. Ziegler wrote in his journal, "Our Union Leaguers proved most rascally coward, running like thieves, horrid. C. C. Haldeman (major pro tem) publicly proclaimed this cowardice. Andy Rambo-cowardly provost-among the first to fly." Rumors flew that certain Wrightsville citizens, including a Mrs. DeWolf, were angry at the hasty retreat of their militia defenders. Some had leveled pistols and even opened fire at Union soldiers. The individuals accused of this unpatriotic conduct denied the allegation, but suspicions persisted for years. Annie Welsh wrote, "I am sorry to say that my old native town was disgraced by some females (they were not ladies, of course) who fired out of the windows at our men when they were retreating and it was said greeted the Rebels with flowers."[51]

A Lancaster newsman judged the majority of the militia to be "of character and high-toned bravery." However, he castigated the First City Troopers, who deserved "considerable condemnation for the cowardly manner in which they 'covered' the retreat from Wrightsville on Sunday." The reporter was only warming up. "Instead of covering the rear, the 'gallant' City Troop reached the east end of the bridge some fifteen minutes in advance of the infantry, thus covering themselves in shame and disgrace." Unaware of Haller's orders to the Philadelphia cavalrymen, he continued, "The troop are an independent body of tacticians, [and] therefore go it on their own hook and skedaddle when it best suits their purposes. It would be far better if such men would remain at home,

---

50 Nichols, *61st Georgia*, 115-16. This account was written in the 1890s, and the old soldier embellished the role of his regiment. He was not present at Wrightsville.

51 F. X. Ziegler diary, entry for June 28, 1863; Annie Welsh to Thomas Welsh, July 1, 1863. Courtesy of Richard C. Wiggin. Columbia resident Andrew M. Rambo had been captain of Company A of the 2nd PVM during the Emergency of 1862. He purchased the *Columbia Spy* in August 1863 from Samuel Wright, who had joined the army.

than be the means of attaching disgrace and ignominy to the service of our imperiled country." By contrast, a correspondent from a rival newspaper believed, "The troop acted splendidly in the fight."[52]

Annie informed General Welsh, "When you read an account of this in the press or any of the Philadelphia papers do not believe one word it may say about the part the City Troop took in the fight. "They were not across the bridge at all. They did nothing but ride about Columbia and are doing nothing but that yet. The Press says too that there were no Volunteers from Columbia, but two Companies of Coloured men. This is a falsehood, also." She added, "I heard a number of people wish that Gen. Welsh were here to command. I said I wished too he was [here], if he had his own men with him, but would not want you to command these greenhorns and take the blame for all their blunders."[53]

A different complaint would be lodged against Frick's militiamen. "When the troops retired to the Columbia side of the river, they brought the tools [borrowed from Cottrell's hardware store] with them, loaded them in the cars and shipped them to Harrisburg, despite the protests of the owners," explained one Pennsylvania paper. "That was the last time Mr. [J. B.] Bachman saw his picks and shovels. If they were ever sold, the money went into the State treasury."[54]

While some residents busily apportioned blame for the bridge burning, others opened their doors to displaced neighbors, relatives, and even strangers. F. X. Ziegler's house was "full of refugees" from York County. Sidney Josephine Myer observed that, while "immense numbers of refugees came to town," there was a simultaneous exodus occurring as "hundreds of poor negroes walked from Columbia. The roads are lined with them."[55]

Eleven miles from the bridge, former President James Buchanan retired to bed after a tense day. He had refused to leave his Lancaster mansion, Wheatland, even when the Rebels approached Wrightsville. For several months, men had left notes at his doorstep, threatening to burn his house. In late June, rumors circulated that the advancing Confederates intended to kidnap Buchanan and use him as a political hostage. Relieved that the threat was

52 *Lancaster Daily Express*, July 2, 1863; *Lancaster Examiner and Herald*, July 1, 1863.

53 Annie Welsh to Thomas Welsh, July 1, 1863. Courtesy of Richard C. Wiggin.

54 *Columbia Spy*, Jan. 16, 1886.

55 Sidney J. Myer diary, entry for June 28, 1863, LCHS.

apparently over, he wrote a friend, "the rebels might have paid a flying visit to Lancaster had not the bridge been burnt down. I remained quietly at home and would not have removed under any circumstances."[56]

The night finally turned peaceful and all was quiet except for the sounds of the provost guards on patrol—Randall's First City Troop in Columbia and Evans' 31st Georgia in Wrightsville. Choking columns of thick black smoke still rose over the Susquehanna River from the embers of the once magnificent bridge. In Harrisburg, a relieved Darius Couch scribbled a terse entry in his diary and then went to bed: "Early was foiled in getting possession of Columbia Bridge his intentions having been to march in the rich county of Lancaster."[57]

56 James Buchanan papers, LCHS.

57 Gambone, *Major General Darius Nash Couch*, 169.

Chapter 12

The Aftermath

A Rebel Dawn in Wrightsville

A heavy fog bank settled over the river towns during the rainy June night. Private Gordon Bradwell of the 31st Georgia and a friend awoke at first light on Monday, June 29, to the shrill blare of an unwelcome reveille. They hastened through the showers to downtown Wrightsville to find their captain and the balance of the 31st's Company I. They located them at an undamaged hotel opposite the burned section of town. A large sign in front proclaimed in large letters "Henry Hunt's Hotel." This was the Union Hotel, owned and managed by Dutchman Henry Hantz.[1]

Entering the office, Bradwell found that Colonel Evans had installed Capt. George W. Lewis as Wrightsville's provost marshal. Soldiers were "lounging around in full possession of everything." The panic-stricken proprietor apparently had abandoned his business and "placed the river between him and us." Lewis assigned one of his most trusted men to safeguard the cellar, where Hantz stored "a large and well-selected stock of liquors." Despite the armed guard, several Rebels had little difficulty in getting as much alcohol as they wanted. George Washington had paused at this same hostelry in July 1791 en route to Philadelphia from York. Now, other Southern guests sampled its liquid refreshments. Bradwell wrote that "a certain wag of a soldier" appropriated a large bunch of keys that Hantz left in his office. He carried them throughout the

---

1 The hotel was just below the bridgehead on the southeast corner of Hellam and Front streets.

war, taking the prized relic of his Wrightsville service home to Georgia after Appomattox.[2]

Virginia cavalryman James Hodam and his comrades were busy "feasting ourselves on the delicacies" in the captured militia camp. As the fog burned off under bright sunshine, he rode into Wrightsville to "look at the place where war had laid his hand of destruction. Here and there on the sidewalks were piled the worldly effects of some poor unfortunate family who had fled from the devouring flames." Hodam marveled at the utter destruction, "On the river bank the remains of iron foundries and mills strew the ground while nothing of the bridge remained except some thirteen great stone pillars with here and there a piece of burned timber clinging to them." On the far bank, he could see "the glint of the Federal sentinels' muskets."[3]

While his men frolicked and went sightseeing, John Gordon accepted Mary Jane Rewalt's invitation from the previous evening. He and his staff arrived at her father's house on Hellam Street, knocked on the front door, and entered the mayor's brick home. His officers, dressed as they were in their worn gray uniforms, were delighted to sit at the bountifully supplied table. Mrs. Rewalt, described as a "modest, cultured woman," welcomed her guests. Despite the fact that she was entertaining enemy soldiers, she was so self-possessed, so calm, and so kind that Gordon wondered if she might be a Southern sympathizer. Cautiously probing for clues as to her political leanings, Gordon was surprised when she did not hesitate to give him a direct answer.

Without a quiver in her voice, but with "womanly gentleness," she replied that she fully comprehended his line of questioning. She cautioned Gordon not to misinterpret her simple courtesy, as she merely wanted to give some token of her appreciation to him and his soldiers for saving her father's house. Poised and confident in her bearing, Mrs. Rewalt closed by proclaiming that, "with my assent and approval, my husband is a soldier in the Union army, and my constant prayer to Heaven is that our cause may triumph and the Union be saved." She also told the general about her brother, Capt. Frank J. Magee, who served in a Federal army in the South.[4]

---

2 Bradwell, "Burning of Wrightsville," 301. Hantz later filed a Federal damage claim for $1594 for his losses.

3 Kesterson, Hodam Manuscript.

4 Gordon, *Reminiscences*, 144. In an 1888 interview with the *Atlanta Journal*, Gordon recalled that the invitation was extended the day after the bridge burning, and that it was for lunch, not

In 1863, Chief Burgess James Magee lived in this house on Hellam Street in downtown Wrightsville. His daughter Mary Jane Rewalt served breakfast on June 29 to General John B. Gordon and his staff. *Author's Collection*

An awestruck Gordon later recorded that "No Confederate left that room without a feeling of profound respect, of unqualified admiration, for that brave and worthy woman." After appropriate thanks for the home-cooked food,

breakfast. His memory clouded, Gordon also stated that the invitation came from town officials, not from Mrs. Rewalt.

Gordon and his staff left to prepare their brigade to march back to York. Almost from the moment Gordon rode away, tongues in Wrightsville wagged about the newlywed Mrs. Rewalt and her open hospitality toward the handsome Confederate general. Some later speculated that she had penned the mysterious note delivered by the little girl in York. For his part, Gordon never publicly rendered such an opinion, although he praised its unknown author "whose evident genius for war, had occasion offered, might have made her a captain equal to Catherine."[5]

With his stomach satisfied, Gordon ordered his quartermaster to compile a list of goods to be requisitioned from local businesses. The supply officer met with the remaining civic leaders in one of their homes. Noting that the homeowner possessed a manual for the Independent Order of Odd Fellows, the Confederate asked if the town had an Odd Fellows hall. Wrightsville businessman Morgan L. Bahn inquired whether the officer was affiliated with that organization. When the Rebel replied that he had indeed been a member in the past, Bahn escorted him to the hall at Front and Locust streets, which had been hit by Tanner's artillery the previous day.

The lodge room was on the second floor of the damaged structure, where two United States flags flanked the Noble Grand's seat. Bahn commented that lodge brothers were pledged to honor their Creator, their country, and their fellow man, and he could not understand why the Georgian dishonored the flag by his rebellion. The quartermaster replied, "Brother, just now we do not look at all things alike." He left the building, but assigned two sentries to guard the hall to prevent looting. Not so fortunate was merchant Jacob G. Leber. Rebels had significantly reduced his inventory. Among his losses were 10 hats, 13 caps, 15 pairs of boots, 20 gallons of molasses, a barrel and a half of sugar, large quantities of spices, and several large boxes of crackers. His entire stock of wooden pails and buckets were also missing, likely used by the Confederates for their bucket brigade the previous evening.[6]

Wrightsville residents were now becoming better acquainted with their "guests" from Dixie. Rachel Bahn wrote, "They behaved pretty civilly while passing here. Hundreds of them came in, one wanted bread, another wanted butter, the next wanted apple butter, milk &c. They wanted to pay everything with their worthless money, but of course we did not take any. A dirtier, more

---

5 Gordon, *Reminiscences*, 150.

6 McClure, *East of Gettysburg*, 74; York County Damage Claims, Jacob G. Leber claim.

motley, obnoxious-looking set of fellows I never saw. The majority of them seem to be tired of this unholy war, & would be willing to lay down their arms & come into the Union again." According to one reporter, "The rebel soldiers then in Wrightsville. . . . acted very humanely. Very little pilfering was done, and aside from demands for food, private property was not molested to any great extent. . . . The rebel officers stationed guards at most of the houses, and no one was permitted to enter without the consent of the citizens. Mounted men patrolled the streets to maintain order." However, he continued, "some houses in the suburbs of Wrightsville, and some farm houses with a radius of a mile or two of the town, were pretty thoroughly sacked. In some cases every portable article was either thrown about the premises or carried off. Much of this work was done by the bummers, who constituted the lawless and irresponsible rabble of both armies."[7]

Residents throughout the region began encountering Rebel patrols as White's men and Waldo's scouts canvassed the area for fresh horses. Sixteen-year-old David Sloat and his father took his invalided grandmother to an uncle's home at Canadochly in Lower Windsor Township. They talked to eleven mounted Confederate soldiers on top of Mt. Pisgah, the highest point along the Susquehanna River.[8]

Across the Broad Susquehanna

While Gordon's Confederates relaxed in Wrightsville, Columbia remained under martial law with the First City Troop patrolling the streets. In a temporary hospital, army surgeon Otto Schittler and his assistant, Edwin G. Martin, tended to seventeen sick and injured soldiers lying on cots on the first floor of the Columbia Classical Institute. A yellow flag floated over the building. Sidney Josephine Myer noted in her diary, "All businesses were suspended in town. The storekeepers [are] all packing up and sending off their goods." Colonel Jacob Frick ordered a strict 11 p.m. curfew and banned the sale of alcoholic beverages and spirits.[9]

7   Rachel Bahn letter, published in *Pennsylvania Civil War Heritage* (2008); *Columbia Spy*, Jan. 16, 1886.

8   1917 newspaper microfilm, YCHT.

9   *Pottsville Miners' Journal*, July 4, 1863; Myer diary, entry for June 29, 1863, LCHS; *Pottsville Journal*, July 18, 1913; *Columbia Spy*, Jan. 16, 1886. Frick's official report mentioned nine

Soldiers and citizens fretted about the enemy artillery. No one could be sure if there were any guns in the hilltop fields across the river, ones that might start bombarding the town at any second despite the yellow flag still waving over the invalids' temporary hospital. A Philadelphia reporter, vainly peering into the thick fog, noted that, "One fact is certain, and the truth may as well be told, Columbia is completely at the mercy of the enemy, who, from the opposite hills just mentioned, can shell every building in the town." To counter this threat, Lt. Delaplaine Ridgway's artillerymen used the horses they had impressed during the night to move the guns to a new position near a blast furnace. However, Major General Couch wired Frick, "Of course you will not presume to fire artillery from [the] Columbia side unless the enemy attempts to cross. The distance is so great that you could not dislodge the enemy with rifled guns."[10]

Frick was also concerned about a possible attack from across the river. There were two boatbuilding factories north of the burnt section of Wrightsville, and a couple of large lumberyards in that vicinity might provide ample wood should Gordon's men choose to build rafts or flatboats. Frick's brother William and his brother-in-law had prospered as canal boat builders upriver from Columbia and, from their example, the colonel knew how quickly a few skilled carpenters could assemble suitable transports. He readied new defensive lines to contest any Confederate crossing. Workers drained the canal between its first lock and the wrecked bridge. Lieutenant Francis Wallace noted, "The water was let out of the Canal so as to make the bank a place of defense. Every one is prepared for the worst."[11]

Frick moved the 27th Militia from the Lockard's Meadow ravine into downtown Columbia. There, he dispersed his men. He ordered his reserve companies A and B to stack arms in an old warehouse. Several other companies lined the eastern riverbank, some as far as the breast of the dam two miles

---

wounded men, including one injured by a horse. Some newspaper accounts placed the number as high as 12 or 15. Dr. Martin, a 27-year-old Allentown native, graduated from the Medical School of the University of Pennsylvania in 1856. After the war he was a surgeon in the Pennsylvania National Guard and prominent businessman, dying in 1893. According to the *Columbia Spy* (Jan. 16, 1886), the field hospital was at Fifth and Locust streets in the first floor of the Columbia Classical Institute. Local physicians assisted the army doctors.

10 *Philadelphia Inquirer,* June 30, 1863; *Columbia Spy,* Jan. 22, 1887.

11 *Pottsville Journal,* July 18, 1913. Frick's brother William had established a successful boat-building business, which their brother-in-law Eli Slifer and younger brother Henry later joined.

downstream. Wallace and a platoon rowed out about a quarter-mile to picket a large island [likely Mifflin's Island, just north of the burnt bridge]. Frick allegedly loaded two companies below deck on canal boats, which carried them two miles upstream past Marietta to contest any Confederate attempt to cross the river when its level receded. However, this flotilla spotted no enemy soldiers. Major George L. Fried proclaimed martial law in Marietta and banned liquor sales. His men and the townspeople began entrenching along the riverbank.[12]

Scouts fanned out from Columbia in the morning fog and intermittent showers, searching for any signs of a Confederate attempt to cross the river. A citizen claimed he had seen five enemy cavalry pickets concealed along the river near Bainbridge, near Col. William Thomas's position. Other civilians reported that a few Rebels had entered the swollen river in that vicinity, but turned back when their horses began to swim as the river depth increased. Another man claimed Rebels had tried crossing the river on a homemade raft.[13]

To better protect their men, Frick and Major Haller impressed "every citizen in Columbia" to assist in constructing wooden breastworks between the canal and river. Frick authorized Corp. Joseph Wood and a squadron of militiamen to enforce his orders. Hugh M. North, a Columbia attorney, was startled when two militiamen approached him with fixed bayonets, ordering him and other passersby to help erect barricades with "huge logs" along Front Street. J. Houston Mifflin recorded that civilians were impressed to construct entrenchments on high ground behind the Pennsylvania Railroad depot, "to command the river above the piers of the bridge in case they attempted crossing by pontoon."[14]

The First City Troop divided into eight squads to collect more workers. The tenuous relationship between the Philadelphians and the townspeople became further strained as they forced unwilling citizens to comply. Hearing rumors the government was about to impress them into the army for six months or more, many of Columbia's able-bodied men fled to the fields, or hid in barns and other places. Young cavalryman Persifor Frazer commented, "Many amusing scenes took place, and many hale, hearty men, who would not

12 *Pottsville Miners' Journal*, Oct. 24, 1863; *Philadelphia Inquirer*, June 30, 1863; *Columbia Spy*, April 17, 1886; *Marietta* (Pa.) *Mariettian*, July 4, 1863.

13 These men likely were from the 17th Virginia Cavalry, which operated in that vicinity.

14 J. Houston Mifflin to Lloyd Mifflin, July 8, 1863, LCHS.

be ashamed to own it, pleaded with tears not to be taken from their dear homes and helpless families." Captain Samuel Randall allowed several to return home for two hours to "arrange their affairs." Of course, many never returned to work. Sergeant M. Edward Rogers judged that the residents seemed to all be "copperheads of the vilest description." He went on to complain, "The citizens seem to detest the soldiers and have nothing to do with them, very unlike Gettysburg, where we were received with much kindness."[15]

The residents and refugees loathed the Philadelphia gentry's "impudent and imperious" attitude and "ridiculous demands." Another source of contention was Frick's General Order No. 3: "Keepers of hotels, beer shops, and restaurants are hereby ordered to close their places of sale, and to refrain from selling spirituous, vinous or malt liquors to citizens or soldiers until further orders." The colonel put the onus of enforcing prohibition squarely on Randall and the City Troopers. What riled the citizenry, according to a newsman, "is that the City Troop had all of the ardent they wanted. It was shipped to them by their friends from Philadelphia."[16]

Meanwhile that morning, the throngs of refugees began to dissipate after a harrowing night in which Columbia's hotels did a booming business (before Frick closed the bars). Now, the eastbound morning trains were filled with crowds heading to Philadelphia. A trio of women from York exemplified the plight of many of the crowd. They had arrived on Saturday in the exodus, "bringing with them their trunks, which contained many valuables." They had implored a gentleman friend to help them secure conveyance, "even if it were a cart," to take them and their baggage farther east. He had been unsuccessful on Sunday in locating any form of transportation. They managed to buy tickets on the first outbound train on Monday morning.[17]

The Threat Subsides

While his ragged soldiers collected supplies in Wrightsville and Federal defenses strengthened in Columbia, John Gordon realized that there were no alternative means for his brigade to cross the still-swollen river. The dam was too far beneath the level of the river to offer suitable footing and, even if they

15 *History of the First Troop*, 76; *JMSIUS* (1908), Vol. 43, 291-92.

16 *Columbia Spy*, April 17, 1886.

17 *Ibid.*, Jan. 23, 1886.

could, his men would have to cross single file while under artillery fire from the fort on the far riverbank. Captain Waldo's patrols had failed to locate any usable fords. With his work in Wrightsville done, Gordon reluctantly formed his men into column and marched out, his eastward thrust into Lancaster County forever stymied.

Many of Gordon's men busily raided the supplies stored in Wrightsville for Frick's regiment. Lieutenant Charles T. Stuart of the 26th Georgia wrote, "We exchanged some horses, took what supplies we needed from the well-filled commissary, and retraced our steps." Private James Hodam of the 17th Virginia, among the last troops to leave, noted that Company C took "a longing look at the blue-coated sentinels on the Columbia shore of the Susquehanna" before returning to York to rejoin their commander, Col. William French. As Gordon watched his lead elements depart Wrightsville about 10 a.m., a committee of civic authorities called on him, extending "the formal thanks of those people for having saved the town."[18]

By 11:00 a.m., nearly all the Confederates had left Wrightsville, slowly heading westward through Hallam in light sprinkles. Rebels seized Henry Stoner's bay horse, harness, and wagon fully loaded with corn. A few Georgians raided the nearby farms of Eli Emig and George D. Ebert, taking several more horses including Ebert's prized 17-hand spotted stallion and an old gray horse. Others visited the Widow Smyser's home, stealing young Albert Smyser's prized 3-year-old horse that he had begged Gordon to return the previous day. Despite Gordon's later claims that his men did not disturb private property on the marches to and from Wrightsville, some residents along his path suffered considerably. George W. Dellinger, on whose Hellam Township property the Georgians briefly rested, reported that his property was a "total loss." Rebels and their horses trampled twenty acres of ripe wheat and twenty acres of oats.[19]

Gordon's veteran infantrymen were exhausted from their long marches, the recent skirmish, and the unplanned firefighting duties that continued late into the evening. Gordon Bradwell summed up the feelings of many of the soldiers when he wrote, "We were all disappointed by the Pennsylvania

18 Stuart, *Autobiographical Sketch*, USMHI; Kesterson, Hodam Manuscript; *Atlanta Journal*, Sept. 16, 1888.

19 York County Damage Claims, reels 30-31. Some accounts state 10 a.m.; Bradwell stated it was closer to 11 a.m. before Gordon left for York. The 31st Georgia, as the provost, likely was the last unit to depart Wrightsville.

'Melish,' who burned the bridge across the river and thereby put a stop to our further progress toward the Quaker City [Philadelphia]."[20]

Across the river in Columbia the fog lifted in mid-morning. Federal officers peered through their field glasses at the streets of lower Wrightsville. Much to their relief, they could see no evidence of boat building or any other potentially threatening military activity. A Reading reporter spied a few Rebels riding about on the far shore, but no enemy flags flew over the town, and nothing pointed to a Confederate river crossing. Columbia now appeared to be safe. As visibility increased, reality set in that the bridge was gone. A Philadelphia newspaperman noted that its only remains were "the piers which stretched themselves across the river like giant stepping stones."[21]

Throngs of curious sightseers, eager to see the charred wreckage of the bridge, began arriving in Columbia. Randall ordered the First City Troop to impress these gawkers to build more breastworks. When the tourists protested and asked that they be allowed to return home, Randall's troopers reiterated his order at gunpoint. The men and boys, not permitted to leave Columbia until nightfall on Tuesday, reluctantly began working. Anxious relatives spread the news that sightseers were being forced into hard labor, and the flow of visitors slowed to a trickle.[22]

About midday, while excited townspeople gossiped or constructed more breastworks, the Federal officers' attention focused on a small boat making its way across the broad river, its occupants straining at the oars to gain speed. When they spotted a flag of truce, the officers issued orders not to fire at the craft as it drew near Columbia. When the boat reached the Lancaster County riverbank, seven weary Wrightsville residents stepped out. The Confederates, they confirmed, had departed, taking Lieutenant Colonel Sickles and eighteen prisoners with them. Frick and Haller openly voiced their opinions in front of reporters. Angry accusations flew at the unfortunate Sickles, including such things as "willful cowardice" and "neglect." The citizens also delivered the sad news that a body had been buried in the entrenchments, as well as the rather

---

20 Bradwell, "Burning of Wrightsville," 301.

21 *Reading Daily Times*, June 29, 1863; *Philadelphia Inquirer*, June 30, 1863. The riders were almost certainly from Captain Waldo's company, which covered General Gordon's withdrawal. James Hodam recalled staring across the water at the blue-clad sentinels on the Columbia riverbank before departing.

22 *Lancaster Daily Evening Inquirer*, July 1, 1863.

astonishing report that two Rebel regiments had formed a bucket brigade to save the endangered town.[23]

After digesting the information, Frick handed an orderly a telegram to notify Major General Couch of the loss of Wrightsville and the destruction of the Columbia Bridge. Couch relayed the news to the Army of the Potomac's new commander, Maj. Gen. George G. Meade:

> My people driven over Columbia bridge. It is burned. I hold the opposite side of the river in strength at the present. I am looking for a considerable destruction on all railroad lines. Twenty-five thousand [Confederates] are between Baltimore and this place. I have only 15,000 men, such as they are, on my whole line—say 9,000 here.[24]

Granville Haller finally enjoyed a well-deserved sigh of relief. John Gordon had chased him out of two counties, but the pursuit had finally ended in a third. Within a month Haller grudgingly described his nemesis Gordon as an "evil genius." Haller did not get to relax for long. In the late morning, he received a telegram from Couch directing him to go immediately to Bainbridge, where he would oversee Colonel Thomas's dispositions of the 20th Militia to defend the fords "at every sacrifice." Before leaving, Haller instructed Capt. Robert Crane to submit a written report, which, after Colonel Frick's perusal and slight corrections, was sent to the major with a copy to bank cashier Samuel Schoch. Haller left Columbia after lunch and, at 2 p.m., passed the Chestnut Riffles, rapids in the Susquehanna River near the mouth of Codorus Creek. He arrived in Bainbridge in mid-afternoon and conferred with Thomas, reporting Sickles' cowardice and capture. Haller also sent word back to Capt. Thomas McGowan in Columbia to have his Patapsco Guards come to Bainbridge to help construct rifle-pits and earthworks.[25]

Word of Gordon's retirement from Wrightsville quickly spread among the militia and the conscripted citizens, still hard at work constructing more barricades. They were relieved that enemy artillery no longer threatened their

---

23 *Philadelphia Inquirer,* June 30, 1863.

24 *OR* 27, pt. 3, 407.

25 Haller, *Dismissal of Major Granville O. Haller,* 74. Chestnut Riffles is now known as Haldeman Riffles. For many years, it was a popular place to catch shad, and was a frequent destination for the volunteers constructing the defenses at Columbia and Wrightsville.

town. J. Houston Mifflin noted that all remained quiet in Columbia and no Rebels had been seen. With each passing hour it had become evident the enemy did not intend to force a crossing, but instead had returned to York. Finally, the civilians' forced toil ceased. Mifflin wrote his son, "You cannot imagine the appearance of the town in expectation of being burned immediately."[26]

After twenty hours of occupation, the Rebels now were gone from Wrightsville. Many refugees still huddled along the riverbank in Columbia, staring at the empty piers from the bridge that had dominated the landscape only a day before. Soon, a small flotilla of boats bobbed in the Susquehanna, carrying citizens home to Wrightsville. Some residents discovered notes of appreciation from Rebels who had lodged in their homes. Others found worthless Confederate banknotes, interesting souvenirs but small compensation for the food and household items taken by their unwanted houseguests. In other cases, homeowners who had left their houses unoccupied returned to find that they had been ransacked, despite the best efforts of the provost guards. A reporter wrote, "Some houses in the suburbs of Wrightsville, and some farm houses within a radius of a mile or two of the town, were however pretty thoroughly sacked. In some cases every portable article was either thrown about the premises or carried off. Much of this work was done by the bummers, who constituted the lawless and irresponsible rabble of both armies."[27]

Some Wrightsvillians discovered that Confederate artillery rounds had struck their houses and churches. These solid shots, as well as shell fragments, became conversation pieces. One family found a rifle on their property, apparently abandoned by a wounded Rebel. The owner of the Washington House came back to find that several bedrooms now had holes in their walls from Minié balls. To their dismay, merchants George W. Harris and Samuel Smith discovered that the Rebels had raided their shop, stealing a prized buffalo robe and arm loads of trade goods and food.[28]

---

26 J. Houston Mifflin to Lloyd Mifflin, July 8, 1863, LCHS.

27 Prowell, *History of York County*, 1, 989; *Columbia Spy*, Jan. 16, 1886.

28 York County Damage Claims, reel 30. A Schenkl round is still in possession of the Presbyterian Church. The rifle is in the National Civil War Museum in Harrisburg. The store was on Hellam Street, near the intersection with Front Street. Other items taken included 60 hats, large quantities of shoes and clothing, 6 dozen pocket knives, 42 pairs of scissors, tobacco, molasses, and 30 pounds of coffee.

Some Georgians had billeted in Smith's two-story residence across Locust Street from the Methodist Church. One of his three sons, 19-year-old Silas, had enlisted in the infantry to go south to fight the Rebels. The youth carried with him a pocket testament that had been given to him as a parting gift. Silas fell mortally wounded in Virginia and died in a Confederate field hospital far from Wrightsville. He was sleeping in an unmarked grave in the enemy's homeland, while Rebels were sleeping in his parents' Pennsylvania home. Samuel and Eliza Smith fled at the approach of the Confederates, but left their door unlatched. Returning the day after Gordon's men had departed, Mrs. Smith was stunned to find her dead son's testament lying on her kitchen table. She trembled as she opened it, finding his name and address inscribed on the flyleaf. A small but precious part of her beloved Silas had returned home.[29]

Nearby, a dozen fire-damaged structures needed significant repair. Several anguished citizens found their homes or places of employment along the riverbank reduced to smoldering ashes. Three buildings owned by Harris were totally destroyed (at a loss of $8,000). His foundry, occupied by Eden Wolf of Baltimore, had suffered $4,000 in damages. Henry Kauffelt's planing mill, operated by Mr. Duke of Baltimore, was a total loss. The wealthy Kauffelt, a director of the First National Bank, was relieved to find that flames had not consumed the town's largest depository. Nearby, Kauffelt and Lanius's massive lumberyard was now only a memory, and they assessed the damage at $8,000. William H. Lanius, an officer in the 87th Pennsylvania, later rebuilt his father's business. Postmaster Alexander J. Thomson filed a Federal damage claim for the loss of the post office and its contents. A reporter 25 years later noted, "Immense quantities of lumber were destroyed, the owners of which, like the owners of the bridge, have never been compensated. Several of these lumbermen were financially crippled for life, and one of the sufferers became embarrassed [bankrupt] afterwards."[30]

Officials estimated the total damage as between $16,000 and $21,000. The economic effect of lost wages and business taxes to the community was even higher, notwithstanding the psychological effect of the loss of prized personal property and family heirlooms. Several residents later hired the York law firm of Cochrane and Hay to represent them, but they recovered no compensation

---

29 Prowell, *History of York County*, 1, 933. The Smiths lived at 315 Locust Street. Samuel and Eliza (both about 50 years old in 1863) had a daughter Mary and sons Ambrose, Silas, and John.

30 *York Pennsylvanian*, July 3, 1863; *Columbia Spy*, Jan. 16, 1886.

from either Pennsylvania or the Federal government. Ironically, Thomas Cochrane was the attorney who had repeatedly questioned A. B. Farquhar before he rode out to Farmers to discuss surrendering York to John Gordon.[31]

York Under the Rebel Flag

While Gordon reluctantly marched his command back from Wrightsville, Elijah White's troopers destroyed hundreds of rails and ripped down thousands of feet of telegraph wires. By evening, Rebel cavalry had destroyed all 24 bridges and trestles between Wrightsville and York. Colonel William French's 17th Virginia Cavalry spent much of the day procuring horses, forage, and supplies from York County farmers, being particularly active in the largely Copperhead area of Dover Township. They camped on Jacob Brillinger's property east of York. During the two nights that hungry men and horses stayed there, Brillinger lost 247 bushels of corn, 68 bushels of oats, 22 acres of hay, and nearly all his fences. Confederates ordered his wife and family to serve 300 meals, washed down with six barrels of whiskey. Other nearby farmers reported that Rebel cavalrymen stole horses, mules, harness, food, forage, and sundries during their stay.[32]

Meanwhile, Jubal Early's infantrymen relaxed in and around York, some strolling leisurely through the streets or visiting old acquaintances. Rebels "scattered their counterfeit trash around freely, paying $5 or $10 for a couple of cigars, and waiting for change." Soldiers entered Charles Spangler's dry goods store, buying notions, ginghams, calicoes, stationery, gloves, and other merchandise with Confederate scrip. N. Lehmayer & Brothers contributed 225 coats, 100 hats, 387 shirts of various styles and colors, 50 undershirts and drawers, 50 pairs of suspenders, 50 pocket handkerchiefs, and 50 pairs of woolen socks toward Early's ransom. Borough officials collected cash and requisitioned goods throughout each ward. They kept George Munchel and other local cobblers busy crafting shoes and boots for the Rebels.[33]

---

31 McClure, *East of Gettysburg*, 68; Prowell, *History of York County*, 1, 933. Henry Kauffelt petitioned in December 1871 for $907 for the loss of personal property and $1858 for his lost business.

32 York County Damage Claims, reel 19. Brillinger charged the government 15 cents per meal in his claim.

33 *Pottsville Miners' Journal*, July 4, 1863; York County Damage Claims, reels 28 and 31.

In some cases when the Confederate raiders found that the Pennsylvanians had previously sent their horses away to safety, they forced them to pay the equivalent value in greenbacks. One York County farmer had to fork over sixty dollars. Just north of York, another countryman who lived near the turnpike gate ran out to meet the oncoming enemy soldiers, telling them that he, too, was a rebel. Not surprisingly, the Southerners looked on with disdain for the farmer and ordered him to hand over his pocketbook. They then forced him to guide them around the countryside, a task he objected to doing. Then, they threatened to hang him from a nearby tree. They had started throwing a rope over it when his terrified wife came to his rescue. She paid a ransom of twenty dollars to stop the proceedings. The Rebels released the man, but threatened to come back and hang him if they lost their way.[34]

Because the telegraph lines were severed throughout much of York County, news of Early's occupation of York was slow in reaching the Union army. S. S. Blair, the superintendent of the Baltimore Division of the Northern Central Railway, happened to be in York when the Rebels arrived. Midday on the 29th, he slipped out of town and walked fifteen miles down the railroad through Hanover Junction to Glen Rock, where he finally located an intact telegraph station and working wires. The operator tapped out a message to the War Department in Washington and officials in Harrisburg confirming Jubal Early's presence in York. Blair estimated that Early had less than 10,000 men under his command. He also related that despite considerable bragging about their planned movements and future conquests of Northern cities, the Rebels seemed "very uneasy—their cavalrymen are in the saddles and infantry resting on their arms."[35]

Jubal Early's plans to invest Harrisburg from the rear evaporated with the burning of the Columbia Bridge. He still had a chance to take the city through a coordinated frontal assault with Ewell, however, but that too ended when the objective was changed. A scout named H. T. Harrison informed Robert E. Lee late on Sunday evening (while the bridge was burning) that the Army of the Potomac was finally on the move and was now across the Potomac River into Maryland. To deter the Federals from advancing father west and intercepting his lines of communications with Virginia, Lee decided to concentrate his army

---

34 *Philadelphia Press,* July 10, 1863.

35 Fishel, Edwin C., *The Secret War for the Union: The Untold Story of Military Intelligence in the Civil War* (New York: Houghton Mifflin, 1996), 513.

just east of South Mountain. Riding into York, Capt. Elliott Johnston, one of General Ewell's aides, handed Early a copy of a note from Lee and verbally instructed him to rejoin the rest of the corps the next day.[36]

Early paroled a few prisoners captured in the army hospital and turned his attention to the Northern Central Railway's operations in York. He ordered his men to destroy all the remaining rolling stock, but he spared the railroad buildings, army hospital, and two railcar factories, believing that the destruction of these military targets would cause the greater part of the town to burn. Notwithstanding the "barbarous policy pursued by the enemy" in similar circumstances, he hoped to establish a good example for his "cruel enemy."[37]

Cassandra Small's family and many other residents spent a restless day, worried that the Confederates might take revenge on the town. Soldiers did burn a few old railcars that had been used by the government, but, generally, everything was quiet. About 4 p.m., to her horror, Cassandra witnessed Gordon's second arrival in York. This time, the weary brigade entered the borough from the east. The Rebels were in an angry mood, because the destruction of the bridge had checked their forward progress. Someone gave Gordon a copy of a York newspaper. He seethed at an injustice to his soldiers, "As evidence of the base ingratitude of our enemies, the Yankee press has attributed to my brigade the burning of the town of Wrightsville."[38]

James Gall of the U. S. Sanitary Commission witnessed the Georgians' second parade through York. "About four P.M., Gordon's brigade returned from Wrightsville, bringing with them some horses and cattle which they had picked up on the way," he wrote. "They had about eight supply and ammunition wagons, and twelve ambulances with them. Many of the latter were marked U.S. The ambulances were all filled with men, who had apparently given out on the way."

Believing that a battle would occur at or near York, Gall arrived their late on Sunday afternoon. Because of the damage inflicted to the Northern Central by White's cavalry, his train could go no farther than Parkton, Maryland. Undeterred, he simply walked the rest of the way to York. Gall left a vivid description of Gordon's road-weary soldiers:

36 OR 27, pt. 2, 317 and 467; *SHSP*, Vol. 10, 543.

37 Early, *War Memoirs*, 260.

38 Cassandra Small to Lissie Latimer, July 8, 1863, YCHT; OR 27, pt. 2, 492.

Physically, the men looked about equal to the generality of our own troops, and there were fewer boys among them. Their dress was a wretched mixture of all cuts and colors. There was not the slightest attempt at uniformity in this respect. Every man seemed to have put on whatever he could get ahold of, without regard to shape or color. I noticed a pretty large sprinkling of blue pants among them, some of those, doubtless, left by Milroy at Winchester. Their shoes, as a general thing, were poor; some of the men were entirely barefooted. Their equipments were light as compared with those of our men. They consisted of a thin woolen blanket, coiled up and slung from the shoulder in the form of a sash, a haversack slung from the opposite shoulder, and a cartridge-box. The whole cannot weigh more than twelve or fourteen pounds. Is it strange then, that with such light loads they should be able to make longer and more rapid marches than our men? The marching of the men was irregular and ill-kept. Their whole appearance was greatly inferior to that of our soldiers.[39]

After paroling the Yankees captured at Wrightsville, Gordon camped his men along the Carlisle Road a few miles west of York. By nightfall, the bulk of Avery's brigade of North Carolinians joined them by nightfall, having marched from York after leaving a strong provost detail. Tanner's artillery parked nearby, while Confederate officers pressed civilian Dr. Jacob Eisenhart into treating their injured and ailing men. He fired up the beehive oven, and his wife and two adult daughters began baking bread and pies for the hungry soldiers. Rebel foraging patrols scoured the area for supplies and horses. Some soldiers headed westward on the Gettysburg turnpike. One party paused at Thomasville to raid a country store. Proprietor Levi Becker later filed a damage claim citing the loss of six pairs of boots, as well as his inventory of tobacco, sugar, groceries, pocket knives, handkerchiefs, and various notions. Confederates also forced him to surrender his silver watch. The same squad took horses from several unsuspecting farmers, including Michael Eyster who discovered that three of his were missing from his stable.[40]

Somehow, a handful of refugees from Gettysburg managed to arrive in downtown York. The Hartzells, having fled their Mummasburg Road farm on

---

39 J. H. Douglas, "Report of the Operations of the Sanitary Commission during and after the Battles at Gettysburg," in *Documents of the U. S. Sanitary Commission* (New York: 1866), 2,78.

40 York County Damage Claims, various reels. The bulk of Avery's Brigade was gone from York before 9 p.m. after posting guards at the taverns and other public places and cordoning off the town.

June 26, sat down to dinner in a hotel. When the proprietor spotted them he shouted, "My God, men, you'll be captured!" Sixteen-year-old Samuel Hartzell, his father, and another family slipped out of town and headed for Wrightsville, where they would cross the river "in little boats" and make their way to Lancaster.[41]

Samuel L. Roth, the persistent Mennonite pastor, finally located General Gordon and demanded that he return his gentle mare that a staff officer had appropriated on Saturday evening. Gordon had already been informed that the horse in question belonged to a minister, and so had sent the animal off to his adjutant for safekeeping. The general informed the grateful pastor that he could indeed reclaim his horse. Roth, justifiably worried that Confederate pickets might stop him and seize the animal a second time, requested a written pass. Much to the Mennonite's surprise, the general instructed his adjutant to personally escort the preacher back to his home. When the mare was finally safe in her stall, Roth invited the Georgia officer to join his jubilant family for dinner.

Reverend Roth's positive results mirrored other instances where plucky civilians confronted the Rebels and insisted that their horses be returned. The *York Gazette* reported on the general subject:

> In several cases the horses were returned on identification and demand of the owners. . . . The time the enemy remained here in force was nearly two days, and long weary days they were, rendered more dark by the gloomy weather which prevailed. The apprehension, excitement, and humiliation at the presence of the enemy, together with the total suppression of business, cast a universal gloom over the place, which we pray we may be spared from ever beholding again. But the people submitted with becoming resignation to imperious necessity.[42]

Gordon Bradwell of the 31st Georgia recalled that, "At York General Early had made a demand on the merchants for a large sum of money as indemnity for destruction of property in Virginia. When they were unable to pay the amount imposed, he seized a large quantity of such goods as the army needed."

---

41 *Gettysburg Times*, July 1, 1938. After the battle of Gettysburg fought on July 1-3, 1863, the Hartzells returned to their farm only to find that all of their cattle and supplies had been stolen.

42 *York Gazette*, June 30, 1863.

The Georgians reached York in the night and camped there following a difficult march from Wrightsville. "The orderly sergeant detailed me and a comrade to go to the quartermaster and draw rations, and our part of the goods coming to our company," wrote Bradwell. "It was surprising to see the amount and variety issued to us, and to get it all to the men consumed a great part of the night, and we found many of them lying about fast asleep, and could not waken them to take anything."[43]

Well to the east across the river Monday night was upon Columbia, which was slowly returning to normal although nearly about 1,000 soldiers occupied the borough. John Q. Denney, one of the Columbia volunteers who had ignited the fuses on the bridge, was reunited with his wife and two children. He had previously sent them away to relatives for safekeeping. The family anguished over the wreckage of the bridge, now a string of blackened and still-smoldering timbers sticking up from the water in all directions. Denney exclaimed, "Well, if we hadn't burned it, the whole Rebel Army would have come galloping across it."[44]

Townspeople were busy gossiping about Sunday's exciting events. J. Houston Mifflin, having returned home at 9:30 p.m., relayed rumors he had heard in Columbia regarding Confederate strength. Mifflin wrote to his son that "the true news at that time was three thousand cavalry & infantry & some artillery. . . . drove our men to the bridge." Mifflin believed that Colonel Frick "commanding our boys, managed well." He incorrectly reported that an enemy battery had killed three men and a little girl. The militia had escaped with not five minutes to spare. Ten minutes after they left, E. K. Smith and Robert Crane had fired "the middle of the bridge," but all was well; "everything burned but the piers. No damage to Columbia or Wrightsville." However, a reporter for *Harper's Weekly* took note of all the artillery pieces sitting in Columbia that, in his opinion, could and should have been used to halt the Confederates. "In a panic the bridge was rashly fired," he wrote, openly calling into question Haller's and Frick's decision. One "distinguished gentleman," as Frick later deemed him, thought he knew military tactics from his days in an antebellum local company. He loudly complained that the officers should simply have taken up the flooring. This ignored the fact that there were in Frick's view "millions of feet of

---

43 Bradwell, "Crossing the Potomac," 371.

44 Spicer, *The Columbia Civil War Centennial*, 20.

planks and boards on the banks of the river, within a few yards of the bridge, ready for use to replace those taken up."[45]

Corporal Daniel Dillman had remained posted with Lieutenant Ridgway's artillery all day. In the early evening, he spotted several shadowy figures moving about on a hill immediately to the north. Dillman and a fellow militiaman, Dr. Howell Halberstadt, climbed the height to make a "reconnaissance in force." The two pickets discovered nothing but some women and children. Relieved, Dillman enjoyed "an excellent view from the eminence. The moon, being near full, the prospect was enchanting." In York, dreading what the night might bring, Cassandra Small's family closed their shutters and bolted the doors. To their relief, all was quiet and their property and possessions were not disturbed.[46]

The Rebels Finally Leave York County

At daylight Tuesday, a cold rainy last day of June, Jubal Early called together his brigade commanders and ordered a withdrawal from York. John Gordon and his staff passed through downtown at 6:00 a.m. "in great haste" to prepare their brigade for the westward movement. "We finally fell down ourselves and had hardly closed our eyes in sleep when we were called to ranks, half dead from fatigue, to resume a hard march to Gettysburg," recalled Gordon Bradwell. "Even when our men awoke they paid no attention to the great piles of supplies we had brought them, and marched away, leaving their portions for anybody who might find them. Among the rations I remember were two hindquarters of very fine beef, a barrel or two of flour, some buckets of wine, sugar, clothing, shoes, etc. All this for about twenty men. I suppose the rest of Early's division got things in the same proportion as our company, all of which would have required quite a train to transport it."[47]

45 J. Houston Mifflin to Lloyd Mifflin, July 8, 1863, LCHS; Harper's Weekly, July 18, 1863. Frick later defended his actions in a letter to the Columbia Spy which the paper published on Feb. 6, 1886: "The enemy reached the west end of the bridge, and then that the safety of the crossing might be assured, no other means being available, 'prudence' dictated the destruction of the bridge. While regretting the absolute necessity for the destruction, the great interests involved and impending, made the duty plain, and I could not forego it. . . . the wisdom of destruction of the bridge is apparent to unprejudiced minds."

46 Pottsville Journal, July 18, 1913; Cassandra Small to Lissie Latimer, July 8, 1863, YCHT.

47 Bradwell, "Crossing the Potomac," 371.

Many of Gordon's men were so as exhausted as to be incapacitated. "By the time we made the trip to the Susquehanna and back to York," James J. M. Smith of the 31st Georgia's color guard recalled, "my feet were desperately sore and bleeding at every step. I, together with a number of our barefoot, disabled men, were relieved from duty and ordered to the ambulances. Myself and a comrade named Glaye were the worst crippled pair of the bunch, and before we could hobble to the ambulances they were filled and we were left without transportation." Smith and Glaye hobbled painfully along Carlisle Road as best they could. A surgeon ordered the soldiers to do all they could to remain with the head of the brigade so they would not straggle behind the column and risk being bushwhacked.[48]

As they were leaving town along the main street, some of Col. Isaac E. Avery's North Carolinians took the opportunity to tear York's confiscated large flag into long strips. Other soldiers tore these strips into little pieces while singing, "We'll Plant Our Colors on a Northern Hill." Jubal Early's Division marched off via Weigelstown and East Berlin to rejoin Ewell's Corps. Elijah White's battalion used the York-Gettysburg Turnpike to screen Early's left flank.[49]

Cassandra Small's mother awakened her daughters with the welcome news that the Rebels were gone. Cassandra rejoiced, "Oh, what a happy people! How thankful we should be that our lives and property are spared." She was also grateful that the men of her family had stayed home, instead of leaving town, as had so many other residents. Her father Philip, Uncle Samuel, and brothers Latimer and Sam "were absolutely necessary here" during the crisis. With the family now safe, Latimer Small, a member of York's Committee of Safety, left for Wrightsville to see the extent of the damage. "No one but those who were eyewitnesses to the occupation of York," M. L. Van Baman wrote, "can have any conception of the extent of anxiety and suspense of our people during the two days' occupation."[50]

48 *The Sunny South*, Sept. 23, 1904. The comrade likely was one of the Glaze brothers in Company K.

49 Gibson, *History of York County*, 174, 210. Accounts differ as to the fate of York's massive flag. See McClure's *East of Gettysburg*. Gibson places the time of Jubal Early's departure from York as between 4:00 and 5:00 a.m. In all probability, this is when the head of the column started on the road, since several accounts claim that Confederates were still in town as late as mid-morning.

50 Civil War files, YCHT.

"The town is now no longer occupied by the enemy in force, but a few pickets and scouts are passing through town as we write, and they are no doubt yet in the surrounding country," editorialized the *York Gazette*. "Let us hope that they are on the retreat, and that the invasion of our fair State by the enemy may soon be at an end, and never again be repeated.[51]

However, not all of Early's men were gone from York. According to the Staunton Artillery's Capt. Asher W. Garber in a letter home to his sister, "[James] W. Fallon—I sent out an inquiry about him. Him & Michael Duneghee [Donaghee] deserted the company in York City and have not been heard of since." Cassandra Small also wrote about seeing enemy soldiers about, noting, "A great many stragglers and deserters are still here." In a few isolated cases these "atrocious villains," as Small described them, took out their frustrations on residences that had been abandoned by their owners who had taken horses and valuables across the river to safety. About 10:00 a.m. near Hanover Junction, Confederate infantrymen shattered several windows and entered the locked house of Jacob Smeich. After stealing an accordion, two ladies bonnets, a woolen shawl, and other property, they ransacked the house, destroying furniture and smashing glassware, pottery, and Mrs. Smeich's looking glass. When then entered the barn they discovered a large supply of oats and corn, all of which they pilfered and later delivered to Elijah White's cavalrymen.[52]

White's battalion, meanwhile, headed westward on the turnpike through Abbottstown. By this time a question was making the rounds through the battalion's ranks: Where was J.E.B. Stuart's column? By now, White's men should have rendezvoused with the horsemen. Captain Marcellus French expressed the prevailing concern when he wrote, "Somehow, in a veteran army, "men divine pretty closely what is going on, and all were wondering, 'Where is Stuart?'" White dispatched a few scouts to search for the missing chief of cavalry, but not a trace of his cavalry force could be found. When he and his men were within ten miles of Gettysburg, White ordered French and ten troopers to ride about one-half mile in front of the column to ascertain if any enemy force was ahead on the road. Before too long Captain French spotted a

51 *York Gazette*, July 2, 1863. The report was written on the afternoon of June 30.

52 Cassandra Small to Lissie Latimer, June 30, 1863, YCHT; York County Damage Claims, reel 30. According to the journal of the First City Troop, thirteen Rebels were captured in York and then escorted to Columbia on July 2.

"considerable body" of Union cavalry in the distance entering the pike from a side road. White sent a message to Early that a cavalry and infantry force had been on the York Road at Abbott's Ford, but had since moved south toward Hanover.[53]

Gordon's infantry headed westward on the next road north of the gravel turnpike, a welcome change for James J. M. Smith and other hobbled foot-soldiers. Glaye had straggled, but Smith somehow stayed with the head of the column. He later claimed that Gordon dismounted and commanded him to mount his horse. Smith did so, and said that the general walked forward and remained dismounted throughout the day.[54]

A few miles west of York, the Georgians heard the deep rumble of artillery fire off to the southwest. Captain William Tanner unlimbered his artillery on a hill on the Henry Ramer farm and prepared to defend Gordon's flank in case of an enemy attack. None came, and the brigade marched out of York County without opposition. Early sent a note (presumably to Elijah White or William French) asking the colonel to "get between Gettysburg and Heidlersburg, and picket at Mummasburg and Hunterstown. Send in the direction of Gettysburg, and see what is there, and report to General Ewell at Heidlersburg. A small body of Yankee cavalry has made its appearance between Gettysburg and Heidlersburg. See what it is." However, some of H. Judson Kilpatrick's cavalry from the Army of the Potomac captured the courier that night on the road to New Oxford.[55]

Arriving again in Adams County, Early bivouacked three miles east of Heidlersburg on the road from East Berlin. His camps were in the area of Round Hill, with Companies A and K of the 38th Georgia on the advanced picket line keeping watch for Yankees. Early's men enjoyed the fresh water of Plum Run while he rode to meet Richard Ewell, who ordered him to march to

---

53 *Richmond Times-Dispatch*, June 19, 1910; OR 27, pt. 2, 467. After Captain French's initial encounter with Kilpatrick's men near Abbottstown on June 30, White sent forward 15 men to augment the reconnaissance and ride to Gettysburg to ascertain if any Yankee infantry was there. Residents along the turnpike told French that 60 Union cavalrymen were directly ahead of him. Cautiously approaching Gettysburg, French spotted a Union vidette 300-400 yards on the turnpike, and soon heard what he perceived as infantry drums "all over the valley." He reported to White that "the Yankee infantry were in Gettysburg."

54 *The Sunny South*, Sept. 23, 1904. Smith claimed that bushwhackers captured and hung Glaye and other stragglers. No corroboration is known.

55 Prowell, *History of York County*, 1: 1047; OR 27, pt. 3, 414.

Cashtown where Lee planned to concentrate the army. The soldiers enjoyed the fruits of the York ransom. Private George F. Agee of the 26th Georgia related, "We spent the night some few miles west of York. We had been faring splendidly in the way of something to eat since we struck the enemy's country, but on this occasion there was something extra in store for us. We drew in the way of extras sugar, coffee, candy, raisins and some good old rye whiskey, which was a rare treat for a confederate soldier."[56]

That same evening in Washington, Secretary of the Navy Gideon Welles penned several sentences of pithy observations in his diary of recent events:

We have no positive information that the Rebels have crossed the Susquehanna, though we have rumors to that effect," "There is no doubt the bridge at Columbia, one and a half miles long, has been burnt, and, it seems, by our own people. The officer who ordered it must have been imbued with Halleck's tactics. I wish the Rebel army had got across before the bridge was burnt. But Halleck's prayers and efforts, especially his prayers, are to keep the Rebels back—drive them back across the "frontiers" instead of intercepting, capturing, and annihilating them. This movement of Lee and the Rebel forces into Pennsylvania is to me incomprehensible, nor do I get any light from military men or others in regard to it. Should they cross the Susquehanna, as our General-in-Chief and Governor Curtin fear, they will never recross it without being first captured. This they know, unless deceived by their sympathizing friends in the North, as in 1861; therefore I do not believe they will attempt it."

Before retiring Welles added the following ominous language:

I have talked over this campaign with [Secretary of War Edwin M.] Stanton this evening, but I get nothing from him definite or satisfactory of fact or speculation, and I come to the conclusion that he is bewildered, that he gets no light from his military subordinates and advisers, and that he really has no information or opinion as to the Rebel destination or purpose.[57]

---

56 Hudgins, "With the 38th Georgia," 161-63; *The Sunny South*, July 20, 1901. In Jackson Township, Thomasville farmer David Witman reported that Gordon's infantrymen robbed his horse, so at least a portion of Gordon's Brigade may have followed the turnpike westward (York County Damage Claims, reel 32).

57 Gideon Welles, Diary of Gideon Welles, Secretary of the Navy under Lincoln and Johnson (Boston: Houghton Mifflin, 1911), 352.

On Wednesday morning, one of General Ewell's couriers arrived with word that Jubal Early was to march his division south to Gettysburg. Early complied promptly with his new orders and his four brigades broke camp and set out at a steady clip. Before long, the distant thunder of artillery fire settled upon the tramping Confederates. Not everyone was with the column. "On the morning [of] the first day of July, General Gordon marched the brigade away and left us standing, and we still have not been relieved to this day," complained Sgt. Francis Hudgins. "[Captains] Miller and Stuffs held a council and very wisely decided to abandon our position and try to overtake the brigade. Bill Jenkins, kettle drummer of Company A, beat the long roll, and we quickly formed and marched with quick step until we overtook our command. This incident," continued the sergeant, "has never been explained to me, and I suppose Generals Gordon and Evans will not court-martial us now for abandoning our position."[58]

Shortly after 2:00 p.m., with the sound of battle upon them, Gordon's Georgians engaged the Yankees just north of Gettysburg as part of a much larger action that was unfolding around the prosperous town. This time the enemy was not Pennsylvania militia but Francis Barlow's division of Maj. Gen. Oliver O. Howard's Eleventh Corps, Army of the Potomac. Although the Confederates as a whole enjoyed a sweeping success on July 1, the fighting on the two days that followed proved bloody and unsuccessful. Jubal Early's Division lost more than 1,100 soldiers in the savage encounter, including more than 500 from Gordon's Brigade alone.

Meanwhile, several stragglers and deserters from Early's Division remained behind in York County. Some of the Pennsylvania militia crossed the river on July 1 and captured a handful of stragglers from Gordon's command, including Pvt. John Ludlaw of the 31st Georgia. Twenty scouts from Judson Kilpatrick's cavalry brigade entered York on Thursday, July 2, the first Union troops to reoccupy the borough. When a sentinel reported that a body of horsemen was approaching from the west, they jumped into the saddle to be ready to respond at a moment's notice. An officer scanning the horizon with his field glasses discerned that the "raid" was only a farmer riding into York from Bottstown with a wagon and six-horse team hauling a load of hay. The relieved citizens

---

58 Hudgins, "With the 38th Georgia," 161-63. Hudgins suffered a severe chest wound later near Barlow's Knoll. The bullet went through his blanket roll, which had thirteen holes when unrolled.

gratefully fed the Yankees, who then rode off to join Kilpatrick's Union cavalry near Gettysburg.[59]

The Susquehanna River receded that same day, and Sgt. Robert E. Randall and twenty-one First City Troopers crossed on flatboats at Marietta. They patrolled York County, occasionally capturing Confederate stragglers and deserters, including thirteen prisoners taken in York. Colonel William Thomas and nearly one thousand men of the 20th PVM reoccupied the county later in the week, and another Federal flag waved high over York's Centre Square as Latimer Small fulfilled his promise to replace the one the Rebels carried away.[60]

For days, York citizens scrubbed and washed the army hospital buildings that Colonel Avery's ragged North Carolinians had occupied. Lice contaminated several structures, as well as the market house where other soldiers had slept. The citizens didn't fully appreciate it, but they were in a race against time. Within a short time wounded Union soldiers from the fighting at Gettysburg would arrive. When informed that the army planned to send injured Rebels to the facility, Dr. Henry Palmer threatened to resign. He had already been captured by Early's men during the occupation, though he had managed to escape.[61]

Dr. Palmer—and most other York Countians—had seen more than enough of the Confederate invaders.

59 Gibson, *History of York County*, 174; White, *A History of the 31st Georgia*, 99. It is not known why Ludlaw lingered so long in Wrightsville. Authorities took him to Columbia for processing, and then forwarded him to Fort Delaware. He remained incarcerated there for two years before being released at the end of the war.

60 McClure, *East of Gettysburg*, 123.

61 Cassandra Small to Lissie Latimer, July 20, 1863, YCHT.

Chapter 13
The Impact of Gordon's Expedition

The Scars of War

Despite the destruction of the Columbia Bridge, many Pennsylvanians doubted that Robert E. Lee could be stopped. Anxious citizens who had not lost horses or livestock to Jubal Early's division now tried to send them off to safety in case of another raid. On June 30, East Berlin farmer Peter Altland drove his six-horse team east toward the Susquehanna River heading for Lancaster County. Reaching Loucks' Mill near York, he heard that the bridge had been burned. After turning around, he was passing the Conewago Creek near Dillsburg when he ran into J. E. B. Stuart's cavalrymen, who were hoping to connect with Jubal Early's infantry. They appropriated his horses. More than 400 York County farmers and townspeople lost animals to Stuart's three brigades on June 30 and July 1. The passage of about 5,000 enemy cavalrymen startled residents who were already nervous after Early's visit.[1]

In York, Cassandra Small's aunt was "terrified beyond all. Didn't take her clothes off at night for more than a week; sat up in a large chair; couldn't sleep at all; looked miserably, and never smiled." Several other residents suffered from similar psychological trauma. Annie Weiser was miserable, believing that "all the excitement [had] injured her very much." She planned a getaway vacation to New York to recuperate in the Catskill Mountains. With the Rebels still a dangerous threat, Governor Curtin was finally able to recruit additional state troops. Thousands of previously apathetic men poured into Harrisburg. By the

---

1   York County Damage Claims, reel 22.

evening of June 29, 16,000 soldiers manned the Department of the Susquehanna, a far cry from the 250 that Maj. Gen. Darius Couch employed just two weeks earlier. However, Couch warned the War Department that just 5,000 regulars would "whip them all to pieces in an open field."[2]

The populace had little faith in the military strategy or the raw militia. York attorney James Latimer penned, "Things look blue. . . . I am afraid the rebs will have but little difficulty in going to Philada or anywhere they please. . . . I may take too gloomy a view of affairs, but things seem at their worst." J. Houston Mifflin complained that the Rebels "may try Harrisburg or Bainbridge, but these may be feints intended to quiet and deceive us, but all the help we expected from Phila. or Washington is vain. They expect us to defend all of the river, when it is here they ought to defend Phila.—here is the place—& only defend themselves." Philadelphia's leading citizens appealed directly to Secretary of War Edwin Stanton to send 20,000 Federal troops to man their city's elaborate earthworks, but he kept them in Washington's defenses.[3]

Among the new soldiers were 1,138 men from York County. Another 2,154 men enlisted in Lancaster County, including many who had served in the various volunteer companies that had dug the first rifle-pits. Captain William A. Atlee re-enlisted, taking along several of his pupils from Franklin & Marshall College. On June 29, 38-year-old Prof. James P. Wickersham, who had previously led his Millersville Normal School students and instructors to Wrightsville, announced that he would take command of all who would follow him. Wickersham raised a "People's Regiment" and enrolled it at Harrisburg on July 2. His new 47th Pennsylvania Volunteer Militia included a pair of professors and a large number of students intent upon "driving back the ruthless invaders of our soil." Colonel Emlen Franklin recruited and organized the 50th Militia with Lancaster County men. His lieutenant colonel was Thaddeus Stevens, Jr., whose father owned the Caledonia Furnace burned by Jubal Early.[4]

2   Cassandra Small to Lissie Latimer, July 20, 1863, YCHT; *OR* 27, pt. 3, 407.

3   James Latimer to Bartow Latimer, June 30, 1863, YCHT; J. Houston Mifflin to Lloyd Mifflin, July 8, 1863, LCHS.

4   *Pennsylvania Volunteers and Militia Called into Service during the Gettysburg Campaign* (Washington, D.C.: Adjutant General's Office, 1885), 8; Millersville Normal School Catalog, 1863-1864, Ganser Library, Millersville University, Millersville, Pa. Colonel Wickersham's 47th Militia was assigned to Col. Emlen Franklin's Second Brigade within Maj. Gen. William F. "Baldy" Smith's First Division of the Department of the Susquehanna. The regiment mustered out August 13.

Another reaction to the Confederate threat came from neighboring New Jersey. On June 29, Gov. Joel Parker, a Democrat, wired President Lincoln that his constituents were apprehensive that the invasion might extend to their state, so the enemy should be driven from Pennsylvania. Believing that Washington was apathetic despite "such fearful circumstances," Parker mentioned that his constituents wanted Maj. Gen. George B. McClellan restored at the head of the Army of the Potomac. At the very least, McClellan should be assigned to command the New Jersey, New York, and Pennsylvania troops already deployed in Pennsylvania. He added, "If either appointment be made, the people would rise on masse." When word finally reached authorities that the immediate threat had been thwarted at Gettysburg, Governor Parker breathed a little easier. However, strong support for McClellan remained, fueling the general's ascendance to the Democratic presidential nomination the following summer.[5]

Once Lee's retreat became certain following the battle of Gettysburg, Pennsylvanians took stock in what they had accomplished. Neither John Gordon nor any other Rebels (except prisoners and a few deserters) had crossed the Susquehanna River. The U.S. flag still flew proudly over the state capital. War-damaged communication lines and railroads could be repaired. Although the military provided the money, labor, and raw materials to rebuild 33 trestles and bridges damaged or destroyed by French and White, the Northern Central Railway spent an additional $234,000 to repair damage to rails and infrastructure. Work crews hauled away burnt timbers, railcars, trackside structures, and huge piles of debris. Officials calculated they had lost $108,793 in normal revenues during the downtime. York's residents did not hear the whistles of locomotives until July 8 when service resumed.[6]

With rail lines severed, it took longer to evacuate the wounded from Gettysburg to Philadelphia, Baltimore, York, or Harrisburg. The only bridge connecting Lancaster and York counties no longer existed, so wagons of much-

5   OR 27, pt. 3, 409.

6   Robert L. Gunnarsson, *The Story of the Northern Central Railway* (Sykesville, Md.: Greenberger Publishing, 1991), 63; Cassandra Small to Lissie Latimer, July 8, 1863, YCHT. The 1863 annual report of the NCRW estimated the loss of trade as $109,000; railcars destroyed at York $12,000; railcars destroyed at Gettysburg $5,600; scale at York $1,800; ironclad car #319 $800. Another $5,000 was allocated to build a new brick passenger station in York to replace one it alleged was burned by Early, as well as a new paint shed and car repair shed. No other account exists that the Rebels burned the station.

needed medical supplies from Philadelphia and Delaware bound for Gettysburg had to be diverted or ferried across the river. Doctors, relief agents, nurses, and other volunteers were forced to use alternate means to cross the river. A ladies aid society from Lancaster was delayed for days because of a lack of available seats on rowboats. Dr. Theodore Dimon of New York stopped in Philadelphia on July 10 on his journey to the Second Corps' battlefield hospital. The next morning, inquiring as to the shortest route to Gettysburg, he was advised to buy a one-way ticket on the Philadelphia & Columbia Railroad to Columbia. Once there, Dimon was ferried in a small rowboat across the river to Wrightsville. There, he found that the Rebels had destroyed much of the Northern Central. The determined doctor took a private conveyance to York, where he finally ate dinner.[7]

The loss of the bridge also negatively affected the canals. Gone were the towpaths that enabled the easy transfer of barges from the North Branch in Columbia to the Susquehanna and Tide Water on the opposite side. Water-borne traffic was totally blocked for a short time, and it would take days to ready alternative plans. A steam tugboat, appropriately named the "Columbia," was pressed into action to pick up the canal boats and tow them across the river to the opposite canal.

Many civilians suffered greatly in the aftermath of the bridge's destruction. Edward Fisher of Peach Bottom in York County penned, "The whole structure was burned down and it was a great loss to the people." Some of the criticism among Columbians was leveled at their neighbor Robert Crane and his bridge destruction crew. Crane apparently had second thoughts about the wisdom of his own actions. In response, Granville Haller wrote to him, "You are aware that I, in response, expressed my approbation, of your conduct and these who stood by you on that occasion. Your party has my warmest thanks for your service. Independent of what I have said to you and written, the written order of Col Frick is full authority for all you have done. Every order from him was valid, unless countermanded by me by order from Major Genl Couch, who had directed me to superintend the military operations for him, in this section of country."[8]

---

7   Theodore S. Dimon, "From Auburn to Antietam: The Civil War Journal of a Battlefield Surgeon Who Served With the Army of the Potomac, 1861-1863," GNMP.

8   Granville Haller to Robert Crane, Oct.17, 1863; Transcribed by Scott Mingus. Files of the Columbia Historic Preservation Society.

As the Confederates approached in late June, refugees had driven thousands of horses to Lancaster County to protect them from Rebel raiders. David Hursh took his horses and a wagonload of hay across the bridge just before it was closed to public traffic. He had to use a flatboat to return to York County. His horses shied at this unusual mode of crossing the river, but Hursh was able to return them to his farm without incident. With the direct commercial route between Philadelphia and York cut, merchants and farmers had to take much longer routes to other bridges or use ferries to take their products to market. Ferry service at Wright's Crossing was quickly restored, and local private boat owners saw a noticeable increase in their monthly gross revenues. At times, a veritable armada of small boats bobbed in the current.[9]

Residents throughout Franklin, Adams, and York counties took the most damage, financially and psychologically. Cassandra Small described the resulting tension between York's Copperheads and Unionists. Some females "who call themselves ladies" had visited and entertained the North Carolina troops billeted at the hospital. The women soon regretted this action, because they became outcasts in York society. "No one will visit them anymore," she wrote, "they must form a party among themselves—a distinct line is drawn... The Rebels, themselves, spoke of them to some of our townsmen and said had they dared they would have put bullets through the hearts of those persons who welcomed and waved to them—that 'friends in an enemy's country are worse than traitors.' They said they held them in supreme contempt." She was shocked to learn that her well-liked neighbor and his family sympathized with the Secessionists and frequently had entertained Early's officers. His sister had waved a handkerchief at them, until a clergyman rushed over and stopped her, saying, "If you have no respect for yourself, have some for the people you live among." Despite her neighbor's hospitality, Small reported that a Confederate officer had deliberately walked through his office and out through the yard to the stable, where he took the sympathizer's horse. The Smalls subsequently shunned their neighbors who had openly welcomed the enemy. Cassandra declared, "Real Southerners are more bearable than these traitors."[10]

Small's neighbor was not the only Copperhead who suffered as a result of the invasion. As Jacob Frick's 27th Militia pursued Lee's beaten army toward

9 *Delta Herald & Times*, December 8, 1916; Gerald Austin Robinson, Jr., *Confederate Operations in York County* (Millersville, Pa.: Unpublished graduate thesis, Millersville State College, 1965).

10 Cassandra Small to Lissie Latimer, July 8, 1863, YCHT.

the Potomac River, soldier-newsman Francis Wallace reported that "Southern sympathizers in Southern Pennsylvania and Maryland have been cured by the Rebel invasion." These Copperheads, he concluded, "are bitter against the Rebels now." White's and French's cavalrymen had raided dozens of farms, destroying crops and killing livestock for food. Many farmers had lost horses needed to harvest their crops. Early's soldiers stole a draft animal from farmer George Rutter, who tried hitching his reaper to his remaining horse and two inexperienced mules. When they bolted, the reaper ran over the 27-year-old Rutter, crippling him for life.[11]

Thousands of farmers along the Confederate route of march had lost their horses, cattle, hogs, chickens, wagons, harnesses, and all their meat and/or flour. Despite Gordon's orders to leave private property alone, many of his soldiers could not resist the temptation to sample the region's bounty. Lieutenant Joseph Hilton of the 26th Georgia admitted he had "a nice time of it" in Pennsylvania, where his regiment inflicted serious injury upon "the corpulent Dutch farmers of that loyal State," including the deliberate destruction or theft of beehives, fowls, eggs, butter, cherries, green apples, cider, and apple butter. Hilton estimated that it would take the Yankee farmers at least three seasons to replenish their stock, not to mention the havoc the Rebels played on their horses and cattle. Cassandra Small simply wrote the Rebels were finally gone, "I hope never to return. May the Lord preserve us from such distress again."[12]

Several Wrightsville families were now homeless (at least temporarily) because of the fire and damaging Confederate shells. Others forced from their homes did not return for weeks or even months, preferring instead to remain in safer locales with relatives or friends. Some had to seek new employment because their workplaces were no longer in existence. A pair of families endured tragedy much worse than the loss of a few horses, a home, or a job. A year after the skirmish a shell taken as a souvenir to East Prospect rolled into a fireplace and exploded, killing two of John Shenberger's children. In another accident, a pair of boys discovered an intact shell along the riverbank a short distance above Wrightsville. When they detonated the artillery round a fragment severely wounded Ashbel Lane. Only the careful and dedicated nursing of his devoted

---

11 *Pottsville Miners' Journal*, July 25, 1863; York County Damage Claims, Rutter claim.

12 *Lancaster Daily Express*, July 11, 186; Joseph Hilton to Lizzie Lachison, July 18, 1863, GHS; Cassandra Small to Lissie Latimer, June 30, 1863, YCHT.

mother and an attending physician saved his life. Lane later became a preacher in Ohio.[13]

The events at Wrightsville did have one favorable outcome—newfound respect for black volunteers. They had shouldered arms alongside the white soldiers and performed courageously. *Lancaster's Examiner and Herald* trumpeted, "The only Columbia volunteers in the fight were fifty-three negros, who after making entrenchments with the soldiers, took muskets and fought bravely." In his official report, Col. Jacob Frick praised the excellent conduct of these black civilians. "After working industriously in the rifle-pits all day, when the fight commenced they took their guns and stood up to their work bravely. They fell back only when ordered to do so." Lieutenant Francis Wallace wrote to his Pottsville paper, "All honor to the colored men of Columbia. They will die in defense of life and liberty, which is more than a majority of the whites here seem disposed to do—the cravens."[14]

Darius Couch had kind words for all the volunteers. "The militia of Pennsylvania raised to resist the invasion was composed of all classes and professions, and was a fine body of men." Thankful for the hundreds of Harrisburg residents who constructed earthworks, he added, "Some of the patriotic citizens of that city volunteered to work in the trenches; others were paid. The colored population were not far behind their white brethren in giving assistance."[15]

Unfortunately, the name of the heroic black volunteer decapitated by Tanner's artillery has been lost to history. No press coverage accompanied his funeral or burial. Columbia's black cemeteries and churches did not maintain detailed records during this period, and the borough did not start keeping civil records on deaths and burials until years after the war. The only existing muster roll for the Columbia volunteers is from November, well after the skirmish. Some blacks who shouldered muskets in the earthworks, including young John Aquilla Wilson of York County and Barney Sweeny of Columbia, later enlisted in three-year U.S. "colored troops" and served in the South. Famed social reformer Frederick Douglass came to Lancaster County in mid-July to encourage black men to enlist. His passionate speech in Marietta's town hall

---

13 *Columbia Spy*, March 3, 1866; Nye, *Farthest East*, 27.

14 *Lancaster Examiner and Herald*, July 1, 1863; OR 27, pt. 2, 279; *Pottsville Miners' Journal*, July 4, 1863.

15 OR 27, pt. 2, 214.

resulted in a group of twenty eager volunteers leaving for Philadelphia to join one of the new regiments. Ironically, four-fifths of his audience was white.[16]

Other blacks left the region for good, their lives forever altered by the Confederate expedition. Census records and property records indicate that in 1860, 186 blacks lived in Gettysburg. By 1870, only 74 of these same citizens remained in the borough. Fearing conscription into slavery, many left the rural counties during the invasion and moved to larger cities such as Harrisburg or Philadelphia, never to return.[17]

Area census rolls occasionally included deserters from the Army of Northern Virginia, including a few ex-Georgians. After seeing the plush farmlands and thriving cities, some war-sick veterans decided that the Rebellion was no longer worth fighting for. Some married local girls and became community leaders. In his official report, Couch recounted the collaboration between some Pennsylvanians and Southerners. His militiamen had taken 1,341 prisoners, of whom nearly 500 were armed, 400 wounded, and the remainder stragglers and deserters. "This does not include a number who escaped through the mountains and went north, being aided in this by the citizens."[18]

Jubal Early commented that the performance of Couch's militia at Gettysburg, Hanover Junction, and Wrightsville in fact had amounted to no resistance at all. The skirmishing was "merely a source of amusement" to his troops because the militiamen were "so utterly inefficient." They presented "little obstacle," leaving the region in a "defenseless condition." This disdain

16 *Marietta* (Pa.) *Mariettian*, July 18, 1863. On January 16, 1886, the *Columbia Spy* noted "it is unfortunate that the military annals of Pennsylvania fail to give the roster of the three white and one colored companies of militia from Columbia, who rendered such effective services in the trenches on the Wrightsville hills . . . Barney Sweeny, who afterwards served honorably in a volunteer regiment, was a member of this [colored] company. So was big George [Smith]. They ought to get the company together again, call a roll, and file a roster in the Adjutant General's office at Harrisburg for future reference… even the names of the officers seem to have been forgotten. . . . The SPY will cheerfully publish a roster of the company, if Messrs. Sweeney and Smith will furnish the names." Unfortunately, as of the date of publication, no roster has yet been located.

17 *Columbia Spy*, Jan. 16, 1886. Wilson, of Fawn Grove in southeastern York County, enlisted in the 32nd U.S. Colored Troops, which helped capture Charleston, South Carolina, in 1865. The last living Civil War veteran in York County, he died in 1942 at the age of 101.

18 1860 and 1870 U.S. Census; Nye, "The First Battle of Gettysburg," 17; *OR* 27, pt. 2, 215. During the skirmish at Witmer Farm, Miles Wilson of the 17th Virginia Cavalry, tired of the war, hid in the Bayly's cellar. He remained with the family until after the war. He married a local girl and settled in the area. According to Nye, Wilson's descendants lived near Mummasburg as of 1965.

influenced Maj. Gen. Henry Heth's leisurely deployment into battle lines on July 1, when he assumed, like Early on June 26, he was encountering "mere militia" on the same ridges west of Gettysburg. Heth may have expected these Yankees likewise to turn and march away, allowing uncontested passage into the borough. Retreating militia was a pattern well established in the Confederate mindset after Granville Haller's slow withdrawal across Adams and York counties. Not once had they stood firm. Instead, Heth engaged John Buford's veteran cavalry and then First Corps infantry. Hence, his men uttered, "Tain't no militia; it's those black-hatted fellows!" when they realized the Army of the Potomac was at Gettysburg.[19]

Brigadier General John Gordon's soldiers who survived the campaign held widely divergent views on their ill-fated expedition to the Susquehanna. One Georgian believed that his sole accomplishment was to gain "very sore feet" which plagued him until he again rested in a Virginia camp. Another private's fondly recalled the girls of Pennsylvania and wished that he could have taken a certain one home to be his bride. Cavalryman Capt. Frank Myers bluntly called the invasion "brilliant, but fruitless." Joseph Truett of the 31st Georgia's "Mountain Tigers" wrote, "I am tireder of warfare than I ever was of anything in my life." Lieutenant Charles Stuart of the 26th Georgia dubbed the Wrightsville trek a "fruitless tour," a useless move that "meant nothing." Lieutenant Joseph Hilton was more philosophic, realizing that much fighting remained in the coming days. "I am once more in Dixie, safe and sound, and ready for anything that may turn up, either to move forward, or backward, run or fight, or anything else Robert E. Lee tells me to do."[20]

The destruction of the Columbia Bridge helped dash the Confederates' hopes of capturing one of the North's most politically important state capitals. In 1892, Jacob Frick penned, "I was fully impressed with the belief at the time that this bridge was General Lee's objective point, and that it was to become the highway of the Confederate army to reach the centers which enabled the Northern army to maintain its position in the field by cutting off the supplies by capturing the eastern ports and plant the seat of war in Pennsylvania instead of

19 Early, *War Memoirs*, 261.

20 Myers, *The Comanches*, 191; Joseph H. Truett letter, Aug. 13, 1863, GDAH; Stuart, *Autobiographical Sketch*, USMHI; Joseph Hilton to Lizzie Lachison, July 18, 1863, Georgia Historical Society. The 26th Georgia guarded Jones' artillery battalion during the first day's fight at Gettysburg.

Virginia." It was a belief he harbored until his death. He had earlier written in 1886, "Surely there are none stupid enough to believe that the Confederate commander, after destroying [the] railroad and bridges between York and Wrightsville, if he did not desire it for his own use, would deliberately withdraw without destroying the grandest and most important structure of them all."[21]

Jubal Early "regretted very much" Gordon's failure to secure the bridge. With nothing to retard his progress, he claimed he would have taken his division across the Susquehanna, cutting the Pennsylvania Railroad before marching on Lancaster. After laying that town under contribution, he would have attacked Harrisburg in the rear while Ewell attacked the front. In the worst contingency, Early planned to mount his division from the immense number of horses taken across the river by the refugees, and then move to the west, destroying the railroads and canals before returning to safety. He lamented, "This project, however, was entirely thwarted by the destruction of the bridge, as the river was otherwise impassable, being very wide and deep at this point."

In February 1892, U.S. Senator John B. Gordon sent a letter to his former enemy Jacob Frick confirming that the destruction of the Columbia Bridge had prevented his crossing. However, Gordon stopped well short of Early's optimistic theories of what may have transpired had it remained intact. "What would have been the course of events after this is impossible for me to depict," admitted Gordon. Two months later Col. Thomas M. Anderson of the 14th U.S. Infantry concurred in a note to Granville Haller. "All theories apart, I should say that would have been better to burn twenty bridges than to have taken any chances," wrote Anderson. "If the burning of the bridge stopped Gordon, it was an important as a battle."[22]

Samuel Wright, the editor of the *Columbia Spy*, agreed. "When the history of our great victory at Gettysburg comes to be written," he argued, "this little skirmish will be found to have sustained an important relation, and with no small degree of complacency will those men who so faithfully watched the rebel approach, reflect on the part they played in the drama."[23]

21 Jacob G. Frick letter, April 1892, Schuylkill County Historical Society, Pottsville, Pa; *Columbia Spy*, Feb. 6, 1886.

22 Early, *War Memoirs*, 260; *Philadelphia Inquirer*, June 16, 1892, quoting Col. Thomas M. Anderson to Granville O. Haller, March 30, 1892. Haller in Seattle relayed Anderson's message to Frick on April 28, 1892.

23 *Columbia Spy*, July 11, 1863.

U.S. Senator John B. Gordon confirmed that the burning of the Columbia Bridge had thwarted his plans to invade Lancaster County, Pa. He would later return to the region on his popular speaking tour covering "The Last Days of the Confederacy." *Library of Congress*

Years later, as modern development threatens the now-forgotten battlefield at Wrightsville, the burning of the wartime Columbia Bridge remains an important part of Pennsylvania's Civil War heritage. The bridge's piers remain a visible legacy of the events of June 28, 1863. That rainy night, the outcome of Robert E. Lee's invasion forever changed as flames raged over the Susquehanna.

Epilogue

The Confederates

Brigadier General John B. Gordon served at Gettysburg with distinction, particularly on the afternoon of July 1 north of town. To artilleryman Robert Stiles, Gordon was "the most glorious and inspiring thing I ever looked upon. He was riding a beautiful coal-black stallion, captured at Winchester, that had belonged to one of the Federal generals in Milroy's army—a majestic animal." Stiles marveled at, "his rider standing in his stirrups, bareheaded, hat in hand, arms extended, and, in a voice like a trumpet, exhorting his men. It was superb; absolutely thrilling."[1]

Gordon's inspired veteran Georgia brigade smashed into the Union Eleventh Corps on Blocher's (Barlow's) Knoll just north of Gettysburg. One of the dead that afternoon was 21-year-old Capt. William L. McLeod, the commander of the 38th Georgia. Captain McLeod was shot in the right temple. His soldiers carried the prostrate McLeod to the Jacob Kime farm, where he lingered for five hours before dying. His slave Moses helped identify and bury the corpse.

Despite his growing losses Gordon pressed his troops southward, breaking a second enemy line near the Adams County Almshouse and driving the blue-clad soldiers backward through the clogged streets of Gettysburg. Despite the stunning victory General Ewell did not order Jubal Early to continue the attack and seize the high ground south of town known as Cemetery Hill. Instead, Early sent Gordon's Brigade eastward to the York Road on the army's flank in

---

1 Stiles, *Four Years Under Marse Robert*, 210-211; Hudgins, "With the 38th Georgia," 163.

support of General William "Extra Billy" Smith. According to a report, enemy troops were seen moving in that direction. Gordon spent a frustrating night on July 1-2 listening as the Yankees entrenched their position on Cemetery Hill.[2]

Gordon's Georgians camped near Gettysburg and were essentially spectators for the rest of the battle. On July 2 they advanced a short distance to support an assault on East Cemetery Hill by Isaac Avery's and Harry Hays' brigades. Jubal Early called off Gordon's attack in the growing darkness. The Georgians skirmished for two more days, but saw no significant action. Several regiments suffered appalling losses at Gettysburg, including many men who had formed the bucket brigade at Wrightsville. Gordon's men saluted him, "You are the best Genl. who ever led men into a fight."[3]

JOHN GORDON'S BRIGADE				
Regiment	Killed	Wounded	Missing	Percentage Lost
13th Georgia	37	75	25	43.9
26th Georgia	2	13	17	10.2
31st Georgia	13	44	8	25.8
38th Georgia	18	62	53	39.0
60th Georgia	12	28	19	19.7
61st Georgia	30	75	6	38.5
Total	112	297	128	29.6

Many of Gordon's wounded were treated at the Josiah Benner farm, Pennsylvania College, and the Adams County Almshouse buildings north of Gettysburg. Late on July 4, the brigade headed back toward Virginia, covering Lee's retreat before finally recrossing the Potomac River in mid-July. Early's

---

2 Hofe, *That There Be No Stain Upon My Stones*, 38-41. Pvt. Reuben F. Ruch of the 53rd Pennsylvania described aiming at a man without a weapon, who was crossing a fence several yards in front of the colorbearer. Ruch suffered two leg wounds and was captured.

3 Busey & Martin, *Regimental Strengths & Losses at Gettysburg*, 286; White, *A History of the 31st Georgia*, 94, citing a letter from Capt. William H. Harrison.

Division left behind 194 of its most seriously wounded men, including dozens from Gordon's Brigade. Eventually, most were transferred to the Andrew and Susan Weikert farm along the Fairfield Road. Several injured Georgians remained in Gettysburg up to six weeks before being transported to prison camps or hospitals. In some cases, arms once used to save Wrightsville now were consigned to piles of amputated limbs. Several soldiers died from their injuries and were buried on various farms. A few may still rest in Gettysburg. Not all of Gordon's men were accounted for in 1871 when crews disinterred several known Georgians and transported them to Savannah for reburial in Laurel Grove Cemetery's Gettysburg Plot.[4]

Gordon survived Gettysburg to ascend through the ranks of the Confederate army, being promoted to major general on May 14, 1864. He finished the war as a corps commander and member of Lee's inner circle. Robert E. Lee selected Gordon to surrender the Army of Northern Virginia in a ceremony April 12, 1865, at Appomattox Court House. His Union counterpart was Joshua Lawrence Chamberlain, also of Gettysburg fame.

John Gordon returned to Georgia. He served three terms in the United States Senate and later became governor. He became involved in the early Ku Klux Klan. His house burned down in the early 1890s, destroying many of his papers and Civil War memorabilia. Gordon throughout his remaining years crisscrossed the country in a series of speaking engagements. On March 6, 1894, the old general again visited York, this time to present his popular "The Last Days of the Confederacy" lecture at the Opera House. At the nearby Colonial Hotel, he encountered old Samuel L. Roth, the Mennonite pastor who had persuaded him to return a stolen horse during the Rebel occupation. John Gordon died at his winter home near Miami, Florida, on January 9, 1904, just three months after the publication of his reminiscences. His body was returned to Atlanta for burial.[5]

---

4 Gregory A. Coco, *A Strange and Blighted Land—Gettysburg: The Aftermath of a Battle* (Gettysburg: Thomas Publications, 1995), 217-19; *Savannah Morning News*, Aug. 22, 1871. Among the dead removed from Pennsylvania and re-buried in Savannah were Lt. C. L. Walker and Pvt. John B. Willoughby of the 38th Georgia and several other members of John B. Gordon's Brigade. Many unidentified Confederate remains were disinterred and reburied in Richmond's Hollywood Cemetery.

5 Prowell, *History of York County*, 1, 997. Roth leased a large portion of his farm to the Conewago Iron Company after the war. Now retired, he and Gordon shared a tearful remembrance of their 1863 meeting.

Two of Gordon's regimental leaders, William McLeod and John Lamar, were killed in action. The four survivors all became prominent in postwar Georgia. Colonel James Milton Smith of the 13th Georgia became a Confederate congressman. After the war he served in the Georgia House of Representatives. A staunch opponent of Radical Reconstruction during Grant's presidency, Smith governed Georgia from 1872-1877, being acknowledged for retiring the state's debt. After an unsuccessful run for the Senate, he served on the Railroad Commission for six years. His former commander, Governor Gordon, appointed him as judge of the Superior Court of the Chattahoochee Judicial Circuit in 1887. Smith died of complications from a stroke on November 25, 1890. He is buried in Gainesville's Alta Vista Cemetery.

Clement A. Evans was promoted to brigadier general and assumed command of the brigade after Gordon's promotion. He survived five wounds during the war. He later became an influential Methodist minister and advanced the "Holiness Movement," a controversial doctrine that eventually split the denomination. He pastored churches in the Atlanta area, some with memberships as large as a thousand people, until his retirement in 1892. Three years later, Evans authored the *Military History of Georgia*, which was based heavily upon his Civil War memoirs. He also edited and co-wrote *Confederate Military History*, a 12-volume compendium. Finally, he co-authored the four-volume *Cyclopedia of Georgia*. Death stilled Evans' prolific pen on July 2, 1911. He was buried in Atlanta's Oakland Cemetery, just a few yards away from the grave of John Gordon.

Colonel Edmund N. Atkinson of the 26th Georgia suffered five separate wounds during the war and survived incarceration at the infamous Point Lookout prison camp in Maryland. It was his second stint as a prisoner of war (he was captured earlier in the war at Fredericksburg). He was elected in 1866 to the state legislature from the Waycross district. His health broken by the war, Atkinson died in 1884 at the relatively young age of 49. His counterpart, W. B. Jones of the 60th Georgia, returned to the newspaper business in the Atlanta region, where he co-published *The Reporter* with Charles Willingham.[6]

Private Isaac G. Bradwell surrendered with the 31st Georgia at Appomattox. He moved to Alabama in 1878 and taught school for more than two decades. He was a longtime member of the United Confederate Veterans

6   Atkinson family records; Confederate service records.

and a prolific author of articles for *Confederate Veteran*. Gordon Bradwell died in December 1934 at the age of 92.

Major General Jubal A. Early continued to serve with passion. Commanding a small, independent army, he launched the Confederates' final incursion into the North in the summer of 1864, invading Maryland and threatening Washington. Delayed for a full day at Monocacy by Lew Wallace's Yankees, Early reached Washington's outer defenses on July 11. Reinforcements arrived in time to deter him from entering the city. His force came closer to Washington than any other formal body of Rebels. Briefly fleeing to Mexico after the Confederacy collapsed, Early returned to the reunited states to practice law. An ardent supporter of the "Lost Cause," he engaged in a series of bitter exchanges over Gettysburg in the press with James Longstreet. Old Jube, who never married or took the oath of allegiance, died March 2, 1894.

Lt. Colonel Elijah V. White and his 35th Battalion, Virginia Cavalry guarded Lee's flanks at Gettysburg, scouting and occasionally skirmishing with Yankee cavalry. After helping bury some of the dead, the Comanches returned to the Old Dominion, still facing two more years of hard service. They performed brilliantly as scouts and raiders, harassing enemy supply wagons and providing valuable military intelligence. When Lee surrendered at Appomattox Court House, White's men refused to capitulate. They rode away from the Army of Northern Virginia, carrying their colors with them. The Comanches disbanded in Leesburg.

With the war over, Lige White returned to his farm and founded a country store in Leesburg. He was elected as Loudon County sheriff in 1866. The Democrat operated a popular ferry on the Potomac River and owned a grain and farm supply company. In 1877, he became an elder in the Primitive Baptist Church, often preaching repentance. After the death of his first wife, he married the sister of a former Union colonel from Philadelphia. Later, White became president of People's National Bank of Leesburg. In 1906, surviving members of the battalion reunited at Brandy Station and exchanged war stories with their former commander. The Reverend E. V. White died from paralysis at his home on January 11, 1907. He is buried in Union Cemetery in Leesburg.

The Courtney Artillery fought at Gettysburg, duelling on July 1 with 19-year-old Lt. Bayard Wilkeson's Union battery on Blocher's Knoll. Captain William Tanner listed two of his Virginians as missing in action. His four Ordnance Rifles expended 595 rounds in Pennsylvania, including the forty shells fired at Wrightsville.

The Federals

Major Granville O. Haller learned in late July that he had been charged with disloyalty and dismissed from the service. While exchanging toasts in Haller's tent shortly after Fredericksburg, naval officer Clark Wells had accused Haller of making unpatriotic remarks, toasting separate Northern and Southern confederacies, at least while Lincoln was in office. Wells also charged that Haller directly blamed the president and his failed war policies for the slaughter at Fredericksburg. In response, Haller warned, "The day will come, I trust, when I can have this matter investigated by the Masonic Lodge in York, and your conduct sifted and stamped as it deserves."[7]

In August, in an effort to counter his dismissal, Haller pleaded with Secretary of War Stanton, "That I am or have ever been really disloyal in word or deed, is utterly and nakedly false. From the time I first entered the army, nearly twenty-four years ago, I have been true and faithful to my country, her government, her constitution, and her laws." To support his case, he solicited letters vouching for his recent military performance from Robert Bell, David McConaughy, Jacob Frick, and others. However, his appeal was denied, and he spent years trying to clear his name. Lieutenant Commander Wells slammed Haller's "utter incapacity, not to say treasonable conduct, while in command of the few brave militia of Pennsylvania during the invasion of that State by Lee." Before the year was over, the two exchanged public insults in a pair of widely circulated pamphlets.[8]

Each had his ardent supporters and equally vociferous opponents. A Philadelphia newspaper lamented Haller's dismissal as "the most pitiful exemplification of political malice and party spite… His is the highest of all crimes against the Administration—he is a Democrat, a friend of General George B. McClellan, of the Constitution as it is and the Union as it was." The angry editor a month later opined, "We have not words to express our utter detestation of his treatment." A Harrisburg correspondent deemed it "one of the grossest cases of injustice on the part of the administration."[9]

---

7   *Harrisburg Patriot and Union*, Dec. 3, 1863; Haller, *Dismissal of Major Granville O. Haller*, 19.

8   Haller, *Dismissal of Major Granville O. Haller*, 21; Wells, *The Reply to a Pamphlet Recently Published by G. O. Haller*, 12.

9   *Philadelphia Illustrated New Age*, Nov. 12 and Dec. 17, 1863; *Harrisburg Patriot and Union*, Dec. 3, 1863.

Major General Darius Couch wrote to Haller in August, "I was impressed with the energy, action and good judgment displayed by you at the time of the invasion. Without any organized force at the commencement of it, you, with the aid of loyal citizens of Gettysburg and vicinity, were enabled to make a show of resistance to the invaders, and keep this department, and therefore the General Government, well informed of rebel movements. Your services were valuable to the country. For this Department I express to you my thanks. You can leave to your children the proud heritage that when your State was threatened by the fearful calamity of rebel invasion you were among the very foremost of its defenders."[10]

Jacob Frick wrote to Haller in October, "You manifested great zeal in behalf of the best interests of the country, and was indefatigable in your efforts while aiding me to make such dispositions of my small force as would enable us to repel an attack of the rebel horde that marched against us from York. At no time did I hear you utter a disloyal word or sentiment. I believed then, as I believe now, that your activity and anxiety to thwart the enemy was prompted by the purest and most patriotic motives. Certainly no one of my command questioned for a moment your patriotism or your sincerity."[11]

Among the contrarians was Professor Michael Jacobs of Pennsylvania College: "But although Major Haller... seemed to be active and industrious, very little of any value was actually accomplished in that respect. Whether it was because of his incapacity for the position he held, or indifference as to the result, was a matter of conjecture. It is singular, however, that so soon after the utterance of the remark, that he would 'first fight the Rebels, but, after the war, the Administration,' should have followed his dismissal from the service 'for disloyal conduct, and the utterance of disloyal sentiments.'" Jacobs believed that because of Haller's repeated command failures "the golden opportunity for efficient preparation passed away." Nineteenth century historian Samuel P. Bates criticized Haller's attempt to defend Gettysburg, "His conduct of affairs was most unfortunate . . . a most suicidal policy."[12]

10 Darius N. Couch to Maj. Granville O. Haller, Aug. 13, 1863, cited in Haller, *Dismissal of Major Granville O. Haller*, 10.

11 Breshears, *Major Granville Haller: Dismissed with Malice*, 16.

12 Jacobs, *Notes on the Rebel Invasion*, 12-13; Samuel P. Bates, *The Battle of Gettysburg* (Philadelphia: T. H. Davis, 1875), 29.

In the spring of 1864 the frustrated Haller returned to the Washington Territory, where he engaged in several business ventures and served as treasurer of Island County. He used profits from potato farming to invest in real estate near Seattle. In the spring of 1873 Congressional friends convinced the Army to convene a court of inquiry. Haller's service had been "wholly and entirely satisfactory," testified Darius Couch, "I do not think that there were any of the fighting generals of the Army of the Potomac, if they had been in York, in the position of Major Haller, that could have done any better than he did. I thought so at the time, and I think so now." Colonel Levi Maish of the 130th Pennsylvania stated, "I know Major Haller to have been at that time active and industrious in communicating information to headquarters; arousing the people to the danger of the invasion, advising them to save their cattle, stock & etc. In many of these things I cooperated with him."[13]

The court exonerated Haller, and President Rutherford B. Hayes helped him secure the regular army rank of colonel. After his retirement in 1882, Haller relocated to Seattle and became prominent in the city's emerging business and social circles. He built a monolithic eighteen-room mansion, "Castlemount," in Seattle's fashionable First Hill neighborhood. After Granville Haller died on May 2, 1897, following a brief illness, the once-beautiful house eventually fell into disrepair. Shortly before World War II, work crews razed it.[14]

Of Haller's three emergency regiments that contested the Gordon expedition, Col. Jacob G. Frick's 27th Militia performed the best. Several officers and men were combat veterans of the 129th Pennsylvania and already familiar with one another. After Gordon's withdrawal from Wrightsville, they drew three days' rations in Columbia before returning to Harrisburg via train. Brigaded with the 31st PVM under Colonel Frick, they marched through

---

13 *New York Herald*, April 5 and June 29, 1879; Breshears, *Major Granville Haller: Dismissed with Malice*, 90. On cross-examination, Couch was asked; "Do you consider that your intercourse with Major Haller was of that familiar nature, during that time, that you could have discovered sentiments of disloyalty had they existed with him?" He answered: "I do not know how I can answer that question except by saying that I cannot conceive that a man could do what Major Haller did for the country and at the same time be disloyal." Haller was commissioned on December 11, 1879, to fill a Regular Army vacancy created by the death of Col. Jefferson C. Davis of the 23rd Infantry.

14 *Seattle Morning Olympian*, May 3, 1897. His obituary notice included this fitting epitaph: "Col. Haller was not only widely known, but was very highly respected by all." G. Morris, Haller's oldest son and a leading businessman, drowned in December 1889 along with two companions while on a duck-hunting canoe trip near Whidbey Island.

Carlisle and passed the smoking ruins of the military barracks. They subsequently entered Gettysburg, where they saw the debris of that battle. Later on its way to Chambersburg, the regiment marched by Thaddeus Stevens' burnt Caledonia Furnace, "destroyed with fiendish malignity" according to Lt. Francis Wallace. Turning southward, the 27th became the first Pennsylvania militia command to enter Maryland, pursuing Lee's rear guard. When no battle developed and Lee escaped into Virginia, Frick's soldiers returned to Harrisburg. After spending two weeks marching, losing three men to disease, the foot-weary regiment mustered out on July 31.

Jacob G. Frick returned to Pottsville and resumed his feud with his former division commander, Maj. Gen. A. A. Humphreys. He charged Humphreys with disloyalty, tyrannical conduct, and drunkenness. The following June, Frick assisted Lt. Col. Henry Pleasants in planning the explosives-filled, 230-foot-long tunnel under the Petersburg entrenchments, which resulted in the battle of the Crater. He remained interest in politics, serving as a delegate to the Republican National Convention in both 1860 and 1868. He remarried after the war, raised a son, authored two books, and manufactured wire screens for the coal mining industry. He had an interest in the Moorewood and Standard Coke-Works in Connellsville, Pennsylvania, and in February 1890 the Republican won election to a term as the chief burgess of Pottsville.[15]

In 1892, Frick received the Medal of Honor for his valor at Chancellorsville and Fredericksburg, but by then his health was failing. He was a "physical wreck" suffering from deafness and nervous prostration caused by injuries during the war when a Rebel shell burst near his head and an iron fragment perforated his ear drum. Six years later, fellow Medal of Honor winner Senator Matthew S. Quay introduced a bill in Congress to grant Frick a speedy government pension. J. G. Frick passed away from chronic heart disease at his home on March 5, 1902, and was buried in Pottsville's Presbyterian Cemetery. He was the first man in Schuylkill County to receive the Medal of Honor.[16]

Lieutenant Colonel William H. Sickles of the 20th Militia received widespread criticism for his inability to prevent White's raiders from seizing Hanover Junction and for his shameful surrender at Wrightsville. After being

15 *Boston Daily Advertiser*, Dec. 24, 1863; *Philadelphia Inquirer*, Feb. 4, 1889, and Feb. 19, 1890.

16 *Philadelphia Inquirer*, March 6, 1902, and March 3, 1989. His obituary read: "On June 28, 1863, he made himself famous by burning the Columbia bridge across the Susquehanna River, at Wrightsville, cutting off the Rebel invasion of Harrisburg."

paroled, Sickles used an overcrowded handcar on June 29 to return to York via a portion of the railroad tracks that had not been destroyed by Lige White. The star-crossed officer fell under the car and fractured one of his legs, completing a frustrating week. He recuperated at the Tremont House hotel in York before returning to Philadelphia, where he tried to put his best spin on his performance during the Gettysburg Campaign. His three companies of the 20th Militia eventually returned to York, where they reunited with Colonel Thomas and guarded York County in case of a Confederate breakthrough at Gettysburg.

The chagrined regiment marched in pursuit of Lee's retreating army. A special correspondent for the *Philadelphia Inquirer*, Samuel J. Rea, wrote on July 10 from Chambersburg, "Colonel Thomas, with his regiment, also looks familiar. Among them I meet many of my fellow townsmen. The officers and men express great anxiety to revenge, in a fair field, and against equal numbers, the Hanover Junction affair, where superior numbers drove them back." They would never get the chance to repay Elijah White for his raid on the junction. The 20th PVM mustered out in Harrisburg on August 10. Sickles was cashiered from the army after Colonel Frick's scathing criticism in his official report to Darius Couch. Frick wrote of Sickles' incompetence: "From information received since the engagement, I feel convinced that if my orders had been promptly obeyed, no prisoners would have been taken."[17]

Splintered by Early's June 26 attack at Gettysburg, one company of Col. William W. Jennings' 26th Militia had accompanied Granville Haller to Wrightsville while the bulk retired to Harrisburg. Jennings continued to look for a way to rendezvous with Haller, sending a soldier to Hanover to telegraph Couch for railcars to transport the regiment. Later, he dispatched Lt. Col. Joseph Jenkins to York to locate Haller, but he arrived after the Rebels had occupied the town. After spending 54 of 60 hours walking after leaving Henry Witmer's farm, Jennings' demoralized band finally arrived in the state capital about 2 p.m. on Sunday, July 28. Some of his parolees also arrived that day, after being captured by Rebels a second time when they encountered Ewell's soldiers near Carlisle. Private John Casler of the famed "Stonewall Brigade" later wrote, "We met the paroled prisoners that Early had captured… General [Edward] Johnson made them pull off their shoes and give them to his men who were barefooted. Some of our men thought this was cruel, but Johnson said they

17 *York Gazette*, June 30, 1863; *Philadelphia Inquirer*, July 15, 1863; OR 27, pt. 2, 279. Frick did not include Bell's cavalryman in his total. Early reported paroling 19 men.

were going home and could get other shoes quicker than he could, as he had work for his men to do."[18] Within a few days, Captain Walker's detachment left Columbia and rejoined the regiment, which was formally mustered out of service on July 31.[19]

Colonel Jennings, despite his feud with Granville Haller over the propriety of his raw militia engaging the veteran Rebels at Gettysburg, maintained the loyalty of most of his men for the rest of his life. Samuel Pennypacker wrote that Jennings "was a fine looking man of about twenty-eight years of age... Everyone liked him, because he understood his business, acted toward his men as an officer should, and from former experience, knew how to take care of them. I never heard a single word of complaint against him, and I think he possessed the respect of every man in the regiment. On more than one occasion, he exhibited considerable military ability." Concerning the June 26 skirmishing, he opined, "I believe Colonel Jennings deserves the highest praise not only for having adopted the sole proper course of action but for the dexterity with which it was conducted."[20]

After mustering out, Jennings returned to his Harrisburg iron business, amassing significant local political and social clout. He was elected sheriff of Dauphin County for two terms and served as president of several business and civic organizations, including two banks, a railroad, a steam heating company, and several others. Jennings died of heart disease on February 28, 1894, at the age of 56, leaving his widow Emma and four adult children.[21]

Some of Jennings' emergency militiamen rose to prominence after the war. Samuel W. Pennypacker became a powerful Republican lawyer and judge. The president of the Historical Society of Pennsylvania, he was a prolific writer before being elected governor of Pennsylvania in 1902. His collection of seven thousand books on early Pennsylvania included 260 from Benjamin Franklin's printing press. He died on September 1, 1916. Drummer boy Henry M. M. Richards served in the 195th Pennsylvania in 1864, and then enlisted in the navy as a midshipman after the war, serving until 1874. He served in the Spanish-American War and became a well-known author and engineer. During

---

18 John O. Casler, *Four Years in the Stonewall Brigade* (Dayton, Ohio: Morningside Bookshop, 1971).

19 Richards, *Pennsylvania's Emergency Men at Gettysburg*, 12; *Philadelphia Press*, June 29, 1863.

20 Pennypacker, "Six Weeks in Uniform," 327.

21 *Baltimore Sun*, March 1, 1894; *Philadelphia Inquirer*, March 2, 1894.

World War I, he invented an electrical circuit closer for torpedoes that became a mainstay of the U.S. Navy during the Second World War. He wrote eight books and applied for several patents. Richards died in his native Easton on September 28, 1935, at the age of 87.

Major General Darius N. Couch retained command of the Department of the Susquehanna for another year, overseeing the defense of Chambersburg when John McCausland's Southern cavalry burned the town. Couch's 25-year-old son, Robert, died in the battle of Cold Harbor and his body was never identified. Transferring to the Western Theater in December 1864, Couch returned to field command, leading a division of the Twenty-third Corps in the battle of Nashville. He finished the war in the Carolinas, a well-respected and much-traveled officer. When the war ended, Couch resigned from the army and entered politics, unsuccessfully running for governor of Massachusetts in 1865. The Democrat became the port collector of Boston, and later, the adjutant general of Connecticut. Couch died in Norwalk, Connecticut, on February 12, 1897, at the age of 75.

Cavalry commander Maj. Charles M. Knox's health was broken by the Gettysburg Campaign, and he received a medical discharge in October 1863. The 1860 graduate of Columbia Law School moved to Springfield, Massachusetts, in 1868 and rose to vice-president of the Massachusetts Mutual Life Insurance Company. Ten years later he resigned because of health issues and philosophical differences, and subsequently worked for the Philadelphia Mutual Insurance Company. He managed their New York City office for several years before retiring to Long Island. Knox died in 1894 at Patchogue, New York, at the age of 56. His obituary described him as "an energetic businessman, positive in his ideas, and well liked by all who came in contact with him." He left a widow and two children.[22]

The Adams County Cavalry elicited the thanks of several Columbians. In mid-July Mrs. John P. Staman and some friends sent "a large box of superb provisions" to Gettysburg for the scouts to enjoy. They had camped in the vicinity of the Staman place while in Lancaster County. Captain Robert Bell stayed in the service and rose to major of the 21st Pennsylvania Cavalry by the end of the war. He returned to Gettysburg, and he and his wife Abigail raised eight children. He joined the board of directors of the First National Bank, being promoted to cashier in 1875. Bell became active in early efforts to

---

22 *Springfield Republican*, Feb. 21, 1894.

preserve and memorialize the battlefield and served on the board of the Gettysburg Battlefield Memorial Association in the 1880s. He died in late June 1904 and was buried in nearby Hunterstown.[23]

The First Troop, Philadelphia City Cavalry remained in Columbia as provosts until July 4, when most of the troopers left for Harrisburg. Sergeant Robert Randall and a 21-man detail had ferried across the Susquehanna on July 2 to collect Rebel fugitives and worn-out horses. They managed to avoid a direct confrontation with J. E. B. Stuart's cavalry, spending a restless evening hiding in a Heidlersburg cemetery as Confederates rode by. According to Jones Wister, they "traversed the beautiful valley near Hanover and York, sleeping in the open. This was anything but agreeable," especially after their comfortable stays in leading hotels. On July 3, four troopers escorted several Rebel prisoners to Fort Delaware. The next day, in a drenching rainstorm, Capt. Samuel Randall led the Troop to Harrisburg, where his brother's detachment soon rejoined the company. With angry crowds in Philadelphia threatening a riot to oppose Lincoln's recent order for a military draft, the cavalrymen returned home on July 15. Major General George Cadwalader relieved them from active duty on July 31 and later gave a speech at a banquet honoring their recent service.[24]

Their relationship with Columbia's townspeople remained strained for years. In 1884, the *Columbia Spy* sneered, "Contrary to military usage, the Troop led the retreat, and was among the first to reach the Columbia shore. Many of the older citizens still laugh at the ludicrous figure the troopers of 1863 cut in the streets of Columbia, and some get angry yet over the recital of their impudent conduct and imperious demands made upon the citizens." The Troop became associated with the National Guard and was activated again during the Spanish-American War. In the early 21st century, it served as peacekeepers in Bosnia.[25]

After the war, Democrat Samuel J. Randall endorsed allowing former Confederates to hold office again. Among his harshest critics was staunch

23 *Columbia Spy*, July 25, 1863; *Philadelphia Inquirer*, June 28, 1904. Bell's obituary deemed him "one of Adams County's oldest and best-known citizens." Many old comrades from throughout the state came for his funeral.

24 Wister, *Reminiscences*, 163; *History of the First Troop*, 77-79. Newspaper accounts indicate that Randall's patrol, along with Bell's Cavalry, rounded up one hundred stray mules and horses, presumably left behind by Stuart's cavalry, and herded them to the York fairgrounds where their owners could claim them.

25 *Columbia Spy*, Aug. 9, 1884, and Jan. 16, 1886.

Republican Jacob G. Frick, who wrote, "I desire to say that I do not train in your crowd, and therefore do not sympathize in the object of your convention. I fought in this war against treason and traitors, and I do not feel now like ignoring the past and helping Copperheads and Republican traitors to place these same men in power again where they can make laws for me, and crack the whip of slavery over the free people of the North." Randall became a prominent statesman and national politician, serving as speaker of the U.S. House of Representatives. He twice ran for the Democratic presidential nomination, losing first to Gettysburg hero Winfield S. Hancock in 1880 and then to Grover Cleveland in 1884. Randall died in Washington in April 1890, while still serving his country as a congressman.[26]

First City Trooper Jones Wister profited from a series of business ventures with his five brothers. He became noted as "the father of American cricket," promoting the British sport throughout the North. After his first wife died, he remarried and raised a second family. He traveled extensively across the world and enjoyed fishing excursions in exotic locations. In June of 1916, trying to revolutionize trench warfare, he patented a rifle that could shoot around corners, with a curved barrel and a periscope sight. Wister suddenly died in Chicago on September 1, 1917, while returning to Philadelphia from a lengthy vacation in California. His unexpected death at the age of seventy-eight stunned his wife and friends, because he was in excellent health and "despite his advanced age, he was a very active man."[27]

In October 1863, 20-year-old Persifor Frazer, Jr., became an acting ensign in the U.S. Navy. He surveyed Charleston Harbor in preparation for the celebrated attack on Fort Wagner. He served in the Mississippi Squadron until the end of the war, rising to command of the gunboat USS *Hastings* despite his youth. He later became an internationally famous geologist, as well as a chemistry professor at the University of Pennsylvania and the Franklin Institute. Frazer was an early advocate of cremating the dead, and he pioneered the use of handwriting analysis to detect forgeries. The celebrated scientist and prolific author died on April 7, 1909, at the age of 64.[28]

26 *Wellsboro* (Pa.) *Agitator*, Aug. 1, 1866.

27 *Philadelphia Inquirer*, Sept. 1, 1917.

28 Ethan Allen Weaver, ed., *Annual Proceedings, Sons of the Revolution, Pennsylvania Society 1909-1910* (Philadelphia, 1910), 44; Persifor Frazer, *The Franklin Institute: Its Services and Deserts* (Philadelphia: The Franklin Institute, 1908), 297.

The York Invalids were ferried across the river to Wrightsville, and, "by easy stages," marched back to York, collecting Rebel stragglers along the way. According to one convalescent, the people of York "were not of the Union loving kind." Now, after Jubal Early's forced levies, "If they did not relish the blue before, they did now, and we were heartily welcomed." The Invalids returned to the military hospital as orderlies and stewards for Dr. Henry Palmer. Hundreds of wounded soldiers from Gettysburg soon joined them. The badly wounded men taken to Columbia before Early's occupation of York stayed there for months before returning to the hospital once it emptied of the Gettysburg victims. Several of the invalids again served in the field in 1864 when Confederate Brig. Gen. John McCausland raided Franklin County and burned Chambersburg. Major Palmer mustered out in October 1865 and returned to southern Wisconsin, where he was prominent in medical circles until his death in 1895.[29]

The Patapsco Guards remained in the Department of the Susquehanna for the duration of the war. On July 7, they marched from their rifle-pits in Bainbridge back to York but did not stay long. They were dispatched to guard Camp Letterman, Gettysburg's temporary field hospital, until Christmas. Couch later assigned the Marylanders as provost guards in Harrisburg and Chambersburg, where they often escorted wounded Confederate prisoners to points of exchange. They helped defend Chambersburg in 1864, skirmishing on July 30 with McCausland's Rebel cavalry. The Patapsco Guards mustered out on August 17, 1865.

The Columbia company of blacks dispersed, with most returning to their jobs at Case's rolling mill. Some of the men joined regiments of U.S. Colored Troops and again faced Confederate bullets. Among them was 15-year-old John Aquilla Wilson, who lived to be 101, the last survivor of Wrightsville's black defenders.

The Civilians

Gettysburg residents Sallie and Joseph Broadhead eventually returned to their native New Jersey, where Joe entered the coal business. When he died in 1903, Sallie returned to Pennsylvania, living with her daughter Macy in the town of Ruthmill. She died May 23, 1910, and was buried in Pleasantville, New Jersey.

---

29 Wray, *History of the Twenty-third Pennsylvania*, 152.

Young Tillie Pierce married attorney Horace Alleman in 1871 and moved to Selinsgrove, Pennsylvania. The couple had three children. Tillie died in 1914.

Arthur Briggs Farquhar, the audacious York businessman who took the initiative to negotiate with John Gordon, volunteered in the Gettysburg hospitals, tending the wounded. He met with a mixed reaction when he returned to York, several townspeople mockingly calling him a Rebel and a traitor. Shortly after Gettysburg, he visited Abraham Lincoln in Washington. Squeezing Farquhar's hand, the president introduced him to his Secretary of War. Lincoln teased, "Stanton, I have captured the young chap who sold York, Pennsylvania to the Rebels. What are we going to do with him?"[30]

Farquhar achieved his dream of becoming a millionaire when his farm implement company prospered, allowing him to venture into other successful businesses. His threshing machines were widely touted as major advances in the science of agriculture, and Farquhar filed for several patents. He advised several presidents on labor relations and led manufacturing's fight against labor unions and the implementation of a mandatory eight-hour workday. In 1894, the Democrat bought a local York newspaper and, to the chagrin of local ministers, began publishing one of the areas' first Sunday editions.

Farquhar, fellow millionaire Michael Schall (Jones Wister's friend), and W. Latimer Small had three of the first six telephones installed in York. In 1922, Farquhar published his autobiography, appropriately titled *The First Million: The Hardest*. The octogenarian died on March 5, 1925, weakened from injuries suffered when an automobile struck him. In 1952, his company was sold to the Oliver Farm Equipment Company. After White Farm Equipment acquired Oliver in 1961, manufacturing under the name A. B. Farquhar ceased, after nearly 100 years of commercial success.

York resident Cassandra Morris Small, whose letters vividly chronicled Gordon's march through town, married Dr. Alexander Blair of the General Military Hospital in 1864. She spent many years as a Sunday School teacher in York's Presbyterian church. Small died in 1891 at the age of 62.

Wrightsville heroine Mary Jane Rewalt stayed at her parents' home when her husband returned to the army for two additional stints. She bore five children, and the Rewalts lived in Wrightsville for decades, except for a brief period when Luther set up practice in Philadelphia. In 1875, after James Magee passed away, Mary Jane inherited the three-story house where she once had

30 Farquhar, *The First Million*, 83.

entertained John Gordon. Dr. Rewalt became the surgeon of the Grand Army of the Republic post at Wrightsville and was elected to the local school board. In 1886, the Rewalts sold the Magee house and moved to Fulda, Minnesota; later they moved to Madison, South Dakota. John Gordon, by now a nationally known public speaker, was scheduled to appear in Madison on July 20, 1895. There, the venerable Rebel was surprised to meet Mary Jane Rewalt again.[31]

Hanover Junction

The *New York Tribune* had sent senior war correspondent A. Homer Byington to cover the story of the Confederate invasion. Finding Gettysburg's and then Hanover's telegraphs inoperable, he headed to Hanover Junction. Young apprentice John Shearer spent Sunday, June 28, with fellow telegrapher Daniel Trone, Byington, an unnamed Hanover Branch Railroad engineer, and Joseph Leib, the freight and passenger agent. The quintet inspected the broken track, ruined bridges, and downed telegraph wires in the direction of Hanover. They found that White's Confederates had destroyed two small bridges on the Hanover Branch Railroad and damaged another one.

By Monday night, Shearer and other railroaders sent to assist him had repaired the downed wires and poles. In short order, the apprentice resumed relaying military messages from various communications centers. Dispatching news stories from Hanover with Daniel Trone's help on July 2, Byington became one of the first correspondents to report on the battle at Gettysburg.

J. E. B. Stuart's Confederate cavalry filed into York County on Tuesday, June 30. They unexpectedly encountered Brig. Gen. Judson Kilpatrick, his subordinate George Armstrong Custer, and their Federal cavalry in a pitched battle that raged through the streets of Hanover. Stuart retired, taking a circuitous route through Jefferson, stealing horses and whiskey along the way. The approach of Rebel cavalry again sent panic through the already jolted residents of the region. Stuart and his principal officers paused at the house of wealthy farmer John E. Ziegler before riding through the night to Dover.

On July 4, crews from the U.S. Military Railroad repaired the burnt Codorus Creek bridge at Hanover Junction, as well as other nearby bridges and trestles. Approximately 7,600 Union and 3,800 Confederate soldiers wounded at Gettysburg were processed through Hanover Junction from July 7 to July 22,

31 Gordon file, YCHT.

enroute to hospitals in York, Harrisburg, Philadelphia, and Baltimore. Heavy rains between July 12 and 14 caused flooding, which washed away several of Brig. Gen. Herman Haupt's temporary bridges on the Northern Central, including that at Hanover Junction. This time, the railroad footed the entire bill for the five-day repair effort. In November, while traveling to and from Gettysburg, President Abraham Lincoln changed trains at Hanover Junction. He planned to make a short address at the dedication of the new National Cemetery on the battlefield.[32]

Telegraph apprentice John Shearer was promoted to operator and transferred to Baltimore, missing Lincoln's visit to Gettysburg. He remained with the Northern Central Railway and its successors, taking on other assignments in Elmira, New York. Shearer died at his home in 1935 at the age of 88. His obituary praised his service in restoring telegraph service after Elijah White's raid.[33]

The Columbia Bridge

Controversy fired up almost immediately. The long-time cashier of the Columbia Bank, Samuel Schoch, officially confirmed the bridge's destruction at the start of business on Monday, June 29. In his report, he elaborated that United States military authorities burned it to prevent the Rebels from crossing the Susquehanna River. The board of directors authorized Schoch to retain counsel to sue the Federal government if needed, and they set the value of the lost bridge at $150,000.[34]

On July 2, as Jubal Early prepared to assault Cemetery Hill, the bank appointed artillery Capt. E. K. Smith and businessman Hugh North to "confer with Colonel Frick, relative to the iron and timber remaining after the destruction of the bridge." On July 8, the Lancaster Daily Examiner reported that the bridge's destruction "has given rise to a rumor that its loss would have the effect of impairing the credit of the Columbia Bank." Seeking to avoid a run on the bank's reserves, officials reminded people that the "the government [is] responsible for all loss" when destruction was ordered by the military, citing an

---

32 *OR* 27, pt. 1, 22-23; Files of YCHT.

33 Hanover Junction file, YCHT.

34 *Lancaster Express*, June 30, 1863.

1849 law. By the end of the month, the bank had solicited sworn statements from Robert Crane, John Q. Denney, and others directly involved in the bridge affair.[35]

Smith and North traveled to Washington and met with Secretary of War Edwin Stanton to discuss the damage claim. No cash was forthcoming, so, on December 15, the Columbia Bank sold the piers and abutments to the Pennsylvania Railroad for $57,000, recovering a third of its loss. The bank sold additional property in 1864 and filed formal claims with the government. Republican Congressman John Scott took up the cause in 1871, presenting "a petition of citizens of the borough of Wrightsville, Pennsylvania, praying for compensation for losses sustained in consequence of the burning of the Columbia bridge during the war for the suppression of the rebellion." The matter was referred to the Committee on Claims, which failed to approve the requested funding. Scott and a succession of other politicians carried the fight well into the 20th century, albeit unsuccessfully.[36]

For five years after the destruction of the bridge, ferryboats again became the primary public transportation when ice did not block the Susquehanna. During the winter, residents often trekked across the ice on foot, while enterprising merchants used sleighs to transport heavy loads of freight between the river towns. Wrightsville lumber dealer John Stoner Beidler walked across the ice to Columbia to buy a $94 sewing machine for his wife, and then paid two dollars to have two men carry it back.[37]

In 1868, the Columbia Bridge Company began erecting a new bridge on the same piers as the previous span. This one contained two large iron spans, connected in the middle, meant to be fire-resistant. The Pennsylvania Railroad bought the Wrightsville, York, and Gettysburg line in 1870 and then purchased this third bridge in 1879. A severe windstorm destroyed the structure on September 30, 1896. Within twenty-nine days, prefabricated iron truss spans were erected on the piers and it reopened in 1897. In 1964, with rail service no longer needed between Wrightsville and Columbia, this bridge was demolished. All but two of the original twenty-seven stone piers still stand today. Ice, fire,

35 Goodell, "The Second Columbia Bridge," 15; CHPS.

36 Prowell, *History of York County*, 1, 930; *Congressional Globe*, Dec. 15, 1871; *Columbia Spy*, Feb. 20, 1886.

37 John Stoner Beidler diary entry for Jan. 25, 1865, YCHT.

wind, and finally the wrecking ball—the four bridges had a history of destruction.[38]

Two modern viaducts now flank the piers of the wooden bridge, burned so long ago. Each day, thousands of motorists pass by, unaware of the story of that rainy June evening in 1863 when flames brilliantly illuminated the sky over the Susquehanna River.

38 *Baltimore Sun*, Oct. 2, 1896. The paper reported, "The damage to York city and York county by yesterday's cyclone is now estimated at one million dollars. Hardly one farm in the whole one thousand square miles of territory escaped. The heaviest loss reported was the destruction of the Pennsylvania Railroad's frame bridge that spanned the Susquehanna River at Wrightsville. The bridge was built in 1868 and cost $300,000. It was lifted bodily from the piers and blown into the river. The structure was over a mile long. No lives were lost when the bridge collapsed. All passengers and baggage are being transported by ferry."

Appendix A

Order of Battle: Wrightsville

CONFEDERATE

Elements of the Army of Northern Virginia,
Ewell's Second Corps[1]

Elements of Early's Division: Maj. Gen. Jubal Anderson Early
(Near York at the start of Gordon's advance, arrived in Wrightsville around dusk)

Gordon's Brigade (1,813 men): Brig. Gen. John Brown Gordon

13th Georgia: Col. James Milton Smith (312 men)
26th Georgia: Col. Edmund Nathan Atkinson (315 men)
31st Georgia: Col. Clement Anselm Evans (252 men)
38th Georgia: Capt. William L. McLeod (341 men)
60th Georgia: Capt. Waters Burrus Jones (299 men)
61st Georgia: Col. John Hill Lamar (288 men)

1   Confederate strength estimates are from Busey and Martin, *Regimental Strengths and Losses at Gettysburg*, 286.

Elements of Division Artillery

Courtney (Va.) Artillery: Capt. William A. Tanner
(four 3-inch Ordnance Rifles, 90 men)

Cavalry Escort

35th Battalion, Virginia Cavalry: Lt. Col. Elijah Veirs White (276 men)[2]
17th Virginia Cavalry, Company C: Capt. Thaddeus P. Waldo (~40 men)

*   *   *

UNION

Elements of the Department of the Susquehanna[3]

Columbia / Wrightsville defensive force: Col. Jacob G. Frick[4]

27th Pennsylvania Volunteer Militia: Frick (650 men)
Columbia company, "Negro volunteers" (53 men)
Columbia artillery: Lt. Delaplaine J. Ridgway
(two 12-pound smoothbore Napoleons and one 3-inch Ordnance Rifle,
estimated at 80-90 members of the 27th Militia and private citizens under
Capt. E. K. Smith manning the guns on the Columbia riverbank).

2   Duty roster. Only a portion was at Wrightsville. The rest were scouting, destroying the railroad, or camping two miles east of York.

3   Union estimates are from the Official Records, newspaper accounts, and regimental records.

4   Frick reported far more members of the First City Troop than were present on June 28. Many joined the troop on June 29 and 30.

Adams County / York County defensive forces:
Maj. Granville Owen Haller

Right flank: Lt. Col. William H. Sickles

20th Pennsylvania Volunteer Militia, Companies B, F, and H (200 men)

Left flank: Lt. Col. David B. Green (27th Militia)

York Battalion: Patapsco (MD) Guards (60 men)
Elements of the 87th Pennsylvania, York Military Hospital Invalids,
and private citizens (238 men)
Bridge guard: Capt. Christopher Wilson Walker
26th Pennsylvania Volunteer Militia, commissary guard (50 men)

Cavalry: Maj. Charles McLean Knox, Jr.
First Troop, Philadelphia City Cavalry: Capt. Samuel Jackson Randall (45 men)
Adams County Independent Cavalry: Capt. Robert Bell (60 men)
Lancaster County Scouts: Capt. Matthew M. Strickler
("a small number of cavalry" according to Frick)

Appendix B

Casualties and Losses at Wrightsville

UNION

- Unknown black volunteer reported by newspapers as being decapitated. Confederate accounts suggest that a body was found in the trenches and buried by citizens.

- Captain Robert G. March, Company B, 20th Militia, wounded in the left leg and arm. He had been colonel of the 4th Pennsylvania Reserves, resigning October 1, 1861, before enrolling in the militia on June 18, 1863.

- Nine wounded soldiers of the 27th Militia:

  Pvt. Max Silverberg, Co. B: slightly wounded in breast

  Pvt. Terrence F. Smith, Co. B –slightly bruised in leg

  Cpl. Henry Reichert, Co. C: slightly wounded in hip by a shell fragment

  Cpl. Michael J. Thomas, Co. C: slightly wounded in neck by a shell fragment. (He suffered pain and discomfort the rest of his life.)

  Pvt. Henry Matthews, Co. C: slightly wounded in the hand by a shell fragment

  Sgt. Henry Brindle, Co. F: trampled by a horse

  Sgt. Joseph Fitzgerald, Co. F: injured by a fall

  Pvt. Allen D. Mohr, Co. H: bayonet wound, right hand

  Pvt. Aaron Tice, Co. H.: slightly wounded in thigh by a shell fragment

- Unknown member, Bell's Cavalry, wounded and captured by Confederates. Paroled June 29 in York.

- Lieutenant Colonel William H. Sickles, 20th Militia, captured along with seventeen of his men (some accounts say twenty prisoners). Paroled June 29 in York and returned to Columbia.

- Two companies of the 20th Militia who fled throughout Lancaster County.

- Corporal Charles H. Voute, Company B, 27th Militia, collapsed with severe heart palpitations shortly after retreating across the bridge.

- Ashbel Lane, a child severely wounded by a shell explosion shortly after the battle.

- Two children of John Shenberger, 6-year-old Caroline and 8-year-old William, who were mortally injured in March 1866 by a Confederate shell taken from Wrightsville. They were playing with the old relic when it rolled into their fireplace and soon exploded.

- The second Columbia Bridge.

CONFEDERATE

- Private C. C. Smith, Company H, "The Bartow Invincibles," 60th Georgia, gunshot wound to the right thigh.

- Unknown number of deserters and stragglers. Private John B. Ludlaw, Company A, 31st Georgia, was among those listed as captured and transported to Columbia on July 1.

- Any hope of capturing Lancaster and investing Harrisburg from the rear.

Appendix C

The Weather during Gordon's Expedition

The Reverend Dr. Michael Jacobs was Professor of Mathematics and Science at Pennsylvania College during the Confederate invasion. He enjoyed meteorology, and kept meticulous notes on the weather at Gettysburg beginning in 1839. These provide an unusually detailed record of the atmospheric conditions encountered by Gordon and Haller's soldiers during the last week of June 1863:

> The entire period of the invasion is remarkable for being one of clouds, and, for that season of the year, of low temperature. From June 15th until July 22nd, 1863, there was not an entirely clear day. On the evening of June 25th at 8 p.m. a rain began… This rain continued at intervals until Saturday June 27th, at 7 a.m., the perception being in inches 1.280. At all the observations made on Saturday and Sunday, and until the nine o'clock observation of Monday night, the entire sky was covered with clouds.[5]

As Lee's Army of Northern Virginia broke camp and marched into the Shenandoah Valley, it did so under a full moon. There was virtually no moon when Early and Johnson's divisions of Ewell's Second Corps reached Winchester. As John Gordon began his march through Adams and York counties, the moon began to wax, reaching full moon status on July 1 during the Battle of Gettysburg.

---

5   Gettysburg College, Musselman Library, Michael Jacobs papers.

Temperatures (°F) at Gettysburg			
1863	7 a.m.	2 p.m.	9 p.m.
Thursday, June 25	59	51	63
Friday, June 26	60	63	62
Saturday, June 27	61	63	67
Sunday, June 28	63	67	68
Monday, June 29	66	72	69
Tuesday, June 30	68	79	71

Appendix D

Chronology

June 3: McLaws' Division of the Confederate Army of Northern Virginia departs Fredericksburg, Virginia, heading northwest to Culpeper. Gordon's Brigade rests in camp at Hamilton's Crossing.

June 4: Rodes' Division of Ewell's Corps moves out. Union observation balloonists spot it and alert Federal commander Hooker that the Confederate army is on the move. Gordon packs his supply wagons and breaks camp.

June 5: The remainder of Ewell's Corps leaves camp. Union balloonists observe them leaving Fredericksburg and alert Washington. At 1 a.m., Gordon leaves Hamilton's Crossing under the cover of darkness. His brigade marches 16 miles in heavy dust past Spotsylvania Courthouse to Gordonsville.

June 6: Union forces demonstrate at Fredericksburg. Gordon stays in camp in a driving rain, ready to countermarch in case of a strong Yankee attack. It does not come.

June 7: Hooker sets his cavalry in motion. Gordon marches toward Culpeper Court House, wading across the Rapidan River at Raccoon Ford.

June 8: Lee reviews Stuart's cavalry near Culpeper. Gordon has a short march of only two miles through Culpeper Court House, camping two miles beyond.

June 9: Federal cavalry surprises Stuart at Brandy Station; bitter fighting ends in a tactical draw. About 3 p.m., Gordon marches at quick time to reinforce Stuart, but arrives after Union forces had retired. Gordon camps on the battlefield. The U.S. War Department creates two new departments to guide the defensive measures. The Department of the Susquehanna, headquartered in Harrisburg, accounts for south-central Pennsylvania.

June 10: Darius Couch is assigned to command the Department of the Susquehanna. Gordon returns to his camp near Culpeper Court House. Other elements of Ewell's Corps leave Culpeper, entering the Shenandoah Valley.

June 11: Couch arrives in Harrisburg. Hooker gets a portion of his infantry in motion, chasing Lee, who has a significant head start. Most of the Army of the Potomac sits in camp awaiting orders to move. Gordon marches north through Sperryville, Virginia, and camps three miles beyond Little Washington, passing through streets lined with ladies serving cold water to the tired soldiers.

June 12: Gordon enters the Shenandoah Valley at Chester Gap in the Blue Ridge Mountains. His brigade marches northward, arriving at Front Royal about 8 p.m. and camping just east of the South Branch of the Shenandoah River.

June 13: Two of Ewell's divisions (Early and Johnson) approach Winchester, guarded by Robert Milroy's Yankees. Initial Confederate attacks force Milroy to concentrate his forces. Couch has 250 men in uniform in the entire 34,000-square-mile Department of the Susquehanna. He requisitions 10,000 rifles and 1,000,000 rounds of ammunition, planning to raise militia. The arms are instead sent to Pittsburgh.

June 14: Early and Johnson crush Milroy at Winchester, forcing him to retire toward Harpers Ferry. Gordon makes a spirited bayonet charge, losing seventy-five men. Rodes passes through western Maryland and approaches Pennsylvania. Refugees start flooding into Franklin County ahead of the Confederates. Hooker finally moves the rest of his army when Rebels are scant miles from Pennsylvania. Central Pennsylvania counties start raising home guard companies. Governor Curtin calls on free blacks to rally around the state flag. Couch fortifies Harrisburg and orders artillery from the War Department. None is sent.

June 15: Early pursues Milroy and cuts him off, forcing thousands of Yankees to surrender. Confederate advance cavalry scouts enter southern Pennsylvania. A. G. Jenkins' mounted infantry brigade occupies positions just north of Chambersburg. Lincoln calls for 100,000 men from Pennsylvania, Ohio, Maryland, and West Virginia to serve for up to 6 months to meet the Confederate threat. Curtin calls for 50,000 Pennsylvanians for six months. There is little response. Couch reports that "there are less than 250 organized men" in the Department of the Susquehanna.

June 16: Chambersburg is still in Jenkins' hands. Wagonloads of supplies are procured and sent south, including blacks into slavery. Gordon remains near Winchester. The First Troop, Philadelphia City Cavalry passes a resolution to volunteer its services. Couch orders Maj. Charles Haldeman to raise troops to defend Columbia and Col. Emlen Franklin to recruit volunteers to protect the Columbia Bridge. Students from two Lancaster County colleges are among the first to respond.

June 17: Cavalry battles are fought at Aldie and Middleburg. Jenkins' horsemen retire from Chambersburg to Maryland. Gordon marches to Shepherdstown on the Potomac River and prepares to enter Maryland. White's cavalry cross the Potomac near Point of Rocks and raid telegraph and rail lines. The 20th Pennsylvania Volunteer Militia is organized in Harrisburg under Col. William Thomas. The Patapsco Guards move from York to Shippensburg. Couch assigns Maj. Granville Haller to organize the defenses of Adams and York counties. The railroad constructs cursory earthworks at Wrightsville to protect the Columbia-Wrightsville Bridge. The Lancaster County college companies receive weapons and march to Columbia.

June 18: The collegians dig rifle-pits west of Wrightsville. Haller heads to Wrightsville to inspect the defenses and then travels in the evening to Gettysburg. Fighting ends at Middleburg, and Union cavalry is repulsed. Gordon rests at Shepherdstown. White returns to his Virginia camp after sacking the B&O railroad depot at Point of Rocks.

June 19: Longstreet's corps enters the Shenandoah Valley and heads north. Hooker's Army of the Potomac halts for six days, allowing Lee to further increase the gap between his army and the Yankees. Gordon rests at Shepherdstown. A group of Gettysburg civilians travel to Harrisburg to enlist. They will later become Company A of the 27th Pennsylvania Volunteer Militia.

June 20: Imboden's Southern cavalrymen enter the Bedford Valley, threatening the Baltimore & Ohio Railroad. Workers begin to remove rolling stock across the Susquehanna toward Philadelphia. Gordon is still at Shepherdstown. Fort Case is completed in Columbia. Engineers stake out more earthworks in Wrightsville near the rifle-pits. Couch reports that he has 499 men in Harrisburg, 419 in York, and 403 in Philadelphia. Ewell is approaching with 22,000 soldiers. Haller swears Bell's Cavalry into state service.

June 21: A cavalry battle occurs at Upperville, Virginia, as Lee continues northward. Federal cavalry still cannot penetrate the Rebel screen and the exact locations of Lee's divisions are uncertain. Gordon stays at Shepherdstown. His brigade cannot cross the Potomac, swollen from recent heavy rains. Robert Bell's Adams County Cavalry is organized. The First City Troop arrives in Gettysburg. An American flag is raised over Columbia's Fort Case, and the workers are treated to an ox-roast.

June 22: Gordon crosses the Potomac at Shepherdstown and enters Maryland, passing by portions of the old Sharpsburg battlefield. William French's 17th Virginia Cavalry joins Early near Hagerstown, Maryland. Rodes enters Greencastle about 12:30 p.m., the first Confederate infantry to march into Pennsylvania. Jenkins skirmishes with New York cavalry, killing a corporal. Jenkins retakes Chambersburg as Yankees withdraw to Harrisburg. The 26th and 27th Militia regiments are organized in Harrisburg under colonels William Jennings and Jacob Frick. Haller sends civilians west of Gettysburg to fell trees to block mountain passes. Rebels fire on them.

June 23: Stuart starts his ride around Hooker's army. Gordon enters Pennsylvania, camping near Waynesboro. The 26th and 27th Militia drill near Harrisburg. Jenkins reaches Shippensburg and spends two days collecting "badly needed drugs and food." White crosses the Potomac at Shepherdstown.

June 24: Rumors reach Harrisburg that Ewell is approaching with 30,000 soldiers. Rodes enters Chambersburg. White's cavalry enter Pennsylvania and report to Ewell. Early and Gordon march through Quincy and Altodale, camping near Greenwood at the western base of South Mountain. Jennings' 26th Militia entrains for Gettysburg. Delayed by a railroad accident, they camp six miles from Gettysburg at Swift Run Hill. Frick moves to Columbia and sends four companies to the Wrightsville defenses. He sends the Lancaster County volunteers home, including the college contingent.

June 25: Rebel patrols secure critical South Mountain passes. Gordon remains stationary at Greenwood. Early rides back to Chambersburg to meet with Ewell, receiving orders to advance to Gettysburg the following day. Additional Confederate divisions cross the Potomac into Maryland. After a six-day halt, the Army of the Potomac finally heads north. Jennings sends one hundred men in the rain to Gettysburg, while the rest of his regiment stays in camp. Frick orders four additional companies of his 27th Militia to cross into Wrightsville.

June 26: Ewell heads from Chambersburg toward Carlisle. Early leaves Greenwood, burns the Caledonia Furnace and marches into Adams County. White and Gordon push back Jennings west of Gettysburg. French then routs Jennings at Witmer Farm, capturing nearly 200 militiamen. Haller retires to Hanover, then York. The bulk of the Union army crosses into Maryland. Curtin calls for 60,000 additional men to defend the state. He only has 4,000 Pennsylvanians and 8,000 New Yorkers in the field, opposing 25,000 Rebels already in his state.

June 27: White enters Hanover. That afternoon, he sacks Hanover Junction. A portion of the 20th Militia falls back toward Wrightsville while the rest head for Bainbridge. Gordon marches through New Oxford and halts at Abbottstown, where Arthur Farquhar unofficially offers to surrender York. Early marches through Hunterstown and East Berlin. His division camps in York County: Early at Big Mount, Gordon at Farmers, and White at Nashville. York officials meet with Gordon and determine conditions for Confederate occupation of their town. Haller leaves York for Wrightsville. During the night, four companies from Columbia, including one of fifty-three blacks, join the Wrightsville defenses. Robert E. Lee enters Pennsylvania. Longstreet and Hill occupy Chambersburg. Ewell reaches the outskirts of Carlisle. Jenkins camps at Mechanicsburg, less than ten miles from the state capital. The War Department dispatches an officer to relieve Hooker.

June 28: At 3 a.m., Meade takes over the Army of the Potomac. At dawn, the three white companies from Columbia return home. The black company stays in Wrightsville to dig earthworks. Mid-morning, a 238-man battalion from York and remnants of the

20th Militia reinforce Frick. Gordon parades through York and then marches to Wrightsville. Early occupies York. Gordon advances about 5:30 and pushes aside Frick's defenders, who withdraw to Columbia. One Yankee is killed and several wounded. Nineteen Federals are captured, and two companies flee in panic throughout Lancaster County. About 8 p.m., Frick orders the Columbia Bridge to be set on fire. Southerners join Wrightsville citizens in battling blazes in the business district. Ewell demonstrates in front of Harrisburg. Cole's Union cavalry skirmishes with Rebels near Fountain Dale in Adams County, capturing 15. Copeland's 5th and 6th Michigan Cavalry occupy Gettysburg.

June 29: The last spans of the burning bridge fall into the river. After breakfast, Gordon marches back to York where the prisoners of war are paroled. Haller departs Columbia for Bainbridge to meet with Colonel Thomas of the shattered 20th Militia. Early stays in York, planning to assist Ewell if needed with an assault on Harrisburg. Ewell reaches Oyster's Point, just two miles from the Susquehanna River and Harrisburg. Lee recalls Ewell to concentrate near Chambersburg.

June 30: Body of unknown Confederate soldier washes ashore along the Susquehanna. Stuart reaches Hanover and battles Kilpatrick's Union cavalry to a stalemate. Ewell leaves the Harrisburg area, fully intending to return after whipping the Yankees. Early hears cannon fire in the direction of Hanover, and a battery is unlimbered on the Henry Ramer farm west of York. Gordon marches to Adams County via Weigelstown and East Berlin. Near Abbottstown, White reports seeing Union cavalry and infantry heading south toward Hanover. Near Heidlersburg, Confederate cavalry skirmishes with John Buford's patrols. Ewell meets with Early and orders him to Cashtown where Lee in concentrating his army. Buford enters Gettysburg after skirmishing near Fairfield. Hill sends Pettigrew's brigade to Gettysburg, but it withdraws when the officers see Federals. Confederate command assumes it is again mere militia, no threat. Harry Heth asks Hill for permission to enter Gettysburg in the morning.

July 1: Ewell orders Early to turn south to Gettysburg. Gordon, in the lead, arrives about 3 p.m. after marching all morning. They form into line, supported by Hays and Avery on their left flank. Gordon smashes into Federal positions north of that town, and 500 men from the Wrightsville expedition are killed or wounded. Heavy fighting west of town collapses the Union lines, and thousands of Federals flood through and around the town to take up new positions. Gordon once again enters Gettysburg, this time under much different circumstances. He is incensed that Early's Division has not been ordered to take the high ground south of Gettysburg. He cannot sleep and spends a fretful night listening to Yankees entrench on Cemetery Hill.

July 2: Assaults against both ends of the Union line are not decisive, and Avery and Hays fail to take a fortified East Cemetery Hill in a determined evening assault. Gordon remains in a support position, but takes no active role.

July 3: Lee's last attempt to break the Union line is thwarted in what history has come to know as Pickett's Charge. Other than some skirmishing, Gordon's men remain relatively idle.

July 4: At 2 a.m., Gordon withdraws westward through Gettysburg to Seminary Ridge, near the turnpike. Lee begins withdrawing toward Virginia using the Fairfield Road. Frick's 27th Militia leaves Columbia for Harrisburg and then Carlisle.

July 5: In drenching rain, Gordon's Brigade starts its long walk home, leaving behind nearly two hundred men in the care of Gettysburg citizens or as prisoners. Gordon has suffered more than 30% casualties. The 26th Georgia fights a rear-guard skirmish against elements of the Union Sixth Army Corps, losing eleven men. Gordon camps near Fairfield. Frick's 27th Militia leaves Carlisle for Waynesboro, a four-day march following the Army of the Potomac at a distance. They capture several Confederate deserters.

July 6: Gordon crosses South Mountain at Monterey Pass, camping near Waynesboro. Frick camps at Pine Grove after a grueling seventeen-mile march. Several men drop by the wayside from exhaustion.

July 7: Gordon marches through Leitersburg, Maryland, and arrives at Hagerstown, camping a mile north of town. Frick's militia marches through Gettysburg. Later, they pass the Caledonia Furnace. Frick camps at Chambersburg.

July 8: Gordon rests in camp near Hagerstown and collects stragglers. The 27th becomes the first Pennsylvania militia regiment to enter Maryland, staying well in the rear of the Army of the Potomac.

July 9: Gordon continues to rest in camp. The 27th Militia moves cautiously along the mountain roads toward Hagerstown and Boonsboro.

July 10: Gordon marches through Hagerstown and camps on a ridge southwest of town on the Cumberland Road.

July 11: Gordon moves to the right near the Williamsport Road and forms a battleline, expecting an assault by pursuing Federals. The Yankees do not attack, showing "more caution than courage" according to a member of the 26th Georgia.

July 12: Gordon remains in a defensive posture. Nearby enemy troops remain stationary.

July 13: At twilight, Gordon abandons his position and retires toward Williamsport.

July 14: Just after sunrise, Gordon's Brigade crosses the Potomac River. The Georgians reenter West Virginia and camp near Hainesville, the bridge-burning affair just one of many bitter memories of a failed campaign.

Gordon's Expedition

Gordon's Approach to Gettysburg and the Skirmish at Marsh Creek

1. To follow Gordon from Winchester, Virginia, take Route 11 to Route 51 east. Turn left on Route 1. Pass through Leetown and cross the Potomac River at Shepherdstown. Gordon crossed downstream at Boteler's (Packhorse) Ford. Take Route 34 to Sharpsburg, where Gordon almost died from five wounds and the Georgia brigade lost hundreds of men. Follow 34 north to Boonsboro. Turn left on Alternate Route 40 toward Hagerstown. Gordon camped along the turnpike three miles west of Boonsboro on June 22 near Benevola.

2. Turn right on Benevola Church Road. Turn left on Route 66, driving north 12.8 miles through Cavetown to Smithsburg, where Early passed through streets filled with Southern sympathizers. Turn left onto Main Street. Drive 3.8 miles to Leitersburg, Take Route 60 north 2.1 miles to Pennsylvania, where the road becomes Route 316; drive 2.9 miles to Waynesboro, site of Gordon's June 23 camp. Take Route 997 twelve miles through Quincy and Mount Alto to Greenwood, where Gordon camped on June 24-25.

3. Take Route 30 east 2.1 miles to Thaddeus Stevens' 1830 blacksmith shop, a vestige of the Caledonia Furnace, burned on Early's order. In 2.9 miles, turn right onto Old Route 30. In 1.7 miles, you will cross a bridge over a small ravine and begin climbing Gallagher's Knob, where bushwhackers attacked the column. Accounts vary as to this incident, with some stories saying a wounded Rebel was carried to the nearby Newman's Tavern, where he expired. In 0.2 miles, note the Hilltown Road where Early turned off with most of his division. The Mary Bruch tavern is in the valley to the north; that is the location of the story of General Early cutting the center out of an 1858 map of Adams County. Gordon's infantry and Elijah White's cavalrymen stayed on the

Thaddeus Stevens' old blacksmith shop is all that is left from the once thriving Caledonia Iron Works, burned on June 26, 1863, by Jubal Early's Rebels. *Dr. Thomas M. Mingus*

turnpike. In 1.6 miles, note the historic (1797) Cashtown Inn (known as the Mickley Hotel during the Civil War era), a command post for Union videttes.

4. In 2.5 miles, rejoin Route 30 toward Gettysburg. Drive 1.6 miles, passing through Seven Stars, to Marsh Creek. A quarter-mile past the creek, carefully pull over to the right. On the left is a small marker to Col. William Jennings' 26th Militia and the skirmish with E. V. White's Rebel cavalrymen.

5. Continue into historic Gettysburg, noting the large statue honoring Jennings' regiment along Chambersburg Street at West Street. 217 Chambersburg was Sallie and Joe Broadhead's home. At the northeast corner of Chambersburg and Washington streets sat the Eagle Hotel, Maj. Granville Haller's headquarters. Christ Lutheran Church is halfway up the block on the

Statue commemorating the 26th Pennsylvania Volunteer Militia along Chambersburg Street in Gettysburg, Pa. *Dr. Thomas M. Mingus*

The Jacob Mickley hotel at Cashtown (commonly known as the Cashtown Inn). *Dr. Thomas M. Mingus*

south side. Here 38 Yankee prisoners rested on the steps, eating food brought by local women.

The Witmer Farm Skirmish and Gordon's March to York

1. Begin in Gettysburg's square. The Gettysburg Hotel in 1863 was the McClellan House, Haller's cavalry headquarters. Head north on Route 34, passing the railroad depot where the First City Troop and, later, Jennings' militia arrived in Gettysburg. In a mile, turn right on Tablerock Road. In 3.5 miles, Bayly's Hill is on your right near the Goldenville Road intersection. Turn right and, after a quarter mile, cross the stream, the location of Captain Carnachan's skirmishers from the 26th Militia. The red brick home on the left as you climb the hill marks the Henry Witmer farm, where Jennings encountered French's "wildcat cavalry."

2. Follow Goldenville Road, turning right on Shriver's Corner Road. Jennings led his remaining men to the left toward Harrisburg. In one mile, turn right on Old Harrisburg Road and return to Gettysburg's square.

3. Head east on Route 30. Gordon's Brigade and Company C of the 17th Virginia Cavalry used the old turnpike to reach York. In 0.6 miles, cross over Rock Creek, where White's cavalrymen skirmished with Federal militia and First City Troopers. Rebels

The center square in Abbottstown, Pa. showing U.S. Route 30 (foreground). *Dr. Thomas M. Mingus*

burned a railroad bridge to your left. Near here was Gordon's June 26 camp. In 4.8 miles, near today's Centennial Road, Rebels burned a warehouse at Gulden's Station.

6. In 1.7 miles, make a left turn onto Swift Run Road. Pause near the railroad tracks (a post-war addition) and walk back to the intersection with Route 30. Across the street to the southwest were the 1863 tracks. A wandering cow caused the 26th Militia's train to derail on June 24, and Jennings' militia camped nearby for a day, delaying their arrival in Gettysburg. Turn around and head east on Route 30.

7. In 2.3 miles, note the New Oxford train station, a post-war structure. A wall plaque commemorates the 26th Militia's rail journey.

8. Continue on Route 30 for 4.3 miles to Abbottstown, where York businessman A. B. Farquhar offered to surrender his town to Gordon. Continue 4.6 miles to Farmers, turning right on Locust Lane. In 0.1 miles, note the long paved driveway on the right leading to the Jacob S. Altland house, where Gordon met with a delegation from York on June 27. Much of his 1,800-man brigade camped north of the turnpike near Paradise Creek.

This heavily modified and updated farmhouse on Locust Lane in Farmers, Pa., in 1863 was the home of Jacob S. Altland. There, General John Gordon met with a delegation of civic leaders to discuss a peaceful occupation of York. *Dr. Thomas M. Mingus*

Gordon Parades through York to Wrightsville

1. Take Route 30 east to Route 462, exiting toward York, 7.3 miles from Locust Lane.

2. Gordon entered York on June 28 via Market (Main) Street and two parallel streets (Philadelphia and King). Park downtown near the intersection of Market and George streets, known today as Continental Square. The Continental Congress spent nine months meeting in a courthouse there in 1777-78, after the British pushed its delegates out of Philadelphia. A replica of this early building (constructed at Market and Pershing streets two blocks from the square) marks the adoption of the Articles of Confederation, the forerunner of the Constitution. During the Civil War, a large 110-foot flagpole stood in "Centre Square" between two market sheds. Rebels lowered the 18'x35' Federal flag and hauled it off. York's Committee of Safety met at P. A. & S. Small's hardware store, which stood on the northeast corner.

3. Turn right on George Street; drive three blocks. Turn right on College Avenue. Within a block, note Penn Common to your left, the site of the General Military Hospital that housed 14,000 sick and wounded Federal soldiers, including hundreds from Antietam and Gettysburg. A bronze relief map depicts where the individual buildings once stood. The York Invalids and the Patapsco Guards marched from here to Wrightsville. Part of Isaac Avery's North Carolina brigade camped at the hospital

York's Centre Square has changed substantially since 1863, when two large market sheds and a 110-foot-high pine flag pole dominated the view. Looking northeasterly toward the corner where the P.A. & S. Small hardware store once stood. *Dr. Thomas M. Mingus*

The National Hotel has changed little externally since John Gordon's Georgians paraded past it on Sunday, June 28, 1863, on their way through downtown York, Pa. Some residents are said to have waved Confederate flags from the porches. *Dr. Thomas M. Mingus*

In 1863 General Gordon paused his horse in front of this house, the home of P. A. Small and his family, to address a group of women which included Small's daughter, Cassandra. *Dr. Thomas M. Mingus*

during the Rebels occupation. After they left, citizens thoroughly scrubbed it because of a fear of lice. The postwar monument memorializes York County's Civil War veterans. To the south is Webb's Hill, where the guns from the Staunton Artillery unlimbered on June 28-30, their muzzles pointed at York. Guns from the Charlottesville Artillery parked at the Agricultural Society's fairgrounds.

4. Circle the block and return to Centre Square. Turn right on Market Street. Before the next traffic light, carefully pull over in front of the Yorktowne Hotel. The house directly across the street (the Lafayette Club) belonged to prominent businessman Philip Albright Small (the grandfather and namesake of Col. P. A. S. Franklin, the vice-president of the White Star Line that owned the ill-fated steamship RMS *Titanic*). Gordon addressed Small's daughter Cassandra and a group of women standing on the porch.

5. Continue east on Market Street. In the next block, note the Presbyterian Church to your left. James Smith, a signer of the Declaration of Independence, is buried here, as is P. A. Small. Somewhere in the next three blocks, Gordon encountered a 12-year-old girl who handed him a bouquet of flowers hiding a mysterious note detailing Wrightsville's defenses.

6. In 1.3 miles, turn right on Elmwood Boulevard and stop in 0.3 miles at Belmont Street. Diagonal right is York Bank director Jacob Brillinger's mansion. He allegedly used its two attics to hide runaway slaves. Turn left on Belmont, then right on Market Street.

7. In a mile, note the parking lot of the York Mall, the location of the Olde York Valley Inn, a 1747-era stone tavern built by English Quaker John Griest. In 1863, this farm served as Gordon's Brigade's resting place after marching through York.

8. In one-half mile, near today's Springettsbury Fire Department on the north side of the road, is "The Cedars," a two-story brick house owned by the Widow Smyser. Gordon had lunch here. Later he had his orderly return one of Smyser's horses that had been stolen by a soldier. Gordon's infantrymen camped near a 125-year-old stone inn a mile farther down the road.

9. Continue on Route 462 through Hallam toward Wrightsville, noting the terrain and slopes that Gordon traversed. The Confederates passed by numerous century-old farmhouses, some pre-dating the American Revolution. Several are still standing.

The Wrightsville Skirmish

1. Two miles east of Hallam, turn right onto Strickler Lane, the site of a prosperous farm owned for generations by the Strickler family, whose old cemetery is on your left. Somewhere along this ridgeline, Gordon peered through his field glass at Wrightsville's defenses. Today, woods that did not exist in 1863 obscure the view. From here, Tanner's guns opened long-range at the militia's lines. North of the pike, one gun unlimbered directly in line with Locust Street in Wrightsville. Several shells struck houses and churches on that street.

2. Continue south 0.6 miles south to Strickler's School Road. Note the old railroad bed, stone culvert, and bridge ahead of you. This was the Northern Central Railway spur used by Haller's train to reach Wrightsville. A day later, White's patrols burned the bridge, one of thirty-three destroyed by Rebel cavalry.

3. Turn left and follow Strickler's School Road for 0.4 miles. Turn left on Bair's Mill Road and drive 0.5 miles. The old mill is in the ravine near Kreutz Creek. Colonel Clement Evans led three Georgia regiments and White's companies along this narrow valley to flank the Federals. Nearby were the NCRW's tracks and another bridge burned by the Rebel cavalry.

4. Cross the creek and head north. In 1863, an open field existed to the east, where Tanner's Battery unlimbered a second time, after moving closer once Gordon ascertained there would be no counter-battery fire. A shell likely fired from here decapitated a black volunteer.

5. Turn right on Route 462. Drive 0.4 miles and turn right on Cool Creek Road (Old Baltimore Road in 1863). A small log-walled tollhouse stood at the intersection. Stretched along the road were Capt. Joseph Oliver and 70 skirmishers from the 27th Militia.

The Huber farm northwest of Wrightsville served as an artillery platform for Tanner's Battery during the June 28 skirmishing. Tanner fired 40 rounds, including several from two guns deployed at this location. *Dr. Thomas M. Mingus*

6. Drive 0.2 miles. Off to your left were 200 yards of earthworks protecting the left battalion of the 27th Militia and a company of 53 black civilians. Hearing the sound of battle, Bell's Cavalry clattered back toward Wrightsville after patrolling two miles south along this road. Artillery fire unhorsed two troopers, one of which was wounded and captured. The other cavalryman hid in a nearby farmhouse. Bell wheeled around and his remaining men galloped south to Safe Harbor, where they crossed the river into Lancaster County.

7. Turn around. Turn right on Route 462. In 0.1 miles, turn left on Eighth Street, following the approximate 200-yard line of earthworks held by the right battalion of the 27th Militia. These fortifications were to your left, between Eighth and Ninth streets. Neither existed in 1863. Rebels wounded nine militiamen after they withdrew from here.

8. Turn right onto Locust Street, then left onto Seventh. In 0.2 miles, turn left on Hybla Road. Behind you were the north-facing extension of the earthworks, ground held by William Sickles' 20th Militia. The old stone farmhouse to the northwest was the J. H. Huber homestead. Tanner's left section deployed on this small knoll, firing obliquely down the main Union entrenchments, as well as lobbing shells at Sickles. Note the rolling Hellam Heights, used by Rebels to flank the Federal position.

9. Turn around. Return to Hellam Street (Route 462) and turn left. Note Fairview Cemetery where several prominent Wrightsvillians are buried, including toll collector William McConkey and Capt. Frank Magee (both near the first traffic circle if you wish to enter the cemetery grounds).

10. Turn right on Sixth Street. In 0.3 miles, turn left on Meadow Lane and descend into the ravine. Near here, the skirmish began along the railroad as fifty dismounted Southern cavalrymen fired at Yankee skirmishers, narrowly missing Maj. Charles Knox. Turn around and return to Sixth Street, turning right. Fields of high wheat and rye covered this area, shielding Colonel Evans' Georgians as they advanced toward the earthworks.

11. In 0.2 miles, turn right on Orange Street. Halt in 0.1 miles at the intersection with Fourth Street. Here was the Detwiler farm. South of the farmhouse (torn down in the 20th century), the York Battalion held the entrenchments. Detwiler's barn was torn down in 1962.

12. Turn left on Third Street and return to the intersection with Hellam Street. A Rebel shot skipped past the 27th Militia, struck a locust fence post, and ricocheted into the side of James Kerr Smith's house near this intersection.

13. Turn left on Hellam Street. Turn right on Fourth Street.

14. Turn right on Locust and park. On the north side between Third and Fourth streets is the Methodist Church. A shell fragment struck the original structure under the second-story window. Additional fragments smashed one of the brick chimneys of the ell-shaped Morrison house across the street. A Schenkl shell hit the Presbyterian Church (since replaced by the modern structure) at the northwest corner of Locust and

Monument dedicated early in the 20th century to remember Wrightsville's role in the Gettysburg Campaign. *Dr. Thomas M. Mingus*

Second streets. The bolt is still in the possession of the congregation. Shells also struck the adjacent Jacob Bahn and Minnich houses. Another one hit the Big Brick Hotel at the corner of Second and Walnut. This building, once the Odd Fellows Hall, has long since been removed.

15. Turn right on Third Street, heading south.

16. Pull over at Constitution Square (intersection with Hellam Street). A monument commemorates Wrightsville as the easternmost point reached by Confederates during the campaign. Turn left on Hellam Street.

17. Note the three-story brick house on the south side of the street as the road slopes downhill (274 Hellam). This was James F. Magee's home, where Gordon breakfasted on Monday. His hostess, Mary Jane Rewalt, was the great-grandmother of author Gore Vidal. Her husband Luther was a Union army surgeon and her brother Capt. Frank Magee served in the 76th Pennsylvania.

18. Go straight toward the river (do not cross the bridge). On your left is a small building housing the Bridge Burning Diorama, open on most Sundays. In 1863, Hellam Street continued straight ahead to the covered bridge. The first abutment (land-based) from the wooden bridge was removed years ago (as was its counterpart in Columbia). However, the remaining twenty-five piers still exist.

Confederates saved the Wrightsville House from burning. *Dr. Thomas M. Mingus*

19. Turn left on Front Street. Park on the right near the large brick warehouse-turned-restaurant. Note the old limekilns on the western side of the street (a block ahead of you) and the stone piers in the river from the old covered bridge.

20. Head south (left) on Front Street. The stone building on your right at 127/129 was the Wrightsville House, a 20-room building that Gordon's Georgians saved from burning.

21. Pass under the modern bridge and stay on Front Street. Note the historical marker for the Susquehanna and Tide Water Canal, which ran south to Havre de Grace, Maryland, on the Chesapeake Bay. The old entrance to the canal is just north of the current bridge. Across the river was the North Branch Canal, which ran from Harrisburg to Columbia. Horses and/or mules used a bi-level towpath on the bridge's southern side to pull boats across the river to the opposite canal. The last canal boat was taken out of service in 1901.

22. Continue on Front Street. This was the Westphalia section of town most immediately threatened by the blaze. A series of lumberyards along the canal caught fire as embers from the burning bridge ignited the roof of one of the buildings. Several houses and businesses soon caught fire, and suddenly residents appeared with buckets and pails. Throughout the evening, Confederate soldiers maintained a bucket brigade to douse hot spots.

23. Turn right on Willow Street. At its end, turn right on Barnes Avenue. The First City Troop patrolled this area, where the Northern Central Railway tracks once entered town (south of the alley between Willow and Lemon streets). The original cut has been heavily altered, having been filled in over the years. Turn right on Lemon Street. Turn left on Front Street.

Wartime Columbia

1. Turn right and cross the bridge into Columbia. Turn right on Second Street. Turn right on Walnut, heading back toward the river. Turn left on Front Street. The Washington House depot was located at this intersection, opposite the present stone Columbia depot. Turn right into River Park (across the railroad tracks). The fire consumed several buildings across the river from you in Wrightsville. The bridge conflagration consumed one house on Columbia's Front Street, but frantic efforts by the fire company, citizens, and soldiers kept it from spreading.

2. Turn right on Front Street. Cross the tracks. Pull over at Mill Street. Along the riverbank to the west was Fort Case, constructed by home defense companies. This fort was partially built of sandstone blocks, and abutted the dam. It was the site of a festive ox roast for the volunteers. Earthworks and rifle-pits once protected the crescent-shaped fort. All have vanished, apparently in 1906 when the Pennsylvania

Railroad constructed the Low Grade branch. Dr. John Denney (son of bridge burner John Q. Denney) stated that the old fort was still recognizable at the start of the 20th Century, although it was in disrepair and filled with rubble. Turn around and head north on Front Street.

3. Turn right on Locust Street and proceed one block. The Columbia Bank, the financiers and owners of the bridge, once occupied the building at the southeast corner of Locust and Second.

4. Turn right on Fourth Street, then left on Union Street. Cross over Fifth Street and look to your left. The area north of Fifth and west of Union streets was "Tow Hill." Many of the blacks that helped construct the earthworks lived in this neighborhood. In Columbia's pioneer years, this was a field where farmers grew flax for use in weaving. The golden (tow) color of the flax gave the area its name. Quaker John Wright donated the land to free blacks. By 1850, Tow Hill had one of the largest black communities in the region. Nearly one thousand blacks lived in Columbia, most of them here. Follow Union Street to Route 462 (Lancaster Avenue) and make a left. Stay on 462 as it turns left onto Chestnut Street.

5. Follow Chestnut and turn right on Second Street. In one block, turn left on Bridge Street, the eastern terminus of the covered bridge in 1863 and the location of a section of Ridgway's artillery, positioned to rake the bridge. The present-day tracks

The Columbia Bank tried for decades to recover money from the Federal government as compensation for the destruction of the Columbia Bridge, but to no avail. *Dr. Thomas M. Mingus*

approximate the old Pennsylvania Railroad, used by the 27th Militia to arrive from Harrisburg. Just beyond the rails was the North Branch Canal.

6. Loop back to Second Street and turn left. The area bounded by Poplar and Cedar streets was the wartime Lockard's Meadow, site of the main Union militia camp. Ironically, Lockard was a devout Mennonite, opposed to the concept of war.

7. Turn right on Poplar. Pass by Third Street. Hundreds of curiosity seekers thronged the hill to your left to watch the burning bridge. Turn left on Fifth Street and drive through the Route 30 underpass. Immediately pull over to your right at an old cemetery. Note the headstones commemorating black Civil War soldiers, some of whom fought in the Columbia black company at Wrightsville.

8. Turn around on Fifth Street and turn right on Linden Street. You are in the middle of Lockard's Meadow. Turn right onto Third Street. Nearby on Grubb's Ridge, volunteers built a two-gun emplacement of timber, backed by earth.

9. Take Route 30 2.3 miles west to the Wrightsville exit. Turn right on Cool Springs Road and follow the signs to the Accomac Inn (the road will become Dark Hollow Road). Turn left on River Road, paralleling the Susquehanna. Stop 1.2 miles north of the inn when you note a small gravestone on the right side of the road. On June 30, citizens discovered a body that had washed ashore, burying it along the riverbank. According to local lore, three Confederate deserters tried crossing the swollen river on a raft. One fell overboard and drowned. However, the June 30, 1863 *New York Herald* reported, "A rebel was shot above this place [Wrightsville] in attempting to cross the

Modern gravestone marking where the body of a Confederate was buried in the days after the invasion of York County. *Dr. Thomas M. Mingus*

river in a boat." When a steel barrel that had long marked the gravesite deteriorated, the Sons of Union Veterans replaced it with the memorial stone.

10. Turn around and return to Dark Hollow Road. Turn right. In 0.3 miles, turn left. In 0.4 miles, cross over Hauser School Road. Turn left when Dark Hollow Road curves eastward. Two Confederate regiments came through this area of Hellam Heights, crossing the road as they flanked the Wrightsville defenses. Follow this for two miles. Turn right at the end of Dark Hollow Road and use Front Street to return to Wrightsville. Gordon retraced his route to York using the turnpike, camping two miles beyond town along the Carlisle Road (today's Route 74). He rejoined Early and marched through East Berlin to Heidlersburg using roads paralleling today's Route 30. White's cavalrymen headed west on the turnpike, screening Early's left flank.

Driving Tour: White's Raid on Hanover Junction

1. Follow Route 30 east from Gettysburg's square to Hanover Road (Route 116), bearing right. Several farmers along this thoroughfare suffered losses as Elijah White's cavalrymen headed toward Hanover.

2. Continue on Route 116 through McSherrystown. White paused to inquire if Yankees were in the vicinity. A farmer rode into Hanover with the warning that Rebels were approaching. At the traffic light, turn right onto 3rd Street. Drive 0.9 miles, staying on 3rd Street when 116 becomes High Street. You are paralleling the old railroad tracks.

3. In 0.3 miles, turn right onto Carlisle Street (Route 94). In 0.3 miles, you will reach Hanover's center square. Note the large brick building on the southwest corner, the Central Hotel in 1863. In front of here, White delivered a speech to the town's leaders. His men rested in Hanover for an hour, visiting local stores to obtain whiskey, food, and sundries. Citizens captured a few Rebels who had lingered behind, taking them to this hotel for processing before they were transported to Winchester.

4. Turn left on Broadway, staying in the right-hand lane. Take Route 116 (York Road) eastward for 1.3 miles. At least one company followed the Hanover Branch Railroad to Smiths Station and Porters Sideling before heading to Jefferson Station. We will shadow White's main force.

(Optional tour to approximate White's companies that traveled along the railroad):

A. Take 116 northward from Hanover. After passing Blooming Grove Road, note the historical marker for Gordon's expedition in 0.3 miles.

B. In 0.6 miles, immediately after crossing the railroad tracks, turn right onto Cannery Road. Drive 1.2 miles to Smiths Station.

C. Go straight on Yingling Road for 0.2 miles.

D. Turn right on Thoman Road. Drive 1.8 miles.

E. Turn right on Porters Road through Porters Sideling. Drive 1.4 miles.

F. Turn right on Krafts Mill Road. The site of old Jefferson Station is on your right in 1.7 miles. Turn right on Jefferson Road. Proceed to step 7.

5. Turn right on Blooming Grove Road (Route 216). Drive 3.0 miles, passing Lake Marburg, created in the 20th Century by damming a branch of Codorus Creek. Turn left on Dubs' Church Road. Cavalrymen stole a horse from William Dubs' stable and then continued to Jefferson. White's original route is now under water, so turn around at the church and return to Route 216, turning left.

6. In 1.2 miles, turn left on Sinsheim Road. Jefferson is about four miles from this intersection. The modern road curves around the lake and rejoins the original route that White used to enter Jefferson from the southwest (Hanover Street). White's men paused briefly in the square, where one of them traded a stolen brooch to a little girl for a cup of cold water.

7. Go north on York Street (Green Valley Road). Drive 4.7 miles to Route 214 and turn right into Seven Valleys. Here, White's cavalrymen raided horses, and several troopers helped themselves at Henry Bott's store (along the railroad tracks on Cherry Street). Carefully turn around and head north. The depot was known as Smyser's Station.

8. In 0.2 miles, turn left onto Route 616 and go south for one mile. Shortly after crossing Codorus Creek, you will enter Hanover Junction. The old depot on your left is a popular spot on the York County Heritage Rail Trail, a bike path paralleling the old Northern Central Railway, which intersected the now-removed Hanover Branch Railroad near the depot. Rebels burned the bridge and destroyed the railroad yard. The three-story brick house (now a private residence) was the John Scott Hotel.

9. Turn left onto Route 616. In 0.2 miles, turn left on Maple Street, crossing the tracks. Sickles' militia fled through this valley to their hillside fortifications, where they helplessly watched as White sacked Hanover Junction.

10. Drive 1 mile to Seven Valleys. Turn left onto Main Street (Route 214). In 0.1 miles, turn right onto Church Street (214 East) and drive 0.9 miles. Note the railroad tracks and Codorus Creek to your left. Carefully stop after crossing Fishel Creek. White's troopers burned the original wooden railway bridge. Several enjoyed whiskey from Henry Fishel's distillery.

11. Turn around on 214 and drive back into Seven Valleys. Turn right on Main Street. In 0.3 miles, turn left on Green Valley Road and return to Jefferson. Turn right at the square on Berlin Street (Jefferson Road). A courier found White and gave him orders to camp near Gordon close to the York turnpike.

12. In half a mile, turn left on Krafts Mill Road. Note the old Hanover Branch Railroad bed to your left. This was Jefferson Station, where a party of cavalrymen

Samuel Roth lived in this house during the Gettysburg Campaign. "Lige" White's Virginia cavalrymen raided the farm for horses on June 27, 1863. *Dr. Thomas M. Mingus*

torched a carload of bark. At Henry Rebert's nearby store, Rebels cracked open whiskey barrels. Turn around and turn left on Jefferson Road.

13. Turn right on Route 116. Enter Spring Grove (Spring Forge in 1863). The sprawling paper mill on your left was a small facility when the Rebels rode by. Drive 0.8 miles.

14. Turn left on Roth's Church Road. White camped June 27 on the 22-acre John Wiest farm at this intersection, just south of Nashville. In 0.4 miles, the Andrew Menges farm is on your left. In 0.5 miles on the right was the Samuel Roth farm, with the Reverend Samuel L. Roth's house down the farm lane to the right. Confederates raided horses from several local farms, including these.

15. Turn left on Locust Lane. Follow this to Gordon's June 27 campsite at Farmers. On June 28, White accompanied Gordon into York, camping two miles east of town on the John Small farm. There, the battalion split into small raiding parties to burn bridges, scout for enemy activity, and steal more horses and mules. Some headed for Wrightsville with Gordon.

For more photographs from these driving tours, visit the author's website:
www.scottmingus.ash.com/photos.html

Bibliography

PRIMARY SOURCES

Newspapers

Adams County Sentinel
Atlanta Constitution
Atlanta Journal
Atlanta Reporter
Atlanta Southern Confederacy
Boston Morning Journal
Chambersburg Valley Spirit
Columbia News
Columbia North Star
Columbia Spy
Forney's War Press
Franklin Repository
Gettysburg Compiler
Gettysburg Star and Banner
Hanover Spectator
Harrisburg Daily Telegraph
Harrisburg Patriot and Union
Huntingdon (Pa.) Journal and American
Lancaster (Pa.) *Express*
Lancaster (Pa.) *Examiner and Herald*
Macon (Ga.) *Weekly Telegram*
Marietta (Pa.) *Mariettian*
Mercersburg Journal
Mobile Advertiser & Register
New York Times
New York Tribune
Norristown (Pa.) *Herald*

Philadelphia Inquirer
Philadelphia Press
Philadelphia Weekly Times
Pottsville (Pa.) *Miners' Journal*
Reading (Pa.) *Daily Times*
Reading Berks & Schuylkill Journal
Reading Eagle
Richmond Daily Dispatch
Richmond Whig
Savannah Daily Morning News
Savannah Daily Republican
Staunton (Va.) *Observer*
York Gazette
York Republican
The Sunny South

Manuscripts and Related Materials

Adams County Historical Society, Gettysburg, Pennsylvania
　　Sarah Broadhead diary
　　Fannie Buehler account
　　Henry Eyster Jacobs account
　　Albertus McCreary account

Bullard County Historical Society, Georgia
　　Benjamin F. Keller, Jr. papers

Columbia (Pa.) Historic Preservation Society
　　Robert Crane testimony
　　John Q. Denney testimony

Georgia Department of Archives and History
　　Joseph H. Truett letters

Gettysburg College, Musselman Library, Gettysburg, Pennsylvania
　　David McConaughy papers
　　William Henry Rupp diary

Gettysburg National Military Park, Gettysburg, Pennsylvania
    William Hamilton Bayly account
    Theodore S. Dimon account
    Joseph Hilton letters
    Michael Jacobs account
    Frederick Klinefelter account
    Jennie McCreary letters
    R. H. Mohr letters
    Henry Wirt Shriver account

Historical Society of Berks County, Reading, Pennsylvania
    Joseph Kaucher letters

Historical Society of Pennsylvania, Philadelphia, Pennsylvania
    Joseph P. Wood letters

Lancaster County Historical Society, Lancaster, Pennsylvania
    J. Houston Mifflin letters
    Josephine Sidney Myer diary

Library of Congress, Washington, D.C.
    Jubal A. Early letters

Loudon County Historical Society, Leesburg, Virginia
    Elijah V. White files

Millersville University, Ganser Library, Millersville, Pennsylvania
    James P. Wickersham papers

Montgomery County Historical Society, Rockville, Maryland
    Joseph H. Trundle letters

Navarro College, Corsicana, Texas
    William D. Lyon Papers

Richard C. Wiggin Collection, Lincoln, Massachusetts
    Annie Welsh letter

Pennsylvania State Archives, Harrisburg
    Border claims, State Adjutant's Office

Schuylkill County Historical Society, Pottsville, Pennsylvania
John Gordon speech, Kutztown State Normal School, Oct. 24, 1896

United States Army Military History Institute, Carlisle, Pennsylvania
George Henszey letters
Elias Hoppes letters
Bentley Kutz letters
Charles Thompson Stuart autobiographical sketch

University of Georgia, Hargrett Library, Athens
John B. Gordon letters

Virginia Center for Digital History, Charlottesville, Virginia
Abraham Essick diary
William Heyser diary

York County Heritage Trust, York, Pennsylvania
John Stoner Beidler diary
James Latimer letters
Cassandra Small letters

Government Publications

The War of the Rebellion: A Compilation of the Official Records of the Union and Confederate Armies, 70 volumes in 4 series. Washington, D.C.: United States Government Printing Office, 1880-1901.

Maps

Shearer's Map of York County, Pennsylvania. Philadelphia: W. O. Shearer and D. J. Lake, 1860.

Articles

Bell, Robert, "Co. B, 21st Pennsylvania Cavalry, Remembrances of 1863," *Star and Sentinel*, January 17, 1883.
Bender, Lida Welsh, "Civil War Memories," *The Outlook*, June 24, 1925.
Bennawit, John F., "Excerpts from the Diary of F. X. Ziegler," *Journal of the Lancaster County Historical Society*. Vol. 105, No. 2 (2003), 49-51.

Bradwell, Isaac G., "The Burning of Wrightsville, Pennsylvania," *Confederate Veteran*, Vol. 27 (1919).

———. "Crossing the Potomac," *Confederate Veteran*, Vol. 30 (1922)

———. "The Capture of Winchester, Virginia," *Confederate Veteran*, Vol. 30 (1922)

Early, Jubal A., "The Invasion of Pennsylvania, by the Confederate States Army, in June 1863," in *The Historical Magazine and Notes and Queries*, Vol. 1, Series 3. Morrisania, N.Y.: Henry B. Dawson, 1872-73.

Frazer, Persifor, Jr., "Philadelphia City Cavalry, Service of the First Troop Philadelphia City Cavalry during June and July, 1863," *Journal of the Military Service Institution of the United States*, Vol. 43 (1908).

Gordon, John B., "The Last Days of the Confederacy: Lecture of Gen. J. B. Gordon, given in various parts of the country, this, at Brooklyn, NY, Feb., 1901," *Modern Eloquence*. Thomas B. Reed, ed. Philadelphia: John D. Davis Company, 1901.

Haller, Theodore, "Granville O. Haller," *The Washingtonian*, Vol. 1, No. 3. Tacoma: Washington State Historical Society, 1900.

Hudgins, F. L., "With the 38th Georgia," *Confederate Veteran*, Vol. 26 (1918).

Yoder, Harold, "Letters from a Civil War Soldier," *Historical Review of Berks County*. Vol. 51, No. 2, Spring 1986.

Books and Pamphlets

Alleman, Tillie Pierce, *At Gettysburg, or What a Girl Saw and Heard of the Battle of Gettysburg*. New York: W. Lake Borland, 1889.

Authentic General Directory: York, Hanover, and Wrightsville for 1877. York, Pa.: Herman, Miller, and Thomas, 1876.

Bates, Samuel P., *History of Pennsylvania Volunteers, 1861-5*. Harrisburg: B. Singerly, State Printer, 1869-1871.

———. *Martial Deeds of Pennsylvania*. Philadelphia: T. H. Davis & Co., 1876.

Directory: Harrisburg, Lancaster, and York for 1863. York, Pa.: Herman, Miller, and Thomas, 1863.

Early, Jubal Anderson, *War Memoirs: Autobiographical Sketch and Narrative of the War Between the States*. Philadelphia: J. B. Lippincott, 1912.

Farquhar, Arthur B., and Crowther, Samuel, *The First Million: The Hardest: An Autobiography of A. B. Farquhar*. Garden City, NY: Doubleday, 1922.

Gibson, John, *History of York County, Pennsylvania: A Biographical History*. Chicago: F. A. Battey, 1886.

Gordon, John B., *Reminiscences of the Civil War*. New York/Atlanta: Charles Scribner's Sons, 1903.

Haller, Granville O., *The Dismissal of Major Granville O. Haller of the Regular Army of the United States by Order of the Secretary of War in Special Orders, 331, of July 25, 1863*. Paterson, N.J.: Daily Guardian Offices, 1863.

History of Franklin County, Pennsylvania. Chicago: Warner, Beers & Co., 1887.

History of the First Troop Philadelphia City Cavalry, from its Organization, November 17th, 1774 to its Centennial Anniversary, November 17th, 1874. Philadelphia: Hallowell & Co., 1875.

Hoke, Jacob, *The Great Invasion of 1863; or General Lee in Pennsylvania*. Gettysburg, Pa.: Stan Clark Military Books, 1992.

Jacobs, Michael, *Notes on the Rebel Invasion of Maryland and Pennsylvania and the Battle of Gettysburg*. Philadelphia: J. B. Lippincott, 1864.

Johnson, Pharris Deloach, ed., *Under the Southern Cross: Soldier Life with Gordon Bradwell and the Army of Northern Virginia*. Mercer U. Press, 2002.

Jones, Terry L., *The Civil War Memoirs of Captain William J. Seymour: Reminiscences of a Louisiana Tiger*. Baton Rouge: Louisiana State U. Press, 1997.

Lee, Robert E., Jr., *Recollections and Letters of General Robert E. Lee*. Indianapolis: IndyPublishing.Com. 2002.

Moore, Frank, ed., *The Rebellion Record: A Diary of American Events . . .* , 7 volumes. New York: G. P. Putnam, 1861-8.

Myers, Frank M., *The Comanches: A History of White's Battalion, Virginia Cavalry. . .* Baltimore: Kelly, Piet & Co., 1871.

Nichols, G. W., *A Soldier's Story of His Regiment, 61st Georgia*. Kennesaw, Ga.: Continental Book Co., 1961.

Pennsylvania Volunteers and Militia Called into Service during the Gettysburg Campaign. Washington, D.C.: Adjutant General's Office, 1885.

Pennypacker, Samuel W., *The Autobiography of a Pennsylvanian*. Philadelphia: The John C. Winston Co., 1918.

———, "Six weeks in uniform," *Historical and Biographical Sketches*. Philadelphia: Robert A. Tripple, 1910.

———, "Dedication of Monument, 26th Emergency Infantry," *Pennsylvania at Gettysburg*. Harrisburg: Wm. Stanley Ray, 1914.

Prowell, George Reeser, *History of the Eighty-seventh Regiment, Pennsylvania Volunteers*. York, Pa.: The Regimental Association, 1903.

———, *History of York County, Pennsylvania*. Chicago: J. H. Beers, 1907.

Richards, Henry M. M., *Pennsylvania's Emergency Men at Gettysburg*. Reading, Pa.: Self-published, 1886.

Scott, William Alonzo, *The Battle of Gettysburg*. Gettysburg, Pa.: Self published, 1905.

Skelly, Daniel A., *A Boy's Experiences in the Battle of Gettysburg*. Gettysburg, Pa.: Privately published, 1932.

Stiles, Robert, *Four Years Under Marse Robert*. New York/Washington: The Neale Publishing Company, 1904.

Stephens, Robert Grier, Jr., ed., *Intrepid Warrior: Clement Anselm Evans*. Dayton, Ohio: Morningside Press, 1992.

Wallace, Francis B., *Memorial of the Patriotism of Schuylkill County in the American Slaveholders Rebellion*. Pottsville, Pa.: Benjamin Bannan, 1865.

Wells, Clark H., *The Reply to a Pamphlet Recently Published by G. O. Haller, Late a U.S. Major U.S.A.* York, Pa.: H. Young, 1865.

Wister, Jones, *Jones Wister's Reminiscences*. Philadelphia: J.B. Lippincott, 1920.

Wray, William J., *History of the Twenty-third Pennsylvania Volunteer Infantry, Birney's Zouaves*. Philadelphia: s. n., 1904.

SECONDARY SOURCES

Articles

Alexander, Ted, "A Regular Slave Hunt," *North & South*, Vol. 4, No. 7 (2001), 82-88.

Billett, Glenn E., "The Department of the Susquehanna," *Journal of the Lancaster County Historical Society*, Vol. 66, No. 1 (1962), 1-64.

Bloom, Robert L., "We Never Expected a Battle: The Civilians of Gettysburg, 1863," *Pennsylvania History*, Vol. 55 (reprinted 1988, Adams County Historical Society).

Brubaker, Jack, "Defending the Susquehanna," *Civil War Times, Illustrated*, Vol. 42, No. 2 (2003), 74-80.

Burger, T. W., "First to Fall," *Civil War Times, Illustrated*, Vol. 39, No. 4 (August 2002), 32-38.

Chapman, John M., "Comanches on the Warpath: The 35th Battalion Virginia Cavalry in the Gettysburg Campaign," in "Gettysburg: Regimental Leadership and Command," *Civil War Regiments: A Journal of the American Civil War*, Vol. 6, No. 3 (1999).

Crist, Robert G., "Highwater 1863: The Confederate Approach to Harrisburg." *Pennsylvania History*, Vol. 30 (1963), 158-183.

Ent, Uzal, "Rebels in Pennsylvania," *Civil War Times, Illustrated*, Vol. 37, No. 4 (1998), 46-52, 64-66.

Goodell, Robert H., "The Second Columbia Bridge," *Journal of the Lancaster County Historical Society*, Vol. 57. No. 1 (1953).

Heisey, M. Luther, "Lancaster in the Gettysburg Campaign," *Historical Papers and Addresses of the Lancaster County Historical Society*, Vol. 43 (1939).

Jolly, James A., "140 Years Ago the Enemy Advanced and the Normal Boys Took Arms: The School Closed," *Friends Folio: The Newsletter of the Friends of Ganser Library*, Millersville University, Vol. 47 (2003).

Kessler, Charles H., "Historic Columbia: Founded 1788," *Lancaster New Era Nespaper Series* (1988).

McSherry, Patrick, "The Defense of Columbia: June 1863," *Journal of the Lancaster County Historical Society*, Vol. 84, No. 3 (1980).

Major, Mark, "Schuylkill County in the Civil War," *Historical Society of Schuylkill County Publications*, Vol. 7, No. 3 (1961).

Nye, Wilbur S., "The First Battle of Gettysburg," *Civil War Times, Illustrated*, Vol. 4, No. 5 (1965), 12-18.

Prowell, George R., "The Invasion of Pennsylvania by the Confederates Under Robert E. Lee and Its Effect Upon Lancaster and York Counties," *Historical Papers and Addresses of the Lancaster County Historical Society*, Vol. 29, No. 4 (1925), 41-51.

Rhoads, Willard R., "Pennsylvania's North Branch Canal," *The Columbian*, Vol. 1, No. 2 (1960).

Roland, Charles P., "Lee's Invasion Strategy," *North & South*, Vol. 1, No. 6 (1998).

Shettel, James W., "The Skirmishes Before the Big Battle," *National Republic*, Vol. 38 (Aug. 1950).

Vermilyea, Peter C., "To Prepare for the Emergency: Military Operations in the Gettysburg Area through June 24, 1863," *The Gettysburg Magazine*, Issue 32, (2005), 39-48.

Weigley, Russell F., "The Emergency Troops in the Gettysburg Campaign," *Pennsylvania History*, Vol. 25, No. 1 (1958), 39-57.

Books and Pamphlets

Anthony, William, *Anthony's History of the Battle of Hanover*. Hanover, Pa.: Self-published, 1945.

Beck, Brandon H. and Grunder, Charles S., *The Second Battle of Winchester, June 12-15, 1863*. Lynchburg, Va.: H. E. Howard, 1989.

Birnstock, H. O., *Wrightsville's Book of Facts: A Souvenir Inspired by the Sixtieth Anniversary of an Event of the Civil War Which Occurred at Wrightsville, York County, Pennsylvania*. York, Pa.: Historical Commission of Wrightsville, 1923.

Breshears, Guy, *Major Granville Haller: Dismissed with Malice*. Westminster, Md., Heritage Books, 2006.

Busey, John W., and Martin, David G., *Regimental Strengths and Losses at Gettysburg*. Hightstown, N.J.: Longstreet House, 1982.

Chamberlain, Martin N., *Granville Haller: Leader*. Bloomington, In.: Trafford Publishing, 2005.

Coco, Gregory A., *A Strange and Blighted Land—Gettysburg: The Aftermath of a Battle*. Gettysburg, Pa.: Thomas Publications, 1995.

Coddington, Edwin B., *The Gettysburg Campaign: A Study in Command*. New York: Charles Scribner's Sons, 1968.

Cole, Philip, *Civil War Artillery at Gettysburg: Organization, Equipment, Ammunition, and Tactics*. New York: Da Capo Press, 2002.

Collier, Kenneth C., *The 13th Georgia Regiment: A Part of the Lawton-Gordon-Evans Brigade*. Atlanta: Self-published. 1997.

Commemorative Biographical Encyclopedia of Dauphin County, Pennsylvania. Chambersburg, Pa.: J. M. Runk & Company, 1888.

Conrad W. P., and Alexander, Ted, *When War Passed This Way*. Greencastle, Pa.: Greencastle Bicentennial, Lillian S. Besore Library, 1982.

Dawson, John Harper, *Wildcat Cavalry: A Synoptic History of the Seventeenth Virginia Cavalry Regiment*. Dayton, Ohio: Morningside Press, 1982.

Divine, John E., *35th Battalion, Virginia Cavalry*. Lynchburg, Va.: Virginia Regimental Series, H. E. Howard, Inc., 1985.

Douglas, Stacy C., *The Fighting Boys of Wiregrass: A Short History of the Ben Hill Guards, 38th Georgia*. Athens, Ga.: Southern Regional Publications. 1996.

Eckert, Ralph Lowell, John Brown Gordon: Soldier, Southerner, American. Baton Rouge: Louisiana State University Press, 1989.

Encounter at Hanover: Prelude to Gettysburg. Gettysburg, Pa.: Historical Publication Committee of the Hanover Chamber of Commerce, Times and News Publishing Company, 1962.

Gambone, A. M., *Major General Darius Nash Couch: Enigmatic Valor*. Baltimore: Butternut and Blue, 2000.

Gerhart, John, Jr., *The Impact of Lee's Invasion Upon Lancaster County, 1863*. Millersville, Pa.: Master's Thesis, Millersville University, 1965.

Gladfelter, Armand, *The Flowering of the Codorus Palatine: A History of North Codorus Township PA, 1838-1988*. York, Pa.: Sesquicentennial Comm., 1988.

Glatfelter, Charles H., *The Story of Jefferson: Codorus, Pennsylvania*. Codorus, Pa.: Jefferson Community Centennial, Inc., 1966.

Gunnarsson, Robert L., *The Story of the Northern Central Railway*. Sykesville, Md.: Greenberger Publishing Company, 1991.

Hall, George D., *Wrightsville Centennial Celebration of the Invasion of Wrightsville by the Forces of General Robert E. Lee and the Burning of the Bridge, June 28-29, 1963*. York, Pa.: Self-published, 1963.

Hefelbower, Samuel Gring, *The History of Gettysburg College: 1832-1932*. Gettysburg, Pa.: Gettysburg College, 1932.

Henderson, Lillian, *Roster of the Confederate Soldiers of Georgia, 1861-1865*, Volumes 1–6. Hapeville, Ga.: Georgia. State Division of Confederate Pensions and Records, Longino & Porter, Inc., 1959.

Hofe, Michael W., *That There Be No Stain Upon My Stones: Lieutenant Colonel William L. McLeod, 38th Georgia Regiment 1842-1863*. Gettysburg, Pa.: Thomas Publications, 1995.

Johnson, Clifton, ed., *Battleground Adventures: The Stories of the Dwellers on the Scenes of Conflict*. Boston and New York: Houghton Mifflin, 1915.

Kauffman, George P., *York and York County and the Civil War, from Glimpses of Historic York*. York, Pa.: typescript manuscript, undated.

Kesterson, Brian S., *Campaigning with the 17th Virginia Cavalry: Night Hawks at Monocacy*. Washington, W.V.: Night Hawk Press, 2005.

Klein, Frederick Shriver, *Lancaster County Since 1841*. Lancaster, Pa.: Intelligencer Printing Co., 1941.

———, *Old Lancaster: Historic Pennsylvania Community: From Its Beginnings to 1865*. Lancaster, Pa.: Early America Series, Inc., 1964.

Lehman, Donald I., Sr., *Wrightsville: Gateway to the West*. York, Pa.: Historic Wrightsville Association, 1976.

Lehman, James O. and Nolt, Steven M., *Mennonites, Amish, and the American Civil War*. Baltimore: The Johns Hopkins University Press, 2007.

Lovelace, David Shriver, *The Shrivers: Under Two Flags*. Westminster, Md.: Willow Bend Books, 2003.

McClure, James E., *East of Gettysburg*. York, Pa.: York County Heritage Trust, York Daily Record, 2003.

Mingus, Scott L., Jr., *The Burning of the Wrightsville-Columbia Bridge*. Millersville, Pa.: Graduate Report, Millersville University, 2003.

Mouat, Malcolm Palmer, *Dr. Henry Palmer: 'The Fighting Surgeon" 1827-1895*. Detroit: Harlo, undated.

Murray, Alton J., *South Georgia Rebels: The True Wartime Experiences of the 26th Regiment, Georgia Volunteer Infantry*. St. Mary's, Ga.: Self-published, 1976.

Nicholas, Richard L., and Servis, Joseph, *Powhatan, Salem, and Henrico [Courtney] Light Artillery*. Appomattox, Va.: Virginia Regimental Series, H. E. Howard Inc., 1997.

Nofi, Albert A., *The Gettysburg Campaign, June and July l863*. New York: Gallery, 1986.

Nye, Wilbur S., *Here Come the Rebels!* Baton Rouge: Louisiana State University Press, 1965.

———., and Redman, John G., *Farthest East*. Wrightsville, Pa.: Wrightsville Centennial Committee, 1963.

Osborne, Charles C., *The Life and Times of General Jubal A. Early, CSA: Defender of the Lost Cause*. Chapel Hill, N.C.: Algonquin, 1992.

Rigdon, John C., *Historical Sketch and Roster of McGowan's Independent Company, Maryland Infantry (Patapsco Guards)*. Baltimore: Self-published, 1999.

Robinson, Gerald Austin, Jr., *Confederate Operations in York County*. Millersville, Pa.: graduate thesis, Millersville University, 1965.

Rohrbaugh, Carroll, Jr., *Operation Underground Railroad in York County*. Gettysburg, Pa.: Gettysburg College, 1953.

Scaife, William R., *The Georgia Brigade*. Atlanta: William R. Scaife, 2d Edition, 2002.

Spicer, John E., *The Columbia Civil War Centennial*. Middletown, Pa.: Wert Binding, 1976.

Stoner, Jacob H., *Historical Papers: Franklin County and the Cumberland Valley, Pennsylvania*. Chambersburg, Pa.: The Craft Press, 1947.

Taylor, Frank H., *Philadelphia in the Civil War: 1861-65*. Philadelphia: Dunlap Printing Company, 1913.

Thompson, Magnus S., *The Service Record of Col. Elijah V. White, From the Ranks to Brigadier General*. (Leesburg, Va., s.n., 1923).

Toomey, Daniel Carroll, *The Patapsco Guards Independent Company of Maryland Volunteers*. Baltimore: Self-published, 1993.

White, Gregory C., *This Most Bloody and Cruel Drama: A History of the 31st Georgia Volunteer Infantry*. Baltimore: Butternut and Blue, 1997.

Young, Ronald C., *Lancaster County, Pennsylvania in the Civil War*. Apollo, Pa.: Closson Press, 2002.

Electronic Sources

Schaefer, Thomas L., Defend or Destroy? The Columbia-Wrightsville Bridge in the Gettysburg Campaign. Videotape/DVD. Rivertownes Pa., Total Magic Video Production, 2003.

INDEX